Old Testament Theology

A Latin American Perspective

Old Testament Theology
A Latin American Perspective

Pablo R. Andiñach

©Digital Theological Library
2025

Library of Congress Cataloging-in-Publication Data

Pablo R. Andiñach.
[El Dios que está : teología del Antiguo Testamento]
Old Testament Theology : A Latin American Perspective/ Pablo R.
Andiñach
334+ xvi pp. cm. 15.24 x 22.86
Includes bibliographical references & Index
ISBN 979-8-89731-000-5 (Print)
ISBN 979-8-89731-001-2 (Ebook)
ISBN 979-8-89731-002-9 (Kindle)
      1.   Bible—Old Testament—Theology
      2.   Bible—Old Testament—Criticism, interpretation, etc
BS1192.5 .A53 2025

www.DTLPress.com

Cover Image: The parchment is a 19th century vellum of the
Samaritan Pentateuch from the DTL print holdings.
Photo credit: DTL Staff

¹³ Moses said to God,
"Suppose I go to the Israelites and say to them, 'The God of your
fathers has sent me to you,' and they ask me, 'What is his name?'
Then what shall I tell them?"
¹⁴ God said to Moses, "I am who I am. This is what you are to say
to the Israelites: 'I am has sent me to you.'"

Exodus 3:13-14

Give me your hand out of the deep zone of your wide-spread
sorrow...
All ye, bring to the cup of this new life your ancient buried
sorrows.
Show me your blood and your furrow,
tell me: here I was punished
because the jewel did not shine or the Earth
failed to yield enough stone or enough corn:
point to the rock on which you fell
and the wood on which they crucified you...
I am coming to speak for and through
your dead mouths.

Pablo Neruda
The Heights of Machu Picchu, XII

Champollion deciphered the wrinkled granite hieroglyphics. But
there is no Champollion to decipher the Egypt of every man's and
every being's face. Physiognomy, like every other human science,
is but a passing fable. If then, Sir William Jones, who read in thirty
languages, could not read the simplest peasant's face in its
profounder and more subtle meanings, how may unlettered
Ishmael hope to read the awful Chaldee of the Sperm Whale's
brow? I but put that brow before you. Read it if you can.

Herman Melville, *Moby Dick*, LXXIX.

Table of Contents

Acknowledgements

This work began to take shape in 2012 when I was living in Dallas, as a Visiting Professor at the *Perkins School of Theology, Southern Methodist University*. Much of the bibliography supporting these pages was consulted at their *Bridwell Library*, an extraordinary place for any book lover. Later, my conversations with students and colleagues at the *Universidad del Centro Educativo Latinoamericano* (the Methodist University in Argentina) enlarged these pages. To both institutions I dedicate this work. And I wish to express my special gratitude to the *Digital Theological Library* for their generosity in receiving this work for publication and to Verbo Divino for allowing this translation of my Spanish original, *El Dios que está*, to be produced.

Abbreviations

AASOR	*Annual of the American School of Oriental Research*
ANET	*Ancient Near East Text Related to the Old Testament*
BDB	Brown, Driver, Briggs, Gesenius, *Hebrew and English Lexicon*
CBQ	*Catholic Biblical Quarterly*
CBI	*International Bible Commentary*
CBL	*Latin American Bible Commentary*
COS	*The Context of the Scriptures*
CuadTeol	*Theology Notebooks*, Buenos Aires
DBHE	*Hebrew-Spanish Biblical Dictionary* (Ed. Trotta)
EB	*Bible Studies*
EstB	*Biblical Studies*, Petrópolis
HSS	Harvard Semitic Series
Interp	*Interpretation*
JBL	*Journal of Biblical Literature*
JSOT	*Journal for the Study of the Old Testament*
OrArg	*Eastern Argentina*
RevBíbl	*Revista Bíblica*, Argentina
RIBLA	*Revista de Interpretación Bíblica Latinoamericana*
TDOT	*Theological Dictionary of the Old Testament*
SJLA	Studies in Judaism in Late Antiquity
VT	*Vetus Testamentum*
VT Sup	*Vetus Testamentum Supplements*

Author's Preface

This "Theology of the Old Testament" is eccentric for several reasons. So much so that we hesitate to subtitle this work "Theology of the Old Testament" because at first it does not seem to respond to what has been called by this name for the last two hundred and fifty years. But at the same time we feel that the force of these words corresponds to the content of this book beyond the fact that they may also correspond to a wealth of works that — although not opposed to our work — interpret its task from different angle than that considered normative and constitutive of traditional scholarly work. The appropriation of a title, in this case the name of a literary genre, to limit it to a particular form of approach to the biblical text is like a net that immobilizes it and has the potential to limit thought and reflection. Every advance in the understanding of the biblical text supposes the freedom necessary to open up to new approaches and new paradigms of reading.

On March 30, 1787 Johann P. Gabler gave his master lecture on "the correct distinction between biblical theology and dogmatic theology" in which he separated the two kinds of theology and thereby inaugurated the brand-new discipline of Biblical theology, although he never wrote such a work.[1] Since then, Old Testament theology (and also New Testament theology) has been a discipline that, on the one hand, critically exposes the content of the text and, on the other, discusses the various approaches that other authors have contributed to the project. From the beginning, it was an intellectual exercise and was developed exclusively in the academic university setting. Although there are nuances, which we will discuss later, the essence of the genre assumed that the author had to be a professor and that the audience of the work was the professor's peers. It was not possible to imagine a different scenario until the 1940s and 1950s. But even so, and without forgetting a work such as Ernest Wright's *The God Who Acts*[2] (which must be considered an

---

[1]See a summary of his work in R. P. Knierim, *The Task of Old Testament Theology* (Grand Rapids: Eerdmans, 1995), 495-556.

[2]G. E. Wright, *El Dios que actúa* (Madrid: Fax, 1978).

exception to the rigor of the rule), the various published works did not intend to go beyond the academic scope of discussion.

In our view, this focus on a professorial audience is not a consequence of the lack of interest of non-specialist readers or of the academic rigor of the works which the books undoubtedly exhibited, but rather a sign that the genre was conceived as an academic exercise from the beginning. The exploration of the text was not pursued in order to improve the understanding of the Old Testament within the community of faith, or with the intention of answering the questions that came from readers not initiated in the rather intricate twists and turns of biblical criticism, nor were the works intended to contribute to spreading interest and love for these texts. Rather the task was posed as the search to respond to the demands of modernity that demanded internal coherence and almost scientific discipline so that the work would be respected and accepted within the rational discourse of the time. Although in recent decades there have been reactions to this position, the works produced up to recent years have not ceased to be books for academic theologians. Both the questions that are assumed and the answers or proposals that are offered consistently derive from and interact with the frames of reference and data sets of the academic discussion of the Old Testament and the origin and evolution of the religion of Israel. The authors answer each other and leave perplexed those persons who approach the book because they are attracted by the titles under the false assumption that they will encounter a work that will help them to reflect on the questions that their faith presents to them when reading of the Bible or when seeking to see more clearly the particular ways that the texts of the Old Testament present God and God's relationship with humanity and creation.

We must say that we do not reject the sophistication of thought or the profound character of a reflection that sometimes demands a language that can be difficult for the uninitiated person — and we in no way deny that such scholarly rigor and intellectual acumen can be applied to works that are written in popular language or for simple reading. Both academic and popular work have their value, but what is needed is for academic writers to share the sophistication of their thought of a broader audience. We wish to pursue precisely this project of broader sharing, as we have already mentioned. We wish to offer a theology of the Old Testament that is unique — perhaps eccentric — when judged by the presumed standards of scholarly composition offered by other theologies of the Old Testament.

This work proposes a double task: on the one hand, it seeks to be a reflection that arises from the exploration of the OT texts to exhibit their internal relationships, their dynamics and generation of meanings, the diversity and unity of its theology; and on the other hand, simultaneously, it seeks to offer lines of interpretation that allow readers or contemporary communities to reread the texts in the social, cultural and political contexts in which they exist. With this said, we begin with a description of the imprint of our work and the distance it has from what is generally understood by theology of the Old Testament. In these pages, we seek to explore the biblical text to reveal its mysteries and ambiguities, to let it challenge us and to open ourselves to recognize our ignorance every time we do not know how to digest a passage. We do not disdain the academy — in fact we hope that the book will be read and discussed in that context — but we are convinced that the theology of the Old Testament is a discourse that belongs to academy in the secondary sense. The first sense of Old Testament theology ought to be found in the personal confrontation of the text with contemporary personal and social reality and in the contemporary readers' inspiration and light in the OT pages to address contemporary concerns.

This demand for a deep (personal) understanding of the message is what should interest biblical theologians. They should put all their interpretive and technical potential at its service to help readers go beyond a simple and uncritical reading and allow them to discover that the text says more than appears on the surface. Between the lines there are secrets that ask to be revealed, but these revelations often demand an attentive and patient reading, two conditions that are not abundant in our busy 21st century lives. Nevertheless, we are called to practice such attentiveness and patience.

The distance we express between our work and what is understood in the academic world as Old Testament theology is not an evil that we suffer exclusively. The same situation is found in so-called "systematic theology" as it is practiced today in so-called systematic theology. *Theology* in the literal sense is absent in the Old Testament. The New Testament includes some theological treatises such as the Letter to the Romans or the Letter to the Hebrews and a few other texts of similar style, but nothing like that is to be found in the Old Testament. One can argue and agree or disagree with Paul because his writings are theological treatises, but one cannot argue with Moses or Ezra because the texts attributed to them do not express their personal thoughts; there is no theology of Moses or Ezra like that which is usually evoked from the apostle Paul or from the Johannine texts. In the pages of the Old Testament other winds blow: there is narration, prayer, imagination, loving passions and despicable passions are expressed; the word of the prophets and the laws that should guide the people are recorded; meditation is done; all said in a testimonial way, which imprints on the text the impact it had on the life of the biblical writers and their communities. By speaking in this way, the Old Testament does theology without seeking to do it.

Old Testament discourse aims to leave life experiences as a testimony for future generations and this record is "theological" because it speaks of the relationship between God, and the believer, and God's people. In this sense, the biblical discourse is closer to art and literature than to the rationality with which philosophy is sometimes identified, and for this reason its discourse is more like a dialogue between friends and confidants than a conference between experts. It is as if these friends get together and in private tell each other their joys and sorrows, share their family stories, the insults to which they were subjected, the deeds of their ancestors, their dreams, their loves, their infidelities, the utopias that excite them, their failures and honors, their humiliations and their expectations for the future, the challenges that frighten them. In all these stories the perspective of faith is a natural ingredient for the simple reason that it is part of their lives and therefore it could not be any other way. Thus, among the many tasks of the Old Testament theologian is also the function of revealing that unspoken theology that lies within its folds.

What has been said up to this point should be enough for the reader to understand why in this Theology of the Old Testament we strive to show the semantic connections within the texts, to trace the lines of meaning that structure each work and its constitutive parts, and to highlight those marks in the stories that reveal the particular relationship with God that each text wants to bear witness to. A notable sign is the plurality of readings that we find in it. We will see that there is no concept that does justice to the totality of the message of the Old Testament. When scholars attempt to impose any singular vision or a paradigm on the whole, they inevitably sacrifice the complexity of the whole for the relative unity of a single part, thus ignoring the importance of the text in this entirety and the diversity between its parts. On the contrary, the unifying elements that link the texts appear after a long process of reflection but not as a unique theological idea that explains the unity of the different sections of the Scriptures; rather in this work we assume that there is a theological coherence of the Old Testament that is perceived in the dynamic relationship between the different parts of the discourse. This relationship is observed between dissimilar texts that share a common climate and flavor that runs through all the pages of the text with more or less emphasis depending on the case.

The reader will notice that sometimes we quote not only theological authors but also other works that are a product of our culture and that help us structure society and life. This is because sacred texts are not read in a different sphere from other literatures that, to the extent that they impact us, are also part of our reading context. We include them as a symbol and do not wish to abuse them. Readers will know how to place those that are related to their experience. Obviously, in most cases we do this not to support an idea but to expand it and show how in areas that are not explicitly theological or ecclesial there is also good theology to nourish our reflection and faith.

The best prize that we can discover is a new word. If we find several, the party will be huge.

PRA

Translator's Preface

Translating, even when one knows both the original language and the target language, is complex. On the one hand, every source language and every author has their own style, idioms, turns of phrase, sentence structures, and linguistic patterns. On the other hand, every destination language and every translator has all the same idiosyncrasies and habits of mind. Mindful translators want to convey the meaning of the original text and its author's intent in terms meaningful and persuasive to the readers of the translated book without importing too much of the translator's own personality and assumptions into the author's carefully composed text.

This translation was completed by the staff of the Digital Theological Library with all of these complexities in mind. No single individual was fully responsible for the translation. Rather the translation was a community project. We will briefly explain the process by which we produced this book. First, we got the original manuscript from Pablo and entered that text into an AI translator. We tweaked the perimeters several times to achieve the tone and readability that we desired in the translation. We set the AI perimeters to adhere as closely to the linguistic patterns and sentence structures of Pablo's Spanish text (we prioritized proximity to the original sentence structures more than the smoothest of English translations). Readers who know Spanish well will recognize that our English translation reflects Spanish language patterns which are less common in English, particularly the extensive use of equative verbs and accompanying pronouns. After acquiring the desired English translation, we ran the resulting translation through another English AI proofreader. Finally, we proofread the translated text with our old fashion human eyes.

A few notes are worthy of mention. First, we have intentionally created—as much as realistically achievable—a gender neuter translation when referring to both God and humans. This translation decision sometimes compromised the beauty and eloquence of Pablo's Spanish prose, but we felt that the decision was justified. (We did retain masculine pronouns in relation to the Biblical authors—on the assumption that most of the Biblical authors were in fact male or least encoded in the Biblical text as male.)

Second, although we did not consult English equivalents for the works which are cited in the footnotes and bibliography, we did translate quotes when they appeared in Pablo's original Spanish publication. This decision to translate quotations involved some risks, since many of Pablo's Spanish quotations were themselves Spanish translations of texts that were originally composed in German, French and English. In effect, we were sometimes translating Spanish translations of English base texts back into English from a Spanish translation — or translating Spanish translations of French and German into English from the Spanish translation rather than from the original language. We did not try to discover and reproduce the original English; nor did we produce our English translation from the original French or German texts. Instead, our English translations are based on the Spanish texts which Pablo was citing or producing.

Third, at Pablo's request, we included the original Spanish phase, *El Dios que está,* after the English translated in each appearance of the expression in order to convey the sense of presence that the Spanish phase infers, an inference which is less notable in English.

Finally, we would like to say that in this translation, we have worked diligently to make Pablo's voice and Latin American modes of thought accessible to English readers without imposing too much of our own thought on his work. We apologize for any errors, misunderstandings, or failures on our part and we trust that our limitations will not reflect badly upon our admired colleague.

The DTL Staff

Introduction

Toward a new reading paradigm

The God who is (*El Dios que está*) here is not a mere spectator of the drama of creation. The Scriptures emphasize that their God is a God committed to human life and that, far from isolating the divine presence, God interferes in the paths that humanity travels and closely follows the destiny of people. This vocation is expressed in God's persistent presence in history and in the events of the world and in the way in which God imprinted on God's people the experience of that presence. This feeling that there is a God who accompanies and is attentive to the destinies of God's people generated God's word, the saying, the voice that tells what God perceives and lives. With time and with the maceration of the centuries that word became a text and today we have the text before us.

The fact that the text is a record of an experience that is presented as intimately linked to historical events meant that, from the 18th century onwards, the study of the Scriptures focused its efforts on rescuing and reconstructing the history that gave rise to it. The project bore incontestable fruit but also reached its limit, perhaps unintentionally, by conditioning the interpretation of the texts to the reconstruction of their historical context, which after much study was understood as a goal that is never fully achieved. In the investigation of the historical facts underlying the biblical narratives, the goal became increasingly complex and the results more provisional.

The more archaeological knowledge advances, the more our ignorance is revealed about the link between the story and the history that is reconstructed from the objects unearthed and evaluated by that discipline;[1] this ends up discouraging the search. A key book in bringing this situation to light is *The Collapse of History* by Leo Perdue; in it he says things like "history should not be the only criterion for reading the Old Testament. Wisdom, many psalms, and legal texts do not have a close connection with

---

[1] I. Finkelstein, "Archeology and the Text in the Third Millenium: A View from the Center," *Congress Volume Basel 2001* (ed. A. Lemaire; Leiden: Brill, 2002), 323-42, with an extensive bibliography on this topic.

history theologically speaking."[1] But even more, he delves into the difficulty of reconstructing the relationship between the text we have today and the events that could be at their origin. His work exposes how Old Testament theology has been unable to assume history in all its complexity, as corresponds to the conception of the 19th and 20th centuries, and thus treats biblical history uncritically. It does so because otherwise its weakness would have been exposed. Perdue makes explicit the loss of the relationship between biblical texts and history as a support for their veracity and raises the question of why we should strive to understand ancient society if we cannot affirm that the migration of Abraham or the covenant at Sinai happened in history, and if they did, we cannot affirm anything about the concrete events as they occurred. Perdue has synthesized in his thinking the product of knowing that biblical texts are not unitary works written at once but a collection of fragments from different periods and contexts, most of them already unrecoverable due to the action of time and forgetfulness. Neither Perdue nor we advocate abandoning historical research but rather recognizing that the texts bear the scars of *various* social, cultural and theological contexts, from which they have already become independent.

Does assuming this situation make the texts unreadable? Does it transform them into mere specters of a past already forgotten and unrecoverable? The answer would be affirmative if we think that the only way to their message lies in placing them in their original context and that reconstructing the moment of their production is crucial to understanding their message. It is not if we change the scope of approach and consider that the first context of reading should not be the historical one but the *literary place* in which that text is found and has been bequeathed to us. Having said this, it is imperative to look for a new conceptual paradigm to support the reading. Each text, each biblical book, is received as part of a larger body of works that in themselves constitute a narrative, theological, thematic universe, of very high literary complexity but at the same time capable of being investigated and approached with a view that is carried out from another place and with tools that help us to open its folds. The consideration of the texts as such and not as a source of information that feeds other disciplines (history, the biography of

---

[1]L. Perdue, *The Collapse of History* (Minneapolis: Fortress Press, 1994), 1-68; our quote is 113-14.

a character, the customs of a period, linguistics, ancient history, etc.) opens up new possibilities of reading and interpretation and allows them to be valued in their very condition as texts and not as an auxiliary work for other interests. As Sacred Scripture for the Jewish and Christian faiths, the biblical text cannot be reduced to being an instrument of information about things from the past, but rather it demands to be read as a work that speaks for itself and whose meaning is discernible from the coordinates present in the text. But even for those who read it as a profane document and as a testimony of antiquity, they will find in this work a dimension that is intrinsic to it and that makes it more than just a material that informs about facts and cultures that no longer exist.

What has changed most with the emergence of new hermeneutics of liberation, whether they are called postcolonial, feminist, ecological, indigenist, transcultural, queer, and other hermeneutics, is the discovery of the plurality of voices contained in the biblical texts. If it was once thought that the experience of Israel's faith was monolithic or at least that it had been transmitted as monolithic by the class that dominated the intellectual and social tools in order to impose its opinion and eliminate others, today we find that the record left in the texts includes what has been called a polyphony of thoughts and praxis. Walter Brueggemann has pointed out that "ultimately, it is clear that the final form of the text, in its process of canon formation, did not represent a total hegemonic victory for any hermeneutical trajectory."[1] This can be seen in the diversity of approaches that the Old Testament offers to such crucial issues as who the Messiah is or what he will be like, or what it means to be the chosen people, or what is the criterion to discern between true and false prophecy, and so on.

Much has changed since the times when it was possible to write a history of Israel like that of John Bright,[2] not only because of his plethora of confidence in the possibility of reconstructing "what happened" based on the conjunction of the biblical text with biblical archaeology, but to a greater extent because of his confidence in the one-sidedness of the thought and theology that structured that single history. Sixty years later, Rainer Albertz's history gives an account of the complexity of the formation of the canon, which is made evident by verifying the presence in the

---

[1] W. Brueggemann, *Teología del Antiguo Testamento* (Sígueme: Salamanca 2007), 744.

[2] J. Bright, *La historia de Israel* (Buenos Aires: Methopress, 1966).

final text of an interweaving of ideas, theologies, testimonies and historical experiences. And that they do not cancel each other out but rather contribute to the mosaic that is the final story.[1]

The task facing a biblical theologian today is primarily to decipher a text. What ancient Israel left us as a testimony of its faith and its past is contained in those pages that, faithful to their reason for being, demand to be read. This task, whether it is carried out in the field of theoretical reflection or in that of ecclesial and community praxis, must take seriously the object before it. That is why it is striking that biblical exegesis has dispensed with a theory of the text, at least without setting it out explicitly. This also presupposes a theory of the reading of the text, and we will address this briefly in our later discussion: "The Word became Literature." On the other hand, the loss of history as an element that structured narration and theology has sometimes led to questioning the very possibility of a "theology of the Old Testament."[2] The weakening of a column that was once a backbone has produced a certain fragmentation in the analysis, and this emergence of the diversity of theologies that inhabit the Scriptures can prevent the elements that amalgamate biblical thought from being distinguished. We will devote the rest of this chapter to these aspects.

Old Testament Theology: An Articulated Whole
Theology and Theologies in the Old Testament

It was Erhard Gerstenberger most clearly questioned the idea that it was possible to produce a theology of the Old Testament. His work is entitled "Theologies of the Old Testament" and with it he seeks to account for the diversity of opinions found in the biblical texts. His central argument is set forth in the introduction when he says "to speak of theology supposes declaring an element, a stratum, an idea as the dominant one of the entire Old Testament" and that "these elements must be subordinated to a [single] idea."[3] He then sets out his understanding of the texts and his task as a biblical theologian by

---

[1]R. Albertz, *Historia de la religión de Israel en tiempos del Antiguo Testamento* (Madrid: Sígueme, 1999).

[2]For an exposition of the place of a biblical theology in the context of theological thinking see J. Barr's article "The Theological Case Against Biblical Theology," *Canon, Theology and Old Testament Interpretation* (ed. G. M. Tucker *et al.*; Philadelphia: Fortress Press, 1988), 3-19.

[3]E. S. Gerstenberger, *Theologies in the Old Testament* (Minneapolis: Fortress Press, 2002), 2.

saying that the texts show "the faith that the Israelites practiced in their daily lives and in their social group" and that the task of the theologian is "to enter into conversation with such expressions of faith" (p. 15). The body of his book then consists of evaluating the various social spheres where the faith of Israel is expressed and analyzing their significance and theological implications. To do so, he uses the tools of sociology and the description of the political tensions that underlie the texts; then he describes the various social spheres of the Israelite community such as the family, the clan, the tribe and their particular ways of producing "theology."

The value of his work lies in the investigation of every day and "real" religion as opposed to that expressed in the "official" texts. Gerstenberger does not discuss the theology of the texts themselves, but the faith that is discovered in the interstices of the texts; It can be said that he seeks to unmask the theology hidden under the cloak of official discourse consecrated by the sectors that dominated theological thought. His contribution is very valuable insofar as it provides a novel vision and an interpretation absent in other works of the same tenor. However, he is not convincing in his criticism of the possibility of a theology of the Old Testament. In his proposal, the author reduces the value of the texts by considering the set of stories as a reservoir of theologies — which in this case could be official or marginal — that must be extrapolated and exposed. By conceiving it in this way, he ignores the hermeneutic process of creating meaning from the concatenation of received texts, which strengthen each other and give each other meaning. Of course, "theologies" coexist in the biblical text, but that does not make them incompatible with each other or incapable of constructing a coherent discourse that encompasses them and gives them a body of meaning. The very fact that they have been preserved together in one work (the Bible) speaks of the community's ability to perceive the relationship that links them despite their notable differences. The task of the biblical theologian is therefore to delve into those pages and explore their way of saying something relevant to our time, a message that is enriched by the diversity of experiences that dwell within it. That Gerstenberger's book ends with a chapter entitled "God in our time" makes evident his concern to show the relevance of the text to the challenges of today and that his project is not far from that which we propose to carry out in these pages.

An author who is now considered a classic, Gerhard von Rad, had already organized his theology without having a center or a concept that would unify the entirety of the biblical testimony.[1] His *Theology of the Old Testament*, published in 1952, conceived the biblical texts as a succession of testimonies of faith that were passed from generation to generation. In this process, each new generation "added" what was necessary for the story to be pertinent to the new situation.[2] Von Rad does not consider that the community assumed as its task the preservation of a finished and definitive text, but rather that of being an active creator of a work in constant production. Another classic, G. Ernest Wright, in his book of the same year, *The God Who Acts*, expressed that biblical theology "is a theology of the narration or proclamation of the actions of God, at the same time as of the deductions that are drawn from them." He then states that "biblical theology is a theology of narrative in which biblical man confesses his faith by narrating the events that made his history the redemptive work of God."[3] It is, as for von Rad, a theology that is conceived in the course of history and is presented in a story.

The biblical authors were not theologians in the modern sense of the term, but rather *they recounted* their life experiences and bore witness to the action of God in them. Wright's book had a tremendous influence on biblical thought in the mid-twentieth century, not only by virtue of its brevity and simple language but also because it presented the content of Old Testament theology as a fluid and constant dialogue with the facts of history. It does not present biblical theology as the confirmation of an established dogma, but as the product of interpreting life from a living and transforming faith. Today we consider that both giants suffered from a certain historical criticality or relied too much on what was then the cutting edge of archaeological discoveries, but both were aware of the theological diversity present in the pages of the Old Testament and stressed that the characteristic of biblical theology was not to have a center or generating theological idea; what was characteristic was its particular way of conceiving and doing theology. Thus, the problem raised by Gerstenberger should not be seen as a challenge to develop a theology of the Old Testament but as a denunciation of all forms of reductionism of the

---

[1]For an overview of the development of Old Testament theology as a discipline and its leading exponents, see W. Brueggemann, *Teología del Antiguo Testamento* (Salamanca: Sígueme, 2007), 15-134; also in N. P. Lemche, *The Old Testament Between Theology and History* (Louisville: Westminster John Knox Press, 2008), 255-64; G. Hasel, *Old Testament Theology* (Grand Rapids: Eerdmans, 1991), includes authors not discussed by the above.

[2]*Teología del Antiguo Testamento I-II* (Salamanca: Sígueme, 2000).

[3]G. E. Wright, *El Dios que actúa* (Madrid: Fax, 1974), 6, 48.

complexity of Old Testament theology to a single idea or principle. His proposal to consider the diversity of theologies is not debatable, but his inclination to deny them the coherence that allows them to participate in the same theological enterprise is. Libraries house generations of works entitled theology of the psalms, of the prophets, of the exodus, of creation, etc. All of them are pertinent and truthful to the extent that they seek to account for the particular way of witnessing to the experience of God in each of these books or sections of the Bible, but that does not mean that they should be considered watertight compartments unrelated to each other. The identification of a work and its theology, even if we refer to particular literary strata (for example, Deuteronomistic theology, or that of the second Isaiah, fragmentary texts that are not identified with a single book) far from limiting its capacity to relate to the rest, enriches it by providing a diversity of perspectives to biblical thought.

The Dynamics between the Sections of the Narrative

The problem posed by the existence of diverse theologies in the body of the Old Testament requires us to take a few steps further in its consideration. If the theology that emerges from Job is quite different from that perceived in Leviticus; if the theology of the Exodus (or of the exodus narrative) that is crucial to the discourse of the prophets and many psalms has had little influence on the wisdom books; if the creation stories of Gen 1-2 are almost absent in the rest of the Old Testament; if the eroticism of the Song of Songs shines alone in the concert of the other books, should we not assume that we are in the presence of an anthology of theologies rather than a theology that accounts for the entire Old Testament? In our opinion, the problem must be posed in another way.

First of all, we must consider the different character of the texts to be compared. But we are not referring to their variety of literary genres—which already give different coordinates for each case—but to their place in the three-part scheme into which the Hebrew Bible is divided: *Torah, Neviim* and *Ketubim*. The first corresponds to what we call the Pentateuch; the second groups the so-called historical and prophetic books; and the third to the rest of the books of the Old Testament. These three parts do not have the same textual value and are conceived of within a dynamic relationship that unites them and at the same time distinguishes them, a relationship that we will discuss later. The *Torah* or Pentateuch acts as a theological source for the Old Testament; it is the Law that governs the life of the people and includes the story from the creation to the delivery of the laws to Moses and his death. Everything that is said there is normative for the life of Israel. Following this first section, the *Neviim* or prophetic books that preceded it (Joshua to 2 Kings) and followed it (Isaiah to Malachi) conceive of themselves as its interpretation and application, as set forth in the legendary narratives of the conquest, the judges and the kings, and in the interventions of the prophets. To a certain extent, they are an exercise in what would later become *midrashic literature*. The prophets compare the conduct of their people in the light of the Law and, by proclaiming "return to God," they call for a return to a healthy observance of the precepts set forth in the *Torah*. The judgment on the kings, which is repeated frequently as "they did not do what was right in the eyes of God," refers in particular to their failure to comply with the commandment prohibiting idolatry, which presides over both versions of the Decalogue (Ex 20:3-6 and Dt 5:7-10). The *Ketubim* are more heterogeneous, but when the sages advise "not to forget the Law" and "to keep in the heart the precepts of God" they are invoking the fundamental law contained in the *Torah* as expressed in Dt 6:3-6:

> Hear, O Israel, and observe this law, that it may go well with you in the land flowing with milk and honey, and that you may increase in number, as the LORD, the God of your fathers, has promised you. Hear, O Israel: The LORD our God is one LORD. And you shall love the LORD your God with all your heart, and with all your soul, and with all your strength. And these words which I command you today shall be in your heart...

The sages, who are not interested in the stories of the patriarchs and matriarchs, are clearly aware that departing from the Law is what corrupts life, and that Law is identified with that recorded in the Pentateuch. To this we can respond that there is no proof of this identity, but the truth is that it is unthinkable that the sages had as a reference a book of the prophetic corpus or another set of normative texts. It is to the *Torah* that they refer, although that does not mean that its text was complete as it was in the first century. The relationship between the *Torah* and the rest of biblical literature is also perceived in that the latter alludes to the former, but there are no cases of the reverse. In the context of this relationship between the parts, the question arises: Can the texts of the Pentateuch be compared with those of the prophets or the wisdom texts as if they were on the same conceptual level so that it can be said that they expound different theologies? We are in a similar situation to that of when we analyze a sermon or read an exegesis and we recognize a distance from the biblical text on which they are built. This prevents us from thinking that this piece has the same or different theology from the passage that it comments on or analyzes; this distance makes us give an opinion on the happy or unhappy interpretation of the text that is analyzed or expounded, but we do not compare their theologies because we recognize the different dimension of both texts; one is the source and the others are its interpretation. In the same way, the theology of a prophetic or wisdom text should not be read at the same level as the texts of the *Torah* because the former assume themselves as an interpretation and application of the latter.

To what we are stating, it can be objected that the order of the three parts of the Hebrew Bible is not chronological and that when the prophetic and wisdom texts were produced — at least a good part of them — it is probable that the Pentateuch was not yet formed. The same can be said of other cases, and all biblical criticism supports this fact; we ourselves share this assertion. But the theological link to which we refer is not in the identity between the texts, as if the latter quoted the former verbatim, but in a way of doing theology. The texts of the Deuteronomistic history (Joshua to 2 Kings) "tell" history but do not seek to instruct on how one should live, or what rules must be followed to be in harmony with God. The same happens with the prophets who, in their oracles and imprecations, invoke a justice and righteousness that they themselves do not formulate; these are part of the ethical and religious heritage of Israel that crystallized sooner or later in the *Torah*. What we say also reveals a guiding line in the formation of the Pentateuch. When constructing this narrative and theological edifice, special care was taken not to leave out any legal text from the tradition of Israel. Even late or repetitive legal texts were included in the *Torah* so that every law appeared to have been received by Moses "in the time of the desert" and the entire rest of the Hebrew Bible was considered an "application" of these laws, which in this way are presented on the narrative level as prior to the prophetic and wisdom texts that must apply them.

Secondly, although it is a mistake to look for a unifying theology in the Old Testament in the sense that modern systematic theology understands its task, that does not mean that the biblical corpus does not have common coordinates. Gabler already established the independence of biblical theology from the schemes of dogmatics in his founding conference, and although it took a long time to make that statement a reality in concrete biblical studies, it opened the door for the texts to be considered in themselves and without the distortion generated by trying to accommodate them to a pre-established rationality, whether dogmatic or philosophical. The Old Testament was formed during a long process of accumulation and discarding of texts that participated in a common "theological climate," a faith in the same divinity called Yahweh and that gave an account of a common past for the believers of that people. That process of formation and its criteria are obscure and largely unknown to us. However, the selected texts and the literary construction they reveal allow us to affirm that they have sought to give an account of and bear witness to the presence of Yahweh in history.

At this point, it is of little use to say that in our eyes the historical criteria that were applied are weak, that there were profound and marvelous texts that were excluded, or that the arguments for such exclusion — when we can glimpse them — may be fallacious and arbitrary for us. What is interesting is that at the time they were grouped together and recognized as Sacred Scripture, they were seen as texts that contributed to the understanding of the action of God with God's people (El Dios que está) and that in no way contradicted the faith that brought them together. It emerges from these that what unites the Old Testament is not a theological idea or a thematic center around which all its thought revolves, but the fact that in each text there is testimony to the experience of the presence of the same God in the most diverse contexts and with a multitude of actors. And we must understand this not as the product of intellectual reflection but as a natural result of the experience of faith of the entire people of Israel. The Jewish man or woman of the late first century — when the texts are almost entirely consolidated — perceives that the God who called Abraham in the land of Chaldea, who freed the Jews from death in the story of Esther in Persia, who forgave the harsh words of Job, who gave the Law to Moses in the desert, who heard the cry of his ancestors who were slaves in Egypt and freed them, who listened to the cry present in numerous psalms, who made the walls of Jericho fall, who chose and blessed David and his descendants, who freed Daniel from death by lions in Babylon, who called Elijah to come out of the cave and listen to God's voice, who, full of anger, let God's temple in Jerusalem be destroyed, is the same God to whom she asks that morning to take care of her life because she is about to give birth or God asks her for fertility for the field with which she will feed her family. What unites the Old Testament is the intimate conviction that in the immense diversity of contexts and people that populate its pages, there is testimony to the blessing received from the one and same God.

Thirdly, what we call Old Testament theology must take into account the dynamic relationship between the parts that compose it. Accustomed to the idea that a theology is a linear and direct reflection "on God," it may be difficult for us to understand that the Bible speaks of God with other categories; if we look closely—and it is necessary to do so—we see that more than *speaking about* God, the texts of the Old Testament *bear witness* to the presence of God. On the one hand, and unlike our current way of articulating a theological discourse, the Bible does not offer definitions of its actors: there is no definition of God, nor of God's love, nor of God's anger; the concept of faith, nor of hope, nor of anguish is not specified. Nor is the theological perspective precise, nor does it seek to justify the fabric of a story because God's action in history is perceived as natural, as that of an actor who underlies everything and who does not require presentation or biography. In none of these cases is there a need to explain anything because biblical rationality does not demand it and therefore it would be an artificial element to the discourse. On the other hand, the biblical textual world offers its own intellectual context and feeds on its own fruits. The Law is enough for the prophet and the wise person, and it is a central part of the Scriptures. And it is striking that although the *Torah* is the heart of the Hebrew Bible, the other two parts (*Neviim* and *Ketubim*, Prophets and Writings) were also incorporated into the set of sacred scriptures. This has not been sufficiently reflected upon. There would be many arguments to support the idea that only the Pentateuch should be considered sacred scripture, as the Samaritan community does to this day.[1] However, in the course of history, the other writings were not considered mere occasional interpretations, but even though they were applications of the Law, they were considered texts through which God spoke to Israel and were included in the canon. This is another biblical eccentricity that disconcerts us when considering its way of doing theology.

---

[1]The Samaritan community recognizes only the first five books as sacred text. They possess a very old manuscript written in paleo-Hebrew characters that includes some variants with respect to the Masoretic Hebrew text, but the narratives are the same. The fact that they recognize only the *Torah* as canonical is often taken as an indication that at the time of the separation between Jews and Samaritans only that part was considered Holy Scripture by the community of Israel.

For biblical theology, the norm is as valid as its application; It is worth promising to fulfill it, but that promise must be validated in the hours and days of each one and of the people of God. For that reason, texts that narrate such circumstantial situations as many of the prophetic texts, certain psalms, or dozens of proverbs were incorporated into the collection of sacred writings. Without these testimonies, the *Torah* would become a set of good examples and better intentions, but by incorporating the other narratives, it becomes clear how God acts and how humans act in relation to those laws and examples of life.

When we go through the pages of the Bible, we find that on many occasions the presence of God is "said" or witnessed to without naming God. Let us think of the narrative in Exodus 1-2, where God is hardly mentioned; in Esther; in the Song of Songs. Another way of speaking about God and "doing theology" is through exposing *human suffering*, as we find it in various psalms, in Lamentations, or in the life of Job. These narratives of experiences that happen to people are clearly what we call human words about life events, personal or social tragedies that unfortunately were and are part of reality, but which in our case constitute a way of "speaking" about God. Job's suffering undoubtedly "says" about Job and his pain, but it also says about the God who is (*El Dios que está*) behind all his drama. The passion of the young people in the Song speaks of how good it is to love, but it also "says" about God's positive evaluation of sexuality and eroticism.

Thus, the Law and its application in the rest of the books act in a dynamic way in the Scriptures. The former does not lose its status as a fundamental text and the latter are affirmed in their contingency to rise to discourse where the action of God is witnessed. The *Torah* is presented as an immutable law given by God to Moses in that primordial time of the desert; it affirms this in such a way that its last lines have the dramatic tone of announcing the definitive closing of an era from which the facts and words will no longer have the same tenor. Later there will be other prophets, but none like Moses; nor will anyone else be allowed to see God face to face as he was in those days; nor will there be signs and wonders like those narrated in the pages that end there. When the circle closes, those days become an unrepeatable normative time. It says it with these words (Dt 34:10-12):

> And there arose no prophet in Israel like Moses, whom the
> LORD knew face to face, no one like him in all the signs

and wonders which the LORD sent him to do in the land of Egypt, before Pharaoh and all his servants and in all his land, and in the strength of his hand and in the great and awesome deeds which Moses did in the sight of all Israel.

What is presented as belonging to Moses is also exclusive to his time. At the level of the narrative, with his death, a central leader disappears and a theological cycle closes, but a change also occurs in the textual nature of the narrative. Prophets and sages recognize their indebtedness to those important pages and will attribute to them the value that they themselves claim. It is no coincidence that a few lines below the text of Deuteronomy that we have just quoted, the prophetic books open with the command to obey the Law, something that will be the guiding principle for the rest of the Scriptures. It says (Josh 1:7-8):

...be strong and very courageous, and be careful to do according to all the Law that Moses my servant commanded you. Do not turn aside from it to the right or to the left, so that you may prosper wherever you go. This Book of the Law must not depart from your mouth, but you must meditate on it day and night, so that you may be careful to do according to all that is written in it...

This text shows a hinge in history and reinforces the change in the textual nature of the story with respect to the Pentateuch. From Joshua onwards, the narratives have a different value and will have the texts of the Torah as a reference. Psalms will begin with the praise of the one who "delights in the Law of Yahweh" (Ps 1:2); Prov 3:1 will say: "My son, do not forget my Law, and let your heart keep my commandments." Isaiah begins by demanding "...listen to the Law of our God..." (1:10). When the prophet Micah seeks to summarize what Yahweh expects from each person, he summarizes it with three acts: to do justice (*mishpat*), to love mercy (*jesed*) and to walk humbly with God, all three are values exalted in the *Torah* and refer to it (Micah 6:8). Note that the first two are instructions while the third — which is what is new in this text of Micah, what this prophet adds to concepts already expressed by other prophetic texts — is in the words of José Luis Sicre "an attitude, a behavior,"[1] as if the dynamics between the law (the first two) and its application in life in the third were reproduced in these brief words.

---

[1]Sicre adds that the first two presuppose the third, since by fulfilling them one is already "in contact with God." *Con los pobres de la tierra* (Madrid: Cristiandad, 1984).

The Word became Literature
The Bible as Literature: What is a Text?

The study of the Bible as literature may seem new to some.[1] However, the first authors of our time who devoted themselves to it were aware that exploring the Bible in its literary aspects was not a new thing. An author like James Muilenburg, who promoted rhetorical criticism, said already in 1968 that the literary approach to the Bible had been carried out "from the time of Jerome and even before, and continued to be carried out by the rabbis until modern times."[2] With this, we wish to affirm that asking ourselves about the literary character of the Bible does not have the purpose of inaugurating a new discipline but rather of resuming a long-standing Jewish and Christian hermeneutical tradition. This approach is very healthy for biblical hermeneutics because it privileges the analysis of the text as such.

The Jewish and Christian faith bears witness to a God who makes the divine self known in historical events. Unlike the deities of other nations, the God of Israel was not identified with an object or a star, as deities were identified by other peoples. In the eyes of others, Israel had no God; they asked him ironically: "Where is your God?" (Ps 42:4, 11; 79:10; Joel 2:17; Mic 7:10) which not only meant that this God had no power to free him from this crossroads but also that God could not be seen, and therefore had no existence. The believers of biblical antiquity ran the disadvantage of not being able to "show" their God to other nations, but their God made up for this with something that was much richer and deeper: Their God could recount the events in which the biblical writers had been rescued and protected by their God. And even though the strict prohibition of images of God embodied in the first commandment was violated on many occasions and would become the symbol of the sin that is behind all sin, in the field of theology, the concept that there was no possible image of God because nothing could contain God's totality still prevailed in biblical times.

Any image was an aberration because it not only distorted the nature of God by reducing him to a physical design but also

---

[1]In the last thirty years, there has much written on this topic, most importantly A. Berlin & J. Kugel, "On the Bible as Literature," *Prooftexts* 2 (1982): 323-32; Robert Alter, *The Art of Biblical Narrative* (New York: Basic Books, 1981); and M. Sternberg, *The Poetics of Biblical Narrative* (Bloomington: Indiana University Press, 1985). For an introduction, see P. Trible, *Rhetorical Criticism* (Minneapolis: Fortress Press, 1994).

[2]J. Muilenburg, "Form Criticism and Beyond," *JBL* 88 (1969): 1-18.

induced the worship of an object that, as such, was destined to perish and degrade. Even if an image were made, it would be nothing more than a spectre of the true God. So the means that Israel had to present its God was to narrate God's deeds, to tell how had accompanied its founding ancestors, to announce how the Biblical God had freed them from oppression in Egypt and how the Biblical God had raised prophets to guide the people every time they deviated from the Law. Without a doubt, narrating facts does not encompass the totality of God, but it does encompass what the Biblical God wanted to show of the divine self. It tells what the Biblical God did and said; It is not *about God* that we speak, but about God's voluntary manifestation in human history. But this presenting God's self in history and then surviving through the narrations of those events has its limits. What happens is that both the historical events and the stories that evoke them suffer from fleetingness; they do not withstand the passage of time and easily fade away. In order to preserve the memory of Israel's faith, it was necessary to put these stories in writing, and thus the testimony of the acts of God became literature.

It was Paul Ricoeur's work on language and hermeneutics that helped clarify this aspect of biblical narratives, although his observations apply to texts in general. In three foundational articles he establishes what he calls the process of "distancing: between language (the set of words, rules and linguistic signs), speech (the act of "saying"), and the text, which is the record of that "saying."[1] Language is a reservoir of words which in turn have various meanings (the word *monte* is an elevation of the terrain and a forest; *giro* is a movement, a way of speaking and a sending of money). In oral discourse, words are selected from the reservoir of language but at the same time they are placed in a linguistic context (the sentence) that allows us to identify from all of its possible meanings the one that applies to that sentence. Ricoeur says that, in speech, only one of the multiple possible meanings of the word is "closed." The next step is that this oral discourse is delivered by someone (an author) to a listener (audience) at a given time (context). Now, when the oral discourse

---

[1]We refer to the articles "La tarea de la hermenéutica," and "La función de la distanciación, y Hermenéutica filosófica y hermenéutica bíblica," *Exégesis* (ed. G. Antoine *et al.*; Buenos Aires: La Aurora, 1975), 219-78; in Ricoeur's work on hermeneutics there are two main titles: *El conflicto de las interpretaciones* (Buenos Aires: Ediciones Megápolis, 1975); and *La metáfora viva* (Buenos Aires: Megápolis, 1977).

is written down, several modifications occur in its environment: the author disappears, we no longer hear the voice; with him, the original audience of the discourse disappears because the reader no longer participates in that group. And with them both, the original context of the dissertation also disappears. So the text, when written, rescues the oral discourse from oblivion and destruction but pays the price of becoming an entity autonomous from its author and from the context that saw it born. This is what Ricoeur calls the second "distancing," which is the one that distances itself from the initial psychological (author) and sociological (context) context so that it can be opened up in other spaces and thus generate new possibilities for readings.[1]

Ricoeur speaks of a third *distancing*, which occurs when the text in question is a fictional narrative, a poem, a drama, and not a dry business report or a machine instruction manual. Fiction does not claim to be a mirror of reality or to give an objective version of it; fiction is an *interpretation* of reality. As a literary work, it recreates reality and offers an opinion on what it narrates. This condition of literary work makes it independent on factual history (objective facts, such as, for example, a police report should describe) to allow it to create a "world of the text" where the actors and situations have a reason for being intrinsic to the text and are in function of a certain message. In a literary work, meaning does not consist of the plain and automatic reproduction of reality, but rather arises from its recreation, where, through figurative language (metaphors, symbols, characters, symbolic acts, etc.), a profound and committed vision of reality is offered. That is why a work of fiction or a poem participates in a density in its approach to reality that is absent in a mere journalistic report, which is due to objectivity and clarity. When we reach the point where we recognize that the text before us offers us a vision of history and life, we are faced with the task of opening it up and interpreting it. Hermeneutics is the last step in a long process that began in language and culminates in reading and interpretation. Speaking and delivering an oral discourse is an event, an act, limited in time and space and with a specific number of witnesses; this discourse when put into text is perpetuated, transcends its

---

[1]For an exposition of the hermeneutical process in all its details, see S. Croatto, *Hermenéutica bíblica* (Buenos Aires: Lumen, 2000); for examples of hermeneutical practices, see A. Botta & P. R. Andiñach (ed.), *The Bible and the Hermeneutics of Liberation* (Atlanta: Society of Biblical Literature, 2009), especially the articles by G. West, H. de Wit and E. Gerstenberger, 13-86.

original context and opens up to the world for whoever comes to read it from then on.

It is interesting to note that while objects degrade and perish (and today we know that even the sun will one day go out and that the stars that seem to be fixed move and some of them we still see even though they have died!), texts do not share this fragility. Burning a book is not burning the text it contains but its support, only paper and ink. A sculpture can be destroyed and even if it is reconstructed in a copy, it will be an imperfect version of what has already been lost; the same happens with an oil painting or a fresco; but a copied text is always an original. Few can enjoy a Van Gogh or a Joan Miró in their living room, but millions have an original by Cervantes, Pablo Neruda or Julio Cortázar to enjoy at all times. And although it is hard and painful for us to say it, our love cannot stop the passage of time that humiliates and insults those works of art that are in our hearts; nor those faces and places that have made us happy; But as long as there is someone who reads a text, it will live and enjoy the freshness it had on the first day. Is not this the direction in which the prophet proclaims:

...for the mouth of Yahweh has spoken.
A voice says: Scream.
And I answered: What do I have to shout?
That all flesh is grass, and all its glory is like the flower of the field.
The grass dries up, the flower withers,
because the wind of the Lord blew through it;
certainly grass is the people.
The grass dries up, the flower withers;
but the word of our God stands firm forever. (Isaiah 40:5-8)

The poet who left us these wonderful verses thinks of the word of God as a message that does not fade and does not die. The opposition he establishes between "the people" who are transient and subject to the ups and downs of history and their own vicissitudes and the "word of God" that does not degrade and is enduring speaks of his conviction that there were things subject to the contingent and others capable of transcending days. It is natural that he interpreted that God is eternal in contrast to human reality, but we must note that in this poem God is present through God's "word." The Lord of Israel is identified by what *God says* ("...the mouth of Yahweh has spoken...") more than by God's actions. And that word in the hands of a poet is shaped until it becomes a text that endures. We cannot help but feel that in his condition, as an artist sensitive to the instrument he uses, the poet

17

who constructed these verses captured that condition of the texts of possessing vestiges of eternity within their folds. This is because texts are not things but rather an intimate relationship of signs that sleep without degrading until a reader approaches to awaken them.

Performative Art of Reading: What is Reading?

Beyond any speculation we may make, any theological system we may wish to establish or refute, and even beyond any idea we may have of what the Bible is or represents, we must confront the reality that the Bible is a text to be read. Therefore, the act of reading is an experience that deserves our reflection. *Performative arts* are those human expressions that are not expressed in a concrete work such as a sculpture or a painting and that require interpretation in order to be presented. A piece of music "does not exist" until it is performed; in the meantime it is a score, a succession of silent signs. A theatrical work requires staging to show what it really is, in the same way that choreography or liturgy do. *Performative arts* are forms of art and human expression that require the participation of someone to perform them and are not expressed in a physical object. They remain virtual until they are performed and become virtual again when their performance is over. We affirm that the act of reading shares this same characteristic.

While a text is not read, it remains dormant, waiting for its signs to be opened in a reading; it is paper and ink with no other reference than being an object that we call a book and that is indifferent to the content it contains. This can be questioned by pointing out that a sculpture also requires someone to contemplate it, but we must note that a sculpture is something forceful, which imposes itself by its own density in space and time. It will impact the environment in which it is found without the need for an observer; its material interferes with others that surround it: the hardness of bronze that will reflect light, the fine or rustic surfaces of marble that will absorb dust over time, the figure that will impose a theme or a force on the environment where it is found; the metal that will corrode over time; a sculpture is something solid. On the contrary, a text, when read, demands that the readers contribute their voice (internal or sonorous) to the story and the characters; The text is a text that provides an intonation for the words that will nuance the reading; the reader or listener is asked to imagine the faces and appearance of the characters and landscapes. It also requires that words that may have different

18

connotations in different readers be decoded. Does the word hunger have the same impact on someone who knows or knew it as on someone who has never suffered that experience? Does the word city feel the same way for someone who lives in one of the large modern cities as for someone who lives in a small village surrounded by countryside? The word "sun" does not evoke the same sensations for someone who lives in torrid areas as for someone who has grown up in cold and cloudy areas. Readers will put into these and other words and realities that the text evokes an important charge of their personal and social experience that makes the act of reading possible and without which all reading is diluted. Without this participation of the reader, the text does not become actualized and remains dormant. Without the reader, the text does not exist.

At this point, we must avoid the hasty assumption that this discussion indicates that reading is a subjective and manipulable act. In reality, what is demonstrated is that reading is not a simple act of passing information from a text full of it to empty readers who passively informs themselves of its content. Aside from this mechanical action, reading is an act of interpretation in which the interpreters do their part so that the text reveals its message and that part includes everything from their condition as persons with unique biographies to the place they occupy in the society where they live and the relationships that this implies. When readers from different times and contexts approach the same text, they will produce different interpretations, but in all cases they will refer to the same text and must give an account of their interpretation in relation to that story and not to another. There will undoubtedly be different reading angles and dissimilar historical experiences, but in all cases they will be challenged by the same linguistic organization, a work that, because it is unalterable, establishes the limits of reading. The polysemy of the text is explored, but respecting the limits that this linguistic organization establishes.[1] Perhaps it is necessary to say something that may seem obvious, but we always read the text that we have in front of us, not another. And that essential part of any reading that is the readers are not there to invent a text but in the act of reading they must accept that they

---

[1]S. Croatto, by emphasizing that polysemy is "*of the text* (not just any polysemy!)" warns about the risk of subjectivity in reading, *Hermenéutica bíblica*, 107.

enter into an asymmetrical dialogue with that concrete reality that they has in front of him and that we call text.

The asymmetry we mentioned arises from the fact that for there to be reading, two parts must meet. We have a text and a reader, but these two parts that converge in the act of reading (the text and the reader) are not equal, nor do they have the same function. We have already discussed above this strange characteristic of texts, which remain unchanged over time and the inclemency of space. A text remains the same as long as it is not modified by the hand of a new "author:" two thousand years ago, men and women of the Qumran community, on the western shore of the Dead Sea, read the same words of Isaiah that we read today. This means that a text is a crystallized reality, which does not change and that the same labyrinth of signs is revealed each time it is opened in reading. It is a fabric (from the Latin textus, "interlaced," "woven") of unalterable threads. On the other hand, the reader is the complete opposite. Readers are changing beings, subject to the ups and downs of personal and social history, and by virtue of their very condition as a social being, they lives in a constant state of transformation, to which in this case the reading they carries out also contributes. Thus, at the end of the reading, the text remains the same, but the reader has been modified by it. Whatever the impact of the text on the reader, they will not be the same after that encounter. The act of reading is therefore the encounter between a consolidated and firm reality (the text) and another unstable and fragile reality (the reader). But both are necessary because the strong part is not realized or comes into being without the help of the weak part; and the weak part is a devourer of signs and has a blessed curiosity about them.

The next step is to ask ourselves what we are looking for when we read. What we are looking for — or what surprises us! — is a meaning. When we read, a meaning is generated, which is the product of the encounter between a text and a reader or reading community. Meaning is in turn a relationship between a signifier and a meaning, between a word and the reality to which it refers. But once we read it, we appropriate that word;[1] meaning becomes

---

[1]We try to avoid technicalities. The correct way to speak is by the lexeme, the word that has not yet been pronounced, as it is in the dictionary. Although an isolated word undoubtedly gives meaning (for example, a sign that says "Silence" or "Move forward") the smallest natural unit of the text is the sentence that is linked with others to form a narrative or the succession of verses that culminate in a poem; we are certainly not unaware of the infinite number of literary genres such as the sentence, the story, the hymn, etc.

what we perceive, what we feel as new in us. Something has been given to us in the act of reading and that something we have received modifies us and makes us think. In technical or scientific discourse, knowledge is transferred, but literary texts appeal to revealing experiences, feelings, and interpretations. Note that in a scientific text or in a report on work activities, the aim is to reduce the ambiguity of language to a minimum; what is said has to be of superior clarity and the knowledge that is transmitted must be as clear as possible so that there is no doubt about what is being conveyed. To such an extent that in a scientific text or a report, ambiguity is a defect that disables the text. In literary texts—and the Bible is one of them—ambiguity and polysemy are a regular part of the discourse and, far from being a defect, we perceive that they enrich the act of reading. This is because, to the extent that they are testimonies of vital experiences, they cannot avoid the ambiguity and cadence inherent to human life and history. What is more, the better they manage to transmit this condition of the experience of life of being oblique and sinuous, the more we feel that it does justice to what we are. The most remembered works are those that openly expose the human condition in all its crudeness, because in this way they can explore the meaning of life in its deepest dimension.

But the search for meaning is not something that can be done without passion. That is why we also say that reading is an art. With this, we distinguish it from other human activities that tend to be repetitive and not very challenging. From what has been said up to here, it should be clear that we consider the act of reading a moment of great creativity and commitment, and it is for this reason that we assimilate it to artistic activity. *Poiesis* (a Greek word meaning action, creation, and hence poetry and poem) and along with it *poietés* (creator, poet) are realities that are present in what happens when we read. In all cases, but especially when reading a biblical text, we wake up to the reality of being interested receivers of a message and that we contribute with our personality to the construction of that message, to the updating of a text that may be distant or even of unknown origin but that demands that we decipher its signs and reveal its secrets. In doing so, we are creators of that "world of the text" proper to the narrative within which the possible and varied interpretations of the same phrase, of the same verse, are played out. It is clearly not a monotonous activity, nor can it be done mechanically. And, at the same time, by describing reading as an art, we wish to point out that readers must immerse themselves in an activity where they will not have all the coordinates at their disposal and where they must accept that they will not be the owner of everything that is created there. In the act of reading they will be an essential but not exclusive actor and they must accept that by interpreting and opening the text they are given the privilege of contributing to creating a meaning but at the same time of being splashed by that reading, which will leave a mark on their life. Narrations, a psalm, an oracle are not texts that can be read with indifference: the moment we go toward them, they awaken and come toward us.

The Bible as Canon and Sacred Scripture

What has been said so far seems difficult to reconcile with a text that is recognized as Sacred Scripture and that therefore has a special authority for the community that treasures it. If a text is not a simple reservoir of knowledge that the reader extracts in order to understand it, but is a literary world where the reader — or the reading community — is an active subject in the construction of the meaning that the encounter with the text produces, we ask ourselves: How can we understand that the Bible is the Word of God, *God's* message for human beings? When we read, are we not introducing our human experience into the text and that obscures God's own message? In the remainder of this chapter, we wish to comment on five points that are a consequence of the textual condition of God's revelation in God's Word.

First of *all*, we must recognize that God's choice is to communicate with human beings in a way that they understand. And in exercising that vocation, God does so in the only effective way: in a language that is akin to human experience. If God had opted for a heavenly language purified of earthly vestiges, it would be an inhuman and incomprehensible language *for* us. So God agrees to reveal the divine self in the narratives and poems that make up the Bible and accepts the limitations of the medium God uses; the biblical narratives are human words, as profound and truthful as all those that testify to core experiences. They are human; but they are the ones that God has chosen to give us God's Word.

The *second thing* is that what has been said up to this point allows us to affirm that when the reader opens the biblical text, what happens is that a space is created where the message is constructed. The message emerges from confronting the text with the reality of the readers and their community and it is a word that penetrates deeply into the readers' lives. Because they go to the text with questions, anxieties, challenges and it reveals to us that these realities are not foreign to the experiences printed in the Bible's stories. The intimate threads within the reader make friends with certain threads within the text that are activated and provoke the irruption of meaning. Thus, the text and its message come to have an existential and concrete value for the reader. Existential because it gives value to their lives and justifies their existences; concrete because it activates the best of the human being by encouraging commitment to that which the story promotes: justice, equity, the reunion between estranged brothers and sisters, reconciliation between enemies based on truth and justice, the recognition of God's love for God's creation. Surely other readers will activate different threads and it is also necessary to mention what Paul Ricoeur calls "the conflict of interpretations." This conflict is also part of the hermeneutic process of reading because just as there is no isolated reading, there is no one interpretation that exhausts the meaning of a text. Polysemy and the reserve of meaning will allow other approaches and in the dialogue (or conflict) between them, this new reality will be built, which is the product of letting oneself be impacted by the message and at the same time being an active actor in the changes that it promotes in the life and society of the reader.

The *third* observation is that the *Torah* assumes itself as a work in which God speaks to the people. This condition of sacred text is a textual fact that does not depend on the opinion of the reader. Of course, one can reject this condition of the text and read it in a profane manner, but the narrative implies this condition and its character as a "text given by God" is a semiotic actor that must be taken into account in the reading. It is explicit in the text that God is the one who gives Moses the *Torah*. Here we are not interested in the historical fact but in its literary and kerygmatic significance; and what is understood at the level of the narrative is that the complete *Torah* was inscribed on those tablets, even if at the time of the writing of these texts the Pentateuch as such did not yet exist. It is interesting that biblical criticism has conclusively demonstrated that that Moses was not the author of the Pentateuch and that he could not — among others — have narrated his own death, as is done in Dt 34.

Today we no longer discuss historicity and we recognize the literary sources and strata that constitute the Pentateuch, but those historical recognitions have opened doors for literary sensitivity. Because it is obvious that no one can narrate his own death, what is affirmed by declaring that Moses "wrote" the Law (Dt 31:24) is a theological statement that has little to do with the historical veracity of the narrated facts. It is true that a literal and superficial reading understands Moses writing the laws on the tablets at the dictation of God, but that is an interpretation that impoverishes the message. What is established in this story is not the tireless task of Moses carving stones but the radical action of God who decides to communicate with God's people and does so through a written text. The *Torah*, as a fundamental work of the faith of Israel, is not presented as the fruit of a privileged mind or a genius of thought, but is presented as given by God to Moses so that he may deliver it to the people for their observance. This condition of a text given by God to Moses acts at the level of the story as sufficient support to confirm its authenticity as a divine text; the facts narrated in these pages have no more guarantee than that which can be granted by the confidence that the narration is true and that which is given by the faith that arises from experiencing that the narrated facts of the history of ancient Israel are a message for our own historical and life experience. What is told there is worth its own weight.

It is curious to see that Judaism that produced the Greek Septuagint translation found it necessary to elaborate a legend like the *Letter of Aristeas* in order to justify the veracity and correctness of this translation.[1] Since it was a translation produced in the diaspora, it must have been questioned and needed a legendary narrative to support it as a legitimate text. Even more curious is to observe that it was Christianity — which adopted the Septuagint as its regular text and caused Judaism to abandon it in favor of other translations — which subsequently produced an altered version of that legend in which miraculous elements, absent in the Jewish text, abound.[2] The most famous of the additions is the one that says that each translator worked alone and upon finishing their work they verified that in a miraculous act they had all agreed word for word in the translated text. This second version of the legend was made in order to show that the Jews had abandoned a version of the Bible that was faithful and that was certified by the miraculous acts of God. Note that the Hebrew text justifies itself and never needed an external legend to legitimize it.

The *fourth* observation concerns the canon. When we approach the biblical text, we recognize some kind of authority in its pages. Whatever our understanding of what a canon is, we do

---

[1] See N. Fernández Marco, "La Carta de Aristeas," *Los Apócrifos del Antiguo Testamento II* (ed. A. Diez Macho; Madrid: Cristiandad, 1983), 19-63.

[2] It is in the so-called *Cohortatio ad Graecos* attributed to Justin Martyr, but today noted as by an unknown Pseudo Justin.

affirm that there is within its pages a general framework of unity that gives coherence to the whole. And although the process of creating the Old Testament canon was progressive, the different parts were not understood as conflicting but as expanding and complementing. The fact that the canon was created gradually does not speak against its unity; on the contrary, it consolidates it by showing that it is not the product of a moment; if the canon was not the product of a personal genius, neither is it the product of a "golden age," but of a slow theological maceration that took centuries.

Nils Lemche questions the existence of a canon by pointing out that it was conceived very late.[1] Lemche's position seems to reflect the fact that he understands the canon only in the sense of a closed collection of texts and does not take into account that the primary characteristic of a canon is to be a literary body that is recognized as having theological authority and, to a lesser extent, a collection of texts. Seen in this light, it matters little if some books were incorporated late in history, or if even some pages can be questioned as to their value and integrity to be part of the canon; what is important to establish is whether there was a textual body with canonical authority and from when onwards. In this sense we find a very solid testimony in Luke 11:49-51 (also in Matthew 23:35) where the evangelist puts into the mouth of Jesus that the Israelites have killed and persecuted the prophets

> ...so that the blood of all the prophets that has been shed since the foundation of the world, *from the blood of Abel to the blood of Zechariah,* who died between the altar and the temple, may be required of this generation...

The murder of Abel is narrated at the beginning of Genesis and that of Zechariah in 2 Chr. 24:20-22; and for both names to be the first and the last, it is necessary to consider that Jesus knew the Scriptures in the order that the Jewish community maintains them until today and which consists of placing 2 Chronicles at the end. This information, repeated by two evangelists, makes it clear that at least in the second half of the first century, the Old Testament Scriptures extended from Genesis to 2 Chronicles, in that order, and therefore included the books that today make up this corpus.

---

[1]Lemche minimizes the value of the canon as a theological subject, and even points out that the relationship between the testaments is of little theological value; for him the gospels and the letters of Paul only refer to the Jewish Scriptures (the Old Testament) on certain occasions. In our opinion, Lemche does not make a correct evaluation or dimension of the immense process of rereading that the New Testament makes of the Old; N. P. Lemche, *The Old Testament Between Theology and History* (Louisville: Westminster John Knox Press, 2008), 270-83.

The fact that the Song of Songs or Esther were questioned, or that in the diaspora some other writings were included, does not affect the reality that at that time the Old Testament was already a forceful literary corpus and a theological authority.

As *a fifth* observation, at the end of this introduction, we do not wish to fail to mention one more topic, without having the space here to deal with it. A challenge for theology is to find the link between Old Testament theology and general theological thought, both with Christian systematic theology and with the Jewish reading of these texts. In general, systematic theology deals with the ambiguity of God in the Old Testament or with the supersessionist temptation that considers the Old Testament to be superseded by the message of the New. In meditating on this topic, Ellen Davis sadly observes that rather than a loss of authority, the fact is that "intimacy with the Old Testament has been lost."[1] She points out that although it is recognized as canon, it is not used in dogmatics, in teaching and very little in preaching. It has been said that, when a fool makes a mistake, it produces almost no consequences, but if someone very intelligent makes a mistake, it can prolong his stumble for centuries. The author of the Letter to the Hebrews was a first-rate thinker and in 8:6-13 he quotes Jeremiah 31:31-34 and interprets it in such a way as to declare the inherited Jewish scriptures ancient and obsolete. He says:

> 6 But now he has obtained a more excellent ministry, inasmuch as he is also the mediator of a better covenant, which was established on better promises. 7 For if the first had been faultless, there would not have been a place for the second. 8 For he rebukes them and says:
> *Behold, the days are coming, says the Lord, when I will make a new covenant with the house of Israel and with the house of Judah, 9 not like the covenant that I made with their fathers in the day when I took them by the hand to bring them out of the land of Egypt; for they did not continue in my covenant, and I did not respect them, says the Lord. 10 Therefore this is the covenant that I will make with the house of Israel: After those days, says the Lord, I will put my laws in their minds and write them on their hearts; and I will be their God, and they will be my people. 11 They will not teach each other his neighbor, and each one his brother, saying, 'Know the Lord'; for they will all know me, from the least of them to the greatest of them. 12 For I will be merciful to their*

---

[1] E. Davis, "Losing a Friend," *Jews, Christians, and the Theology of the Hebrew Scriptures* (ed. A. O. Bellis and J. S. Kaminsky; Atlanta: Society of Biblical Literature, 2000), 83-108.

unrighteousness, and their sins and their iniquities I will
remember no more.
[13] In that he saith, There is a new covenant, he hath made
the first obsolete: and that which is obsolete and waxing
old is ready to pass away.

It is from this reading of Hebrews that we call the texts
from Genesis to Malachi "Old" and that the "New" Testaments are
published separately because they are considered the Christian
Scripture par excellence and therefore superior to the "old" ones.
But Jeremiah 31:31-34 (in Hebrews the quote is in vs. 8b-12) does
not suppose the writing of a new text in place of the "old" one, nor
the replacement of one people of God by another, but rather it is a
declaration of the radicalization of the place occupied by the Law
in the life of Israel. It says that in the future the novelty will consist
in the fact that the Law will be "in their mind and in their heart"
(v. 33) and that it will not be necessary to teach it from generation
to generation because "all will know it." Jeremiah does not speak
of a law different from the one they had at that time but of a
different way of establishing the link between the Law and the
believing people. Old Testament theology, whether it is a Jewish
or Christian reflection, must be understood as a complete
discipline in itself. In many of its pages, one can perceive that it
aspires to another horizon, but this aspiration is part of its being,
not a lack. Its theology is modeled on the expectation of a God
who still has things to say, and although with different responses
and expectations, this is how the synagogue and the church
understood it.

The Pentateuch
Instructions for Caring for Life

The Creation of a Cosmos

The most impressive verse contained in the Scriptures is at their beginning and consists of a radical affirmation: "In the beginning God created the heavens and the Earth" (Gen 1:1). Such is the magnitude of this affirmation that the Rabbinic tradition saw in the form of the first letter of the first word (the Hebrew letter ב "beth") a sign that there was nothing before it and everything after, since its shape with the open side facing left — the sense of the Hebrew writing — supports this sensation. With these words, it is established that everything created, everything known and yet to be known, and everything that human thought can come to concoct is included in the creation of God. God speaks forward because God supposes that there is no behind and if there were, it would also be contemplated in the expression "in the beginning." As such, this first affirmation opens the description of the creation of the stage where the adventure of life will unfold from that time until the end of time. There are three things to comment on in this text. The first is that it makes no sense to discuss whether creation is from nothing (the classical Latin expression *creatio ex nihilo*) or whether the text should be considered saying that God organizes pre-existing matter. The discussion — which, for some, has been essential and for us futile — motivated different translations of the text. It was Rashi in the 11th century who first questioned the classical translation and proposed translating *"When God created..."* with the intention of suggesting that there was already something created and that it is not a full creation.[1] But this clashes with the overwhelming sense of the words that follow "...the heaven and the Earth" which imply that nothing is left out of the work of God. On the other hand, the story does not seem to be concerned with this dilemma between creating from nothing or organizing what already exists from the moment that it goes on to speak of a formless, chaotic and abysmal space on which the word

---

[1]Following this tradition, *The Jewish Study Bible* translates *"When God began to create..."* A. Berlin & M. Zvi Brettler (eds.), *The Jewish Study Bible* (Oxford: Oxford University Press, 2004); for an exposition of the options see C. Westermann, *Genesis 1-11* (Minneapolis: Augsburg Publishing House, 1984), 82.

of God begins to work. If God had had that approach in mind, God would have been careful not to speak of an abyss and a lack of form, realities that in the syntax of the discourse could be considered pre-existing to creation.

The second thing that this story tells us is that God creates from God's word. God "says" and things "are created." That this condition is remembered and exalted in numerous texts throughout biblical literature is a sign of its importance and a sign that alerts us to what will later be the centrality of the word in the biblical message, a word that will become a text to be transmitted from one generation to another. Notably, Psalm 29 mentions the voice of God seven times as a sign of God's presence and action on nature; in Ex 19:19 the voice and the word of God are the privileged means of communication with Moses that will extend to the entire *Torah*. The response to Job's questions that God makes from the whirlwind (38:1 and 40:6) will be in the form of two speeches loaded with dense words; and in the stories of the vocation of the prophets the word or the voice of God will be the way in which God will make known the plan for their lives (Isa 6:8; Jer 1:4). In turn, this condition of creating through the word is a significant fact about the conception that biblical theology has of God and of God's relationship with humanity. Psalm 28 says on two occasions that whoever suffers expresses it with God's voice (vv. 2 and 6) and uses the same Hebrew word (*kol*, voice) in the following psalm and in numerous other cases to express the will and action of God. God, who at times is conceived as the unnameable and who cannot be looked at without perishing, is also conceived as the one who comes to terms with language and assumes a voice and a word — very human realities — to approach the problems that hurt God's creatures and compromise their destiny. Thus, presenting creation through the word is also a way of speaking about God. Although much has been said about "the God who acts," what biblical theology shows us is more of a God who speaks and communicates to encourage people to act. Although God brings about changes in history in a concrete way (God frees slaves; makes and gives the Law; calls prophets; trains God's servants; etc.) the way God works is usually the act of communicating the action that the listener must undertake. In these cases, saying is God's way of acting.

The third thing that emerges clearly from this text is monotheism. Israel will go through different stages before arriving at a monotheistic conviction at a late point in its history, probably during the Babylonian exile or the beginning of the Persian period;

but this text reflects a monotheistic theology. It is accepted by most authors that Gen 1:1-2:4 is a text that belongs to the priestly tradition and that this part of the Pentateuch is the last to be formed and produces its texts.[1] Thus, this story, which is located at the beginning of the narrative, was composed much later than most of the narratives of the rest of Genesis; it was composed when monotheism was already a reality in the theology of Israel and it seeks to consolidate this thought and avoid any vestiges that could give rise to ambiguities. David Petersen has called attention to the importance of monotheism for the faith of Israel, which is largely built on "theological traditions embodied in clear monotheistic formulas."[2] The radical nature of Israelite monotheism is its strongest pillar and what allowed it to survive successive religious crises. When, centuries later, Islam makes this principle even stricter, it will not be creating a new way of thinking but rather bringing to its culmination a concept already present in primitive Yahwism.

In turn, it is necessary to say something more about the scope of this first act of creation. The hermeneutical process of writing and rewriting means that a text that initially referred to a certain literary context could later be reused to give meaning to a larger or different literary context. In the case of Gen 1:1, it is likely that at the beginning it referred to the narrative of 1:1-2:3 and that creation was concluded there. However, it was later placed at the beginning of the entire Pentateuch. So now it expands its influence and gives its meaning to this new literary reality that is not limited to the initial act of creation of the cosmic order, but extends into the narrative of the formation of the people of God. In its new location, "heaven and Earth" includes more than just the setting: it is history, life that expands, human conflicts and the relationship between other peoples.

The Language of Myths and Symbols

The symbol is the privileged actor in discourses that present the sacred. The use of the symbol is inevitable because any

---

[1]It is not necessary to subscribe to every detail of the documentary theory in order to accept the existence of traditions or schools identified with currents of thought within the Scriptures. The discussion is still open as to whether the Deuteronomist tradition is later than the priestly one or vice versa; the fact that the Genesis narratives do not contain any relevant Deuteronomic elements seems to incline the faithful toward a final priestly redaction.

[2]D. Petersen, "Israel and Monotheism," *Canon, Theology and Old Testament Interpretation* (ed. G. M. Tucker *et al.*; Philadelphia: Fortress Press, 1988), 92.

discourse that emanates from the experience of faith must refer to spheres that do not always admit the simple description of words. They refer to realities that would otherwise be impossible to name. But it is remarkable to note that religious discourse does not create new words to express realities that are not present in the usual vocabulary. One would expect it to do so, just as it does with any new object that human industry generates and that does not yet have a name. Science and technology generate new names at every moment. However, the fact of redefining existing words by giving them a differentiated value has an explanation in the process of elaborating the experience of faith. The perception of God's action in life and in history takes place in the midst of everyday experiences, not outside of them.

The biblical discourse does not come close to that of mysticism, which seeks to access a sphere that is to some extent different and alien to ordinary experience, and thus likes to distance itself from the noise of life and culture in order to better hear the voice of God in silence. On the contrary, the experience of faith present in the Scriptures perceives the action of God in the midst of everyday acts and seeks to express it with the same regular words but loading them with an extra meaning. By acting in this way, the word becomes a symbol.[1] For example, the Hebrew word *ruah* means "wind" in its plain sense, but it is given a particular value when used in the Old Testament with the sense of spirit. The same happens with the Hebrew word *kabod*, which means "glory" but applied to God in many cases expresses the presence of God and in others God's eternity. It is worth noting that not just any word is chosen, but rather one whose first meaning offers something that is sensitive to human feeling and at the same time that it admits being expanded to be taken toward a second, deeper and more complex meaning. We perceive the invisibility of the wind, its strength and mystery, then its name is used to refer to that other, deeper and less accessible reality, but as real as the first one, that impacts the human being. We know of the warrior who dies in battle or the just king who, upon dying, is glorified for God's conduct; honest kings and brave warriors deserve glory and will remain present in the hearts of the people as an expression of gratitude. From there, the meaning of the word extends because the "glory of God" is a superlative condition of that which is named for human beings. God's "glory" is greater because it does not depend on the opinion of people nor will it

---

[1] S. Croatto, *Experiencia de lo sagrado* (Estella: Verbo Divino, 2002), 79-104.

fade away the day that memory fails and the once glorious hero is replaced by a new hero. There are hundreds of cases like this.

When the symbol becomes a story, it becomes a myth.[1] A myth is not, as is generally understood, a false or fanciful story, but rather a narrative that speaks of the origins of things, of their meaning and depth. If it narrates the origin of the universe, it is called cosmogony (from the Greek: "birth of the universe"), and if it refers to elements of culture (the origin of human activities such as song, dance, war, love, etc.) they are called etiological myths. In all cases, the myth develops in a primordial time, outside the temporal coordinates of factual history, and in a physical space also dominated by imprecision and ambiguity. Another characteristic is that in myths, God or the gods act, who can interact with other celestial beings and with human beings. The most important thing about symbols and myths is that while they transmit knowledge and information about the origin of something in particular, they do so by offering an interpretation of the facts that are narrated and therefore offer a particular understanding of the events narrated. As they are anonymous stories and macerated by generations, they reach us purified and give us the meaning that the community that created and cared for them perceives about their very origin. Myths and symbols say more about the way a people identifies itself and positions itself in the world in which it lives than about the supposed facts it narrates. They speak with a language akin to poetry about those things that if we did not have this language we would be condemned to remain silent about, because everyday words aspire to precision while symbols and myths enjoy ambiguity and chiaroscuro. That is why symbols and myths do not have a direct language but are oblique, sometimes enigmatic, and ask us to learn to interpret through them the deep meaning of life and human experience. Through them — and through symbols — we discover aspects of our inner being. They summon up deep feelings and experiences that no other language can access. There are few myths in the Old Testament and the few that there are concentrated in Genesis 1-11.

Why Two Creation Accounts?

Creation is not limited to the first chapter, nor even to the first two stories, which together reach Gen 2:25. The creation story

---

[1]S. Croatto, *Experiencia de lo sagrado,* 207-306 and L. Widengreen, *Fenomenología de la Religión* (Madrid: Cristiandad, 1976), 135-88.

includes not only a physical setting and the human beings who inhabit it but also the formation of the human condition itself in its personal and social aspects. Creation involves the totality of what is human, but in the biblical sense this implies nature (animals, plants, seas and lights), the social (culture, ancestors, social and political relations) and the personal or psychological sphere (desire, fears, imagination, passion). Feelings, the ability to dream, the experience of the interior, are also part of what is created. Hence, the creation story includes genealogies, fratricide, the experience of fear in the face of nature that runs wild in the flood and the rejection of imperialism in the story of the Tower of Babel. The creation story is extended and is only completed at the end of chapter 11.

The reader is first surprised to find in 1:1-2:3 and 2:4-25 two versions of the creation of the cosmos.[1] The narratives differ from each other in such a way that they are incompatible because they follow different literary designs. Suffice it to say that while in the first story the human couple is created at the same time and at the last moment, in the second story a sexually undifferentiated "terrestrial" being is created at the beginning (not the male, as is interpreted in most commentaries); after several experiences, from a portion of the creature's flesh and bone, the couple is created and only at that moment can we speak of them as a woman and a man.[2] In the first story, time is detailed day by day; in the second there is no time, but there is a garden that does not exist in the first. Furthermore, if we were to present these two accounts in chronological order, we would have to reverse their order, since we know that the first is from the priestly school and was composed after the Yahwistic account, which includes much older traditions and, without a doubt, before the exile.

In our opinion, the survival of the two accounts speaks of the inclusiveness of biblical theology. If there was a strong theological discussion in the post-exilic period between those who postulated an exclusivist model of relationship between Israel and

---

[1]Many claim that the first account ends in 2:4a; however, the expression "this is the story" (Heb. *elle toledot*) is the beginning of a new unit. As such, this expression both closes and opens the account so that although it is part of the new narrative, we consider it a hinge between the two accounts.

[2]We must abandon the idea that man was created first and woman second. This is not what the biblical text says. Only from 2:23 onwards is there talk of *ish* (man) and *ishah* (woman). This "discovery" of exegesis is recent and we must recognize that in our commentary on Genesis written a decade ago we had not yet realized this significant fact, see P. R. Andiñach, "Génesis," *CBL I* (ed. A. Levoratti; Estella: Verbo Divino, 2005), 372-74.

its God and those who advocated a more open and inclusive relationship in the writing of the Pentateuch (the former represented by the books of Ezra and Nehemiah, Ezekiel, the latter by works such as Jonah, Ruth, Isa 56:1-9, among others), the balance shows that the open line prevailed. Even if we take into account the variety of texts and positions that make up the Pentateuch, it is possible to confirm that the final balance will show that the attitude is one of openness to diverse forms of thought. It would have been easy for those who put together the final text to choose one of the two pieces and discard the other. This is likely to have happened on many occasions with parallel or conflicting texts from different traditions. It is common to find the opinion that the Elohistic tradition did not have a creation story, but that seems to us to be an excessive statement. We may never know for sure, but it would not be foreign to the dynamics of the formation of the biblical text if it had one that it was discarded at some point in history. It is not unreasonable to think that after the fall of Samaria into Assyrian hands in 722 BC, when a group from that city fled and was received in Judah along with its texts, there was an attempt to make the narratives of Judah compatible with the recently arrived Elohistic one, and in that situation it could have yielded its heading in favor of the Yahwistic story. This could have been due to power relations or literary or theological preferences, we do not know.

Now, even though the two creation stories were preserved, they are not on an equal footing. The priestly editor retained the Yahwistic narrative but placed the seven-day creation story before it in order to give it a privileged place. So if a distinction is established from the formation of the story, it is necessary to ask how this distinction is reflected in the construction of the meaning of the larger text. From the semiotic point of view, it is not correct to speak of two creation stories, because in a linear sequence such as the entire Pentateuch is laid out, there is no room for two narratives of the same event.[1] From this, it follows that Gen 1:1-2:3 is reinterpreted not as the first story but as a preamble to the entire Pentateuch. Consequently, 2:4-25 is incorporated into the narrative that follows it, which extends to 4:26, where the expression "these are the generations of Adam"

---

[1]Note that the parallel narratives of the books of Kings and Chronicles were preserved separately; joining them would have meant the subordination of one to the other.

(Heb. *elle toledot*) in 5:1 closes the story that had been opened with the same expression in 2:4 and leads us to the next unit.[1]

The Preamble to Everything Else (Gen 1:1-2:3)

The most diverse interpretations have been made of the statement "in God's own image he created them, male and female" (1:27). The difficulty in understanding what the image imprinted on the human being consists of does not reside in the text but in an alleged esotericism attributed to it, for which the key to interpretation must be sought somewhere adjacent but foreign to the story. Is it not easier to imagine that those who composed this story are referring to the God they have just presented? The text shows an active God, with imagination, good will and whose activity — in which God puts all the divine effort — is to create. This description of God and the affirmation that the human being carries this image in his body speaks to both sides. On the one hand, it establishes that the creative and imaginative capacity given to each human being, more than a gift from God, is a link that binds us to God's divine condition. It establishes that each human life, at the moment it acts on reality to improve it, beautify it and elevate it, reveals the mark of the divine that it bears and that was given by the creator; This mark also says that all human beings have an inherent value proportional to the image they carry in their flesh. There is no deeper way to declare the sacred character of the body and life of each person. At the same time, on the other hand, it also speaks of the nature of God. God, from the very beginning, wants to establish a bond with humanity. God does not present God's self as an immaterial, distant, and incomprehensible being. Nor as a powerful warrior who, with God's omniscience, humiliates the creatures that populate the Earth. The text tells us that when we seek to identify the image of God, we will not find it in pristine things like the sun or the stars, with their appearance of eternity, but in the fragile bodies of brothers and sisters who share with us the destiny of life, bodies whose fragility is evident but in which both the human and divine condition is revealed to us.

This primordial, sexual, creative human being is given creation to manage. The mandate does not authorize humans to destroy or deform creation, and in no way can the expression "fill the Earth, *subdue it*" (from the Hebrew root *cabash*, to subdue, to

---

[1]For an exposition of the structure of the *Toledot,* see P. R. Andiñach, *Genesis,* 364-69.

dominate) be understood as a blank check for humanity to do with creation whatever they see fit. The divine image imprinted on humanity establishes the limit and condition of their dominion over creation by indicating that their management has to be done within the framework of the conception present in the entire act of creation.

The translation of the Hebrew expression *ki tov* as "it was good" is correct but poor; this expression is said in this story at the end of each act of creation. It is undoubtedly correct but requires some clarification because the word *tov* also carries the concept of beauty and should be translated as such in these cases. In many texts, the word *tov* is translated as "beautiful" and yet this concept has been elusive when translating the story of creation.[1] By saying six times that creation was *tov*,[2] what is being said is that every object and created being is beautiful. Thus, in the act of creation, the ethical dimension (the good) is added to the aesthetic dimension (the beautiful) and it is established that God is also interested in the realm of the senses and shares the passion for beauty. There is something profound and fascinating in this statement. We notice that beauty and unpleasantness are not inherent characteristics of things but consist of our perception of that which we feel at the moment delights or repels us; and this does not depend on the object itself but on our perception of what we have before us. The moon, a solitary tree on the plain, the profile of the mountain peaks against the sky, are mute and indifferent objects, but we perceive them as beautiful to the extent that they impact our sensitivity. In saying that every created thing "was beautiful," God grants a primordial value to human sensitivity by establishing a parameter that is exclusive to it — recognizing beauty — as an intrinsic element of its creation. Of all created beings, only a woman or a man can feel overwhelmed by beauty or horror.

On the first day, light is created. With it, God confines darkness to the night from which it cannot escape. This destiny will later be taken to its maximum expression by the prophet

---

[1]They translate as "good" the entries in *TDOT*, V, 296-317; however *tov* has an aesthetic meaning in Gen 6:2; 24:16; 26:7; 41:26; Ex 2:2; 1 Sam 9:2; 1 Kings 20:3 and many other texts. The adjective *yapheh* (beautiful, beautiful, lovely) is more limited because it has the direct sense of beautiful but not the ethical value of "good."

[2]On the sixth occasion, at the conclusion of the creation of land animals and human beings, a superlative expression is used for the only time: it says, "it was *very* good [beautiful]" (*tov meod* 1:31).

Isaiah, who declares "I form the light and create the darkness" (45:7), indicating that even the latter is the work of the creator. But in Genesis, the aim is to show God's dominion over darkness, which goes from dominating all reality to being limited and dominated by the will of the creator. Then there will be two privileged days in the narrative: the fourth and the sixth. On the fourth day, the luminaries of heaven are created, "the greater" and "the lesser." They are not named as sun and moon because the Canaanite deities were called by these names (Heb. *shemesh* and *yareah*) and it was necessary to omit their mention. In this way, the stars are placed under the sovereignty of the creator God as instrumental objects to God's project; Thus, they are stripped of all power other than that given by God so that they may fulfill a function that will be essential to the life of the people. The Biblical authors perceived the importance of the sun and the moon for the fertility of the fields and the crops, even for the much desired fertility of women, but they do not deify them nor will they be celebrated for it. The fourth day, the central one in the seven-day week, is chosen because the stars will be those who establish and regulate the calendar and will allow the recognition of sacred dates. This particular interest in ensuring the correct identification of religious festivals reveals the priestly character of the document, a fact confirmed by the insistence that the stars "separate the day from the night, the light from the darkness," pointed out on two occasions (v. 14 and 18). Light and darkness, as symbols of profound realities in human experience, are presented as created and subject to divine sovereignty.

The sixth day is occupied with the creation of land animals and then the human couple. Birds and fish had already been created on the fifth day, which establishes a difference in degree with the previous ones that expresses the idea that land beings are those that most fully dominate the Earth. The successive creation of animals and human beings in a single day speaks of the indisputable biological identity that unites them in the biblical conception. It will take centuries for humanity to arrive at the same conclusion in another way in the works of Charles Darwin, which, being of a scientific nature, do not have to confront biblical thought because they describe reality with their own tools.[1] What Darwin describes in no way undermines the

---

[1]Charles Darwin says in the "Historical Sketch" appended to the later editions of his work *On the Origin of Species*: "I see no valid reason why the opinions expressed in this book should offend the religious feelings of anyone. It is enough, in proof of the transience of such impressions, to remember that the

dignity of the human couple but on the contrary places them as the product of a long creative process that culminates with their most precious piece, the one that shares their image. But the resistance to seeing in the Genesis account that the human being is a member of the animal family has obscured the profound meaning of the message of creation and has had as a disastrous consequence the systematic destruction of nature and the exercise of extreme cruelty toward animals. These have not received any respect for their life because it was understood that their essential condition — creation — separates them with a wall from the human family.

This strict separation of animals from humans is not a naive conception but loaded with ideology and had two consequences: the first is the criminal justification of the extinction of species in pursuit of progress and profit, an activity that, to the shame of our civilization, has not yet ceased. The second is more subtle and atrocious. Drastically separating the human condition from that of animals was used throughout history to consider as such the millions of slaves who with their work and life built the great empires from the dawn of humanity to the present day: they were considered animals and they have no rights.[1] A clear and humiliating example is the fact that during the first years of the conquest of America both Spain and the rest of Europe questioned the human condition of the original inhabitants of America, a discussion expressed in the dispute at the Valladolid Council in 1550 between Bartolomé de las Casas and Juan Ginés de

---

greatest discovery ever made by man — namely, the law of gravity — was also attacked by Leibniz 'as subversive of natural, and consequently of revealed, religion.' A famous author and theologian has written to me saying that 'I have gradually come to understand that it is an equally noble conception of the Deity to believe that he has created a few primitive forms capable of developing themselves into other forms...'"

[1] Today, not in theory, but certainly in practice, millions of people continue to be considered inferior and subhuman. On June 20, 2000, the world's newspapers announced the death by asphyxiation of fifty-eight Chinese immigrants trapped in a hermetically sealed container that arrived at the English port of Dover from Zeebrugge, Belgium. It had crossed the clean roads of Europe where sophisticated radars and all-seeing cameras had not detected the "merchandise" that the truck was transporting. A failure in the ventilation system caused them to die and exposed the regular trafficking and sale of people within the Europe that considers itself *post*- modern. A few days earlier, in Spain, it had been reported that a truck with thirty-six Maghrebians in a state of dehydration had been found. On October 3, 2013, a ship sank near Lampedusa, Italy, carrying people fleeing hunger and poverty, killing 309 of them, many of them mothers clinging to their children.

Sepúlveda.[1] The importance of the discussion did not lie in the fact that it sought to elucidate a philosophical enigma or one more curiosity of the many that the world to which the Europeans had just arrived presented to their science and thought. What was at stake was to find the biological support to then give legal and theological form to the subjugation and extermination of these people. If the natives were not human beings they were classified among animals and consequently not only did they not have any rights but they had been created to serve the human being—white and European human beings—and to satisfy their oppressor's needs. The inhabitants of these lands had to take their place alongside the useful and docile oxen, goats and camels. The ultimate irony is that after the dispute, in which European scholars, theologians and thinkers confirmed that the inhabitants of Mexico—who had built pyramids superior to those of Egypt—the Incas and other peoples of these lands did not belong on the same level as iguanas or seals, and their unequivocal status as human beings and their right to life and to have their property respected was affirmed, they continued to be exploited as if they were animals.

All this contrasts with the delicacy of the story, which focuses on the diet prescribed for the first people, a fact that may seem minor but is not. It is said that animals and people are created sexually and invited to join together to populate the Earth, while they are given plants as food (1:29). This diet has to do with the rejection of violence and especially the shedding of blood, a proposal that must be modified in 9:3 after successive experiences of violence lead to a new dynamic of human existence in relation to animals. But on the sixth day of creation, it would have been an affront and nonsensical to create animals and human beings at the

---

[1]It has been said that Sepúlveda did not deny the human condition to the indigenous people since this was already established in the bull *Sublimis Deus* of Pope Paul III in 1537; however, see this paragraph from his *Treatise*: "Being by nature slaves, barbarian, uneducated and inhuman men, refuse to admit the domination of those who are more prudent, powerful and perfect than them; domination that would bring them great benefits, being also a just thing, by natural law, that matter obeys form, the body the soul, appetite reason, brutes man, woman husband, children father, the imperfect the perfect, the worst the best, for the universal good of all things. This is the natural order that divine and eternal law commands to always be observed. And such doctrine has been confirmed not only by the authority of Aristotle, whom all the most excellent philosophers and theologians venerate as a teacher of justice and of the other moral virtues and as a most shrewd interpreter of nature and natural laws, but also by the words of Saint Thomas." *Tratado sobre las justas causas de la guerra contra los indios* (Mexico City: Fondo de Cultura Económica, 1986), 153.

same time, to say that both were "very beautiful," and then to instruct the latter to kill the former for food.

Limits and Transgressions

After the preamble, the narrative begins with a description of the relationship between God's plan and the attitude of human beings. This is described as a distance established by four successive transgressions of the order of creation. But it should not be understood in the sense of a "fall" — a word absent in the biblical text and which is not the best description of what is presented — but rather as a description of the human condition in its fullest reality. Biblical theology does not believe in the existence of a stage of brilliance and harmony that would later be overshadowed by the descent into a rudimentary and sinful stage. On the contrary, the four transgressions arise from the simple observation of human behavior and from comparing it with the divine plan. In all cases, God's response consists in affirming the necessary acceptance by people of their own human condition with its limits, but also with its possibilities.

They will be like Gods!

The memorable cunning of the serpent consists in discovering the fissure that exists in the human spirit. The human condition is characterized by the natural limitations of time and space, of its cognitive and relational capacity, and by its awareness that it must die. It can be said that the human being is the only being who knows its limits, but at the same time, the only one in creation who rebels against them. The human being wants to be more. The Greeks called this feeling *hybris*, which means excess, and they narrated it in their myths as that in which Icarus managed to escape from the island of Crete by rising with God's wings of feathers joined with wax; but it was not enough for him to have left his prison and gained freedom and in his *hybris* he wanted to reach the sun; the story culminates when, as he approached the sun, the heat melted the wax and he fell to Earth to die.[1] The story of Genesis begins by describing the essential break, the one that is at the bottom of all anguish and uneasiness. The first transgression is to seek to abandon the human condition and aspire to be God.

---

[1] This is the case of Penelope's suitors, who do not deserve her; in Greek tragedies, *hubris* is usually an infringement of one mortal against another, but it also applies to a mortal's dispute with the gods.

The consequence of this transgression will be two curses and two words to remember. The curses are directed at the serpent and the Earth; they use the Hebrew word *'arur*, which means rejection, repudiation. What had been created "good and beautiful" now becomes dark and stops being primitive to become part of cultural reality, the way human beings perceive nature. The serpent will be feared but also desired because it is both a symbol of death and life; death because of the poison it transmits with its bite and life because by changing its skin every year it gives the sensation of dying and being resurrected. The Earth is cursed and therefore will require redemption; it will not yield its fruits with generosity but will demand to be worked and a great effort will be necessary for it to produce food. The words to remember are directed at the woman and the man. In both cases, they describe the most intimate human condition of each one and not—as has been said—a new situation where the original image inherent to their essence has deteriorated. They are told that they were created as humans and that this is their destiny; a condition rich in almost infinite possibilities but with its natural limits that they must accept in order to develop all the potential that they have.

Women are reminded that childbirth hurts and that their sexual drive ties them to the man. These words reflect the difficulty of giving birth, even the fear that childbirth caused in women due to the risk of losing their lives in it.[1] Women perceived childbirth and its subsequent moments as the most critical of their existence due to the weakness and vulnerability of their state. And, on the other hand, it was understood that the goddesses did not suffer during childbirth and that they did not need a man to conceive. Women are not goddesses, they need a man to conceive and they must face childbirth. The subjection to the male as a consequence of her sexual drive is the product of experiencing the inclination that led her to seek sexual union to satisfy a desire, an action that remains enigmatic, as indicated in Proverbs 30:18-19 ("Three things are hidden from me… and the inclination of the man toward the woman…"). Although Proverbs points it out from the masculine side, the text of Genesis also serves to observe how the patriarchal model is based on a biological need that is true of both sexes, but interprets it as a need only of the woman; in this way, she becomes a slave of her body and is at the mercy of the

---

[1] Rachel dies giving birth to Benjamin, Gen 35:18-19.

41

man who thus subjects her to his will.[1] The woman at the end of this passage is described as a being who suffers and is dominated by the man. Croatto points out that this domination is not limited to the field of sexuality, but encompasses the totality of her existence.[2]

In the words dedicated to man, he is reminded that he was created to work and to obtain food in order to live; that this will cost him effort, but that this is the meaning of his life. This distinguishes him from the gods, who do not work nor need food and who are served by human beings. The Earth by itself will produce thistles and thorns unfit for food; if up to this moment it seemed that food had to be gathered from the trees of the garden (2:16) with the ease that they suppose, now it is revealed to him that his destiny will be to cultivate the soil. But cultivating and producing food is more than the biological need to incorporate energy; it is that which allows him to develop his creative activity and therefore the development of culture (the industry that generates objects, the imagination that is expressed in texts, in music or in paintings and sculptures, the love that demands the conquest of the loved one, etc.) all is achieved with effort but with an effort for which he is capable. The discourse closes with the most painful statement: you are of dust and you will return to it. This phrase is nothing other than the crudest reality, said directly and without mincing words. We must note that the text is not interested in speaking about death in the sense of what happens at the end of life; what it seeks to establish is the limit of human experience and in this sense, returning to dust is announcing the end of the limits imposed on the body and thought. For biblical theology, the human being is a marvelous and unrepeatable combination of dust that, at the end of its days, will return to that origin.

An assessment of these passages should not overlook the fact that, despite the patriarchal social and theological context in which the events take place, the narrative does not establish a difference between the condition and destiny of the man and the woman. Both suffer from knowing that they are fragile and limited, both aspire to what they are not, and both will return to the land from which they were formed. Our culture and theology

---

[1]This assertion of unilateral subjection will be reversed in Song of Songs 7:11 where it is the man who is subject to the woman by his sexual attraction, see P. R. Andiñach, *El fuego y la ternura* (*Buenos Aires*: Lumen, 1997), 17-19; 139-42; "Un amor clandestino," *Poética* 31 (2010): 89-112.

[2]S. Croatto, *Crear y amar en libertad* (Buenos Aires: La Aurora, 1986), 143.

failed to see these values in the story and undoubtedly contributed to relegating women to a secondary and sometimes humiliating role.

Fratricide as Deicide

God blesses the first couple by giving them two children, and these will be the characters of the second transgression. Human experience shows that life is not the same for everyone, and while some enjoy tranquility and prosperity, others find the same life complex and full of problems. This was understood as a destiny guided by God, and the story expresses it through the story of two brothers. Cain cannot accept that the light of acceptance shines on his brother and that his offering is considered differently.[1] A feature of Old Testament theology is the preference for the weak and despised. The name Abel means "vapor" and conveys the idea of a being lacking entity, of emptiness; he also carries the condition of being second before the firstborn Cain. Abel represents nomadism and a poorer life than that of landowners and sedentary people like Cain; These two modes of production that coexisted in ancient times reflected cultural and economic forces in conflict, since sedentarism was socially more dynamic and tended to dominate over nomadic peoples.

The power that each brother represents is implicit in this story. When each one presents his offering to God, he leans toward Abel, the weakest, and arouses the envy of Cain who, without considering all the privileges he enjoys, sets a trap for him in the field and kills him. The fault is very serious. If in the preamble the shedding of the blood of animals had been avoided, now the story shows us the murder of one brother by another. Because of its quality as a primordial myth, this story has an archetypal dimension and refers to all intentional shedding of human blood to declare that every time the blood of a person is shed, a brother or sister is killed. It does not matter if it is the blood of an enemy or an adversary, it does not matter if the victim is innocent or guilty of a crime, however serious it may be. The murderer is always Cain and the dead man is always his brother Abel; the strong takes the life of the weak and does so for the sole reason of desiring the little that the other possesses. This

---

[1]An extraordinary novel that addresses this issue is *Abel Sánchez, Historia de una pasión* by Miguel de Unamuno; in his recreation of the drama of Cain and Abel, both lives are questioned.

theological statement should be enough to stop all war, all violent action, all violation of life; however, historical experience shows that the story acts as a testimony of a tragedy — of every tragedy — but it does not deter the aggressor since humanity will continue to mourn peoples with more and more massive shedding of innocent blood. Even so, the text still reserves one statement. To mortally wound a person is to destroy the image of God imprinted on that one. It is God who is attacked and who finally dies with every murdered person.

There is something unfathomable in the contemplation of a dead human body. In the novel and testimony *La noche* by Elie Wiesel there is a scene where in an extermination camp a distressed character asks another while contemplating bodies hanged by the Nazis "Where is your God?" The other answers: "there, on the scaffold." The body of the tortured person is the body of God and their languishing life is the life of God. The theology underlying this story tells us that the premeditated destruction of human life is also a form of deicide. There is less God in the world every time someone is killed and humanity loses a new opportunity to encounter the divine in that face that is now deformed and degraded. The phrase is impressive: "The voice of your brother's blood cries out to me from the Earth" (Gen 4:10); blood has a voice and with that voice it cries out; it cries out to God, its creator and giver of the life now cut short; and the victim does so from the Earth that receives it, the Earth that has been defiled and that stands as an incorruptible witness to the crime.[1] Such is the magnitude of this statement that after the flood it will be insisted that God must demand the life of the murdered neighbor because it is the image of God that has been attacked (9:5-6).

But, at the same time, the realism of the biblical discourse does not ignore the fact that murder has a price for the murderer's life. The assailant believes that by killing a problem has been eliminated and that the aggressor has won over their adversary in the fight for life, but in reality the murderer has unleashed a tragedy that will leave a mark on the murderer's own body for the rest of their days. To the question "Am I my brother's keeper?" the

---

[1]Abraham J. Heschel, who witnessed the Holocaust in Nazi Germany and the violence and murders against the black community in the United States, said on many occasions in the face of the impunity of thousands of murderers that "the blood spilled will cry out *forever*," an idea present in the sense of the biblical text that leaves no room for forgetfulness. Without a doubt, Heschel's words have a universal value and apply to all aggression against human life.

answer is "yes, you are, but you have already killed him." Cain will bear a sign to protect his life from eventual revenge, but that same mark will identify him as the one who cut short his brother's life. The mark is protection and denunciation. It preserves his life but reveals his crime. The protection that comes with the warning that he will[1] have to pay fourteen times if someone dares to kill him does not prevent him from being identified as the one who was the first murderer and the first man who, for his actions, deserved to be cursed by God. In his descendant Lamech, the aggressiveness of his lineage and the contempt for the life of others will be confirmed (4:23-24). Mythic language works with archetypes, not with real people. Cain is not a criminal from the past; he is the human being of yesterday and today every time one human plans and executes the death of another.

Violence on Earth

The experience of violence is not only individual but also collective, and the story reflects this. Introducing fratricide as a practice among human beings gives rise to further investigation into the origin of evil. A new story will help us in this task, one that shows that human beings go from being a first couple and their few children to a multiplicity of being—and with that growth in numbers comes more violence which spreads over the Earth. This fratricide is the third transgression. This story is foreign to the general style of biblical narratives, but it has been used because it was part of the stories that allowed the experience of evil to be explained. Although it has the flavor of Canaanite mythologies that suppose a polytheistic conception of reality, this Canaanite flavoring does not prevent it from being reread in terms of the theology of Israel. We refer to Gen 6:1-4 (plus 5-7) that speaks of when men had daughters and they joined sexually with the "sons of God."[2] The latter are frequently mentioned in the myths of the period to represent the minor gods that made up the Canaanite pantheon.

This sexual theme serves several purposes in the re-reading of the faith of Israel carried out by the biblical editor of

---

[1]The Hebrew text says "twice seven;" also in 4:24. Seven is a symbolic number that in this case indicates a high value; its double is a radicalization of that meaning, an uncountable value.

[2]See the myth "The Handsome and Beautiful Gods" in which the God *Ilu* unites with women who give birth to beautiful gods; this Canaanite myth has been linked to Gen 6:1-4, see G. del Olmo Lete, *Mitos y leyendas de Canaán según la tradición de Ugarit* (Madrid: Cristiandad, 1981), 427-56.

this ancient story. First, it allows the introduction into the narrative of the figure of celestial beings who, by uniting with human women, produce a distortion of nature. They are not children of God in a physical sense, but rather take part in the celestial sphere and possess a divine element that does not correspond to human beings. Attempts have been made to determine who these characters were, but this speculation does not take into account that in mythical literature there are many so-called intermediate beings, who are not gods but share some characteristics of the divine. Hence, by telling of their union with earthly women, a generation of hybrid beings is created that disturbs the human condition tied to the Earth and the perishable. It happens that the divine in the human being is established by God's decision to give a sacred character life and imprint God's image on it, but not because it possesses an essence or a physical feature that belongs to God; the human being is created from dust and does not rise beyond that destiny and for that reason the union of celestial beings with human women gives humans an element of divinity that is not their own and that must be eradicated.[1] It should not surprise us, therefore, that the same text introduces the existence of beings that are in a certain way abnormal, such as the *Nephilim*, later mentioned in Num 13:33.[2] These *Nephilim* indicate the existence of deformed beings, which do not correspond to the harmony of creation, but we must read them as a sign of the inner deformity that has occurred in the human being who has departed from the order in which he had been created.

Third, the story directs the reader or listener's attention to the reality of widespread violence due to the expansion of humanity and establishes that the crime of Cain has now become generalized toward all forms of violence and has expanded to the whole of creation; violence is now a fact of human conduct that cannot be ignored and on which God has the will to act. Fourthly, it opens the door to the wrath of God, who for the first time shows divine discontent with the creation that God had made and announces that God will destroy it, a fact that will be made effective through a universal flood. It is destruction by water, distinct from the destruction by fire that will be applied to Sodom

---

[1]See the study by M. Delcor, *Mitos y leyendas de Canaán,* 67-78.

[2]The Septuagint translates the Hebrew word *nephilim* as giants, which is misleading because it actually refers to abnormal, strange beings that do not conform to what God has designed; in myths they represent evil, the deformed; see W. Brueggemann, *Genesis* (Atlanta: John Knox Press, 1986), 71.

and Gomorrah. V. 8 acts as a link between the previous story and the one that follows; in it Noah ("the most righteous and upright man of his generation") and his family are introduced and with them the story of the flood is inaugurated, anticipating that the destruction will not be total because there will also be an ark with pairs of animals that will make the repopulation of the Earth possible. The mythical and symbolic character of the story is made evident when observing that the destruction of "every living thing" does not include the death of fish, animals that were considered so inferior in the scale of living beings that they could be omitted without causing a problem to the argument.

The recourse to a Canaanite text (6:1-4) and to mythical figures (Heb. *Nephilim*) is something that makes us think. The biblical narrative is not exclusivist and seeks in other traditions and other stories ideas that allow it to understand the reality before it. It takes texts that are foreign to it but recasts them in a new theological entity that is akin to its thought.[1] In the case we are dealing with, this narrative serves to give rise to the story of the flood that was understood as an effort on the part of God to rescue humanity that had confused its role in creation. If the previous story was of Canaanite origin, that of the flood dates back at least to the 22nd century BC and is of Sumerian origin.[2] This ancient Sumerian legend is reread in the key of the theology of Israel to point out that the destruction is not total and that it concludes with an alliance where God promises not to try to destroy creation again. It is the first of several alliances that will be revealed throughout biblical history, but in this case it is not established with a particular people but with "every living being" (9:15).

The Condemnation of Imperialism: A Tower in Babylon

Chapter 10 explains the existence of the various peoples as a result of the repopulation of the Earth by the three sons of Noah.

---

[1]This is a constant in biblical literature as it was in the composition of the texts of other religions. The story of the birth of Moses, the story of Joseph's sexual harassment, the flood, and dozens of prophetic and wisdom texts are indebted to the literatures surrounding Israel. A closer example is the Qur'an's re-reading of biblical narratives, notably the sacrifice of Isaac which is narrated as the sacrifice of Ishmael with important theological consequences; see *Quran*, surat 'as-saafat 37:111-112; A. Yunis, "The Sacrifice of Abraham in Islam," *The Sacrifice of Isaac in the Three Monotheistic Religions* (Jerusalem: Franciscan Printing Press, 1995), 147-57.

[2]See the text of the story in *ANET*, 42-44; the Sumerian text we have is brief but was later taken up by the 7th century Akkadian legend known as the Epic of Gilgamesh, tablet XI, *ANET*, 93-97.

Chapter 11 will explain the diversity of languages as a consequence of the confusion of languages promoted by God among those who were working on the construction of a city and an immense tower. With this resource, God sought to prevent its construction because it was perceived as a new act of excess and a transgression of the laws of God. In order to give continuity and coherence to the historical line, the story of Babel will be presented as a new stage in the development of events. Behind the story of the Tower of Babel is expressed the experience of Israel captive in Babylon and projects it toward the beginning of time, combining the theme of languages with that of imperial power. The captivity took place from 597-539 BC and the contemplation of the *ziggurats* (immense stepped pyramids that served as temples and places of sacrifice, the ruins of which can still be seen today) provided the raw material for this story; in these constructions, they saw the symbol of power and pride, and they perceived that in their eagerness to build them the Babylonian monarchs were sending a message to the world they oppressed. With the tower they told all the other peoples that only they had access to heaven and could communicate with the gods; the others were left with the only option of contemplating the greatness of their oppressors, the magnificence of their works, and accepting the crumbs that these gods had for them.

For Israel, this was the tower that led to the foreign gods, those of the others, the gods that blessed the power of the oppressor. For Israel, as for other nations, Babylon was the empire to which they were subjected and their vocation to dominate was symbolized in that colossal tower that sought to reach heaven.[1] As happens with every significant experience, a word will emerge from it that expresses it and prolongs it in time to bear witness to what they have lived. Here, the contrast is with the faith of Israel, which interprets that God rejects all forms of oppression and seeks to unmask injustice; consequently, it confuses the languages of those who build it to prevent them from becoming "prestigious"[2] and fulfilling their imperial desire. In the story, the work is left halfway; the tower seems to have been built but the construction of the city is abandoned. It is logical that this should be so since the will to oppress is denounced, but it cannot be prevented that this oppression is carried out. This narrative records the fourth

---

[1] S. Croatto, *Exilio y sobrevivencia* (Buenos Aires: Lumen, 1997), 353-83.

[2] The Hebrew says "let us make a *name for ourselves*" with the sense of being famous and acquiring prestige, which would place them above people with vulgar names.

transgression of God's will: peoples were created to unite in harmony and peace, but some have sought to oppress others and have created imperial structures with which they humiliate their neighbors.

No story can prevent a historical project of oppression from being carried out, and this one is no exception. We must not think that the Israelites believed that writing a story would conjure up the tragedies of history; they live and suffer the oppression of the powerful and they write this story as a form of protest against reality, while also to bear witness to God's rejection of the dominating and oppressive project of one people over another. The story of the Tower of Babel is a denunciation of the reality of their present and is a proclamation of God's choice for the oppressed, so that future generations may know it. From the moment that one becomes aware of the situation of oppression, the origin of injustice and the actors who sustain it are perceived more clearly; for that reason, the word that this situation generates is usually simple but poignant. In the case at hand, the greatness of the theology printed in this text consists in not remaining in the anguish of oppression or in the condemnation of the specific imperialism that they suffer at that moment, but rather in constructing a story that involves all forms of imperialist oppression of the past and the future. By becoming part of the mythical literature that establishes the foundations of reality and of the human adventure, its message transcends the historical experience that gave rise to it and becomes a denunciation of imperialism and its abuses at all times and places.

The fact that the anti-imperialist instrument is to confuse languages is very significant and speaks of the sharpness of biblical thought. Peoples who dominate others impose their culture, their laws, their religion and their language on the oppressed. But the story reveals to the reader that at the base of all subjugation is language and speech, which could not go unnoticed by a people whose God creates the cosmos from God's word. Whoever imposes language and speech imposes God's authority and dominion. The *lingua franca*, beyond being a necessary instrument for communication between nations, becomes a vehicle for imperial ideology and for the single thought to which all must conform. Then the oppressor establishes that the oppressed speak a vulgar and rustic language, not suitable for literature or poetry, a language that has no words for elaborate thought and is not suitable for addressing God. Consequently, the oppressed must learn the language of the dominator if they want to communicate and perhaps they can do so. However, there will always be a difference between the general knowledge that can be acquired through study or practice and the learning of a language. The foreign language will always be spoken in a defective manner, with an accent that reveals foreignness and the condition of an upstart user. Many cultural traits can be concealed (clothing, food, architecture, etc.) but at the moment of uttering the first word the pronunciation of the acquired language will exhibit the condition of being subjugated or the poor quality of the lineage (Judges 12:6). For this reason, the story of the Tower of Babel is a condemnation of imperialism and is not a condemnation of the diversity of languages. It establishes that all languages are legitimate and suitable for communication and that languages are not the product of sin but are God's response to prevent sin from abounding.

Theology in Genealogies

From a literary point of view, genealogies serve the function of making history "move forward" by linking separate stories and, at the same time, linking characters with those who follow them in the narrative. This literary function and their evident monotony have contributed to little investigation of their theological value. It is surprising to see that we find five genealogies in the creation story. The first is the descendants of Cain (4:17-24); the second is that of Seth (4:25-26); the third links Adam with Noah (chap. 5); the fourth links Noah's sons with the different peoples of the Earth after the flood (chap. 10); the fifth takes up the descendants of Shem and goes directly to Abraham (11:10-32). They are not mere lists; all of them are used to do theology in a subtle way.

The genealogy of Cain vindicates his life. The man who murdered his brother is blessed with a life and a family. This should not be understood as a reward but as the recognition that fratricide is part of human nature and that the development of life is not stopped by the sinful character of the creature. Cain is said to have built the first city. This is a founding sign of civility and if we add to this that his descendants will be the creators of music, the metalworkers and those who first build tents and move their cattle (4:20-22) we see that he is placed as the one to whom God entrusted the continuation of the creative project. It is from Cain that culture develops. However, the text has a surprise in store when it presents Seth, the third son of Adam and Eve who replaces the deceased Abel, as the one through whose descendants (his son Enosh) the name of Yahweh will be invoked for the first time. The text states that human culture comes from the line of Cain but cannot allow the initiation of the link with God to come from that lineage. Thus, it is through the line of Abel's replacement (the one who was left behind, the victim of violence and injustice) that it is revealed that Yahweh seeks to relate to human beings. The only reason for the genealogy of Seth is to rescue Abel's life and show that although God accepts and even blesses the life of Cain, he does not hesitate to take sides with the one who was killed by his brother. The mention of Lamech in the genealogy of Cain as that aggressive character who multiplies revenge places this lineage in relation to the violence that will soon be unleashed to the unthinkable—the destruction of all creation with the flood. Given this scenario, the aim is to show Abel's descendants as those who recognize and invoke God.

The antediluvian genealogy of chapter 5 leads from Adam to Noah. It does so through the line of Seth and Enosh—Cain and Abel are not mentioned—and includes Enoch, a character who gives prestige to the lineage. It is said of him that he "walked with God" and that one day "he ceased to be" (in Hebrew it says "and he was no more, because God took him"). The years of his life spanned 365, a sign of blessing that is marked by the coincidence with the number of days of the solar calendar.[1] The lineage of Abel and the sacredness of Enoch anticipate the condition of Noah. But the text surprises us with the appearance of Lamech (5:29), Noah's father, who proclaims that his son will console us for the fatigue produced by inhabiting a land that has been cursed by Yahweh. The explanation given by the story of the forms of Lamech's presence in this place is that it responds to a Yahwistic text interpolated in the narrative that is of a priestly character. This statement is as true as it is insipid. What is interesting to investigate is what theological deficiency there was in the story that motivated the author to interpolate that text there. In our opinion, the presence of Lamech places the theology of the passage again in the line that God continues the divine project for creation despite the setbacks of humanity. Lamech is the violent one and is the descendant of Cain but God does not abandon him but it is through him that God's plan is now developed. In his

---

[1]This condition of Enoch will make him a privileged character of Jewish apocalyptic literature. In the Septuagint, 1 Enoch is included, but his figure stands out among the pseudepigraphs; A. Díez Macho includes five works referring to Enoch, see *Apócrifos del Antiguo Testamento* (vol. IV; Madrid: Cristiandad, 1984); A. Ricciardi, "Apócrifos del Antiguo Testamento," *CuadTeol* 17 (1998): 129-46.

words, the present situation is linked to the curse of the ground in 3:17 to indicate that Noah will be the one to help his generation to carry on life on that ground condemned by God. But this has a double value, because on the one hand it remembers the curse of the ground but on the other it constitutes it as a legitimate stage of human life. Furthermore, the story anticipates that a tragedy is coming and emphasizes that it is from the land that Noah inhabits that the rescue will come; it will not come from celestial beings or from a miraculous intervention of God; nor from a human being purified of their faults.[1] It is from the root of the bond between human beings and the land they inhabit that the Creator will provide the person who will preserve the rest of the creation destined to repopulate the Earth. Noah is the most just, but he is still a human being subject to all natural limitations, including sin.

The genealogies of chapter 10 describe humanity from the perspective of Israel. Like all peoples who draw a map, they place themselves in the center. From there, the universe is drawn. In this case, the three families that derive from Noah and his sons intersect in Judah. Japheth is the peoples of the sea, the Greeks and Phoenicians; Ham is the father of the Egyptians and the peoples of the south and also of the nations of Mesopotamia; Shem will be the father of the Hebrews (*Heber*) and the Aramaean peoples. It is believed that this text reflects the political situation and the relations with the other peoples during the time of Solomon (961-922). We observe that Japheth is little developed because Israel had little contact and knowledge of them at that time. But it is in Ham where the text is concentrated. From him comes Kush, who begot Nimrod, who is characterized as the arrogant and is associated with various cities. The intention is political, since all the imperial capitals to which the Israelites were subjected are mentioned in relation to Nimrod: Babylon, Akkad, Nineveh and Kalach—the ancient capital of the Assyrians. Another of Ham's sons is Mitzraim (the name of Egypt in Hebrew) and from him the Philistines are derived, perhaps a people with whom they once confronted each other. The evocation of Nimrod anticipates the story of the Tower of Babel, constitutes the literary context for reading it, and announces the social and political conflict that this story will bring to light. If we consider the list of peoples in a geographical sense, it is impossible to unite Egypt with

---

[1]W. Brueggemann points out that this fact shows how rooted in the human the biblical story is, to the point that he considers it as an element that leads us to think about the theology of the incarnation present in the New Testament, see *Genesis* (Atlanta: John Knox Press, 1982, 69.

Mesopotamia; neither does a common policy unite them since they were rivals for centuries. But if we look at it from Israel, both reigns are a symbol of submission and oppression at different times in their history. The genealogy has grouped together in Ham the enemies (those peoples who had oppressed Israel) and has established an alliance with the Aramaean peoples with whom it is probable that they shared the same oppressions. We cannot force the text too much because we do not know the reason or the historical context of this alliance; perhaps it was a particular moment in history that later faded away and yet left its mark on the story. But from a theological point of view, what it says is that Israel, in drawing the division of peoples, distinguishes between oppressors and oppressed.

The last genealogy is that of Shem and takes up the theme of the lineage of Abel. It serves as a connection between the story of creation — to which it belongs — and the history that will follow it. It is structured in such a way as to follow a single line toward Abraham and it does so in a consistent manner until reaching his father, Terah, about whom it offers more familial details. Part of preparing the story to move on to another story is the gradual decrease in the age of the characters in order to link them with the following stage, where the ages will be regular.[1] Note that Shem lived five hundred years, but Terah two hundred and five; this decrease has been explained by the growth of sin, so that the greater the sin, the less blessing in years of life. That may be an explanation, since imperialism has just been condemned in the figure of the Babylonians and the universal character of the myth refers to human nature, not to a particular people. It would not be contradictory to consider that, while considering the seriousness of the human condition, one seeks to make the narrative compatible with the necessary transition to factual history. Terah's age (205 years) still includes him among the characters who take part in mythical language and where time has a symbolic and not a factual value.

From Mythical to Legendary Language: The Human Condition

Words, when they become narratives, demand a form. We call this form a literary genre, but in anonymous and popular literature it is not a conscious decision of the author but an

---

[1]Abraham and Sarah will act as a transition because they will die at 127 and 175 years of age respectively (Gen 23:1; 25:7), but we must remember that great figures are credited with a long life as a sign of blessing, see Job 42:16.

imposition of the theme. It is not possible to discuss the origin of the universe and of all creation without using the figurative language of myths. It is enough to try to tell the primordial origin of some aspect of reality for symbols and myths to emerge without us even looking for them. Disdained during the reign of positivism, it is remarkable that a rationalist and positivist thinker like Sigmund Freud had to resort to myths to describe the intricate paths of human behavior in its most intimate and original fibers; and he had to do so in order to give it a linguistic form that would allow him to organize his thought and—even more—to communicate it to others. At the moment in which the biblical narrative seeks to tell the family stories that present the founding fathers and mothers of God's people, it abandons the mythical discourse and enters the one more akin to our daily experience, which is the discourse of legends. But there are several things that have been established before taking that step and that constitute the general framework for the development of the events that follow.

1. The beauty of creation has not been violated, nor has human life been rejected. Despite transgressions, the universe continues to be a cosmos—an organized and harmonious whole—and displays its splendor before the eyes of all. There is a harmony in nature that can be perceived, and a human being who, although recognized as a sinner, is also a creator of culture and can live in society. In simple words, it can be said that after the experience of the flood and the repopulation of the Earth, the message is that not all is lost and that God does not cease to bless and support the human adventure.

2. Creation and transgressions have established human nature. What has been established is that this existence will be marked by conflict with God's plan and—consequently—with other human beings. It inhabits a generous but arduous and demanding land, which does not yield its virtues without great effort; a land that awaits to be redeemed. The woman will approach the man and will be able to love him but will also feel that he establishes a certain distance; the man will seek the woman and will find her, but something deep inside tells him that she keeps things to herself, that there are silences and moments that are not shared. The bond will be deep but conflict will dwell there. There is an unsatisfied desire to be God and an aspiration to eternity that has not been eliminated and that does not find a

54

channel of resolution. One will live with these contradictions forever.[1]

3. It is pointed out that human beings are social, gregarious, and city-builders, but this condition leads them to conflict expressed in fratricide and imperialism. Their personal and political relationships will be complex and will both bring them together and separate them from their brothers and sisters. The experience of injustice is incontestable and the texts express anguish but also the possibility of opposing it. Justice between human beings is aspired to and the theology of the Old Testament identifies the will of God with it. This justice appears as a challenge to peoples who must work on its construction, while at the same time being aware that full justice exceeds human will and strength and belongs only to God. The experience is that different peoples can be friends, exchange goods and project themselves together in solidarity, but also kill for the possession of territories, cattle, or women, as revealed in the story of Dinah (Gen 34) or the abduction of young women (Judges 21:8-25). It is said that one can live in peace but also that the horror of war or domestic violence will haunt the lives of people and individuals.

As Chapter 11 concludes, the cosmic stage has been set. The human drama has already begun and must continue.

The Creation of a People: Family Stories

The formation of the people of God is gradual and develops throughout the rest of Genesis, although Israel is only constituted as a people at the beginning of Exodus (there it is said of it that it is "a numerous and strong people" Ex 1:9). To get to this point, the stories of Genesis present us with the origin through a series of family stories. In reality, the beginning of humanity is narrated as a family story: Adam and Eve form a stable couple; Cain and Abel are brothers; Noah and Shem are father and son; Terah took his son, his grandson and his daughter-in-law to leave Ur of the Chaldeans and stop in Haran.[2] These family stories are archetypal and as such, they represent times, ways of life, styles of

---

[1]The Old Testament will not take up this contradiction explicitly. The theme of the human aspiration to eternity will be taken up again with a new theological perspective in the New Testament.

[2]D. Petersen considers this a distinctive feature of Genesis that separates it from the book of Exodus and gives it literary autonomy, "The Genesis of Genesis," *Congress Volume: Ljubljana 2007* (ed. A. Lemaire; VT Sup; Leiden: Brill 2010), 27-40; in our opinion this autonomy represents the stage prior to the formation of the Pentateuch. Within it the book of Genesis gives up its autonomy and is both a giver and a debtor of meaning with respect to the entire work.

relationships and reveal the characteristics of the people that will be formed. For this reason, at this stage, promises, alliances and the weaving of ties are crucial, since these elements will be the foundation of the relationship of the people of Israel with God for the rest of its history. The concept of covenant is complex in the Old Testament and goes through several stages; in fact, there are several covenants. It is notable how in these family stories successive elections are narrated — we will see them below — in which each one shows a different and complementary nuance of the relationship of God with God's people and in turn of the relationship between people. The intention is to show that the concept of election is present in all spheres of life and that it is not exclusive to the election of Israel. On the other hand, it makes it evident that choosing one does not always mean rejecting the other, but rather giving it a different role in God's plan.

We must discard the idea that these stories describe the historical period of Abraham or that they have a degree of historicity. It is true that they were conceived and read as history, but what in antiquity was considered history is closer to our legends than to a critical history. They were not interested in precision but in the force of the symbols that became the foundations of faith and the entity of the nation. When we try to place Abraham in history, we do so in the 17th century, which corresponds to the period of the Middle Bronze Age (2100-1150), but this is due to the data we have regarding the demographic situation in the Near East at that time, where migrations from Mesopotamia to Canaan of nomadic peoples are perceived. However, the story — whose core may be very old — was reread and rewritten at the beginning of the post-exilic period, which corresponds to the period of Persian domination over Israel (539-333). From that time, we have an illustrative text of the situation of Judah in Nehemiah 9:36-37:

> Behold, we are servants today; behold, we are servants in
> the land which you gave to our fathers, that they might eat
> its fruit and its goodness. And its fruit is multiplied for the
> kings whom you have set over us for our sins, who rule
> over our bodies and our cattle, according to their will; we
> are very distressed.

This is the situation of the people at the time when the narratives of Genesis were written in their final form. They inhabit the land but do not own it. They work but do not enjoy the product of their labors. They are a nation but do not have political freedom to decide their future. For this reason, we should not be surprised by the material and earthly character of the promises to

Abraham. One might expect that, coming from God, these should be of an immaterial character, treasures for the soul and less tied to human desires. However, sexual fertility is promised to achieve numerous descendants and the possession of the land, those things that are constitutive of every organized people but that also express the aspiration of a people who suffers oppression and wishes to be free and enjoy its land. Both elements must be read in the light of the poor people that Israel was throughout its history with only less than a century of certain political and economic brilliance around the reign of David and Solomon, and some years in the time of Jeroboam II (786-746) in Samaria. Abraham himself is a "landless man," an immigrant and subject to the inclemency of the climate, as Gen 12:10 indicates. Josef Blenkinsopp has described his condition as that of an immigrant who arrives in a new land and meets those who already inhabit it; with them, he will establish a relationship of cooperation, even buying a portion of land from them.[1]

The Election of Abraham and the Destruction of Sodom

The stories of God's covenant with Abraham and the destruction of Sodom and Gomorrah are stories that were not originally linked, but in the current version they were placed one after the other for a specific hermeneutical purpose. The covenant is presented in chapters 15 and 17. Both stories respond to different schools, the first being a combination of Yahwistic and Elohistic texts and the second a clear priestly text. The promises are the same (the descendants and the land) but what changes is that in the first story a text is inserted that announces the slavery of Egypt (15:13-16) and in the second story circumcision is introduced as a commitment of the Israelites. The advance on the suffering of slavery shows that the narrative is unaware of the future slavery, but in the post-exilic rereading it is introduced enigmatically, which emphasizes the importance that this experience had in the history of the faith of Israel and in the formation of its theology. Thus, although it announces the possession of the land, it also warns of the difficulties that they will have to endure, a way of saying that the election does not mean that Israel is free of anguish and sorrow. Circumcision is also an example of re-reading and adapting a text to a new context. As a rite, it is not linked to the cult of Israel, nor is it

---

[1]J. Blenkinsopp, "Abraham as Paradigm in the Priestly History in Genesis," *JBL* 128 (2009): 225-41.

mentioned in the oldest legal codes, such as the Ten Commandments or the Code of the Covenant. It happens that in the post-exile, circumcision became a sign of identity and belonging to the people of Israel and therefore its prescription was added in this and other texts, making it appear as an ancient practice. It acquires a value of its own when it constitutes a mark of the relationship with God and therefore everyone must be circumcised, including non-Israelites who live on its land. Thus, God's election is reflected in the covenant by which he affirms "I will be your God and the God of your descendants" (17:7) and in return Abraham is promised that he will be the father of a nation and that his descendants will receive the land where he lives today. This choice is contrasted with the rejection of Sodom and Gomorrah.

The account of the destruction of these two cities is a unit of excellent literary workmanship. In all its breadth, it covers chapters 18-19. There are several elements at play in this account. The first is that it contains reminiscences of a widespread destruction such as that which occurred with the flood. Destruction by water and fire is common in the mythical accounts of numerous cultures and it has been speculated that this would be a story of Canaanite origin as opposed to the Mesopotamian account of the flood. In any case, on this occasion it is not presented as a universal destruction but only that of an evil people. The second observation is to ask ourselves about the evil that motivates the destruction. From this reading, it emerges that one of them is the lack of hospitality toward foreigners. It is remarkable to observe how the text prepares for this by showing Abraham's abundant generosity with the foreigners who visit him (18:1-15) as well as that of Lot when he arrives at his home in Sodom (19:1-3). The text contrasts these displays of hospitality with the attitude of the men of the city. Another element is more difficult to pinpoint. It has also been understood that it refers to a sexual fault and has been related to homosexuality. However, the text says that the men ask to "get to know" the foreigners. This expression generally has the meaning of having sexual relations in biblical narratives, but it is not its only meaning, since it is also used with the meaning of dominating in order to subject a person to mistreatment. In addition, the atmosphere of the text — if it is accepted that it refers to a sexual fault — presents it more as a rape carried out by a gang that seeks to humiliate the foreigners than as the consensual exercise of homosexuality. It is worth noting that the same biblical authors, when in other texts they refer to Sodom, do not mention homosexuality but other faults: injustice (Is 1:10; 3:9); general disorder (Jer 23:14); and pride and gluttony (Ez 16:49).[1] In our story, everything is exacerbated by the fact that the use of force—because there are many against few—leaves the victims defenseless and because even the inhabitants of Sodom reject Lot when, in order to avoid the attack, he offers his virgin daughters to be raped in exchange for not attacking the visitors.[2] The sign that characterizes the situation is widespread violence and the trampling of the dignity of other people.

Abraham is going to intercede for Sodom in order to avoid the shedding of innocent blood. The game of lowering the number from fifty righteous persons to ten is a way of presenting Abraham as concerned about a possible injustice and God as agreeing to the request of the one with whom he has just sealed an alliance. Abraham stops his request when he reaches ten righteous people because it is the smallest unit that would save the city as a whole; for less than ten they would be rescued individually, which is what really happened because according to the story there were four righteous people (Lot, his wife and his two daughters) and they were forced to leave the city before the destruction.[3] This intercession reveals the personal character of God, the divine willingness to listen to human beings and the divine willingness to discuss the feelings of those who address God. For readers of this text in ancient times, it was an affirmation of God's good will toward God's people represented in Abraham.

At the end of the story, it is pointed out that Abraham and Lot were preserved (19:29). Both express God's choice, while Sodom and Gomorrah represent evil and the rejection of God. As with the flood, on this occasion the role of Noah is played by Abraham and, to a lesser extent, Lot, who are rescued from the destruction of the wicked. The violence that motivates the flood is

---

[1] W. Brueggemann, *Genesis,* 164.

[2] The offering of daughters has a parallel in Judges 19:15-25 where the master of the house first offers his daughter and then gives away his concubine who is raped and dies. From the texts it follows that at that time the life and integrity of a woman was worth less than the right to hospitality of men.

[3] The novel *Cain* by the great Portuguese novelist José Saramago makes this destruction the crux of his moral argument against God. He points out that even if the righteous were saved, the children in the city, who were undoubtedly innocent, died anyway. We celebrate the literary and humorous virtues of the novel, but we believe that Saramago reads the story literally without realizing that it is a play on symbols about the destruction of widespread evil (violence, injustice, contempt for others) and that at no point does it refer to an individual sin for which specific people will pay. The destruction of the city is a symbol that expresses God's rejection of such attitudes.

not different from that which leads to the destruction of these two cities. The fact that the birth of Isaac and the offspring of Lot's daughters are then narrated—through incest, although justified in the text by the lack of men—speaks of the will to continue with the expansion of life now through these new actors. Of these two, Abraham and Sarah will be the chosen ones.

Choice and Protection: Ishmael and Isaac

The family stories presented are realistic situations in every family. When Sarah is infertile, she offers her Egyptian slave. This practice is recorded in ancient legislation and as planned the son will be considered the wife's and not the slave's.[1] It is likely that Sarah was happy with her son Ishmael, but he will still be the son of another woman. This was also understood by the theology of that time because after the alliance a son is promised to Sarah. When Isaac is born and as a child he plays with his half-brother, Sarah's jealousy toward her slave arises and she manages to get Abraham to expel her into the desert to certain death. The scene that follows is one of the saddest in the entire Old Testament. After walking in the desert and running out of water, the mother leaves the child under a bush and walks away so as not to see her son die. The text in its hermeneutical projection evokes the deep and indescribable pain of all mothers who see a son or daughter die. The contrast is between Sarah's harshness and Hagar's anguish. It is notable that the text emphasizes that God heard the voice of "the child" and after encouraging Hagar promises her that a great nation will come from him, the same promise that God had provided to Abraham about Ishmael (17:20). In this text, God confirms that God will choose Isaac but will also protect and magnify Ishmael. To justify this choice, the text had hinted at certain limitations of Ishmael. In 16:12 it is said that he will confront his brothers; 17:18 Abraham's words suggest that Ishmael is not entirely on good terms with God; in 21:21 it is reported that Hagar—who was Egyptian—gave him an Egyptian woman as a wife. These traits disqualify him from being the leading line of the people of God, but on the other hand he is not rejected from the Abrahamic lineage and it will be said in his favor that he buried Abraham together with Isaac (25:9) while his genealogy will be offered later (Heb. *ve'elle toledot*) and the

---

[1]E. A. Speiser published a document from Nuzi which legislates on a situation like this. In such a case the husband can only take another wife if his own wife does not bear him offspring, see *AASOR* 10 (1930): 31; the document is found in *HSS* 5 (1929): 67; also *COS*, III, 251-52.

information of his death (25:12-18). Ishmael is not chosen but his life and descendants remain under God's protection because in biblical thought not being chosen for a mission does not mean being rejected but that another will be the assigned place in God's plan. His descendants will be identified with the Arab peoples of the desert,[1] which is confirmed by mentioning that Esau — another character who will take a backseat — took Canaanite wives, among them Mahalat, daughter of Ishmael (28:29).

Choice and Discord: Jacob and Esau

Two children live in the womb of their mother and the first to be born will be the father's favorite and the second the mother's. The story of the two brothers evokes that of Cain and Abel. The second is the chosen one and the first will see his aspirations frustrated. The story is etiological and justifies the existence of Edom — the descendants of Esau — and the choice of Jacob who will continue the line of succession. There are various details that the text gives us to warn of Esau's shortcomings and justify his relegation. On two occasions, we are told that he takes foreign women as wives; in one case, Hittites (26:34) and in another the daughter of Ishmael, the Canaanite with Egyptian blood (28:6-9). But the most compelling fact against Esau is his sale of the birthright. The story highlights his disdain for what he must have considered a precious and non-negotiable gift. The narrative of the sale carefully shows that Esau is not hungry, nor does he have a pressing need to eat. Just a few scenes later, it shows him preparing a stew for his father himself. The recurrence of data seeks to establish that Esau was not worthy of receiving Isaac's blessing and wearing such an investiture. In contrast, it avoids commenting on Jacob's obvious ethical shortcomings when he takes advantage of a moment of weakness of his brother to buy his birthright and then agrees to follow Rebecca's plan to deceive Isaac and present himself as Esau. In that scene, Jacob violates the commandment to honor father and mother (Ex 20:7) and — perhaps even more serious — the commandment to invoke the name of God to support a false and deceitful action, an act condemned in Ex 20:7.[2] The story tells us none of this. But it can also be read from

---

[1]The Islamic tradition recognizes itself as a descendant of Ishmael. We have already mentioned that this tradition reinterprets the story of the sacrifice of Isaac as if the son to be sacrificed had been Ishmael.

[2]Another reading — this time positive — of Jacob's response to his father has been suggested in the commentary of the *Jewish Study Bible*; it is interpreted that the words "For the Lord your God has set him before me" (27:20) could

another perspective. On the narrative level, the laws of Exodus do not apply to Genesis because they are later, and that is the explanation why the story tolerates such transgressions by Jacob. But there is something even deeper at play. It is the irony that the blessing on which Israel will be founded as a people was given to someone who by right did not deserve it because of his deception. How can this be? The narrator understands that behind the characters' actions God is working to lead history where he wants it. For that reason, there is no moral condemnation of Rebecca or Jacob because, for the narrator, they are not aware that what they do is decided from before. Thus it makes sense that in 25:23 Rebecca is told "there are two peoples in your womb... and the younger will rule over the older," an expression that is a preview of the events but which the story interprets as being fulfilled in these scenes. This also makes sense why Isaac refuses to bless Esau after learning of the trap he has fallen into.[1]

The blessing is expressed in the form of a poem (27:27-29). It combines the wish for a prosperous future with a strong political tone. It grants him property, land, economic prosperity and dominion over the surrounding peoples. It places him above his brothers — in this case Esau — and adds the spell that whoever curses him will be cursed and whoever blesses him will also receive a blessing. The crisis occurs when Esau arrives with his food and Isaac discovers with horror that he has been deceived. His intimate feelings of suspicion told him the truth and, without wishing it, he left his favorite son without the blessing that was rightfully his. At Esau's request that he also be blessed, Isaac remains silent because he knows that the facts exceed his capacity to decide and administer blessings. God has made God's choice. The discord between brothers has been consecrated and the story will continue through Jacob.

Election and Competition: Rachel and Lea

This story shows another family scene. Jacob falls in love with Rachel, but through a trick of his father-in-law he receives as his wife her sister Leah, who was older, unattractive and therefore

---

mean — even though Jacob does not know it — that it is not Isaac's will but God's that is being carried out at that moment by blessing Jacob instead of Esau. However, the text does not seem to support that Jacob acts according to a plan of God but rather according to a plot organized by Rebekah in favor of her favorite son.

[1]W. Brueggemann, *Genesis*, 233.

difficult to marry.[1] Disappointed, he negotiates with his father-in-law and succeeds in getting him to marry Rachel later on. The narrator's theology conceives of God observing all this; God saw Leah was unloved and made her fertile while Rachel, the desired and beautiful, was made sterile. In these two women, the future of Israel is exposed and both compete with each other to give children to Jacob. At one point, out of desperation, they follow the same custom that Sarah followed of giving her husband her maid so that she would conceive in her name; thus both sisters give their maids Bilhah and Zilpah to Jacob so that they could have children with him. At the end of the story, it is perceived that God chose Leah but did not abandon Rachel.

The competition is established from the first day. Rachel, the despised, gives four sons to Jacob. In biblical theology, giving children is always a blessing from God. It is God who opens the womb or closes it. For this reason, sterility was an affront to women because it cast a shadow of suspicion on their lives: it was thought that they had done something to make God close their womb. In those times, people lived in the confidence that good and bad always came from the will of God.[2] Consequently, Rachel bursts with jealousy and accuses Jacob of being the sterile one: "give me children or I die," she says. Jacob answers: "Am I God to deny you fertility?" (30:2). Then Rachel gives him her slave with whom he will have two children who will be considered hers. But—as with Sarah—this condition of putative mother did not stop giving him a bias of inferiority, even though it was legal and accepted. After Jacob had two more children by Leah's slave, Rachel returned in her desperation to try to get pregnant. She negotiated with Leah to leave her husband for a few nights in exchange for some mandrakes that the firstborn Reuben had brought to Leah, since these fruits were considered aphrodisiacs and with them he wanted to strengthen himself sexually. Leah slept with Jacob and conceived two more boys, now Dinah, the only daughter mentioned. Perhaps because Rachel's humiliation was already deep or because the unloved woman of yesteryear now boasted of having given birth to six sons and a daughter, the text says that God remembered Rachel, "heard her," and granted

---

[1]The Hebrew text says of Leah that her eyes "were soft" but the context dictates that this be understood as "dull," "unattractive;" the custom of marrying daughters in order of age meant that Leah's single status prevented the marriage of her younger sister, see C. Westermann, *Genesis*, I, 463.

[2]W. Holladay, *Long Ago God Spoke* (Minneapolis: Fortress Press, 1995), 144.

her a son. The story continues along other paths, but in time Rachel conceived again and gave birth to Benjamin, the last of Jacob's sons. During this birth, Rachel died and a stone on her grave will remember her forever in a warm place, today remembered near Bethlehem. Leah will be buried in the cave of Makpelah, where Abraham, Sarah, Isaac, Rebekah rest and where Jacob will rest. God chose Leah but also blessed Rachel, and the slaves Bilhah and Zilpah.

Old Testament theology is not built on the lives of ideal people but on realistic ones. The threads with which God weaves the divine plan are not of gold or silver, they do not shine for their purity. They are rustic threads but woven by God. None of the characters presented is exempt from faults, missteps, and baseness. None stands out for their purity or moral perfection. Jacob's father-in-law deceives him and trick and marries him for his own interest in the wrong woman; the beautiful Rachel does not rejoice in her sister's blessings; Leah, the once ugly and second, humiliates her sister Rachel by boasting of her fertility before her, who is barren (30:20). The women and men of God are of flesh and blood and for that reason they expose the human condition in all its aspects. They only shine if illuminated by God's plan they reveal human destiny and advance history one step further in the endless caravan of nights and days.

Jacob and the Creation of God's People

Chapters 48-49 of Genesis testify to the final days of Jacob and give shape to the last details that prepare for the constitution of the people of Israel. This is so at the level of the narrative, although not in history, since the text itself contradicts what it seeks to affirm. What is described is not a unified people, but it will be so, as the subsequent narrative will present it in that way. Everything begins with the need to resolve the situation of Joseph, who will be the first to die and will be supplanted by two of his sons. Jacob opens his speech and narrates his experience in an almost pedagogical way. There are four elements in Jacob's words in 48:3-4 that speak to the theology of the story: 1. He evokes the God who appeared to him and who lives in another land, in Canaan; 2. He remembers he was blessed by that God; 3. He expresses that the content of the blessing was fertility and offspring until forming a multitude of peoples; 4. He points out that God promised him the land of Canaan for his descendants.

Jacob then adopts Ephraim and Manasseh for himself and distinguishes them from the other sons of Joseph. They will each form a tribe as if they were his sons, although they are his grandsons; the other sons of Joseph will be counted for the purposes of inheritance, but will not have the status of tribes. This liberty that Jacob takes to modify the criterion of biological reality — namely, that each tribe is made up of one son of his — is in keeping with the choice of Isaac over Ishmael and his own choice of Esau, where the biological connections were also altered. In this case, this alteration will also be reflected in the blessing of Joseph's sons. Jacob will cross his arms in order to bless the youngest with his right hand and give the eldest a blessing with his left. In response to Joseph's complaint that his blindness is causing him to make an involuntary mistake, Jacob tells him that he knows what he is doing and announces that it corresponds to the destiny of the children, since the youngest will be superior to the eldest. The blessing offered to Joseph's sons is significant, especially if we consider that it takes place in Egypt and is intended for two young men whose mother is Egyptian (41:45, 50), who do not know Canaan and perhaps little of Jacob's traditions. The gesture seeks to ensure the status of the Israelites for Joseph's sons.

What lies behind this is the conviction that, although God speaks through descendants and their order, this is not the only way in which God expresses the divine self. And even further, it is revealed that God's action is sometimes incomprehensible to human beings who often act without knowing that they are carrying out God's plan. After Jacob's death, Joseph's brothers fearfully go to prostrate themselves before him because they believe that he might now take revenge because they had sold him when he was a child; Joseph answers them:

> Although you intended to harm me, God intended it for
> good to accomplish what we see today: the preservation of
> *a large number of people* (Gen 50:20).

Jacob has just died and for the first time in the narrative the Israelites are described as "a numerous people." A new turning point in history has begun.

This narrative is followed by chapter 49, which has been called "Jacob's blessings" to his sons. However, there are no blessings in this poem, but words that define each of them. From a formal point of view, it differs from the previous story in that the former is part of the narrative and advances the story, while the latter is not narrative and interrupts the succession of the historical line to insert a poem. The text cannot be dated precisely because it presents themes from before the monarchy and others from after. For example, the words to Reuben refer to situations in the past, while those dedicated to other sons (Dan, Joseph, Benjamin) suppose a later period. It is undoubtedly an ancient work that received updates with hermeneutical intentions.

We can imagine Jacob's concern in his final days when he saw that until then the succession had been conducted in a single-person manner from father to son, but now there was no one to succeed him. His firstborn son (Reuben) does not have a leading role, and the rest are not shown as leaders. Jacob's words to his sons in chapter 39 show his family as a mosaic of different tones. Each son has his own characteristics and none of them appears as a unifying figure, rather he describes them as not very keen on the organization of a community. Reuben, Simeon and Levi are treated harshly because of their violent backgrounds;[1] Zebulun and Issachar are dedicated to other tasks and show no interest in leading their brothers; Dan will be judge of his people — his name in Hebrew means "judge;" Gad, Asher and Naphtali are barely mentioned; the longest of the paragraphs is dedicated to Joseph, who will die in Egypt and will be represented by his sons who are not named; Finally, Benjamin is mentioned crudely as a warrior, as Judges and the story of King Saul, who belonged to that tribe, will show.[2] From a sociological point of view, we might think that we are on the threshold of a disintegration of the sons of Jacob into small nations. However, in 50:24, before dying, Joseph prophesies to his brothers that God will make them "go up from this country to the one he promised to Abraham, Isaac and Jacob;" in those words, there is no room for a rupture between the tribes. They arrived as a family and, although the differences between the tribes are highlighted, making it difficult to think of a political and cultural unity, the narrative goes in the opposite direction and shows us that at the end of this time they will leave Egypt as a people.

The Oppression and Liberation of Slaves

For Old Testament theology, history reaches its climax with the exodus that led to liberation from slavery. This is the point that we arrive at and from this point, we begin to define the rest of the events where God is linked to humanity. It is the fundamental fact of living as slaves without our body belonging to us and discovering that the God we invoke is on our side and acts

---

[1]Reuben committed incest, 35:22; Simeon and Levi murdered the people of Shechem against their father's will, 34:25-31.

[2]Later histories of Benjamin show it as a brutal tribe as in the case of the crime of Gibeah (Jdg 19-20).

in our favor to free us from all oppression. We also discover that God is active in seeking to demolish every structure that oppresses us and takes away our right to life with dignity and freedom. The story will describe the exodus as the center of the world and of time, that moment where divinity showed itself more clearly than ever in its vocation to sympathize with human pain.

Slavery was a social and political reality in the life of biblical Israel and in that of all peoples of antiquity and — in sometimes subtle forms — of our days. Being a visceral experience, it could not be absent in the construction of the theology of the ancient Scriptures. As a historical fact or as a memory of a historical fact — and the entity of the events that may be behind a memory is of little interest, since this is worth its own weight — it generated anguish and that anguish generated a word that, when written down and becoming a text, gave it transcendence. It is the word that is born from the anguish of the oppressed but that does not generate a theology of the oppressed but one of liberation.[1] Oppression is the situation, but the cry is for liberation from pain and the expectation is that God will be on the side of the one who suffers to do justice in his life. A theology that is built only on the experience of oppression or captivity would be quietist and would comfort the victims but would not call them to rebel, as does a theology that knows that justice and liberation are possible and driven by God.

Human pain is by definition punctual and historical, but it rises in the groan to a cosmic and universal dimension. When this happens, the event of slavery becomes a symbol and for that reason the biblical text puts on the lips of God "I have heard their cry in the presence of their oppressors" (Ex 3:7). The text refers to the cry (Heb. *tzea´qa*) of the Israelites, but its words are valid for all times and peoples who suffer oppression and anguish, because if it were not that way, the story of the Exodus would have value only as information about an event that happened in the remote past to a Semitic people. But the God who freed Israel is the same one who today hears the cry of those who suffer oppression and cry out for justice. What we are saying is not a mere declaration of our good wishes toward those who suffer today, but it is what the text says and does when it transforms a specific, passing and forgettable event — like hundreds of acts of justice and injustice

---

[1]See the works of L. Boff, *Teología desde el cautiverio* (Bogotá: Indo América, 1975); *Teología del cautiverio y de la liberación* (Madrid: Paulinas, 1978); in these early works Boff discusses the place of the oppressed and the theology that arises from their anguish.

suffered by women and men that vanished in time – into a story with mythical characteristics and therefore with a narrative density that makes it transcend all times. The word about Israel's slavery speaks of our slavery, pain and injustice. If it were not so, it would have no place in the Scriptures.

The Hardness of the Oppressor's Heart

In Exodus 1:9, Pharaoh describes Jacob's descendants as a "numerous and strong" people. With this statement, one of the promises made to Abraham is fulfilled: that he would be the father of a people. The writer does not miss the fact that the other promise, that of possessing a land, is still pending. And not only pending, but given the situation of slavery and distance from the promised land, it seems that it will never be fulfilled. Pharaoh's strategy of extermination leads to the already arduous days of work becoming a horror. The Israelites are sought to be eliminated because of the burden on their bodies and the consequent loss of fertility. But it does not work out that way, the plan fails and the Israelites continue to grow. Then Pharaoh orders the midwives to kill the children at birth. But the midwives Shiphrah and Puah lead the first act of rebellion against the oppressor: Not only does their strategy prevent the death of the children, but they also save their own lives by lying to Pharaoh about the physical capacity of the Hebrew women. In this way, women are the protagonists of the first act of liberation that will lead to the freedom of the slaves.[1] When this fails, the new order is to kill all the male children born by throwing them into the Nile River, where the cold and the crocodiles will do their work.

This violent and cruel attitude of the Pharaoh is a preview of what will happen later when he meets Moses and the plagues occur. The name of the Pharaoh is not given because the text understands that cruelty has no identity or time and is identified by the damage it inflicts on others. His cruelty is all the cruelties of history. The fear of the slaves that the Pharaoh shows has political roots and also shows the irrationality of the oppressor. He harangues his people and warns them of the risk that the slaves, in case of war, will join the enemies against them. That is quite improbable, but it is a good argument to put his own people in conflict with foreigners; let us remember that the poor and the

---

[1]For an expansion of the role of midwives see C. Houtman, *Exodus* I (Kampen: Kok Publishing House, 1993), 250-65; P. R. Andiñach, *El libro del Éxodo* (Salamanca: Sígueme, 2006), 36-39.

common people formed the armies that were taken to war by their masters. In reality, the Pharaoh perceives the slaves as a threat to his power and privileges, but he has the ability to transfer that fear to the also oppressed Egyptians who constitute his own people. The resource of pitting the poor against other poor is not an invention of our time but has been used with great skill as a tool of submission by the powerful throughout history.

Women Save Moses

The figure of Moses is the most important in the entire Old Testament. His life spans the four books of Exodus, Leviticus, Numbers and Deuteronomy. Before him, the outstanding leaders are Noah and Abraham, but neither of them had the relationship with God that Moses had nor were they figures who mediated between God and the people. Through this link, we see that Moses is more than a prophet, since he not only transmits what God tells him but also dialogues with God and discusses alternatives.[1] No other figure is given so much space in the biblical narratives. With the exception of Genesis, his figure dominates the entire rest of the Pentateuch.[2]

Like every story about the birth of a hero, the narrative has a strong hermeneutical tone. Each detail is intended to express a meaning that has to do with the literary situation of the birth or with the future life of the character. In the case of Moses, an ancient Akkadian legend is used in which King Sargon had been abandoned by his mother in the river, in a basket, and was rescued by a goddess who received him as a lover; later, this child would become king of Assyria.[3] What the biblical author does is use the plot of a popular legend and recast it in the context of the theology of Israel. So there are common elements in the story but modified to express a different theology. For example, Sargon's mother was

---

[1] R. Rendtorff adds that the figure of Moses shows that Israel can only be led by someone who has a direct relationship with God; he sets the standard for other leaders although none reached his stature. *The Canonical Hebrew Bible* (Leiden: Deo Publishing, 2005), 93.

[2] An excellent study is J. Van Seters, *The Life of Moses* (Louisville: Westminster/John Knox Press, 1994).

[3] It refers to Sargon the Great who ruled Assyria in the 22nd century BCE; the text of the legend is in *COS* I, 461; the best study of the Sargon legend is B. Lewis, *The Sargon Legend* (Cambridge: American School of Oriental Research, 1980); also P. R. Andiñach, "Estudio de la leyenda acádica de Sargón," *OrArg* 11 (1994); 67-84; and *RevBíbl* 55 (1993): 103-14. There are other stories where the child is abandoned by his mother and becomes a great hero, such as Romulus and Remus, Oedipus, Hercules, and Cyrus the Persian.

a priestess who was forbidden to become pregnant and therefore the child was unwanted; on the contrary, Moses' mother loved her son. In the story of Sargon there are supernatural elements and the intervention of a goddess who rescues him from the river and receives him as her lover, while these elements are absent in the story of Moses, which takes place within the regular coordinates of human life. What both narratives will agree on is that they grant legitimacy to the character; but even so, the sign is opposite in each case. While Sargon is a commoner who through this story acquires nobility through contact with a goddess and the right to occupy the throne — which he will usurp militarily — in the case of Moses the narrative establishes that he is an Israelite who has been raised in the palace and who, by showing solidarity with his people, returns to his original condition of slave and outcast. His story gives legality to his condition as a Hebrew, belonging to the people of slaves, something that could be in doubt for some. We must bear in mind that his name was Egyptian (Moses); His physical appearance and clothing were confusing (2:19 says, referring to Moses: "an Egyptian rescued us from the shepherds"); and it is likely that the text assumes that his accent when speaking Hebrew was that of someone whose first language was Egyptian (4:10). Thus, the theology of the biblical story reveals that God acts through natural events and privileges the one who makes a commitment to the enslaved people when, as the adopted son of the princess, he could have chosen the serene and uneventful life of the palace.

The birth of Moses is full of ironic elements. Pharaoh ordered that girls not be killed because he considered women socially harmless, and yet it is women who save Moses. The midwives were powerless people, but they were the first to defy Pharaoh's order; with their rebellion, they inaugurated the process of liberation. It was a maid who, in response to the child's cries, protected him and, instead of throwing him into the river, took him to her mistress. It was Pharaoh's own daughter who rescued the child and violated his order to throw him into the river. It was Moses's real mother who breastfed him through the intervention of her daughter. It is remarkable to note that God unites women from two peoples who were at that time in conflict in his project to save the child; they showed compassion in the face of the threatened life of a defenseless baby and that sensitivity united them above their rivalries. The irony reaches its peak when we are told that Pharaoh will unwittingly pay a stipend for Moses' upbringing, who, when he grows up, will defy him and free his slaves. These and other ironies make it clear that the story wants to show that God's will is behind everything that happens, even the Pharaoh's actions. God's plan is fulfilled even when God's participation is carried out in a surreptitious manner, without fanfare and without intervening ostentatiously in the events. Everything is narrated as if it happened by chance, but when we look at the details, it is revealed that the author wants to show that the hand of the God of Israel directs history. This is a feature of biblical theology that includes few cases of direct intervention by God, but lets us see here and there that divine action is carried out without violating the laws that God created.

The Fight Between the Gods: The Plagues of Egypt

Working for justice and encouraging the processes of social conquest have always been human activities as was the escape from slavery in the story of the liberation from Egypt. However, at that time it was assumed that the struggles that took place on the surface of the Earth had their counterpart in the heavens where the gods of each people fought. The people whose god was the most powerful in heaven prevailed on Earth. Misfortunes were understood as caused by the weakness of the god who was supposed to protect the people from them. There are several examples of this thinking in the Old Testament; in Joel 2:17, when suffering a military invasion symbolized by locusts, God is called upon to intervene because the other peoples mock the apparent inability of the God of Israel to protect him by saying "where is your God?" (also Ps 79:10; Mi 7:10). This way of understanding social dynamics is the source of the temptation to "go after other gods" that the prophets denounce. These other gods — Canaanite, Egyptian, Assyrian or Persian — appeared to the Israelites as more effective and successful in the task of protecting and blessing their people and therefore they perceived them as stronger than the God of Israel.

The story of the ten plagues is built on the conviction that it is a struggle between gods. The word "plague" is not the best translation. The Hebrew says *nega'* which means "blow," "mark" (Lev 13-14 applies it to "mark of leprosy") and *deber* which means "pestilence." This indicates that they are not understood in the sense of calamities, but of events that point to another reality that is beyond the situations posed. The classic denomination of these events as "plagues" is already an interpretation of them. In this way, their relevance is limited to what historically could have happened and their transcendental dimension is lost sight of. In fact, as specific events, they could not have been very relevant since no Egyptian source gives an account of them nor were there any allusions found in the documents of other neighboring peoples. It is assumed that a succession of acts of this nature would have left its mark on official or popular histories. Nothing of the sort happened. So everything indicates that the correct reading must be sought in its symbolic and mythical value, which is in itself much deeper and has greater hermeneutical value than mere history.

If we delve into it, we see that the first nine plagues have to do with elements that make the land and its inhabitants impure or that distance them from the blessings of God. The river made of blood, the sores, the frogs, the locusts, the carcasses of animals are all elements mentioned in the Code of Purity (Lev 11-16) among those that inhibit human beings from a fluid relationship with divinity. Contact with any of them separates the person from the blessings and turns them into a threat to the community. But in this case, in the eyes of Israel, the entire people of Egypt are affected by impurity and therefore the message is that they have lost their link with the God who was supposed to protect them. What happens with the plagues is that they are signs that the God of the slaves is stronger than all the Egyptian gods; When Pharaoh's magicians tried to reverse the plagues, they only succeeded partially until the third plague, when they could no longer counter it and recognized that they were not simple acts of human magic but came from God (Ex 8:14). The ninth plague is that of darkness (10:21-29). The narrative evokes the time of creation when God created light and separated it from darkness. Therefore, it means that the Egyptians are sent to nothingness, to a time when light had not yet been created and life did not exist. Attempts have been made to explain this plague as an exaggerated account of a solar eclipse or the irruption of a wind that raised sand from the desert and darkened the sky for three days. Neither of these explanations serves the account, which on the one hand clarifies that the darkness was selective and occurred only in Egyptian homes while there was light in Hebrew homes. Nor do they do justice to the account that shows in the last plague that the God of Israel dominates over the sun, which means that he defeats the Egyptian god Aton. Of him it is said in *The Book of the Dead*, "I am he [Aton] among the gods who cannot be defeated."[1] To leave the Egyptians in darkness is to take them back to the time of

---

[1] See *ANET*, 4.

72

creation, to the time when there was neither language, nor cities, nor science, because human beings did not yet exist; it is to lead the oppressor people into non-existence, a state in which only slaves were condemned. And finally, what this sign reveals is that by establishing a selective darkness, God has taken the side of the weak and exploited.

The tenth plague differs from the previous ones and is distinguished both by its literary form and its effect. The succession of nine signs has revealed a growth of tension. Each one increased the pressure of the Hebrew God and the implicit divine declaration of being the one who dominates the forces of nature. Now the distinction between Egyptian and Hebrew houses requires a mark with blood on the doorposts and lintels. The mythical elements surface again: a destroying angel will pass from house to house and kill the Egyptian firstborn, which is the reversal of the Pharaoh's order from the first chapter. The measure is of such magnitude that the writer shows no joy nor signs of vengeance in recounting this plague. It is as if it is assumed that the Pharaoh's harshness led to this tragedy and that as a result of this attitude the innocent will be affected in the outcome. The aggression is carried out on the firstborn because they were the beloved sons of every family.

Our sensibility rejects this type of action as cruel and unjust. The same thing was said about the destruction of Sodom and Gomorrah. But we must not lose sight of the fact that we are not dealing with historical events but mythical ones, the meaning of which is expressed in the creation of a climate for theological reflection. Unfortunately for the life of humanity, having read these stories in a historical way gave rise to justifying wars, violent actions, genocides and murders with the biblical and religious argument that in certain circumstances even God resorted to violence and the death of the enemy. But what is said here cannot be interpreted as an authorization to unleash our own violence. On the contrary, it says about God that only God has power over the life and death of every person, and about the Pharaoh it says that in his arrogance he has shown that even with all his power he could not preserve even the life of the most protected young man in the kingdom, his son, the crown prince. The strength of God revealed the human frailty of the Pharaoh and the fallacy of his supposed divine condition.

The Identity of God: The God Who Is (El Dios que está)

In the biblical stories, theology is done in names. In the Old Testament — and in many other cultures — the name of a person or place usually expresses its sign and identity. In the stories, due to their literary constitution, proper names are always significant and say something about the person or the place. When Esau discovers that Jacob appropriated the blessing that was due to him by putting himself in his place, he links this action with his name and says: "Therefore he is called Jacob..." (Gen 27:36); the popular etymology of the name Jacob relates it to the Hebrew verb for "to supplant." The psalms evoke the place called Meribah, which means dispute, argument, dispute, because there the Israelites questioned Moses and God (Ex 17:7; Ps 81:7; 95:8). As with people and places, knowing the name of God was a fundamental issue in establishing a stable and faithful relationship. In the narratives of the ancestors, we find some names built on the word *'el'* which is the generic term for God in Semitic languages. We find ' *el olam* (whose meaning is "eternal God," Gen 21:33); also *'el shadai* (which means "mighty God," Gen 28:3; 49:25; outside the Pentateuch, it is only found in Job and a couple of times in Ezekiel); *'el elyon* (God most high, Gen 14:18 *passim*); other forms derived from the latter are *'el-al* (Hos 11:7) and *elyon* (Lam 3:35) with the same meaning. In these cases, it is not clear whether they refer to God as *'el* and then add an adjective or whether they are complete names. From this form will arise the name *'elohim* which we will talk about later.

The key text for considering the name of God is in Ex 3:13-14:

> Moses said to God, "If I go to the children of Israel and say to them, 'The God of your fathers has sent me to you,' they will ask me, 'What is his name? What shall I say to them?' God said to Moses, "*'eheyeh asher 'eheyeh*." And God said to Moses, "Thus you shall say to the children of Israel, ' *eheyeh* has sent me to you."

Moses asks about God's identity and God answers him with an enigmatic phrase that still arouses astonishment today. He answers *'eheyeh asher 'eheyeh* whose most common translation is "I am who I am." This expression does not seem to be an answer to the question and does not make sense unless we consider it a way of saying "I do not have to tell you my name," an improbable answer from a God who throughout the passage (3:1-4:17) shows the God is patient and interested in clearing up every doubt that Moses may have. The Hebrew phrase has a certain dynamic and also admits the translation "I am who I will be" and, the one we

74

adopt, "I am who I am."[1] The Greek Septuagint translation is more rigid and yields *egó eimí ho ón* whose meaning is the classic form "I am who I am" and which has influenced the translation that has become habitual in our language over and above the Hebrew text.

The first thing to say is that in the narrative aspect, in 3:14, the name of God is not "revealed" — as is often claimed — because that name was already known and God was named by it since Gen 4:26 where it is said that "from that time on, the name of Yahweh began to be invoked;" furthermore, in this same unit it is mentioned in Ex 3:2, 4, 7 which makes the supposed revelation nonsensical. What happens in 3:14 is that in response to Moses' complaint, he is given an *explanation* of the name and God's identity. To understand this text, it is necessary to distinguish between name and identity; they are usually confused, but we must note that names are repeated in persons and places, but identity is unique and that is the revelation that this text provides. As in other passages, reading the literary context will help us understand the meaning of God's response. In 3:11, God tells Moses, "I will be with you…" and gives us a key to understand what follows. Moses then insists and asks God to tell him what he must answer when he presents himself as sent by "the God of your fathers" and the Israelites ask him about the identity of the God who sends him. To this question God answers: "I am the one who *is*" in the sense of the one who accompanies, gives strength and does not abandon God's people.

This interpretation is consistent with the second part of v. 14 which adds "the one who is *sent* me to you." What has been made clear in this verse — and that is the novelty it brings — is not the name but the identity of God. If the name as an expression of identity speaks of the intimate nature of the one who bears it, in this case, what is affirmed is the vocation of God to accompany God's people in everything that may happen to them. Being said in the middle of the narrative between slavery in Egypt and what will later be the process of liberation, it is a way of anticipating the liberating sign of God's action that will develop during that process.

Remarkably, the Old Testament does not offer a definition of God; this is so in part because every definition conditions the defined object and pigeonholes it; partly also because the Semitic

---

[1]For an expansion on the meaning of this expression see our *The Book of Exodus*, 82-85 and the bibliography cited there; a key article is that of S. Croatto, "Yavé, el Dios de la 'presencia' salvífica," *RevBíbl* 43 (1981): 153-63.

spirit is not given to precisions and is very given to describing beings by their behavior. When God's power was perceived, he was called 'el shadai, "God almighty;" when God's transcendence was 'el olam, the eternal; the text that we read now shows that before the invitation to a hard and complex project God has revealed God's self as the one who will be and accompany God's people, this is the God of presence and for this reason God instructs them: "tell them, I am the one who is." This condition of "being" is so strong in the theology of the Old Testament that in Ex 17:7 on the occasion of suffering thirst in the desert they question God and they do so by putting God's presence in doubt:

Is Yahweh in our Midst or Not?

What has been revealed is the condition of the God of Israel as being present. In the speech that Moses must present to the Israelites, the central thing is to convey to them that it is the presence of God that characterizes God's way of relating to God's people. The God of Israel is not the God of war, fertility, or destiny. It may be that at times and in different literary contexts, God is something of each of these characteristics. But what makes God different from others and defines the divine identity is that the God of Israel is the God of presence.

A second proof that there is no such revelation of the name is that from 3:14 onwards, the other names continue to be used, especially the generic 'elohim. It is plural and could be translated as gods, but while it is probable that the form comes from a time when primitive Israel recognized various gods, the truth is that in biblical Hebrew it acts as singular in all cases except for those texts where it refers to foreign gods (e.g., Dt 4:7), which happens in many cases but which are not ambiguous for understanding. A related form that never ceases to amaze us is the expression Yahweh Sebaot, which means Yahweh "of the armies," undoubtedly in reference to the heavenly hosts of minor gods of the Canaanite pantheon. This expression is absent in the Pentateuch but is abundant in the prophetic books which re-signified the reference to the gods by placing them under the authority of the God of Israel. But it is difficult to know whether what was done by bringing them under God's rule was to subordinate them to the god of Israel or whether the expression confirms the principle that there is no other god and therefore precludes the existence of those gods. Given the slow process by which Israel passed from monolatry to monotheism, it is likely that the former is true.[1]

The God of the Ancestors and the God of the Place

The God of the Hebrews was described as "the God of Abraham, Isaac, and Jacob" in the biblical narrative. This expression grows in importance as the characters succeed one another. He is the God "of Abraham, your father" for Isaac (Gen 26:24); he will be "of Abraham, your father, and of Isaac" for Jacob (28:13); and for Moses he will be "the God of your father, God of Abraham, God of Isaac, and God of Jacob" (Ex 3:6). The God thus described is a deity who walks with the believer, goes where the believer goes, and has no place of settlement. It is difficult to determine whether this nomadism was a historical or literary fact. Archaeology does not agree on whether or not there was a nomadic period in biblical Israel. In any case, in the narrative, the stages of nomadism and sedentarism are clearly exposed. Before altars were prohibited, it is said that the patriarchs and matriarchs sometimes built them to worship God; this was done by Noah (Gen 8:20), Abraham (12:7; 13:18) and Moses in the desert (Ex 17:15).[2] But the story gives signs that they are temporary altars and that a regular place of worship is not being established. The same can be said of the altar built by Joshua (Josh 8:30) and by the tribes of Reuben, Gad and Manasseh (22:10), although it is probable that these altars began to be stable places of worship for Yahweh. At an earlier time, a further step was taken when the Tent of Meeting and the Ark where the law was deposited were built in the desert (Ex 35-40); the detail of being a portable device continues the tradition of the God who moves, although now identified with a particular structure.

It is with the settlement in Canaan that the transition takes place from the God of the ancestors to the God of the place. This process may be a literary construction, but in any case it reflects a social truth. A people who resides permanently in a land tend to create fixed places of worship and identify these places as the

---

[1] See Ex 15:11; monolatry or henotheism is the acceptance of the existence of several gods but the worship of only one; this is the case of the first commandment that demands the worship of only one among several "you shall have no other gods *before* me," see P. R. Andiñach, *El libro del Éxodo,* 327-29.

[2] H. Preuss points out that although there are many references to the God "of the ancestors" it cannot always be assumed that it refers to Yahweh and that it is probably a very old expression referring to the God *El* who would later have been assumed by Israel. *Old Testament Theology II* (Louisville: Westminster/John Knox Press, 1992), 5-7.

residence of God. A notable example of this way of thinking is found in 2 Kings 17:26 where it is said that the new inhabitants of Samaria are attacked by lions because "they do not know the Law of the God of that land." The interest is twofold: on the one hand, the need to express faith and comply with the prescriptions of religious law; on the other, there is a political interest on the part of the authorities since the temple becomes the place of collection of funds for the crown and of national identification.

By the time of the prophets, those provisional altars built by the patriarchs and matriarchs had already been confused and assimilated to Canaanite places of worship and, therefore, had been transformed into places of idolatry. This motivates them to be criticized in prophetic harangues (Am 3:14; Hos 8:11). However, it does not seem that their preaching was very effective because idolatry continues to abound and it was not until a century later that King Josiah, in the year 622 BC, would produce the most important religious reform in the history of Israel and would order the demolition of all the altars that populate the territory of Judah and the already non-existent Samaria (2 Kings 23:4-14). God's order calls for compliance with the document found in the temple—we presume it was an embryonic version of Deuteronomy—and in accordance with it God will establish the temple of Jerusalem as the only place of residence of God and of legitimate worship (Dt 12:2-7).[1] This reform ends by confirming that the God of Israel does not migrate but resides in Jerusalem.

Only in Daniel and Ezra do we find the expression "God of heaven." Both books are among the latest in the Old Testament, and the fact that this expression is abundant in them indicates it is a new step in the understanding of God. It is likely that it reflects a certain Persian influence, but if so we should ask ourselves why we do not find it in other books from the same period, such as Esther, Ecclesiastes, and Job. What we can infer is that the post-exilic literature is little affected by the favorite themes of the priestly source (the law, the temple, the observance of the festivals, etc.) and that in it a concept that could have come from another culture was crystallized, which consists of considering that God

---

[1]There is a debate as to whether the "Book of the Law" found was actually a protodeuteronomy, whether it was another document, or whether it never existed and was merely a ruse to justify the reform, see N. Na´aman, "The Discovered Book and the Legitimation of Josiah´s Reform," *JBL* 130 (2011): 47-62; the author concludes that, in accordance with the strategy of other monarchs of the ancient Near East, there existed a document of which we can affirm nothing about its specific content and which was used to legitimize the religious reform.

dwells in heaven. But this expression seems more a challenge to the other one that affirms that God resides in the temple than a declaration about the physical space where the divinity dwells. Everything indicates that the expression "heaven" does not refer to a place but to three elements that are a theological novelty for its time: the universality of God who "sees" everything from heaven, which is also a way of testifying to the monotheism already consolidated at that time. The second is the conviction that by living in heaven there is no terrestrial place where divinity can be "captured" and thus be politically manipulated in favor of regional or class interests. The third is that by living "in heaven" the space is freed so that it can be invoked from any place.

One last observation must be made. In Israel, the name of God acquired a sacred value. Hence, the prohibition of taking it in vain, in a frivolous manner, or of invoking God's name for a purpose contrary to God's will was absolute. Such was the zeal that, in order to avoid even doing so carelessly, it was stopped being pronounced altogether. The custom—and later obligation—of avoiding pronouncing it and its replacement by *Adonai* (in Hebrew it means "Lord") occurred at an unknown date but in biblical times.[1] The theology behind this is fine and deserves to be considered: it says that the name of God was revealed to Israel for its redemption, as a positive and promising value; making it an element that can be manipulated for personal or regional ends distorts its meaning and puts the relationship with divinity at risk.[2]

The God Who Liberates

The narration of the moment of liberation is presented within a liturgical structure in chapters 12-15. It begins with the celebration of the Passover and ends with the thanksgiving of the Song of Moses and Miriam. This reveals to us that the story assumes itself not as a history of events but as an interpretation of them. The discourse is not journalistic—external and passing—but rather one that seeks to expose the meaning of what happened and, for this reason, it resorts to liturgical language that is symbolic and mythical. The narration happens in this way because an event grows in meaning when it is seen from the experience of

---

[1]The Septuagint translation dating from the 3rd century BCE already avoided naming him and translated instead "the Lord," indicating that the prohibition already existed by that time.

[2]B. Childs, *Old Testament Theology in a Canonical Context* (Philadelphia: Fortress Press, 1985), 39.

faith, and when narrating it from that experience one must seek the words that allow one to express it. We have already mentioned that this tendency should not be understood as a decrease in the veracity of what is narrated, but as an expansion and deepening of the experience. The plain account of a fact says almost nothing about its meaning, but the experience of faith *sees* in the facts of history the intervention of God and therefore incorporates into the narrative that which is captured by faith and which makes an eventual and passing fact become a message for its time and for posterity.[1]

Beginning with the Passover narrative, the liberation from Egypt is placed in the larger project of Israel's redemption. The distinction is subtle, but we must make the effort to understand that the historic act of leaving slavery to go toward freedom is understood as the first fruits on a path that leads to the redemption of Israel and the final rescue of humanity. This does not detract from the historical and factual liberation wrought upon the slaves, because without it the entire story would lose meaning and value. Furthermore, it is necessary for those who are enslaved to experience the veracity of God's will to free them from that situation so that they themselves are the ones who generate the word that will transmit that message to other generations. The story of liberation arises as a testimony of what God has done for the oppressed and, as such, as a word of hope for all the oppressed in history. Now, the horizon of mere history must be surpassed so that every act of injustice that has gone unpunished and every oppression where liberation has not been realized can be understood not as a weakness of God's plan but as a sign that redemption is not limited to that sphere nor is it annulled by it. But this must not lead to the numbing of consciences or to faith becoming evasion of reality, the "opium of the people."[2] For those who suffer oppression, a God who saves their soul but who has no intention of freeing them from earthly chains is more the attitude of a cynic than that of a God who claims to love and commit the divine self to those who suffer. God's presence makes sense if the

---

[1]For an expanded understanding of the theme of the exodus as a hermeneutical key, see S. Croatto, *Liberación y Libertad* (Buenos Aires: Mundo Nuevo, 1973); despite the years that have passed, his reflections are inspiring and have not lost their relevance.

[2]This expression was widely used in the 19th century and was made famous by Karl Marx in his *Contribution to the Critique of Hegel's Philosophy of Right*; there he considers religion as a numbing of the conscience but at the same time as an unconscious form of protest against real misery, see Karl Marx-Friedrich Engels, *On Religion* (Salamanca: Agora, 1974), 94.

God who is (*El Dios que está*) there is the God who liberates. That is why looking beyond the facts themselves must encourage us to understand that in social and political liberation there is a sign and advance of that full redemption that will overcome all anguish.

Easter thus becomes the feast of the memory of liberation from slavery.[1] This is how it will be understood in the subsequent reflection of the biblical texts and how it will also be understood in the New Testament in the accounts of the passion of Jesus. These are located in the week of the celebration of this feast in Jerusalem and thus bring about a rereading of its themes in the context of the revelation of Christ. What is interesting to highlight in the account of the Exodus is that from it onwards Easter concentrates the memory of an event of the past in which God's will to be with the oppressed and to promote their liberation was revealed in history. So that every time Easter is celebrated in the liturgy, what is done is to update the message of liberation and redemption of God for the moment that the community lives, which will experience it in its own and contextual sufferings, oppressions, challenges and anxieties.

It should not surprise us to find that at the time close to the liberation, we hear words of doubt and recrimination to Moses (Ex 14:11-12). These are the so-called murmurings that appear here for the first time, but that will continue throughout time in the desert. They express the fear of freedom and the longing for a past that, from a distance, seems better than the present. From a theological point of view, their function is to make it clear that liberation and redemption are acts of God and not of human beings. It is God who shakes the human conscience and calls us to take on a project that overcomes injustice, even if those who suffer from it prefer to stay as they are. Human beings mobilize and act by modifying projects and societies, but in the theology of Israel it is God who is behind everything and who gives the strength to carry forward the liberation. In Moses' response to these reproaches, this emerges with total clarity; he tells them: "Do not be afraid; stand firm, and see the salvation *that the Lord will accomplish* for you today... The Lord *will fight for you*, and you shall hold your peace" (vv. 13-14). Once the crossing of the sea has

---

[1]From the point of view of the history of the Israelite religion, the Passover went through various stages before becoming a festival of liberation. It was an agrarian festival and was also a conjunction of two festivals; for further information see R. de Vaux, *Instituciones del Antiguo Testamento* (Barcelona: Herder, 1976), 610-20.

taken place and after experiencing the action of God, the word of gratitude will spring forth expressed in a song (Ex 15).

In a high-quality hermeneutical game, the narrative of the exodus from Egypt is concluded with the Song of Moses and Miriam. It is likely that as a poem it is very old (v. 11) and that it has been rewritten in a new version to apply it to the events of the liberation from Egypt. On the other hand, its current version reflects the time of Israel already settled in Canaan and looking back at its history, which is made evident in the mention of Edom and Moab—which were later classic rivals of Israel—and of the Temple Mount (Ex 15:15-17). But noting this distance in time between the event and its word, far from diminishing its value, strengthens it by showing that after the years, the memory of the exodus as an act of liberation was in good health and was celebrated with one of the most beautiful songs in biblical literature.

The song that brings together Miriam and the other women at the end (v. 20) is a prayer of gratitude for the salvation they have already experienced, and that makes it more valuable than if it were a song composed at the time. If it had been so, it would express the joy of the recent event, but over time the experience matured and grew in intensity as an evocation of a fact that endures in memory and in life. It reveals that the need to celebrate liberation remains in force as a memory of the past but also as an expectation of the present in the face of any other form of slavery into which one may fall. It confirms that the act of liberation was the work of Yahweh and only of him. The poem announces that the Lord put all God's power to defeat the Egyptians and free Israel and does not hesitate to exalt God as a warrior who sank God's enemies in the sea. This language may produce rejection in our current sensibility, but it must be understood in the context of celebrating an act that was violent because the circumstance demanded it. The reason for the violence in the narrative is the Pharaoh's stubbornness in not allowing the slaves to be freed, and the responsibility for the death of the Egyptian soldiers falls on him. We have already pointed out that this type of text does not allow us to use violence as we please, but it does speak of the fact that the biblical story has a delicate sensitivity to identify the origin of social violence and to recognize the dynamics that are presented as inevitable in order to overcome them.

As a synthesis and conclusion of these reflections on the theology that emanates from the story of the Exodus, we wish to highlight the following points:

1. The project of redemption, which is universal and eternal, is expressed in this particular and fleeting deed. But it generated a word that became a text and thus became a message for all generations. As such, we are called to update it in the context of our own challenges.

2. The story shows that liberation is an act of God, but also that God raises up leaders to carry it out. Moses' objections to the mission, which he initially rejects and his later acceptance, are a testimony to the fact that God does not act alone, nor does God wish to do so. If the Israelites had not loaded their bags and left Egypt, God would not have forced the liberation.

3. God's identification with the oppressed and the divine proposal of a plan of liberation announces that God's vocation is to be with them and free them from the yoke they suffer. This action transcends the liberation of Israel and becomes universal when it is crystallized in a story that will later be recognized as canon. This canonical status not only recognizes the sacred value of the text but—more importantly—says of it that it speaks to all the oppressed wherever they are. The liberation of the slaves of Egypt is an archetype of God's plan for all injustices and sufferings of any time and place.

4. The message of liberation must also be read on a personal level. The God who liberates through an act of collective liberation such as the exodus also invites us to reflect on the search for liberation from other forms of oppression that people suffer. That is why the call to freedom of the exodus has implications for the life of each person, to explore the personal aspects of our bonds and to free ourselves from those things—selfishness, pride, gender violence—from which we sometimes do not wish to be liberated. The exodus points in this direction and offers a complete message; for Jews and Christians, this liberation is not exhausted in the past but is presented as a liberating archetype for future history. Breaking with slavery and looking toward freedom is a challenge that God places before each person.[1]

---

[1]G. Gutiérrez understands liberation on the social level and also as an "inner liberation, in an individual and intimate dimension" that he characterizes as psychological (p. 58); later he summarizes liberation on three levels: economic, social, and the liberation that Christ brings that "frees man from sin, the ultimate root of all rupture of friendship, of all injustice and oppression" and points out that the three should not be separated because they occur within a "unique and

The Creation of an Order: The Law

We have not always stopped to observe the central place that laws have in the Old Testament. It is probable that Christian theology, which emphasized grace over law, has influenced this neglect, especially some texts of the apostle Paul that are very hostile to the law or perhaps it is better to say to the concept of law (Rom 4:13-15; 7:6; 1 Cor 3:3; Gal 5:2 among others) although he equally values it in what it contributes to revealing sin ("the law is holy" Rom 7:12). The gospels have also contributed to this neglect (Mt 9:14; 12:1-8; 15:1-9; Mk 7:19 and others). But a careful reading of the Pentateuch reveals that more than one hundred chapters — of the 187 it has — are occupied by legal texts. Genesis is the only one of the five that does not contain laws, and one of them, Leviticus, is entirely a legal text. Although it is difficult to prove, the feeling one has is that Leviticus is located in the center of the five books due to its condition of representing the law in its most complete sense.[1] The laws are associated with the figure of Moses, whose life expands from Exodus to the end of Deuteronomy, and who is responsible for receiving them from God and transmitting them to the people. This solid presence of the laws in the Pentateuch could not be otherwise, since they constitute the core of God's covenant with Israel.[2]

After the story of the liberation from Egypt, the alliance at Sinai takes place, the second great act that will outline the history and consequently the theology of Israel. Both were originally separate narratives that came from two different traditions that at some point joined to form the current story. This union was not mechanical but rather a weave was created between the theologies of both traditions that created a new texture that surpasses each individuality, which makes it impossible to speak of two theologies in the current text.[3] The truth is that the story tells that

---

complex" process, *Theology of Liberation. Perspectives* (Salamanca: Sígueme, 1972), 68-69.

[1]To investigate the structure of the Pentateuch and its division into five books, see P. R. Andiñach, *Introducción hermenéutica al Antiguo Testamento* (Estella: Verbo Divino, 2012), 61-80.

[2]An excellent presentation and discussion of topics can be found in the work of J. L. Ska, *Introducción a la lectura del Pentateuco* (Estella: Verbo Divino, 2001), 61-74.

[3]The distinction between two traditions was preserved in some texts such as Joshua 24, which summarizes the history of Israel but ignores the Sinai covenant; Psalm 78, which also omits the Sinai in the historical narrative (vv. 53-55); the same

after a few days they camp at the foot of Mount Sinai and there the revelation of the laws to Moses will take place; this episode is a continuation of the liberation program and gives a new facet to the social, political and religious conformation of Israel.[1] From this moment on, and until the emergence of a different paradigm in wisdom literature, the theology of Israel will be a dialogue between the evocation of the benefits received from God during the event of the exodus from Egypt and the observance of the laws revealed on this occasion, a dialogue that yearns for balance but which at times will lean toward one or the other of both components.

The Alliance on Mount Sinai

Although the theme of the alliance dates back to Noah (Gen 9:9) and Abraham (Gen 15:18; 17:1), the development it acquired in the story of Sinai will surpass the previous ones. Álvarez Valdés will postulate the existence of two alliances, one without laws (the alliance with Abraham) and another with laws, the one that was conceived in Sinai.[2] The second would have been imposed by the force of the priestly tradition in the post-exile and would have been established as the main alliance in the later theology of Israel. However, what the reading reveals is that the alliance in Sinai takes up the theme of the possession of the land and includes it as an essential part of its discourse. It is important to note that the literary form of the laws, whether they use the imperative apodictic formula ("You shall do..." or "You shall not do...") or the casuistic conditional ("If someone does such a thing... you shall do such another thing..." or "When it occurs that... you shall act in such a way..."), is not compatible with a declaration of the type "they shall possess the land," which is a promise, not a law. What happened is that in order to remedy this situation, expressions that recall and link the first covenant, in particular the promise to possess the land, were inserted in dozens of key places in the Sinai covenant. We select only some of the most significant cases from this resource:

---

in Psalm 105. However, in our opinion, it is forcing the texts to describe a theology based on these vestiges.

[1] J. Collins points out that the liberation of the exodus finds its "fulfillment" in the laws of Sinai and that from there both elements will feed off each other. We understand that Collins' opinion is incomplete since liberation does not culminate with the reception of the laws but continues with them; the laws add the legal aspect to a liberation process that is long and complex; *Introduction to the Hebrew Bible* (Minneapolis: Fortress Press, 2004), 121.

[2] A. Álvarez Valdés, "Levítico 26," *EB* 61 (2003) : 155-81.

At the end of the Code of the Covenant, there is mention of God's guidance—through God's messenger—toward the promised land (Ex 23:20-23).

There are a series of laws introduced by the formula "When you have entered the land of Canaan, which I give you to possess..." (Lev 14:34; 23:10, 22; 25:2 etc.)

Others use the formula "to the land where I will lead you..." (Lev 18:3; 20:22, etc.)

In the context of the rejection of Canaanite religious practices, it is stated that they should not do as they did because "you will possess their land..." (Lev 20:24).

The phrase in the mouth of Moses "to the land to which you swore to their fathers..." (Num 11:12; Dt 1:35; 34:4).

There are some with a negative meaning: "Aaron... shall not enter the land that I gave to the children of Israel" (Num 20:24).

Another negative formula is the instruction not to conquer certain territories because they have been given to other peoples, which supposes that there is also a territory for Israel. This happens with "the sons of Esau" (Edom) in Dt 2:1-7; with "the sons of Lot," the Moabites (2:8-13); and with the "sons of Ammon" in 2:16-19.

God tells Moses before his death: "Go up this mountain Abarim, and you will see the land that I have given to the children of Israel" (Num 27:12).

The formula "go in and possess the land which the Lord promised to your fathers..." (Dt 1:8.21).

In this sense, one of the most important texts is Dt 6:1, since it indicates that the laws and decrees received are for "you to put them into practice in the land to which you are crossing to take it..." This text explicitly involves the alliance made with Abraham with the legal alliance presented through Moses.

The Hebrew word *berit*—which we translate as covenant or alliance- has a dense meaning.[1] It implies two parties who agree to respect an agreement; it also implies the creation of a bond between the parties; this bond is sealed with a document but in other cases it is done through sharing a meal. In Gen 26:26-31, we have an example of a pact between equals whose purpose is to preserve peace and well-being among peoples (Heb. *shalom*) and is confirmed with a dinner. The common biblical expression is "to

---

[1] A detailed etymological analysis can be seen in W. Zimmerli, *Manual de teología del Antiguo Testamento* (Madrid: Cristiandad, 1980), 51-52.

cut a pact" (Heb. *carat berit*, Gen 15:18; 21:27; 26:28, *passim*) which, with pity for our language — something we do not always do in biblical translations — we translate well as "*to establish* a pact." This use of the verb to cut may be in reference to the act of dividing food, to the ritual described in Gen 15:8-11 where Abraham cuts several animals in half as a covenant ritual, or to the sense of distributing something equitably. Whatever the case, what is evident is that "to cut" conveys the idea of an action that recognizes the existence of two parts that are linked.

It has been widely studied and today there is a consensus in recognizing that the structure of the biblical alliance is linked to the so-called vassalage or sovereignty pacts of the ancient Near East, which abounded during the second millennium and the beginning of the first. In these, the sovereign king offered protection and assistance to a king of lesser power. The vassal agreed to the pact and benefited from the fact of being part of a larger political structure while agreeing to pay its taxes. These pacts reflect the dominance of the larger states over the weak but also a creative way of survival of the small kingdoms. What Israel did was to adapt the model of these pacts and use them to express its relationship with God. The people agreed to comply with certain codes and God acted as protector and benefactor.[1] In Ex 6:6-7 there are three elements of the pacts: 1. The name of the sovereign is offered ("you *will say to the children of Israel: I am the Lord*"); 2. Concrete acts of protection are promised for Israel ("*I will bring you out from under the heavy burdens of Egypt, and I will free you from its servitude*"); and 3. The commitment to uphold the covenant over time is announced ("*I will take you as my people and I will be your God*"). Note that this quoted text is at the beginning of the Exodus when the Law has not yet been revealed and therefore defines the rest of the narrative that follows it. So Israel is going to expose the Law in the salvific context of an alliance to be made between a powerful God who acts as protector and a weak people who will be protected. Everything that follows will be read as the acts of liberation that the protective God works in compliance with the announced covenant.

---

[1]S. Croatto postulates that "the alliance is the legal expression of the spiritual reality that Israel lives" and points out that the vassalage pact is the form that best suits a weak nation that recognizes its need for God's protection. *Historia de salvarsa* (Estella: Verbo Divino, 2000), 66, 68.

The Law Given to Moses

Classical exegesis has insisted on dividing the set of laws according to their antiquity and belonging to a particular source. This approach has yielded certain fruits by allowing us to distinguish periods and emphases within them and, in particular, their relationship with the legal codes of the ancient Near East. The cost of this option was that the theological unity that groups them together and that is expressed in the uninterrupted succession in which they have been placed was lost sight of. It is a theological and hermeneutical fact that there are no laws in any of the other books of the Old Testament, even in those such as Ezra and Nehemiah that show a special zeal for legal issues. What happened is that even when there are legal bodies that show their post-exilic color (Lev 27) they were always understood as given by God and this delivery was identified with the time of the desert. From there, each new set of laws that was formed was inscribed as having been received through Moses in the desert. In this way, its foundational value was affirmed and the laws were granted the authority of belonging to that privileged period in which God governed Israel and they lived, sustained only by divine grace and love.

Today we know the text to be idealized by the passage of time and the deformations of memory, but that makes the real or imaginary historical reference but not its symbolic value, which is what contributes to the development of the theology of Israel. This hermeneutical procedure combines two elements; one has roots in the conviction that everything that is good comes from God and therefore the laws cannot be the work of legislators or human kings; second, that those things that established the rules by which every Israelite founded their relationship with God had been given in the desert, a time evoked as ideal by the close relationship that existed in that scenario between God and Israel. In Judaism, this corpus was so important that it is called in the singular as the Law (*Torah*). It does not matter that there are internal divisions, repetitions, or contradictory laws; For the Old Testament itself, these texts are not "the laws" but the Law.[1] This speaks of the

---

[1] An assessment of the use of the expression the Law in the New Testament and in Christianity can be found in J. Klawans' article, "The Law," *The Jewish Annotated New Testament* (ed. A-J. Levine & M. Zvi Bretller; New York: Oxford University Press, 2011), 515-18.

theological value they possess and of the transcendence attributed to them. But words have weight and a clarification is necessary.

The Hebrew word *Torah* means "teaching," "instruction;" its etymology leads us to "throw an arrow" and from there the sense of "give direction," "instruct." When the Hebrew Scriptures were translated into Greek (in the so-called Septuagint translation of the 3rd century BC), *Torah was consistently replaced* by *nomos*, which in Greek means "law." This was probably because in those times the *Torah* was perceived as a plethora of laws and is even described as such in 1 Kings 2:3. But it is important to distinguish between what is an instruction that guides and a law that is indisputable; between a teaching that opens paths to thought and a law that limits them. In Lev 11:46 ("This is the law [*torah*] concerning beasts, and birds, and every living thing...") it becomes clear that *torah* in this case does not mean law but "instruction" and should be translated as such. However, the tradition created in the diaspora of calling the set of texts grouped in the Pentateuch law prevailed, giving them a certain degree of rigidity that we should avoid.

From Exodus to Deuteronomy, the laws are organized in codes or collections, with the addition of some loose texts. Listing them allows us to understand the forcefulness of these texts. They are:

1. The Ten Commandments, in two versions (Ex 20:2-17; Dt 5:6-21)
2. The Code of the Covenant (Ex 20:22-23:19)
3. Laws on sacrifices (Lev 1-7)
4. Laws on the clothing of priests (Lev 8-10)
5. Code of purity (Lev 11-16)
6. Code of Holiness (Lev 17-26)
7. Deuteronomic Code (Dt 12-26)

From a theological point of view, it is necessary to affirm that the laws have been given to Israel for their joy and fulfillment and not as a burden for their faith. Psalm 119 — which is the longest of all the psalms — is dedicated to exalting the value of the Law; the stanza of vs. 97-104 exalts the benefits of being close to it and loving it ("How I love your law! It is my meditation all day long..."); Psalm 19:8-13 says it with deep conviction: "The Law of the Lord is unequaled..."). Deuteronomy 6:3 proclaims that observing it "will do you good and will multiply you in the land..." Thus, the Law was not understood as a limit imposed on the enjoyment of the beauty of life but on the contrary as those norms that, when fulfilled, allowed access to rejoicing in the gifts of God and the blessings of each day. The theology of the Old

Testament is far from considering the laws as a mechanical obligation; Rather, observance of the Law is the gateway to maintaining a creative relationship with God and with one's neighbor. In Gen 2:16, God instructs the first couple to live in freedom and to feed on everything in the primordial garden except for one of the trees; in this way, it is established that a characteristic of life is freedom exercised within the framework of accepting the imposed limitations. To observe the Law is to live in plenitude; thus the wise sage declares: "Keep my commandments and you will live, and my law as the light of your eyes" (Prov 7:2).

Second, what we have just said is based on the fact that there is a coherence in all the codes in that the laws express the will of God and are identified as ordinances with God. In the biblical discourse, to know God is to know God's will; there is no prior or independent knowledge of God of mystical, spiritual or interpersonal origin, which is later completed with the knowledge of the divine will.[1] The prohibition against killing a human being or the punishments for eventual crimes committed are not, as we would understand them today, civil laws that regulate life in society. They are as closely linked to faith as those that prescribe the manner of offerings to be brought to the temple or the observance of the Sabbath. The relationship between law and worship is so close that the prophets denounce that its non-compliance causes the distortion of worship even if it is carried out under a correct liturgy and leads Amos to say: "I detest your festivals... your sacrifices and oblations..." (5:21-27); Natural tragedies such as drought and social misfortunes such as bribery and injustice are attributed in Is 5:23-24 to the contempt for "the *Torah* of Yahweh Sebaot." Observance of the Law is the way to be right with God, but this state cannot be reduced to an individual relationship with the Creator — which it certainly is as well — but rather points to the fact that fulfilling the Law is the way to ensure justice and equity in society.

Third, we observe that the laws contain both promises and threats. Like all laws, they ensure well-being for compliance and punishment for disobedience. Again, in this case, the punishment is not of a police nature, but consists of falling into a state of impurity, a way of saying that persons are separated from the benefits of being close to God until God has restored their

---

[1]B. Childs points out that knowing God and knowing his will are a unique act in his self-revelation, *Old Testament Theology in a Canonical Context* (Philadelphia: Fortress Press, 1985), 51.

previous state through the corresponding rites. It is interesting to observe that each fault corresponds to a means of restoring the correct relationship with God, which indicates that the intention of the Law is not to punish transgressors but to give them the opportunity to correct their conduct. The Law highlights the fault and demands that it be corrected. In this respect, there are few laws that do not allow the reconstruction of the broken bond and are consequently punished with death; those that do so are linked to specific cases. They refer to those who kill or offer human sacrifices (Ex 21:12; Lev 20:2-5), where in both cases the punishment follows the practice of applying the law of Talion of "an eye for an eye" (Ex 21:23-25), but is self-limited by recognizing the right to asylum in cities designated for that purpose when the homicide has been involuntary (Ex 21:13; Jos 20); in turn, death is prescribed for other crimes such as mistreating parents or disobeying them (Ex 21:17; Dt 21:18-21); or the practice or consultation of sorcery (Ex 22:17; Lev 20:6). Some sexual offenses are also punishable by death, but in this regard there are laws with some ambiguity. In Lev. 18 it is considered that sexual offenses produce impurity and although it is stated that the offenders must be extirpated from the people, it is not done with the same force as in Lev. 20:8-21 where several of the same offenses are explicitly punished with death.

It should be noted that we do not have too many biblical examples where the death penalty is exercised effectively and consistently. The cases that there are seem more a product of the anger of the moment than of a reasonable application of the legislation.[1] On the other hand, there are passages that cast doubt on the meaning given to the word death in these texts; In Lev 15:31 it says "you shall remove the children of Israel from their impurities, so that they do not die of their impurities by defiling my tabernacle" but this verse is the conclusion of 15:1-30 where the impurities of women and men are described and the means of purification are indicated without implying any irreparable fault. The mention of the tabernacle does not establish any difference because it refers to the fact that it is located in the center of the camp, not to the person entering it, since that was forbidden to the common people. In any case, the death penalty is very restricted in the biblical codes and there does not seem to have been a

---

[1]See Ex 32:27; Jdg 4:17-22; in 2 Kings 23:4-14 Josiah destroys idolatry and burns the altars but does not kill the priests of Judah although he does kill those of ancient Samaria (23:20).

consistent practice in its application. Our opinion is that the mention of death as a punishment expresses the seriousness of the fault and seeks to act as a deterrent rule.

Finally, it is quite significant that the reception of the laws is literarily associated with the act of liberation from Egypt. The Sinai—the place where the laws from Exodus to Numbers were received—and the steppes of Moab from where Moses announced the laws of Deuteronomy, are still part of the exodus and this should not be forgotten when evaluating the laws. They themselves are placed in tune with the deed by which the slaves go toward freedom, and from the semiotic point of view, the laws are an integral part of that event. But although semiotics helps us to visualize the relationship, what is at stake is the theology that supports this relationship between Law and liberation. In Dt 6:1 it is said that the laws are to be put into practice "in the land that you are going to take possession of;" so that the delivery of the laws is done in the expectation of achieving possession of a land to live and develop. Without the land, laws have no meaning, since most of them presuppose a sedentary life and the ability to operate on social reality with a judicial, religious and political system that slaves lack. This contradicts the idea of 19th century theologies— which also have their representatives today—that there was an opposition between laws considered rigid and the dynamics of the Genesis narratives or the preaching in favor of justice by the prophets. This opposition forced one to choose and, therefore, devalued the legal bodies. However, in the canon, one presupposes the other and separating them based on their sources or a chronological order leads to weakening their message. In the process of constituting an order that organizes life, belonging to a land goes hand in hand with a legal body that regulates the coexistence of the community in all its aspects.

An unresolved discussion—and one that we do not have the space to address here—is the nature of the biblical legal bodies. Are they laws as we understand them today, or did they have another function? The scarce presence of concrete legal judgments in the biblical narratives deprives us of examples where we can observe whether the laws were applied in the courts as a judicial tool or whether they played a symbolic role, as a reference to what was God's will without implying their use as a basis for verdicts. Bruce Wells compares the biblical laws with the codes of the ancient Near East and concludes that we can affirm that some laws were effectively applied while others were not.[1] Certainly the laws relating to rites and liturgies were effective as were those related to food, sexuality and health. Doubts remain about those relating to slavery, those proposing the death penalty and certain laws on the ownership and administration of land; Even so, the trend is that a good part of them acted as laws applicable to everyday life and in the courts.

The Laws on Purity

Of the legal codes, the one that is most difficult for our sensibility to understand is the one on purity. The texts are concentrated in Lev 11-16 but the theme extends to 17-26 and the Deuteronomic Code (Dt 12-26) as well as other shorter texts. The classification of animals into clean and impure and placing under the same category important areas of daily life such as sexual practices, diet and health often perplexes the reader. Various explanations have been offered. We note three that summarize the others:

a. There are those who understand these laws in a symbolic, but very mechanical, sense. Thus they consider that the value of animals that chew the cud consists in evoking the act of meditating on the things of God; or the separation between pure and impure foods reminds Israel of its condition as a separated people; or the regulation of sexuality the need to distinguish between sacred and profane times.

b. More comprehensive is the idea that the prohibition of eating certain animals has to do with issues of hygiene and health. In some cases, it could be thought that they transmitted diseases and in others it was believed that they did. The rules would have arisen as a response to the experience of contracting diseases that were attributed to the meat of certain animals, which for that reason became considered impure.

c. A third interpretation is that proposed by Jacob Milgrom, which consists of understanding that the limitation on killing and eating certain species is an ethical norm to prevent human beings from becoming brutalized. By limiting the killing, society is forced to think about the act of killing animals and leads it to do so with care and prudence. Norms would be a way of

---

[1]Wells believes that the codes were drawn up to serve as examples to be consulted by judges in difficult cases that allowed them to base a verdict on them as legal "antecedents," "What is Biblical Law?" *CBQ* 70 (2008): 223-43.

civilizing human behavior and avoiding the indiscriminate shedding of blood.[1]

These explanations may be part of the phenomenon, but our position is that this type of rationalization or symbolic reading does not take into account that the community that reads and applies these laws considers them a sacred text and therefore is not subject to the need to give a practical account of the meaning of each law. In the case of the laws, these are justified in themselves because they express the will of God and the path that he has traced so that human beings remain close to God. They are assumed as conventions established by God for the good of Israel and for that reason alone they must be assumed. However, even when their rationalization is rejected, certain tendencies can be inferred in the laws that guide us regarding their meaning. One group of them expresses the rejection of any mixture of elements that, at first sight, result in conflict, such as sowing seeds of different plants together, plowing with a donkey and an ox at the same time, or weaving a cloak and interspersing linen and wool (Dt 22:9-11). The prohibition of homosexuality and sexual relations with animals (Lev 18:22-23) and the prohibition of boiling a kid in its mother's milk (Ex 23:19) respond to this same principle. Another group of laws rejects what is understood as a form of deterioration of the natural, such as skin diseases (leprosy, eczema, Lev 13-14) and the loss of bodily fluids such as semen or menstruation (Lev 15). The prohibition of adultery and various forms of incest (Lev 18) seeks to organize the economy of sexuality in order to preserve coexistence in society. Since the wife was considered the property of the husband, clear rules against adultery had to be established to avoid conflicts and violence over the possession of a woman between men.[2] The androcentric nature of ancient Israelite society meant that only sexual relations between a married woman outside her marriage were considered adultery, and therefore these laws acted as a way of preserving the property and honor of men. Today, we see that the dignity of women was ignored by denying them equal treatment and turning them into sacrificial victims in order to preserve the sexual peace and economic balance of men.

---

[1]The central text for this study is J. Milgrom, "The Biblical Diet Laws as an Ethical System," *Interp* 17 (1963): 288-301.

[2]C. Edenburg concludes that the laws on sexuality are an application to Israel of norms common to the legal bodies of the ancient Near East, which in all cases sought to preserve social harmony, see "Ideology and Social Context of the Deuteronomic Women's Sex Laws," *JBL* 128 (2009): 43-60, esp. 57.

No justification is offered for the rationale behind the food laws. One exception is Lev 18:22-23, which instructs not to eat meat with blood because "in it is life," a very ancient concept and the product of the simple perception that when the blood runs out, breathing and life cease. From the lack of justification, it can be inferred that the authority of the law resides in the one who promulgates it and in the commitment of having assumed a covenant. We will look in vain for a rational or cultural explanation for an indication to abstain from eating certain terrestrial or aquatic animals; in the dynamics of the laws, these prescriptions are those that show the degree of commitment to the Law and the will to observe it. It does not matter whether pork is bad or good for health; what is at stake is respect for an instruction that comes from someone who has shown that he seeks the best for the life of the people of God and that has led them to liberation from slavery. If the instruction comes from someone who leads them to freedom, there is no room for discussion and it will be healthy to observe it as much as not doing so will have consequences for the life of the transgressor. Seen in this way, it is clear that they do not refer to the virtue of proteins or the feared cholesterol of a certain food but to its symbolic meaning as it is part of the alliance with God. The diet must be understood as a rite that, when observed, confirms every day the will to continue being part of the alliance with God and therefore its observance has to do with a deep relationship between human beings and their God, a relationship that is always at risk of breaking and that is preserved by this means.

The form and dimension of the laws in the covenant presuppose a profound understanding on their part of the radical nature of human sin. In the covenant, the sinful condition of the human being is challenged by the redemptive will of God. For this reason, the means to cleanse the stain are established and a system of purification of the body and life is offered. To interpret as external acts without greater value, the ritual baths prescribed in Lev 15 for men who suffer from seminal flow or in the case of women the waiting of seven days after the cessation of the flow of blood for their purification is to fail to understand the theology that lives in them. Just as we said above about the diet, in this case the lustral waters and time act in the depth of the relationship between the person and God; they are the means by which God provides a path of redemption for sins and the door to reconcile with God. And there is no one who is exempt from the need to meet God again, because sin has distanced us all from God and from our neighbors and is still at work in us. But this awareness that human beings are in conflict with their Creator is so clear that even after offering the means for reconciliation, a greater space is still reserved for meeting God again. We are referring to the day of forgiveness (Lev 16).

The story begins with the memory of the death of Aaron's sons, an event that occurred because of the incorrect sacrifice. The rite of the sacrifice of a ram and another that is released in the desert seals God's will to offer a means of redemption to Israel. Even if the ablutions and penances had not been carried out in detail, sins could still be cleansed by observing this Day of Atonement. There are also rules to follow: rest must be complete as must fasting. These are liturgical gestures of preparation because what is at stake is the proclamation of the forgiveness of the sins of the whole year: it says "you will be clean from all your sins before Yahweh" (16:30). After Aaron lays his hands on the goat, the animal will carry on itself toward the solitude of the desert and the sins of all the people and there they will be expiated for their purification. In the theology of Deuteronomy, the day of forgiveness is an exclusive act of God for the benefit of human beings who, although they have failed to keep the covenant, are still touched by divine love and the divine will to redeem them.

The Theology of Deuteronomy

The Book of Deuteronomy is a literary hinge. It lives in two spheres at the same time and gives and receives meaning in both. Although any historical reconstruction is hypothetical and generally unnecessary, to satisfy our curiosity, let us say that it is most likely that it was originally the first part of the history that goes from Joshua to 2 Kings and that has been called the Deuteronomistic Historical Work. Deuteronomy would have acted as a theological introduction and therefore left its mark on the creation of that history of Israel.[1] To do so, it is necessary to assume that there was a "Deuteronomistic school" responsible for the writing of the work, something that is accepted today without further discussion. At a later stage, this book would have been incorporated into the Pentateuch and separated from the group of historical books (Josh-2 Kings), called "former prophets" in the Jewish tradition. This must have happened before the translation

---

[1]The OHD is not a homogeneous work either, but rather composed of various documents that were grouped, made compatible and in some cases rewritten according to Deuteronomist theology.

of the Septuagint (c. 250 BC) because by then the Pentateuch was already distinguished from the rest of the scrolls. In this position it fulfills the function of ratifying the laws already received, but what is more significant is that by incorporating Deuteronomy into Gen-Num and thus forming the Pentateuch, the entire life of Moses and the entire laws received by Israel through him are grouped within one and the same work. In this way, the *Torah could be defined* as the heart of the Scriptures because it contains all the laws given by God at Sinai so that from it the prophetic books (Joshua to Mal) and the Writings will be interpreters of the reality, history and life of Israel.

The ever-reviving discussion on the formation of the Pentateuch leads to some who postulate a tetrateuch, a hexateuch, and even an Enneateuch.[1] Sometimes arguments are heard in favor of a hexateuch, such as that the cut in Deuteronomy is abrupt because the Pentateuch supposes the conquest and settlement in the land and therefore the work must include Joshua. Added to this is the fact that Joseph's bones are mentioned in Ex 13:19 and buried only in Jos 24:32. The weakness of these arguments is obvious. The reason for an abrupt conclusion is theologically supported by the fact that what is important to highlight is the absence of the land, not its possession. At the center of their theology, there is an expectation for the land that remains as the engine of all hope for future generations and as a promise of a place that transcends our reality. Every people that throughout history has felt that they are being denied a place or that they have been alienated from their land can see themselves reflected in the story that speaks of a people whose possession of their land is ahead in their history, not behind them. Israel will always be a poor people without land or, when they conquer it, they will hardly have time to enjoy it because it will be cut off from them at successive moments; that is why it is important that in the Pentateuch the land remains as a promise. The argument about Joseph's bones only shows the literary insensitivity of the person who wields it. It is clear that those who gave final form to these writings were masters of literature and placed not these two writings but hundreds of cross-references throughout the Old Testament as links to unite works of different origin. Note, for example, the three successive opening formulas in 6:4 "Hear, O Israel: The Lord our God, the Lord is one;" then 4:44 "This is the

---

[1]See F. García López, "La formación del Pentateuco en el debate actual," *EB* 67 (2009): 235-56.

Law that Moses set forth before the Israelites;" and 1:1 "These are the words that Moses announced to all Israel beyond the Jordan." Each of these could have been the beginning of the work in stages prior to the present one, but beyond all speculation, what is interesting is to note that the canonical redaction did not exclude the others but incorporated them into a larger and new work.[1] This speaks of an inclusive theology, of desires for expansion, of building on what has come before, of valuing what has been received and rereading it in the light of a new context that demands a new theological discourse. It is therefore not alien to this feeling that Deuteronomy, which, based on the liturgical celebration described in chapter 27, seems to come from Samaria, was adopted in Judah and incorporated into the body of Scripture.

The greatest impact of Deuteronomistic theology was that it was the theology of the so-called reform of Josiah (2 Kings 23). While the artisans were working on the repair of the temple, they found the "Book of the Law," took it to the king, who, amazed by its content, undertook a reform to adjust religious practices to the content of that book. We have already mentioned the different theories about what this discovery consists of, but we assume that it is a document that basically expresses the theology that we have today in Deuteronomy. This reform meant a radical change in the religion of Israel, in its practice and in the conception of its relationship with God, but it also had significant political and social consequences. We note the following points about this reform and its links with Deuteronomy. First, the reform helped to strengthen the path toward monotheism. Josiah perceives that idolatry is spreading in Israel and instructs the closing of the Canaanite altars scattered throughout the country and dedicated to the goddess Asherah and the god Baal, as well as the liturgical objects dedicated to them in the temple of Jerusalem. It is noteworthy that sanctuaries that enjoyed the prestige of having been erected by the patriarchs and matriarchs are closed, as is the case of Bethel established by Abraham (Gen 12:8). This speaks of a theological courage worthy of imitation.

Second, the reform consecrated the exclusivity of the temple of Jerusalem as a place of sacrifice, which implied a series of changes in the way of living the faith. For example, due to the new provision that the lamb had to be sacrificed in the temple of

---

[1]It can be inferred from these "beginnings" that the Dt began in the time of Josiah (640-609), continued its expansion during the exile (586-539) and crystallized into the present text sometime during the Persian period (539-333), see W. Doorly, *The Laws of Yahveh* (New York: Paulist Press, 2002), 27-28.

that city, the Passover festival went from being a family festival to a festival that required a pilgrimage to Jerusalem (Dt 16:2). This brought about a lack of meat outside Jerusalem, which led to the authorization of slaughtering for family food (Dt 12:15). For the first time in Israel, the slaughter of animals was permitted outside the scope of a religious rite.

A third consequence has to do with the centralization of the temple and the growing unemployment of the Levites. They officiated in the sanctuaries and altars that were closed. The Deuteronomist addresses this situation and establishes that if a Levite goes to Jerusalem he will enjoy the same rights as the local Levites (18:6-8). However, this provision did not bear the expected fruit, since 2 Kings 23:9 states that the Levites must abstain from approaching the temple. The tension created between the Levites and the priests will last for centuries.

Finally, the reform produced — intentionally or not — a strong concentration of power in Jerusalem with its corresponding capacity to dominate the political and ideological aspects of society. The fact that its temple was elevated to be the place where God dwells and therefore the only place where one can worship and communicate with God led to the priesthood of Jerusalem growing in its capacity to control the life and faith of the people. The condemnation of the so-called false prophets in chapter 13 may mean a purification of idolatry, but it is also the elimination of potential competitors of the priests. The harshness of the punishment — death — gives the impression of being excessive and we do not know if it was actually applied or if it could serve to establish the seriousness of the act in order to eliminate the practice. The king's power is also curtailed in 17:14-20; the clauses give the impression of having been written with Solomon in mind: he is advised to have few wives "for they will lead him astray;" he is instructed to own few horses and little wealth; and he is to copy and read the Law every day in order to "learn to fear God." It may not have been composed with Solomon in mind explicitly, but it does reflect the priests' view of the monarch and his lifestyle.[1] Underlying this legislation is a suspicion of monarchy, which is regarded by Deuteronomy — and the Deuteronomistic Historical Work — as a form of government that led to the disaster of the destruction of the temple and the captivity of Israel.

---

[1]According to J. D. Pleins, it is a "covenant of fidelity" that characterizes God's relationship with Israel and this covenant applies not only to the king but to the people in general as seen in 1:34-40; 3:18-29; 31:1-29 and 32:44-47, see *The Social Visions of the Hebrew Bible* (Louisville: Westminster Press, 2001), 100.

The Law and Life

One more reflection on the Law and life is in order. It is a limited interpretation to think that legislation was made so that by complying with it people have the opportunity to please God or to have a way to comply with God and test our zeal. Rather, the laws have as their main objective to be right with God and to establish the limits for human conduct by outlining the field within which life must develop and thus prevent the human spirit from running wild and unleashing a tragedy. In other words, if there is a commandment that says "you shall not kill" it is because in the human being there is a desire to kill one's sibling and the capacity to realize that desire; if there are laws that regulate sexual activity, it is because there is a tendency to sexual imbalance in adultery or incest; and if respect for parents is required, it is because there were sons and daughters who truly mistreated their parents. Consequently, the law is a guiding element for the person regarding the conduct that favors life in the community and a parameter to establish the seriousness of the fault if it is violated.

Without law, there is no transgression and without transgression there can be no corrective measure. This positive sense of the role of biblical laws in the dynamics of life must be rescued. When Isaiah rejects religious services and says "I am fed up with burnt offerings... and your grain offerings" (Is 1:11-13) and demands "seek justice... give justice to the oppressed and do justice to the orphan and the widow" (v. 17) he is not proposing a disjunctive between formal observance of the law in rituals and, on the other hand, doing justice that pleases the Lord. Isaiah does not reject the Law nor propose abandoning sacrifices and offerings, but rather denounces that it is not observed because observing it is doing justice to the poor and the orphan. The prophet does not ask to abandon the law in order to do justice, but rather calls for returning to it and fulfilling it so that the law spreads and the poor are respected. In Dt 6:6-9, the place of the *Torah* in life is stated in a forceful manner: "And these words that I command you today shall be *in your heart*, and you shall teach them to your children..." The heart, in biblical language, is the place of the will.

Contribution of the Pentateuch to Biblical Theology: Preliminary Conclusions

It would be contrary to our principles to assume that we are expounding on the theology of the Pentateuch as if there were no other possible interpretations. Rather, these pages express a well-founded reading and seek to extrapolate those elements that we understand stand out from its theology and apply to our own theology. The richness of the Pentateuch—like every text that deeply penetrates human experience—is inexhaustible and susceptible to successive rereadings. At the same time, our words are preliminary and inconclusive because we formulate them while the course of reading the Old Testament is still ongoing. Only at the end of the road can we stop to observe and evaluate the contribution of each section to the totality of the work.

The Creation That Never Ceases

The literary form of the texts marks thematic divisions and approaches to the facts. The first chapters of Genesis present the account of creation; we saw that the expression "In the beginning" could also be understood as a formula that covers from 1:1 to chapter 11 or the entire book. There is an evident intention to close the creational work by concluding the account of the Tower of Babel and adding the genealogy that connects with Abraham. But the succession of events contradicts the idea that God stopped creating from that moment on and rather shows that God does so in a different way. The creative activity is expressed first in the formation of the people of God. It is not Abraham and Sarah who seek God, but it is God who calls them. The pilgrimage of the patriarchs and matriarchs is marked by acts in which God guides history and opens or closes doors according to God's own will. The creational elements during the plagues of Egypt, whether positive or negative, allude to a God who creates reality at that very moment. It is not Moses who asks God to act and free the people, but rather it is all a creative response on the part of God to the groaning of the people (Heb. *ne'aqah*, Ex 2:24; 6:5).

Groaning is a sound that is not intended to communicate. A cry, like a word, yearns to be heard and—consciously or not—expects a response. However, a groan is something rustic and prior to the word, it is that which comes from the depths and does not expect a response because it does not believe that there is anyone who can hear; it is the lament of the hopeless, of the one who has lost all hope. What the text reveals is that God went out to meet that groan and acted in a surprising way, first for the slaves, but then also for the powerful Pharaoh. From the oppressor's understanding of life, there is no place for anyone to respond to the cry of a weak and poor person like the oppressed; in the face of their groaning, the oppressor feels like a victory has been won as if the oppressors were able to subdue their intimate will to rebel. And that is true if we evaluate it from the mere social dynamic and the place of those subjected to it, but the story shows that God acted creatively in responding to that groan. By appearing before Moses and calling him to the task of liberation, God creates conditions that could not have been glimpsed before. The God revealed in these stories is one who has not ceased to create and who has no intention of doing so. Surely this speaks to our own practice of faith, whether personal, within the community, or in the social and political realm. The God who made heaven and Earth is the one who never sleeps and does not cease to create.

The God Who Chooses All Peoples in One People

One contribution of the theology of the Pentateuch that will permeate the entire Old Testament is the concept of the chosen people. At first, it was understood as a relationship of exclusivity, but with the passage of time it was seen that God's love and attention extended to other nations; that Yahweh watched over God's people but also extended the divine gaze to the other nations (Jonah 4:11). Hence, the meaning of choosing a people is that God chooses them all because that act seals God's commitment to the destiny of the entire human community. God's irruption into history was to be done through a people, but by calling upon a specific one, God creates a space of relationship between God and the people from which all peoples will be blessed. However, we note that in the Pentateuch the link established in the alliance with Israel is of a greater density than that of the protection of other nations. It is interesting to observe that the link does not legitimize the power relations that could exist within Israel, whether that of the priesthood of Jerusalem or the monarchy. Other peoples use this type of alliance between the monarchy and the divine to strengthen the bonds of oppression of the dominant classes toward the poor of their own nation. This is not the case of Israel, where it is said in Dt 7:7: "It was not because you were more numerous than any other people that the Lord set divine love on you and chose you, for you were the fewest of all peoples."

Israel's smallness is pointed out to prevent it from supposing that it has deserved to be the chosen people, and it is affirmed that it is God's love that is the origin of the election. This concept will be repeated again and again by the prophets when they announce that those who long for the Day of Yahweh because they believe it will be to congratulate them for their fidelity will discover with horror that it will be a day of judgment for transgressing the Law and breaking the covenant (Am 5:18; Joel 2:1-2; Zeph 1:14-15). The same is said regarding the possession of the land; It is not Israel's virtues that make it deserve the land, but rather God's love that gives it to them effortlessly (Dt 9:5-6). The fact is that the choice has a positive value and a counterpart: the positive is that they will receive the land as a gift from God; in this, Israel will know that God is faithful and will be faithful not only to Israel but also to "God's purpose for Israel," which will not change despite their rebellions.[1] The counterpart is that they must be loyal to God. This loyalty is defined in the terms of the first commandment that orders to reject other gods and serve only Yahweh.

This condition of chosen people contributes to theology being an unfinished discourse, still in the process of being realized. If Israel has been chosen, what is the situation of the other peoples? We have already seen that the descendants of those who remained outside the line of election, such as Cain, Lot, Ishmael and Esau, were also blessed; these references are advances of an even broader understanding that has not yet crystallized in the Pentateuch but that will do so in a later theology with a more universalist tone. It will be necessary to reach the end of the Persian period for the understanding of God's love to be expanded and for it to become clearer that the election that is a privilege for Israel does not mean the rejection and much less the condemnation of the other peoples of the Earth. But at this moment, the theology of the Pentateuch celebrates the election and proclaims the responsibility of being the people of God.

The Link Between Liberation and Alliance

We saw at the time that the act of liberation and the giving of the Law in the covenant are part of a single social and religious process. Reading them as if they were in competition impoverishes both and distorts the reading. It is necessary to highlight the political and social dimension of the liberation of the slaves in order to avoid spiritualist readings of these narratives

---

[1]P. D. Miller, highlights the Hebrew concept applied in 7:6 of *segulah,* a word from the economic field that means very valuable property and that could be translated as treasure; see Ex 19:5; Ps 135:4; in Mal 3:17 one can observe the presence of this concept in one of the last prophets; *Deuteronomy* (Louisville: John Knox Press, 1990), 110-14; also W. Zimmerli, *Manual de teología del Antiguo Testamento* (Madrid: Cristiandad, 1980), 47.

that transform them into mere examples of interior life. The concreteness of what is narrated cannot be ignored, and it is only by assuming it in this way that the transcendence of its message can be understood. If the deed of the exodus is significant for the oppressed of today, it is because it narrates a real and concrete liberation, an act of God in favor of those who suffered injustices, which does not require that they be precise events in factual history. Now, if the spiritualization of the story reduces its meaning, a triumphalist reading that understands it as the narration of the success of a slave revolution against institutional power is also limiting.[1] Reading it as a fact of the past that tells how well it was for those slaves when they were freed and taken to a new land transforms it into a specific historical example and as such unrepeatable. The text itself shows in the murmurings and complaints that the Israelites are not the active initiators of liberation and that their laments at times seem more like a theology of captivity in which they cry over their misfortunes than one of liberation that compels them to fight for their freedom.[2] In the story, they accept liberation but do not lead it. The appropriate reading is one that allows the text to challenge our reality at the same time that we challenge it. That God has promoted a real and historical act of justice speaks about divine action in our days and how divine preference is placed on the side of the marginalized and oppressed.

Israel is now a free people with responsibilities that it did not have when it lived under slavery. To constitute itself as a people requires it to organize itself, and laws come to its aid. Slaves who previously supported the lives of their oppressors with their work have now received the blessing of being free and will be able to support their family, their loved ones, and plan their future with the product of their body. This new concrete and social reality demand a legal body like all other peoples of antiquity had. Israel will also have them, but they will be understood not as a collection of regulations but as an alliance that God proposes to them. The norms that will regulate daily life will be based on the memory of the exodus and will not be laws in the strict sense, to the extent that laws are rules agreed upon by society and mandatory. These will be instructions (*Torah*) accepted

---

[1]A valuable work for its simplicity and popularity, such as Jorge Pixley's *Historia de Israel desde la perspectiva de los pobres* (Mexico City: Palabra Ediciones, 1993), 15 seems to require historical success to give rise to the message.

[2]See the work of L. Boff, *Teología desde el cautiverio* (Bogotá: Indo América, 1975), 13-39.

in freedom as a response of gratitude for the liberation received. Israel can accept a legal body in this way because it perceives its God as the one who freed it from slavery and who now continues to support it in the new challenges posed by life in the desert and the construction of a nation whose mission is to respond in fidelity to its God. The society of freed slaves requires a legal body that supports the liberating project. Liberation is not an eschatological ideal but a historical reality, undoubtedly perfectible but concrete and that must be sustained over time. It is the dynamic relationship between liberation and alliance that supports this theology of liberation. Thus, there is no effective liberation without a law that gives it form, which will demand loyalty and compliance. This loyalty must be radical because the very existence of Israel will be at stake (Dt 6:14-15).

Law and Gospel

If by gospel (*euangelion*, "the good news") we understand the abundance of God's love and God's liberating and redemptive will, we must affirm that in the Pentateuch there is no contradiction between Law and gospel. Terence Fretheim pointed out the relationship between laws and God's creative action and goes further by relating creation to the giving of the Law at Sinai by saying that "the statutes are rooted in God's creative work... and serve the creative purpose of life, stability, and the well-being of people and the community."[1] The creative act has no other sign than God's love for the creature; if God creates them, it is for the benefit of the human being, not to humanity's regret. However, we have already pointed out that the Christian reading of the legal texts has been colored by the strong polemic of Jesus, and then of the apostle Paul, with the legalism of the Pharisees of the first century. Both reacted to the ritualism that led to the mechanical application of the Law that marginalized from holiness and condemned to impurity the majority of the people of their time, especially those who had less access to the knowledge of the Scriptures or to the economic resources for purification.

In the discussion with the Pharisees because his disciples gather grains of wheat to eat on the Sabbath and because he then heals a sick person in the synagogue, Jesus does not reject the sanctity of the Sabbath rest (Mt 12:1-13). On that occasion, Jesus does not speak out against the Law but applies it in a non-automatic way and for the benefit of the spiritual and physical

---

[1]T. Fretheim, *The Pentateuch* (Nashville: Abingdon Press, 1996), 163.

health of the people. He acts in a way that frees them from the theological bond that prevented them from gathering food on the Sabbath and enables them to respond to a physical need such as satisfying hunger. In the first case, Jesus alludes to an act of David when he eats consecrated bread to satisfy his and his soldiers' hunger (1 Sam 21:2-7) and makes himself the guarantor of the Sabbath in terms of his messianic condition; he does not exercise this condition to violate the Sabbath, but to respect it in the greater context of attending to the needs of others. In the second, it is based on the freedom to "do good on the Sabbath." At times Jesus exalts the Law as when he says "I did not come to abolish the Law and the Prophets... but to fulfill it" and then declares that the Law will not become obsolete as long as heaven and Earth exist (Mt 5:17-18). Jesus' conception that the Law should be rescued from legalistic distortion makes him a defender of the Law.

It is noteworthy that the position of Jesus and Paul, who reject the external ritualism that is imposed on the exercise of faith is not essentially different from the claim of the Old Testament prophets. The difference is that in the theological horizon of the prophets their "return to God" meant reconnecting with the laws of Moses and fulfilling them. The theological context of the prophets is the radical criticism of idolatry, where in most cases the inclination to foreign gods was combined with the neglect of justice for the poor and respect for the rights of one's neighbor. In Jesus or in Paul, this "return to God" is expressed in terms of the new theological reality inaugurated with the revelation that points to Jesus of Nazareth as the Christ.

The reader will have noticed that the person writing these lines does not adhere to a rejection of the Law as the Old Testament Scriptures present and consider it. Nor are we given to labelling as legalism everything that exceeds our tolerance level. There is a message in the meticulousness of the laws of Leviticus as there is in detailing in Exodus how each object of the Tent of the Presence should be made and then narrating in mirror image almost the same texts changing the verbal form of "you shall make" (Ex 25-31) to "he made" (Ex 35-39). The bells of the mantle are of such importance that they cannot be left unmentioned in the instructions for the seamstress, who will make it and only insensitivity can overlook this detail.

> And you shall make on its hems pomegranates of blue, purple, and scarlet, and between them bells of gold on its hem, a bell of gold and a pomegranate, a bell of gold and a pomegranate, all the way around the hem of the robe. And

it shall be upon Aaron when he ministers; and the sound of it shall be heard when he goes into the holy place before the LORD and when he comes out, so that he will not die. (Ex 28:33-35)

We do not agree with the note in the *Jerusalem Bible* that attributes the ringing of bells to the ancient idea that demons were driven away by this. The sanctity of the place was sufficient guarantee of protection against any foreign force and that is why there could not be demons in the tent, just as there would not be in the temple. Our opinion is that the ringing warned those who might be near Aaron that a sacred rite was being performed and that any error could cause his death and that of others. The bells were not an ornament but a way of warning everyone that life was at stake in what was done there. The ringing prevented involuntary error and reminded that the things of God were sacred and required full attention to them to the point that making a mistake led to death.

The rules of the purity code must be considered by the practicing Christian. We do not say this in a mechanical sense, but in their deep meaning. They establish a way of relating to God and a path of repair in the face of failure. The stain is the symptom of the breakdown of the relationship and the state of estrangement. It is at that moment (which can be understood as produced by contact with something impure but nothing prevents the state of enmity with one's neighbor, the lack of love and mercy toward the weak, lying to gain advantage from also being considered ritual impurity) where the law that sets the limit also offers the path of repairing the stain. Is this not the gospel of Jesus? Is not the irruption of Christ for the Christian the new opportunity that God gives so that those who are separated from God can access to meet their creator again and not die as Ex 28:35b indicates? The law in the theology of the Old Testament has the purpose of preserving life and giving it a meaning.

The theology of the Pentateuch is an invitation to recognize that God is in the midst of God's people and accompanies them in their struggle for justice, to abandon all forms of slavery and in the act of building a more just and egalitarian society, where life is cared for and flows in abundance. As instructions (*Torah*) are those that will guide the people along their path and that the prophets and sages will have as a reference to judge and correct them when they stray from them. And it is an invitation to observe the laws of the covenant and consequently to love one's neighbor, which includes the most unprotected of their time, such as the orphan, the widow and the foreigner. According to their understanding, love comes from observance and separating them leads to distorting the will of the creator.

Inauguration of History
The Narratives of Ancient Israel

History is Born

In the Hebrew Bible, the existence of two histories of Israel is somewhat hidden by relegating the second, composed of the books of Chronicles, Ezra and Nehemiah, to its third section (the *Ketubim* or Writings) and separating it from the first history, which includes the books from Joshua to 2 Kings. The latter are located in the second section (called *Nebiim*, Prophets) and are therefore considered part of the prophetic books, of a higher hierarchy than the *Ketubim*. This physical distance in the text and the fact that Chronicles and Ezra-Neh[1] are located in an order that is not chronological (in the Hebrew Bible the order is Ezra-Nehemiah, then Chronicles) further dilute the possibility of identification and comparison.

A radical change occurs in the Septuagint and in the Christian Bible where the books that begin with Joshua are called "historical books" and include Joshua through 2 Chronicles. The fact that both stories are located in the same section and one after the other facilitates the perception that we are dealing with two stories (from Joshua to 2 Kings and from 1 Chronicles to Nehemiah) that are largely parallel and that describe the same periods at a certain time but with a different theological bias. Both the structures of the canon have theological presuppositions and consequences. They presuppose that inclination toward the inclusiveness of biblical literature that we have already seen in the texts of the Pentateuch and in the vocation to rescue the testimonies of the past, even if we see contradictions between them that cannot always be reconciled. A first consequence is that giving them the name of historical books and ordering Chronicles and Ezra-Neh chronologically express a different conception of history, more critical and proper to the Judaism of the Israelite diaspora that incorporated other cultural horizons to its experience of faith.

---

[1]The two books of Chronicles are one work in the Hebrew Bible, as are Ezra and Nehemiah; that is why they are abbreviated as Ezra-Neh. The separation was made in the Septuagint because the Greek script takes up much more space than the Hebrew and exceeded the limits of a single scroll.

The Hebrew Bible has a strong appreciation for the condition of the text as a word that must be read and proclaimed; hence one of the names that Judaism gives to the Bible is *miqra*, which in Hebrew means "that which must be read," "proclaimed," with the connotation of doing it out loud. In turn, it identifies the books that go from Joshua to 2 Kings as prophetic books (it calls them "earlier prophets" to distinguish them from the "later prophets," those that go from Isaiah to Malachi), a name consistent with the indicated conception since the sign of the prophets is the voice, the word that is announced. And this reveals a characteristic of Israelite historiography, showing that the biblical author is not interested in history as an objective narration of the events of the past; we confirm this by observing that he was not concerned with altering the chronological order of the books of the Chronicler with the sole purpose of having the closing of the canon contain words of hope. In doing so, he succeeded in making the final words of the book announcing the rebuilding of the Temple of Jerusalem and the end of the Babylonian captivity with the return of the people to Jerusalem (2 Chr 36:22-23). However, the intellectual context and theological challenges to which Alexandrian Judaism was exposed were different. When it was influenced by Hellenism, it understood the value of history differently. This led it to reorganize the order of the canon by grouping the narratives of the past into one section and presenting both narratives as history. This also explains the transfer of Ruth after Judges and of Esther after Nehemiah, both works in the Hebrew Bible grouped in the Writings but considered by the LXX as historical works.[1] Bringing Jos-2 King closer to Chro-Neh — in the physical sense in the order of the books but also conceptually, by giving them the same canonical value — allowed them to be compared on equal terms. This change had hermeneutical consequences on three levels:

a. Historical literature is more clearly distinguished from prophetic literature. Separating the prophetic books (Isaiah onwards) from the historical narratives helped clarify the prophet's role as interpreter and critic of history. Prophetic literature is embedded in historical events but is not a record of them.

b. The Septuagint format confirms the privileged value of the Pentateuch as *Torah* (Law) and the heart of the Scriptures, but

---

[1]Ruth was associated with Judges because of the reference to them in 1:1 and Esther because in 1:1 it is situated in the time of Ahasuerus (Xerxes).

the category of all the rest of the books is leveled by giving the Prophets and the Writings the same level of authority.

c. *Torah* becomes clearer. Joshua culminates with the commitment to fulfill the "decrees and norms" and places a stone as a witness to that covenant (Josh 24:25-28). The successive kings will be evaluated by their appreciation or distancing from the Law and their inclination to violate or fulfill the first commandment that prohibits idolatry. The Deuteronomistic history will conclude that the final disaster is due to the massive disobedience of the Law by the monarchs (2 Kings 23:26-27).

This new conformation of the canon, which Christianity would later inherit, can be said to inaugurate the presence of history as a particular narrative within the Bible, even when history is understood as a relation of past events with a strong interpretative bias of a theological nature.[1] Before this conception introduced in the Septuagint, it was not possible to speak of there being a historical narrative in the Scriptures.

The novelty of "discovering" that history had a place in biblical thought was that it had important consequences for the interpretation of the rest of the works that make up the Bible. The pluralism of traditions allowed the two stories to coexist curiously without hiding their differences, and to be offered as a menu of choice for the reader. But they also acted as an alternative version that showed that a society acquires maturity when it diversifies and when it accepts that it does not have the only true word and that there can be a different version of the facts as they have been narrated since ancient times. The very attitude of recognizing the existence of another version is already a liberating act of thought and promoter of a dialogue between traditions that enriches all social practice. The fact that four versions of the life and sayings of Jesus coexist in the New Testament is nothing more than the continuation of this spirit that already prevailed in the ancient scriptures.

The idea that historical narrative involves ideology and theology, that it is not a neutral text since there are other texts that challenge the hegemony of the former, is a lesson that the Jewish community of biblical times learned and practiced. That we have Yahwistic and Elohistic psalms, that we find repeated prophetic texts, that we have two accounts of creation, is sufficient proof that

---

[1]A. Soggin characterizes it as "a historiography that we might call theological" and adds that this applies not only to historical books but also to prophetic ones, *Introduction to the Old Testament* (Louisville: John Knox Press, 1989), 40.

those who created these texts were aware that pluralism and diversity were constitutive elements of social reality.[1] In the theology of the Old Testament as it emerges from the historical books, the zeal is not placed on precision regarding "what happened" but on seeking an understanding of the facts. Hence, the double source, the double space of interpretation, is necessary so that in the confrontation the meaning of history and of the lived events can be glimpsed. The difference does not relativize the perspective but rather strengthens it.

The History of the World: The Enneateuch

If we consider the narrative thread that runs from Gen 1:1 to the end of 2 Kings, we discover we are dealing with a history of the world. It is a block of text that is often called the Enneateuch because it groups together nine books, in contrast to the five of the Pentateuch. The nine are made up of the five books of the Pentateuch plus Joshua, Judges, Samuel, and Kings.[2] It is a history that does not contemplate the events that occurred in the vastness of the world but only those that are of interest to the future of Israel and that are understood as God's plan in relation to the divinely chosen people. It is the history that shows how God is at the beginning and at the end of days. It begins with the creation of heaven and Earth and culminates with what is understood there to be the end of the covenant between God and Israel: the disappearance of the temple and the dissolution of the Davidic monarchy. These events leave in nothing that alliance agreed upon in the desert of Sinai with the slaves freed in the midst of wonderful signs. Jacob's generous descendants have been scattered and no longer exist, and the promised land no longer belongs to the descendants of Abraham. It is the end of history. This pessimism and this tragic conception of events are in line with the Deuteronomistic theology, which understands that God has been faithful to the divine promises and has protected Israel throughout the centuries, but the response of the other party has not been what was expected.

When reflecting on what happened, the narrator will identify the monarchy and the kings as those responsible for the breaking of the covenant. It is worth noting that, unlike other peoples, in the theology of Israel the successive kings were never

---

[1] See the Yahwistic psalms (1-41; 90-150) and the Elohistic ones (42-83); see Is 2:4; Mic 4:3 and Joel 4:10; Gen 1:1-2:3 and 2:4-25.
[2] For a presentation and discussion of the Enneateuch see J. L. Ska, *Introducción a la lectura del Pentateuco* (Estella: Verbo Divino, 2001), 24-27.

deified nor did they acquire a value greater than that of all mortals. A pharaoh, a Mesopotamian monarch, was considered an almost divine being with a particular connection to divinity that differentiated him from the rest of the people and made him untouchable. In Israel, this concept did not exist and the connection with God was always in the hands of the prophets who were called by God and not designated by dynastic succession. This allowed the prophets — and by extension the theology they bequeathed to us — to be critical of the monarch without their judgment affecting the divinity. On the other hand, their declared human condition did not allow the king to invoke his office as a person set apart by God to lead the people in order to justify his actions and prevent the often devastating criticism of the prophets. In Israel, God speaks through the prophets, not the king, and one of the most recurrent criticisms of the political and religious authorities is that of "silencing the prophets" (Is 30:10; Jer 11:21; Am 2:12; 7:12-13) and this happens because their words irritate the rulers. In 1 Kings 22, it is narrated that King Ahab declared that he hated the prophet Micah son of Imlah because "he does not prophesy good to me but evil." There are numerous texts to this effect.

This reading of history as an Enneateuch makes sense in the succession of the books, but we must be careful not to consider it a literary or theological unit. It arises from the concatenation of the works, but it was not understood as a historical line without more since the moment that the Pentateuch acquired a higher theological value as Law and therefore is placed above the rest of the texts. Even considering that there are literary links such as, for example, Jos 24:32 with Gen 50:26, where the transfer of Joseph's remains to be buried in Canaan is narrated, the link is narrative but not necessarily theological. In the Introduction we pointed out that the relationship between the *Torah* and the rest of the books is asymmetrical and that it is linked in a dynamic way with the rest of the Scriptures, where the first acts as a norm and the second understand themselves as the record of the application of the norm. If we consider that the historical books (Josh. 2 Kings) in the oldest tradition of the Scriptures are considered prophetic (the "previous" prophets), it emerges that they are conceived as interpreters of the Law and as practical evaluators of the application of the Law and not as continuators of it. For the prophets, the Law had been given to Israel in the desert and was already closed; they do not discuss the Law but rather watch over its application. Hence, the historical books judge the kings, the people, and other characters to the extent that they are faithful or not to the Law and to the covenant that promulgated it, understood as *Torah* and whose content is the Pentateuch.

It is necessary to point out that the formation of the Pentateuch could have been simultaneous or even in its final redaction later than some of the historical texts, but what is called Law always refers to that theological body regardless of its redactional state. The same must be said of the discussion about whether Deuteronomy should be considered part of the Deuteronomistic Historical Work or the Pentateuch; in relation to what we are considering, this question is irrelevant. From the canonical point of view and as constitutive of the Law, it belongs to the Pentateuch, without the need to specify the moment in which it was incorporated into that textual body. As a work whose theology inspires the narratives from Joshua to 2 Kings, it can be considered a preamble to the history of the conquest and the monarchy until its end. Recognizing this does not necessarily force us to opt for only one of these possibilities, since the Deuteronomistic school is broader than Deuteronomy and left its mark on almost all the biblical books, so that Deuteronomy may well be the theological support of the story without being disconnected from its place in the Law.

This condition of books that watch over and judge human acts from the Law is established from the first moment in the Deuteronomistic history. In the first lines, when nothing had yet been said and the feat of conquest is about to begin, Yahweh tells Joshua "be strong and very courageous, and be careful to do according to all the law (*Torah*) that my servant Moses gave you" (Jos 1:7). And at the end of the capture of Ai, Joshua gathers all the people on Mount Ebal and reads the law (*Torah*), which is received by "the assembly of Israel, including women, children and foreigners..." (8:30-35). From the narrative point of view, this reading is unnecessary because the people already knew it, but its reading has the symbolic value of reaffirming it as the theological basis of what was done and what was to be done. From now on, the history of Israel will be passed through the sieve of fidelity to the Law, and no political or religious hierarchy, however high, will be exempt from being evaluated and judged by this criterion.

We need to reflect on the theological meaning of creating a history of the world. Given the fragmentary nature of the texts and even the differences between the books that make up the narrative, it is evident that this history was not received by tradition but quite the opposite: it was constructed despite the fact that they reflect notable literary and historical dissonances with the received traditions; let us recall as an example the account of the full military conquest according to Joshua 6-12 and the very different one of Judges 1, where not only is it not made effective in a definitive manner but it says that they were not expelled and that they continued living in Canaan with the Israelites.

Every history is written in the perspective of the present and the future. The past is presented, analyzed and criticized, but always in terms of a never-ending development that is sufficiently exciting to justify the effort to construct a complex narrative whose sole purpose is to give meaning to reality and the challenges it presents. We say this to show that we do not think, as is often said, that the Deuteronomistic history connected to the Pentateuch in the form of the Enneateuch was composed on the occasion of the destruction of the temple and the city. Although there is not much evidence to date the final writing of this work, with the sole assertion that it is after the beginning of the Babylonian captivity, it is necessary to point out that what is of interest is not the date but the intellectual and theological climate in which it is written. It is true that the narrative expresses the combination of the theology of the covenant with that of the election of the house of David; the former is the basis of the "people of God," the same people who break that covenant on successive occasions; The second shows God's mercy and the divine will to preserve the link with the house of David. But that combination had been destroyed and everything seemed to indicate that there was no future for Israel. It is from this conviction that we must affirm that the fact of composing this history of the world supposes that the trauma of the loss of Jerusalem and the temple has already been overcome and that it is narrated in terms of a future that begins to be reconstructed. It is about testifying that history did not end with those unfortunate events. Once the anguish of the moment when the tragedy seems endless has passed, Israel begins a double task. A slow but persistent process of rebuilding its relationship with God begins and at the same time, its understanding of the lesson of history is revised. The Enneateuch is the fruit of this new understanding of its place in history.

Conquest of the Land and Fulfillment of the Promise

The book of Joshua narrates the conquest of the land and creates a theology that supports it. The theology is imprinted in the story and merges with it, so we should not expect an explicit theological reflection, but it is necessary to delve into the interweaving of the texts to bring it to light. The book begins with the entry into Canaan and ends with the tribes settled after having distributed the territory among them. Chapters 1-12 are dedicated to the conquest while 13-21 recount the division of the land. The final chapters (22-24) are reserved for the last days of Joshua and the so-called Covenant of Shechem. The three parts act in harmony and give meaning to each other. The division supposes the conquest in the same way that the covenant in Shechem supposes the effective possession of the land. Furthermore, the entire story supposes the narratives of the patriarchs and matriarchs because the promise of the land dates back to Abraham and has been present as an expectation throughout his history. So close is the link between Yahweh and the promise of the land that the conquest is considered an inevitable act of God. In ancient times and in biblical thought, every people was constituted as such in relation to a land and for that reason exile was the most feared punishment because it implied the rupture with that which gave meaning to life. In the same way that Israel considers itself as a people and not a sum of tribes, in the same way it conceives itself with a land, without which the link with its God would be pale and would end in nothingness.

The first thing that draws attention is the fragmentary nature of the story, the irruption of legendary elements, and the evocation of the feat of the liberation of Egypt. Although the triumphalist spirit manifests a complete and militarily effective conquest, the simple comparison with the story in Judges 1 shows that this was not the case. In Judges 1:27-36 it is pointed out that not all the peoples were expelled, nor all the battles won, which shows a panorama that seems to be more truthful from the historical point of view than the narrative in Joshua.[1] The stories in Judges show that Canaan continued to be inhabited by Philistines and other native peoples. This alerts us to the fact that we are dealing with a text with a strong theological imprint and little zeal to reproduce the events as they happened, which leads us to confirm that the narrative in Joshua is a story that relies on history to construct a theological discourse whose purpose is to transmit a message about the action of God in historical events. The author observes events, perceives the presence of God acting in them and

---

[1] B. Childs points out that these inconsistencies reflect that the text of Joshua is the product of a process of redaction and compilation of sources over an extended period of time; this would have eroded historical accuracy, *Biblical Theology of the Old and New Testaments* (Minneapolis: Fortress Press, 1992), 143-44.

writes history as he lives it: the human and the divine are indivisible parts of the same reality. Proof of what we say is found in the first chapters, where among the historical accounts we find an abundant quantity of liturgical and homiletic elements. We list them:

1. Yahweh addresses Joshua to encourage him in his mission (1:1-9).
2. The crossing of the Jordan River is reminiscent of the crossing of the Red Sea (3:14-17).
3. A memorial with twelve stones is built in Gilgal (4:1-9).
4. All the Israelites who were born in the desert without being circumcised were circumcised (5:2-9).
5. Passover is celebrated in the fields of Jericho (5:10-11).
6. The manna that had nourished them for forty years in the desert ceased to appear. This was a sign that the Lord considered that they no longer needed it; and that day they ate for the first time the fruits of the new Earth (5:12).
7. The scene of the conquest of Jericho is organized like a liturgy. It begins with the appearance of an angel of God and then continues with a procession that for six days circled the city until on the seventh day they circled the city seven times and at the sound of trumpets the city fell into their hands.

All these elements aim to show that it is God who gives the land into the hands of the Israelites. This theology of the gratuitousness of blessings and of total dependence on God's generosity is clearly expressed at the end of the book when God declares: "I gave them the land for which they did not toil; I gave them cities which they did not build, in which they dwell; I gave them vineyards and olive groves which you did not plant, and from them they feed themselves" (Jos 24:13). This theology underlies the entire narrative and is expressed in an embryonic way in 1:2 when Yahweh tells Joshua to cross the Jordan "into the land which I give you" and in other texts where God's intervention to grant the land is made explicit, such as 6:2 when he says "I put Jericho into your hands." Because the land and the cities are given by God and belong to God, the first city conquered — and then the rest — is declared herem (*anathema*).

The concept of *herem* is associated with war, which is done in honor of Yahweh, who is recognized as the one who orders and directs it. Consequently, everything obtained as booty must be deposited in God's honor in the temple. This law is a way of consecrating that which was contaminated by foreign hands and which would contaminate whoever used it in Israel. In the case of

Jericho, all living beings, people and animals, are killed, and all objects in the city are burned. Only metals were kept and offered to Yahweh, although it is not explained by what means. Since there was still no temple — in the narrative line this would be built by Solomon much later — it seems to be a tolerated anachronism that does not bother the legendary story whose purpose is to affirm that the law of *anathema* was fulfilled. In a paradigmatic way and as a warning to others, the violation of the *herem* by Achan is mentioned, who kept precious objects from Jericho. When he is discovered and confesses his fault, he is stoned by Joshua and all the people along with his family. The defeat of Ai — because the *herem* had been violated — now turns into triumph and they conquer the second city of Canaan.[1] Liturgical elements are then repeated with the construction of an altar, and the solemn reading of the Law by Joshua in an unprecedented act where six tribes are located on the slope of Mount Ebal and another six in front of them on Mount Gerizim from where they listen to the blessings and curses of the people.

Protected Foreigners: Rahab the Prostitute and the Gibeonites
Two cases will be an exception to the mechanical application of the *herem* to the subjugated peoples. It is surprising that the first ally that Israel will have in the land of Canaan is a woman who practices prostitution. We remember that at the beginning of Moses' story women also played a central role (Ex 1-2). The midwives, the sister and the mother, the princess, the princess's servant, are those who save Moses from dying. The midwives lie to save the lives of the children; Moses' mother and sister hide their relationship from the princess; now Rahab lies to her king to protect the two spies. Mika, Saul's daughter, will lie to save her life and that of David (1 Sam 19:17). The lie in these cases is understood as the shrewdness of women to favor God's plan. The figure of Rahab is more than that of an occasional ally out of sympathy or fear and her dimension grows as we analyze her words; she says that: a. She knows that Yahweh has given them the land; b. That the peoples of the region fear them; c. She knows of the departure from Egypt and the splitting of the sea; d. That they defeated Sihon and Og in battle (Numbers 21: 23 and 33); then she adds an astonishing statement made by a foreigner (v. 11):

---

[1]See below for a description of the law of *herem*.

When we heard this, our hearts melted; no breath
was left in any man because of you, for the Lord your
God is God in heaven above and on Earth beneath.

The text then presents a detailed strategy on her part so that the spies can flee and continue their journey of exploration in the land. At the same time, she seals a pact of fidelity and mutual protection that will be fulfilled after the capture of the city when she and her family are freed from the *anathema* and incorporated into Israel (6:22-25).

It seems no coincidence that the story of Rahab also echoes the contrast between the peaceful attitude toward the Gibeonites and the massive destruction of the other peoples. The recollection of the deception of Gibeon (chap. 9) acts as a justification to explain why in this case peace is made and the Gibeonites are incorporated into Israel, even if only as workers in the service of the community and the temple. Once again, the promises made cannot be reneged on (9:19) — we saw this in the stories of the patriarchs and matriarchs — and this nation is exempt from suffering the *herem* that forced them to exterminate. The words of explanation that they give when their deception is discovered echo those of Rahab (9:24):

When it was made known to your servants that Yahweh
your God had commanded Moses God's servant to give
you the whole land and to destroy all the inhabitants of the
land from before you, we were greatly afraid for our lives
and did this thing.

They recognize the ability of the God of Israel to fulfill the divine promise to deliver the land to the Israelites.

The narratives about Rahab and the Gibeonites reveal theological features that qualify some statements:

1. They show that the Canaanites can be welcomed into Israel.[1]
2. In the case of Rajab, it is clear that despite the patriarchal culture that runs through the Old Testament, there is sensitivity to recognize the human value of a woman. In this story, she is the one who "makes history" by carrying forward the plot of events.
3. Loyalty is privileged over blood belonging to the people of Israel and they are incorporated, even if they are foreigners.

---

[1]Because of their foreign status, they must be added to the Calebites who will receive land and be incorporated into Israel (14:6-7); these are the descendants of Cain who lived in the southern desert area and came from Edom (Gen 36:11). In this case, it is also their fidelity to Yahweh that defines their belonging to Israel, as they declare in 14:8.

4. The latter reveals that the demand to exterminate the Canaanites is not absolute but is relativized to the extent that the acceptance of the God of Israel comes into play.

5. There is an underlying theology in which dialogue and negotiation allow us to get to know the other and thus avoid violence.

The stories of Rahab and Gibeon still contain a message. The story of Rahab contrasts with that of Achan, which we have already mentioned, in that the foreigner is preserved for her fidelity, while Achan the Israelite is condemned for his infidelity.[1] Both reveal that it is not only participation in a social, ethnic or political group that determines belonging to Israel, but that fidelity is also a means of being part of the people of God. The Christian tradition understood it this way and mentions Rahab as a model of faith in Hebrews 11:31 and as an example of how her actions earned her entry into the community in James 2:25.

The Law of Herem or Anathema

We have mentioned the law of *herem* on several occasions.[2] It is recorded in Dt 7:2-5 and 25-26 in relation to objects and in 20:16-18 to people and animals. This last text indicates that it applies to the cities of Canaan because for the "distant" cities there is another legislation that consists first of all in trying to make peace on the condition of submitting to Israel (20:10-15). If this proposal is rejected, a military attack is carried out and once the city has been subdued, the men are killed, but the women, children and cattle are left alive as war spoils; in these cases, the city is outside the concept of *herem*.

It should be noted that a*nathema* is not a law *per se* but a classification. Any object can fall into this category, just as it happens with the state of impurity or the condition of a sacred object. That which is declared *anathema* becomes an object that belongs only to Yahweh and that must not be used by regular human beings, which in practice implies that it must be destroyed or given to the temple for use by the priests (Ez 44:29). In general,

---

[1] It has been noted that in both cases Rahab and the Gibeonites are astonished and convinced of Yahweh's intention to hand over the land and they glimpse that a new social and religious order is about to be inaugurated, see Birch, Bruce *et al.*, *A Theological Introduction to the Old Testament* (Nashville: Abingdon, 1999).

[2] An extensive study in P. Stern, *The Biblical Herem* (Atlanta: Scholars Press, 1991); Y. Hofmann, "The Deuteronomistic Concept of the *Herem*," *ZAW* 111 (1999): 196-210; see N. Lohfink's article in *TDOT*, V, 180-99.

any object that comes from the spoils of a battle is *anathema*, both living and inanimate beings, although there is ambiguity regarding cattle and domestic animals, since in Jericho (6:21) the entire population and cattle are killed, but in Hazor (11:11-14) the cattle are preserved for use by the Israelites. However, it is not only the spoils of war that are *anathema*, but it also occurs in other contexts such as a field that has been sold and cannot be redeemed, or objects that once consecrated can no longer be sold and must be delivered to the priest (Lev 27:21, 28-29). In turn, the *herem* is contagious (Josh 6:18 and 7:12) and therefore its violation is punished severely, as happened in the case of Achan, for fear that the curse would spread to the entire community. Roland de Vaux points out that outside of the narratives of the conquest in Joshua, the *herem* was hardly applied, and that it is not mentioned in Judges (with the exception of 21:11), a book where wars are permanent, and only on one occasion in 1 Sam 15 during the war against the Amalekites. In contrast, the most prized spoils of a battle were the survivors, both male and female, who were taken to work as servants and slaves, and the belongings of the conquered people, which were shared among the combatants. But the fact that it exists as a concept presupposes that to some extent and at some times *herem* existed as a practice. Richard Nelson points out that the total extermination of the enemy, which repels us, is celebrated in Joshua "as an example of obedience to the laws of Yahweh."[1]

We are forbidden to retrace history in order to modify its facts or alter its record and rewrite the Bible. We would have liked that just as the Gibeonites were integrated through a ruse in a peaceful manner, so too would have happened with the other Canaanite nations. That the most benign instruction for the distant cities would have been the same as for those that were close and that at least an effort would have been made to arrive at a negotiated peace.[2] It is difficult to reconcile the cruelty of this law toward the enemy with the love of God expressed in the stories of the Pentateuch; a God who protects the life of one who murdered his brother like Cain or the life of the despised in his house like Ishmael.

---

[1] *Joshua* (OTL; Louisville: Westminster Press, 1997), 20.

[2] M. Noth's theory of a peaceful invasion by transhumant shepherds in camps is more reliable from a historical point of view—although it is still disputed—but that does not mean that the text narrates and celebrates this type of war violence independently of its historical value; see his *The Deuteronomistic History* (JSOT Sup; Sheffield: Sheffield Academic Press, 1981).

The narration of the humiliation of the defeated and his execution has no other meaning for us than to recognize that this was how things were done in that era, encouraged and justified by this law that instructed not to leave the defeated alive. There are a variety of extra-biblical texts and images on friezes that describe acts of this kind against enemies after a battle. The wars of antiquity were no less cruel than ours, where civilian populations suffer the consequences of war decisions made by people they do not know and whose interests are alien to them. An example can be found on the stele of King Mesha; this Moabite king of the 9th century BC tells how he exterminated all the Israelites who lived in the city of Nebo as *herem* to consecrate them to his God Kemosh:

> ...I went out during the night and fought against them
> from dawn until noon, dominating them and killing them
> all, seven thousand men, young men, women, girls and
> maids, because I made them as *herem* to Ashtar Kemosh...[1]

The Distribution of the Land and the Covenant of Shechem

The order of the themes in the remaining chapters of Joshua is striking. The account of the distribution of the land begins with the list of all that was not conquered (13:1-7), and the distribution itself places the division among the Transjordanian tribes before the Cisjordanian ones; and within the latter, Caleb — a foreign group — is mentioned before Judah. The impression one gets is that the less important actors are deliberately placed before those who, over time, gained prestige and power.

Reuben, Gad and the half-tribe of Manasseh are mentioned first. Reuben, Jacob's firstborn, had become a minor tribe over time and had given up its place of privilege to Judah. The fact that they lived on the other side of the Jordan and not in the promised land was due to an unavoidable historical fact; they lived there and the reason for this strange situation had to be explained. The episode of the construction of an altar (22:9-34) in order to preserve the memory of the belonging of these three tribes to the rest of the Israelite community reflects that the situation was not completely resolved, even in those times. The fact that it almost unleashed a war between brothers indicates that the relationship between the tribes was harmonious as long as there was no conflict that put the security of the other tribes at risk and that they still had fresh in their memory the episode of the *anathema* of Achan that had brought them so many problems. The

---

[1]See *ANET*, 320; *COS* II, 137-38.

resolution of the conflict by the declaration that the altar was not for celebrating sacrifices is unconvincing and seems more like a compromise solution. A large altar (v. 11) that was not a real altar is unlikely. Alberto Soggin offers two possible explanations; the first is that the altar was actually a tower that served as both a temple and a fortress, constructions for which there is archaeological evidence; the second is that the word for "testimony" should be understood as "covenant" or "alliance," so that the construction would be a memorial of the agreement between the tribes on both sides of the Jordan.[1] It is difficult to resolve the problem, but what is evident is that soon after the tribes were established we find the first conflict between those who live on one side and those on the other side of the Jordan River.

Then comes the drawing of lots for the territories of the remaining tribes. The use of lots indicates that Joshua and the priest Eleazar leave the assignment of each territory to God, just as the text is careful to detail that the sons of Joseph (Ephraim and Manasseh) each received a portion but that Levi did not receive any land, so that with this device the number of plots is kept at twelve, a number appreciated by Israelite tradition. Caleb's claim that we have already mentioned comes first, and then comes the delimitation of the territories of the three most prominent tribes: Judah (which receives the most attention, but it is surprising to see that Jerusalem is not mentioned),[2] Ephraim and the half-tribe of Manasseh. Next come the remaining seven; of these it is noted that Simeon received a portion within the tribe of Judah, and of Dan it is said that he was given a territory that had not yet been conquered, so that he could not take possession of his place.

We will have to wait until Judges 18, where their exodus to the northern region is narrated, where they will actually settle. As an account of the division of the land, it highlights the inconsistencies regarding the total and definitive conquest described in 11:23: "Joshua took possession of *the whole land,* just as Yahweh had told Moses…" At the same time, it warns of the risks of a reading that does not contemplate the ambivalences of history, which on the one hand is presented as triumphant and without blemish and on the other cannot hide the incompleteness of its result when at least two tribes (Simeon and Dan) do not

---

[1] *Josuah* (OTL; Philadelphia: Westminster Press, 1972), 213-14.

[2] J. Creach interprets this omission as deliberate in order that Jerusalem might be preserved as David's exclusive conquest; *Joshua* (Interpretation; Louisville: John Knox Press, 2003), 102.

receive land like the others. However, in the ideology of Israel that will be reflected in the theology after the conquest and division of the land, it will be considered complete, final and definitive. We should not be surprised by this distortion of the very facts narrated in the Bible, since every event that establishes the history and the very existence of a people must be clothed in solidity and cannot be presented as something indefinite or capable of being reversed. From this moment on, Israel considers that the land has been received from God and therefore that it will never be taken from it, which allows us to understand the dimension of the social and religious trauma that will be produced by the fall of Jerusalem, the destruction of the temple and the beginning of the captivity in Babylon in the year 586.

The Covenant in Shechem is the seal that legitimizes the conquest and the distribution of the land. Like every alliance, it is made in the heat of significant events that have impacted the sensitivity of the people. Let us remember the alliance with Noah after the flood and the rescue of his family and the ark; and the alliance of Sinai after the liberation from Egypt: On this occasion, the covenant is based on the recent conquest and possession of the land. It begins with the description of the acts of Yahweh in favor of Israel; in two sections, it concentrates the entire history from the beginning to its days. Vs 2-7 narrate from Terah, Abraham's father, "who served other gods," to the exodus; and then 8-13 narrates the events of the desert until the conquest. The sign is the constant presence of Yahweh, who leads history to complete the liberation begun in Egypt.

Croatto points out that every evocation of the past is done in terms of a future project and, by reviewing the wonderful events of liberation, the aspiration for the continuity of the presence of God in the accompaniment of God's people is expressed.[1] It is a way of expressing the hope that the God who has brought them there will not now leave them to their fate but will continue to bless them in the challenges that lie ahead. The verse that summarizes the theology of the conquest is verse 13, which resonates deeply in the spirit and sensitivity of the first listeners by saying that they inhabit and possess lands and cities for which they did not have to work hard. It is undoubtedly an exaggerated interpretation if we evaluate it as a historical fact,

---

[1] S. Croatto, *Historia de salvar* (Estella: Verbo Divino, 1995), 108; Croatto highlights that the pact of Shechem includes a return to the origin and to the fortunate days of the exodus and Sinai.

since in effect they had to fight hard to possess them, but if we look at it from the perspective of faith, it acquires another dimension: it says that everything that Israel possesses and dominates has been received as a divine gift and ultimately belongs to God.

Joshua sets before the people the condition for being under God's protection. This is defined in terms of the first commandment to observe fidelity only to Yahweh and to abandon all acts of idolatry. The evocation of the gods of the ancestors before Abraham—of whom they only have a vague image—is an indirect way of referring to the Canaanite gods who are honored in the same land where they now live and who will be a real temptation. The organization of the scene in which the people respond that they will follow Yahweh (vv. 16-18) and Joshua's immediate reaction by pointing out to them that "they will not be able to fulfill that promise" due to their rebellions, acts as a resource to emphasize the alliance but at the same time as a warning that anticipates the dangers that will come. In the face of the people's insistence on following Yahweh, Joshua's words are once again a veiled denunciation of what will happen: "You are witnesses against yourselves that you have chosen Yahweh to serve him..." Eutheronist theology does not miss the opportunity to leave a record of the will to be faithful but of the weakness of that promise. We must not forget that on the horizon still distant in the narrative but present in theological thought is the loss of the land and the condemnation to captivity, facts that will be understood as a result of Israel's sins manifested in going after other gods and clinging to idolatry.

Canaanite Peoples, Peoples of America, and the God of Israel

Since this work was written in the extreme south of Latin America, we cannot help but reflect on the relationship between the God of the Bible and the Canaanite peoples, who, like the original peoples of our America, were subjugated and destroyed in the name of faith and the love of God—love that seemed to be manifested toward the conqueror but not toward the conquered—a fact that has also been repeated on other continents. The question we ask ourselves is: *What is the meaning of God offering a people of slaves the ownership of a land that already has people living on it?*

We do not consider the attitude—which sometimes appears—of settling this problem by assuming a reading "from" the peoples of Canaan to be correct. It would be a reading that rejects Israel's vision of the text and therefore seeks to see the situation through the eyes of the defeated and thus question the ideology of the book and, with it, its vision of the adversary. The problem with this position is hermeneutical: the texts are not written from Canaan but from Israel and they do not aim to show how the Canaanite gods relate to their people but the God of Israel to its history. We can abandon the text and stop reading it, but we cannot read it from a place where it was not written. The attitude of taking the side of Canaan would be considered correct if we were analyzing historical facts or historiographies that demand that we assume one or another political position in solidarity and defense of a sector, in this case the subjugated one; but here we deal with canonical texts, not with the history that may be behind them. Showing solidarity with the victims is a praiseworthy and necessary act, but it is carried out in historical reality, which, as such, is variable and contradictory.

In reading texts, the function of biblical theology is not to analyze what happened in history — that is the task of the ancient history of Israel, a discipline that should not be interested in the theology of the texts — but how these stories transmit to us a certain message about God's action in that history. For example, in Lamentations, it is the Canaanites who murder the inhabitants of Jerusalem by collaborating with those who besiege the city; in Lam 4:21, Edom is mentioned — and in other texts, Ammon and Moab — as those who took advantage of the fall of the city and profited from its misfortune. What we observe is that the canonical text has already chosen the perspective and we cannot change it, but we can try to understand what is behind this narrative that seems so foreign to us from the rest of the Scriptures because of its cruelty and violence toward other peoples. It is not our interest to justify the text — because it does not need it — nor to postulate a secret goodness of its narratives; we are interested in pointing out some aspects that can help us better understand this narrative.

Our view is that the narrative we call the "history of conquest" is strongly influenced by the fact that Israel lived most of its history suffering territorial losses, threats of invasion, and the firm risk of disappearing as a nation. We understand that this book, and especially its narrative of conquest, is a product of this situation of social weakness and at the same time a form of response to it. We must bear in mind that already in the time of Solomon territories were lost to the south and east (1 Kings 11:14-25), and that in the time of Jehu the Transjordanian territories were lost to the Syrian king Hazael who invaded Canaan and came to besiege Jerusalem (2 Kings 10:32-33; 12:17). The fall of Samaria in

722 will cause Israel to lose two-thirds of its original territory in the north, while the pressure of Edom had further reduced its territories in the south during the time of King Ahaz and reduced its dominion to a small area, undoubtedly smaller than the original Judah (2 Kings 16:6). Upon returning from exile, the restored Judah is even smaller than it was before 587 when it had been eliminated by the Babylonians and its surface did not expand much beyond an area around Jerusalem. So those who wrote these stories, and those who read them as part of their own community life were people who lived in a territory that had been constricted over the years and who suffered the constant threat of losing everything; or they were truly a people without a land as Israel was during the Babylonian captivity.

Richard Nelson points out that Israel was more often a people victimized by the atrocities of the political and imperial forces to whose power and whim they were subjected than a nation capable of inflicting military damage on its neighbors.[1] In this cultural context, the grandiose battles of conquest with their complete victories where nothing of the enemy was rescued, where all adversaries were killed and where there was no mercy for the defeated, can well be understood as a literary revenge exercised several centuries after the events.

It was a tragedy for the world that Christianity did not understand the texts of conquest in this way and used them to justify the ideology of subjugation from the time of the Crusades to the Holy Land to the conquest of territories belonging to indigenous peoples in the modern era. We cannot resurrect buried cultures or their dead, but it is our responsibility to ensure that the Scriptures are never again used to justify oppression and dispossession.

The question with which we opened this paragraph (What is the meaning of God offering a people of slaves ownership of a land that already has people living on it?) is answered from a broader theological perspective than the text of the conquest itself. From the beginning in Genesis, we see that God acts in real history and chooses a real people. The social dynamics that are played out in the history of Israel are those that apply to all peoples; in their

---

[1] *Joshua,* 18. He adds that the account of the conquest was not the only way of justifying their right to the land but it was the main one; stories of conquest are already found in Gen 34; Num 13-14, 21, 32 and in Judges 1 and 17-18. Among the previous acts that granted possession we have the story of Jacob and Laban who set the limits of their territories (Gen 31:52) and Dt 32:8-10 which mentions the distribution of the land to all the nations of the world including Israel.

development and cultural evolution they are not modified by God to adjust them to a flawless and heavenly performance considered more appropriate for a people that recognizes itself as "of God." If God had created special sociological conditions for Israel, it would not have been fair to the rest of the nations.

We know that at the time of the conquest of Canaan there were no more empty lands in that region and that all peoples had to displace others to establish their own place. The future of the people of God did not have to be different. But the biblical stories show us that beyond the grandiloquent narratives of the conquest, at the end of Joshua, we see that Israel actually settles and shares the territory with the peoples who were there before their arrival. The same biblical text on several occasions indicates that the Philistines were never completely expelled, and that Israel lived with them as well as with other different Canaanite peoples. The alternative account of the conquest presented in Judges 1, where not all the peoples are expelled, shows this reality (Judges 1:19-21, 27-36). The narratives give an account of this by pointing out their presence in numerous events and the prophets denounce their influence on the faith of Israel at every step.

Creating the Need for a King: The Book of Judges

The book of Judges presents a series of formal and theological problems to the reader. Within the historical line constructed by the Deuteronomist, it occupies the place of the transition between the time of the conquest and the establishment of the monarchy. However, this condition of narrating an intermediate period does not inhibit it from offering a profound theological reflection. Its value as a theological document has sometimes been disdained, generally because it does not lend itself to a moralistic reading that expects the text to provide practical and direct instructions for our conduct today.[1] On the other hand, from the formal point of view, its literary integrity has been questioned, in this case not because of the history of its writing but because of its internal coherence. It is pointed out that 1:1-26 should be included in Joshua and that the remaining narrative

---

[1]Richard Nelson argues that when reading it, one should emphasize its condition as a textual space where cultural and literary values are expressed in the characters and that it would not be correct to assume it as an authoritative text just because of its canonical condition. The vices and virtues presented in the characters are evaluated by the narrator in the same text that with its theological perspective allows to distinguish between the acts of God and those that do not represent him, see "Judges," *WW* 29 (2009): 397-406.

(from 3:7, except for 1:27-3:6) is a continuous text up to 1 Sam 7, which reaches the doors of the establishment of the monarchy; this would include Samuel among the judges as he is named in 1 Sam 7 in vs. 6 and 15. This questioning presented by Serge Frolov supposes a different division of the canon but does not question the text itself.[1] However, the figure of Samuel will emphasize his role as prophet rather than judge, as seen by the later tradition present in Ecclesiasticus 46:13 and Acts 13:20.

The Work of the Deuteronomistic Editor

In his theology, Roelf Rendtorf points out that there are three phases of "Israel without Moses:" that of Joshua's leadership, that of the judges and the monarchy.[2] Of these three, the one we are dealing with is the only one that shows a disaggregated Israel, dispersed and without a vision of unity. The condition of the people of God present in Joshua and ratified in the Covenant of Shechem (Josh 24) has no representative in this book, which seems to have collected popular traditions with a certain degree of historical veracity, at least in its thematic cores and in the condition of its leaders. But this disaggregation required the Deuteronomistic editor to carry out a fine creative work to adjust the narrative to the objective of this part of the work, which is to offer the foundation for the establishment of the monarchy. To this end, he carried out a work of unification that is revealed in certain aspects of the story that we note below.

First, he created the figure of the "judge." The Hebrew word *shofet* has no other translation than judge, but we do not know the reason why they are called that way. The twelve figures who are called judges, with the exception of Deborah, are not really judges who judge in a court or who preside over a table of elders as there are examples in other biblical stories (Ex 18:24-26; Ruth 4), but rather they are transitory figures of a different kind and who will not be repeated again in the later history of Israel. They are called to free them from an enemy who oppresses them,

---

[1]Frolov places himself outside the division of the canon (or "before" it) and considers the so-called Enneateuch (Gen-2 Kings) to be a work, which he understands as a story that existed before its division into the books we have today; he offers an interesting justification for diluting the limits of Judges, but his argument that there was originally an extensive text that was later divided into books is not convincing, see "Rethinking Judges," *CBQ* 71 (2009): 24-41.

[2]R. Rendtorf, *The Canonical Hebrew Bible* (Leiden: Deo Publishing, 2005), 95-98.

so their function is to lead armies and govern, so it would be more correct to call them "liberators" or "leaders."

Secondly, it creates an artificial succession of judges. In the account, twelve judges follow one another in a chain, but without dynastic ties and without a time gap between each one of them. It is noteworthy that only six judges are given sufficient information to be able to characterize them, which means that the remaining six (they are called minors because of the brevity of their narratives) have been added to complete the preferred number of the Israelite tradition. This is highlighted when we see that after the isolated mention of Shamgar in 3:31, the remaining five minor judges are grouped together in two very brief texts (10:1-5 and 12:7-15). A simple observation of the rest (the so-called "major" judges) shows a great heterogeneity among them: Othniel is a Calebite, who by that time had become part of Judah; Ehud is a Benjamite and acts alone to assassinate Eglon; Deborah was a woman, a prophetess, and she served as an effective judge ("under a palm tree, between Ramah and Bethel," 4:5). Deborah decides to summon Baraq, an experienced soldier, but she puts herself at his side to lead the actions; Gideon is from the tribe of Manasseh and comes into conflict with the inhabitants of Succoth and Penuel, whom she will later punish harshly; Jephthah is from Gilead, the son of a prostitute and, for this reason, expelled from his family, which leads him to emigrate and become a criminal; finally, Samson is a Danite, a Nazarite priest and possessor of colossal and mysterious strength. This diversity of tribal origins, characteristics, and personal histories suggests that they were local and isolated figures, who appeared in their respective regions and who did not govern over the entire Israelite territory. Thus, to the temporal chain constructed by the editor, we must add the creation of a model of leadership of the national dimension that they never actually exercised.

The third element, and perhaps the most daring, was that the Deuteronomistic editor created a common design for each judge and a literary framework that embraces the narratives and generates the theological context for interpreting them.[1] In the central body where the history of the judges is narrated (3:7-16:31) the legends remain unchanged but his task consisted of making small adjustments that described the circularity of Israel's conduct

---

[1]Brevard Childs considers this last function to be the first and central one, since it forms the normative structure for reading stories that in their origin did not respond to the Deuteronomist theological plan, see *Biblical Theology of the Old and New Testaments* (Minneapolis: Fortress Press, 1992), 149-50.

and highlighted the moral and religious decadence it had reached. Each of the stories of the major judges was given a literary structure of six parts:

It begins with "they did what was displeasing to Yahweh" which in all cases means clinging to idolatry.

Then Yahweh delivers them into the hands of an enemy people who mistreats them.

They cry out to God to free them.

God appoints a judge who frees them and gives them tranquility and peace during the time in which that one judges (governs) Israel.

God supports the judge's actions.

In several accounts, God delivers the enemies into the hands of Israel.[1]

When the judge dies, the cycle is repeated in all cases, although the six elements are not always explicitly stated. The text seeks to convey the message that Israel will not be able to escape alone from the circle of evil in which it is trapped, which anticipates in the reader's perception the need to seek an alternative form of government. The judges rescue Israel but fail to correct it.

In turn, the Deuteronomistic editor saw the need to give a general framework to these stories and created an introduction and conclusion with strong theological content. The introduction states that the conquest has not been complete (1:27-36) which collides with what Joshua indicates, but goes further and gives a theological explanation of this fact by pointing out that not all the peoples were expelled "in order to test Israel" (2:20-3, 6). The mention of the permanence of foreign peoples contradicts and challenges the text of Joshua and possibly this gap is an essential part of the explanation of why the two literary works are divided. Even more surprising is the conclusion (17-21). In it, the demand for monarchy becomes evident every time that after a blunder in Israel's conduct, the phrase "at that time there was no king in Israel" is repeated four times (17:6; 18:1; 19:1; 29:25), followed in the first and last cases by the lapidary phrase "and each one did what seemed best to him," an expression that is highlighted and therefore chosen with that intention to conclude the book. The creation of private sanctuaries, the anointing of paid priests, the

---

[1]Susanne Gyllmayr-Bucher, "Framework and Discourse in the Book of Judges," *JBL* 128 (2009): 687-702, notes that the repetition of this scheme in each judge contributes to the feeling that these are not isolated rebellions but a pattern of Israel's conduct.

casting of silver images, are all acts unacceptable to Deuteronomistic theology and show the religious deterioration that Israel has reached, which the text attributes to the lack of a leadership designated by God.

Added to these early differences are the horrible events of the murder of the Levite's wife by the Benjamites and the subsequent revenge that leads to the fratricidal war against Benjamin until its near disappearance. The rape of the woman that leads to her death, the mass murder of the tribe of Benjamin and then of the inhabitants of Jabesh Gilead; the theft of the women of Shiloh to give them to the surviving men of Benjamin and the false argument that justifies it are acts as infamous to the thinking of today as they were to that of that time. The conclusion of the book leads us to think that the people of Israel, who witnessed God's acts in their favor in Egypt and Canaan, the people who accepted a covenant of fidelity and protection with God, now behave like the most vile of peoples and are incapable of resolving their internal problems in a peaceful manner. No one in it has the authority to say what is right and what is wrong. The intention of the story to create the conditions for the emergence of the monarchy can be seen in the fact that in the face of these events there is not a single word that leads the gaze to the glorious moments of God's relationship with Israel. It does not look back in search of a solid foundation on which to rebuild the broken relationship; It does not seek inspiration in the example of the faith of the patriarchs and matriarchs or in the profound experience of Sinai. The story looks forward toward the new model of political organization that it wishes to establish.

Hermeneutical Value of the Story of King Abimelech (Judges 9)

In the entire narrative of Judges, the only text that seems dissonant is the story of Abimelech. Two elements contribute to the dissonance: that Abimelech is not a judge and that he does not reign over Israel, but that his story is limited to the city of Shechem. On the other hand, if we have pointed out that this book seeks to induce the acceptance of the monarchy, it is striking that this experience of a king is not rescued in the continuation of the story. Having said this, it is necessary to point out that his presence has a specific purpose in the whole book. The plot and the outcome are clearly pieces of fine theology.

It is necessary to summarize the story of Judges 9. Abimelech is the son of a concubine of Gideon (8:31) who also had seventy children with his wives. The link with the judges is established by his father, but the story does not present him in the line of succession but as an ambitious person who offers himself to be king in Shechem and pressures the elders with his kinship to appoint him. They accept him and his first measure is to kill all his brothers, of whom only Jotham survives. Before fleeing, Jotham presents a poem in the form of a fable where he predicts bad times for Shechem for having enthroned a murderer. The story shows Abimelech as a violent person, who comes into conflict with his subjects and destroys the very city that elected him king; later his cruelty will lead him to commit even more crimes. His end comes when during the siege of the city of Thebez he is wounded by a stone thrown from above by a woman. Faced with what he considers a humiliation, he asks his squire to kill him, who will do so without delay. Let us observe the following theological data:[1]

His father Gideon had refused to be named king, after which he declared, "Yahweh is your king" (8:23). In contrast to his father, Abimelech asks to be appointed king.

There is irony in his name, for Abimelech means "my father is king." It may refer symbolically to the fact that God has chosen him as king, or in a concrete sense to the fact that he is the son of a king. Abimelech is neither of these.

The parable of Jotham is a subtle criticism of the monarchy as an institution and the designation of Abimelech by the people — aand not by God.

Abimelech dies at the hands of a woman. As had happened to Sisera at the hands of Jael (4:17-23), of whom it is said, "thus God humbled Jabin."

Apart from the link with Gideon — which may be the author's own creation — we see that this story has no connection with Judges. However, 9:22 states that "Abimelech ruled over Israel for three years" and adds that "God sent a spirit of enmity between him and the inhabitants of Shechem."[2] The Deuteronomist attributes to him a reign that never existed in order to use this story to warn of the risks of a king ruling in Israel who has not been appointed by God. The story seeks to avoid the risk of establishing a Canaanite-style monarchy in which — in the eyes of Israel — the appointment of the king was a mere human act. The

---

[1]Susan Niditch, *Judges* (Louisville: John Knox, 2008), 114-15.

[2]V. 22 must be considered editorial and that is why it is important; it is this condition that makes it key to understanding its function in the work from the moment it is incorporated into the central body of the book *because* he has been a king although in truth he never was. Its inclusion would not have been justified if he were mentioned as just another judge.

emphasis on Abimelech proclaiming himself and on the violence he unleashes toward his brothers indicates to the listeners that the eventual king for Israel must receive the anointing of a prophet provided by God. Since in this case he is crowned by his own will, the spirit that God sends him is "of discord" and unleashes all the violence that will lead to his death. The last verse rescues — without naivety — the figure of Jotham who had questioned his designation (9:16-20). In the narrative of Judges, the figure of Abimelech acts as an anti-king, the model of a monarch who should not be.[1]

The Monarchy: Rise and Burial

We have already pointed out that the historiography of biblical Israel is a theological narrative. However, the transition from Judges to Samuel gives us the feeling that something has changed in the narrative.[2] The history of the first chapters (1 Sam 1-7) is a literary transition, but as we move forward the flavor of the story becomes more solid. If for the texts of Judges we speak of legends without more, in the case of the histories of the kings, we begin to find a certain climate that makes us think that there is a historical core that reflects real events.

Without a doubt, in the narratives dedicated to Saul, David and Solomon there is much legend, but increasingly the text becomes closer to what could have really happened. From another angle we must point out that for this period archaeological evidence begins to appear which, although it does not prove the veracity of the texts in their details, does allow us to confirm the existence of the main characters, the societies mentioned and to glimpse that the narrated conflicts are not foreign to those that are presumed to have occurred in the social history of Canaan in the 10th or 9th century.[3] It will always be an open debate how much

---

[1]Richard Nelson considers that this story prepares the reader for the monarchy but at the same time made him think about what kind of king would be suitable for Israel, *The Historical Books* (Nashville: Abingdon Press, 1998), 103.

[2]The book of Samuel was divided into two scrolls in the Septuagint because the Greek text takes up twice as much space as the Hebrew and exceeded the length of a scroll; the same was true of Kings, Chronicles, and Ezra-Nehemiah. Here — as with the other books — we refer to it in the singular although we cite 1 or 2 Samuel as appropriate.

[3]For an overview of the current state of historical and archaeological research and its reflection in biblical scholarship, see Richard Hess *et al.*, *Critical Issues in Early Israelite History* (Winona Lake: Eisenbrauns, 2008); Neil Silberman & D. Small, *The Archeology of Israel* (Sheffield: JSOT Press, 1997); Lester Grabbe's *Ancient Israel* (London: T&T Clark, 2007) is an excellent assessment of the literary and archaeological tools for Israelite history. a work that offers an overview of the

there is of history and how much of literary construction, but if until now the story in his imagination was not indebted to an external criterion—the factual events—from this moment on the historian will also have to give an account to this new semiotic actor which is reality, or at least what the society of his time understood were the events as they had happened and expected them to be recorded that way. This explains in part why there are narrated events that contradict the theology or ideology of the author; Saul is chosen by God but is a weak and pusillanimous king; David is the ideal king, but his crimes and adultery are narrated; Solomon is the wisest, but he falls into pride and idolatry. All these examples and others are the result of the author's need to offer a story that is coherent with reality and acceptable to his contemporaries, although this does not mean that he will cease to leave his theological mark on the texts.

It is not unrelated to this that we are facing a new social and political conformation of Israel, which goes from a period of fragmentation to forming a monarchy that unifies it. After a few years, Israel is again under a single-person authority, as it was with Moses and Joshua, which generates a series of changes. A centralized government generates local and international correspondence that needs to be archived. The authorities want their achievements to be recorded in annals and that the laws they must enforce are written and published so that everyone knows them. The construction of a temple leads to liturgies, prayers and songs being written down to be passed on unchanged to new generations. Every monarch longed for history to be written down to see his name printed in it, even if, as was customary, events and feats were distorted in his favor. Finally, a centralized government found it easier to accumulate economic power and scientific knowledge to build buildings, roads, sophisticated weapons, better quality everyday utensils and housing. All these leave their literary and sometimes material traces.

The texts reveal that the establishment of the monarchy in Israel was not a simple process. From the beginning, there were tendencies for and against it. The account of the establishment of the monarchy (1 Sam 8-12) is constructed by alternating texts that favor it with those that reject it. The scheme is as follows:

---

entire history of Israel according to archaeological evidence is Amihai Mazar's *The Archeology of the Land of the Bible* (New York: Doubleday, 1990). See the discussion of different points of view between I. Finkelstein and A. Mazar, *The Quest for the Historical Israel* (Atlanta: Society of Biblical Literature, 2007).

8:1-22	against
9:1-10,16	in favor
10:17-27	against
11:1-15	in favor
12:1-25	against

The side texts and the central ones are those that stand out for their structure and are hostile to the establishment of the monarchy. But the other two texts also reflect the thinking of a sector of Israel that was in favor of it. For a time it was thought that the Deuteronomistic editor had been responsible for the texts that were against the monarchy, but today it is considered that both tendencies were present in Israel and that the editor merely highlighted the one that was more in line with his preferences. It is therefore exaggerated to speak of monarchical and anti-monarchical texts because the course of history will reveal feelings and words that are very favorable to David and then to Solomon, but it will also make it clear that this fabric of texts expresses the inner conflict of the Deuteronomistic editor who writes in the post-exile period and on the one hand loves and appreciates the house of David and all that it means for Israel but at the same time writes convinced that the project of an Israel with justice and balance came to an end because of religious infidelities and social deterioration resulting from the greed of the kings themselves. Thus, the editor navigated turbulent waters since he had to be faithful to the received traditions, narrate them in a credible way for his contemporaries, and at the same time include his own theological perspective that oscillated between love and criticism of the monarchical institution.

The history of the writing of the book is a complex subject and perhaps destined never to be resolved. But we are not far from the facts if we consider that the first collection of materials was made during the reign of Solomon. At that time, the social and cultural conditions for the writing of the ancient histories were in place. This material grew over the years and it is likely that it was significantly revised during the time of King Josiah (640-609). This king, who reigned after the fall of Samaria over a small and weak Judah, sought to reconstruct the model of Solomonic Israel and restore the vast territory that was under his dominion. He understood that idolatry was incompatible with respect for the Covenant that the ancestors had forged with God, and he undertook the most ambitious religious reform in ancient history. To carry out this restoration project, it is likely that he had the chapters on the unified monarchy written, with its military glories, geographical dominance, and great heroes who were at the same time a model of fidelity to God. This narrative served as an ideological and theological support for his political project, which was based on religious reform. His untimely death — and perhaps political difficulties — ruined this project and prevented its realization (2 Kings 23:28-30).

The Deuteronomistic Historical Work was completed in the post-exilic period in the light of the destruction of the city, the temple and the loss of the land given by God to Israel, which led to the burial of the monarchy. This last version is the one we have and in it the great figures of the history of the monarchy appear before God in their human dimension, imperfect, faithful and at the same time fragile.

Saul, the King in Darkness

Horst Preuss, in his *Theology*, has rightly pointed out that the Israelite monarchy does not go back to its origins, it does not have a mythical birth, nor is it linked to the patriarchs Abraham or Moses; on the contrary, it is presented as a product of historical development in response to a situation of lack of protection that required a military structure to overcome it (1 Sam 8:20).[1] This condition of not being part of the primordial creation weakens the Israelite monarchy in its essence, but it is slightly rescued by the resource of the election by God of the first two kings, Saul and David (let us note the degradation that implies that Solomon was not chosen by God but designated by David). Even so, this does not prevent it from being considered a political institution created by human initiative and therefore liable to be criticized and even eliminated without affecting God's plan on a long scale. The anguish that the destruction and exile will produce, expressed in texts such as Psalm 137 or Lamentations, is not so much for the end of the monarchy but for the demolition of the temple of Jerusalem, the place chosen by God for the divine dwelling. Although there are some psalms considered "royal," none of them is a full exaltation of the monarchy and few of the king as such.[2] It is worth noting that the expectation for the restoration of the "house of David" does not respond to the longing for the

---

[1] *Old Testament Theology II* (Louisville: Westminster/John Knox Press, 1992), 19-21.

[2] See Psalm 45 is dedicated to the king's wedding; 72 exalts the king but closes with a blessing to Yahweh. Psalm 151 (LXX) is an exaltation of the person of David, but that is probably the reason why which has not been included in the canon of the Hebrew Bible.

monarchy but to that of a messiah-king savior with strong eschatological connotations. With the passage of time, the "house of David" has become a future reality rather than a memory of the past.

Saul was anointed by Samuel and was confirmed as leader of Israel for his action in the battle against the Ammonites. But the following events made Samuel think that Saul was not the king that God wanted for Israel. There are two moments where Samuel distances himself from Saul. The first break occurs in chapter 13 when Saul offers burnt offerings to Yahweh and is reprimanded by Samuel. It is not clear what the fault was. There are those who think that Samuel was looking for an excuse to damage Saul's image, while others consider that the fault was acting without Samuel's presence.[1] From the beginning there is an ambiguous presentation of Saul in 1 Sam 13:1 where the dates of his age and time of government do not match the reality of the stories and because the capital city is not mentioned; this culminates when Samuel announces to him that his reign has no future and that God has sought another person for king; The close relationship between Samuel's words and the anonymous oracle against the house of Eli (1 Sam 2:30) has been rightly emphasized.[2]

The second break is clearer and occurs in chapter 15 and has to do with the violation of the *herem*[3] by Saul and his soldiers. The *anathema* was obligatory because it meant the recognition that everything obtained belonged to God and to ignore it implied an offense to the divinity. Saul violated it by leaving the Amalekite king alive and keeping all the valuable cattle. After a dialogue, Samuel judges, "since you have rejected the word of Yahweh, God has rejected you from being king." Even though Saul gives a reasonable explanation for his attitude by saying that he preserved the animals to offer them in sacrifice, what emerges from the dialogue is that for Samuel obedience to the law is more important than the sacrifices and that is what distances him from the king. This will distinguish him in the Deuteronomistic narrative of

---

[1]The first opinion is that of P. Miscal who points out that Samuel refers to "his reign" and not to the monarchical institution, see *1 Samuel* (Bloomington: Indiana University Press, 1986), 88; the second opinion is held by D. Jobling, *1 Samuel* (Collegeville: Liturgical Press, 1998), 79 and R. Gordon, *I-II Samuel* (London: Paternoster, 1986), 134, who adds that there may have been fear that Saul was seeking to establish a dynasty.

[2]R. Heller, *Power, Politics and Prophecy* (London: T&T Clark, 2006), 121-22; the author adds that the judgment on Eli fell on Saul, since both are marked by disobedience to Yahweh's instructions.

[3]See our discussion of this concept, *supra*.

David who, despite his shortcomings, will be described as the one who is ultimately faithful to God, obeys the divine commands and respects the divine will. While Saul seeks to kill David on several occasions when he had already been anointed by God, David, on the contrary, respects Saul's life only because he has the condition of being "anointed by Yahweh" although the divine person and reign were already in darkness (chapters 24 and 26). The king who inaugurates the monarchy in Israel and knows the brilliance of the anointing and of power ends up consulting a necromancer (28:3-25) in flagrant violation of the Law[1] and questioned in his own house by his sons in the episode in which they meet David. When David arrives for the first time at Saul's house, it is mentioned that Michal, one of his daughters, fell in love with him (1 Sam 18:20); In the same scene before her, Jonathan had fallen in love with David (18:1-4). This situation generates a competition between brothers for her love that will end up pitting them against their father Saul when Michal helps David escape from Saul's clutches and Jonathan seeks to protect him from his wrath (see 19:11-17 and 20:30-33). David Pleins adds that Saul's suicide is the culmination of all his mistakes and the confirmation of the error of having appointed him king.[2]

David: One Crown with Two Kingdoms

The figure of David stands out in the Old Testament as much as that of Moses, although for different reasons. No other character is given forty-one chapters (from 1 Sam 16 to 2 Kings 2) nor will he be mentioned again in dozens of other texts. It is no coincidence that his name means "the beloved" in Hebrew and it can be said that with the exception of his declared enemies, everyone else admires and courts him. The figure of David possesses that attraction that is difficult to define because his person combines violence and tenderness, beauty and aggressiveness, leadership and friendship, to which must be added his condition as a musician and artistic composer. The narratives about him seem to hide nothing of his life—even his dark sides—and yet at the end of it his figure remains solid and lasting, capable of creating a messianic tradition that, like all idealization, is built with the projection of contained desires and

---

[1]See Lev 19:31; 20:6; Dt 18:11.
[2]D. Pleins, *The Social Visions of the Hebrew Bible* (Louisville: Westminster Press, 2001), 104-05.

generally blurring real history.[1] The idealization of David begins with the first narratives but reaches its culmination in Chronicles, where his reprehensible behavior will be minimized or omitted. This can be seen in a text such as 2 Sam 21-24. These chapters are usually considered an appendix and there is a tendency to devalue them when their textual function is relevant in the construction of the character, since it shows how the image of David has already acquired the ideal overtones in the Deuteronomistic narrative that will later be expanded to form his messianic imprint.

The editor had literary sources at his disposal, which he reproduced with few changes. There are two large cycles of texts that are divided at the time of his enthronement over Samaria. The first (1 Sam 16-2 Sam 5) narrates his life up to and including his reign over Judah; the second runs until his death (2 Sam 6-1 King 2) and includes what is called "the history of the succession to the throne of David" (2 Sam 9-1 King 2) because it is considered one of the most coherent and literarily solid narratives in the entire biblical text.

From a sociological point of view, David must be considered the founder of the kingdom of Israel.[2] Saul's government does not record any major institutional events, but with David's arrival to the throne, it is for the first time that the existence of a political division within Israel is assumed. Today we would speak of two states in the sense that the south and the north were not considered a single political piece, but this is not realized until the reader is surprised with the information of David's appointment as king in Judah, with the seat of government in Hebron, which did not include governing the northern tribes. For this, it was necessary for those tribes to summon him and offer him to be their subjects, which is narrated in 2 Sam 5:1-5. From that moment on, we have a crown with two nations, a political and social reality that in written discourse tends to be diluted in favor

---

[1] It is remarkable how the figure of David was received in our culture. Note the differences in Michelangelo's sculptures of Moses and David. The former is seated, covered in heavy clothing, and holds the Book of the Law while his gaze expresses anger at the idolatry of the people; on the other hand, David is naked and standing, he is beautiful, he is strong, he exposes his body with serenity and his gaze expresses firmness and intelligence. Michelangelo sculpted the real man in his Moses, but in the marble of David he imprinted all human aspirations.

[2] We are referring to the social dynamics imprinted in the story, which may have little to do with the real story. This is what has been defined in semiotics as "the world of the text" where the characters must adjust to the coordinates of that reality. W. Brueggemann, who relies on Amos Wilder and Paul Ricoeur, calls it "narrative world," *Teología del Antiguo Testamento* (Salamanca: Sígueme, 2007), 83.

of political unity, but that at the level of historical reality will never cease to exist.

It is in this new context that David seeks an alternative seat to Hebron as the seat of the crown and finds it in a small, well-fortified city that had the virtue of being located almost on the border between Judah and Israel. Jerusalem is a city without tradition in any of the tribes and that, due to its geographical location, gave the impression of being part of both nations. David takes the city and—like every king of antiquity—gives it his name; this is how it will be called "the city of David," although it will never lose its original name. To this political fact, he will add a religious institutional fact—and no less political for that—which is the transfer of the ark to the new seat in Jerusalem (2 Sam 6). Severino Croatto has pointed out that the importance of this transfer lies in the fact that the ark is the witness of the ancient traditions of Israel. It had been deposited for twenty years in Keriat Yarim and now it is once again located at the center of the religious and political scene of Israel.[1] In this way, the new stage inaugurated by David was influenced by the traditions of the Sinai desert—the Law and the Mosaic tradition—and by the conquest of Canaan, where the ark played a fundamental role.

This event in the history of Israel should not be minimized. The fact that the narrative of the transfer of the ark includes several striking elements indicates the importance that the text gives to what is told. In the Israelite tradition, there was no other object with the same sacred value and this is expressed dramatically in the death of Uzzah for merely touching it, even though he does so to protect it. In the face of this event, David is afraid and sends her to the house of Obededom who, by sheltering her, begins to receive blessings from God. When David finds out about this, he decides to take her to his own house and organizes a colorful procession, with music and dance in which he dances in front of the people in an ostentatious manner, which earns him the contempt of Michal, that woman who had once said she was in love with him, and who after this event is said to have "no children until the day of her death" (6:23), information that seeks to show David's untouchability. All this is not narrated to construct a beautiful literary piece, which it undoubtedly is, but to emphasize that the city without tradition now becomes part of the

---

[1]S. Croatto, *Historia de salvarla* (Estella: Verbo Divino, 1995), 127-28; he adds that in this fact we must see the origin of the theology of Zion that will later be strengthened by the construction of the temple.

long history of the bond between God and God's people. The presence of the ark confers its sacredness and turns it into the "holy city." The political significance of this sanctity favors the king and is reinforced by the narrative that leads one to think that everything is due to David's action.

David's greatness did not prevent his dark sides from being narrated. Although the murders of the soldier who announced Saul's death, of Abner, Saul's general, and of Ishbaal, his son, who had been proclaimed king over the northern tribes, create a certain precedent for violent acts, these do not weigh on his conscience. But the death of Uriah, the husband of his neighbor Bathsheba, will mark a turning point in his biography. The first deaths are lamented by David and although a reading from the reverse side of the story could suggest that his tears are a political strategy, there does not seem to be any textual support for such an assertion. In fact, the deaths of Abner and Ishbaal do not occur by his hand or instruction. But what stands out in the narration of Uriah's death is the contrast between Uriah's integrity and loyalty and David's ulterior motives. When David is told that Bathsheba is pregnant, he tries to get Uriah to go to his wife and sleep with her in order to hide his paternity; But to his misfortune, Uriah refuses on two occasions because he feels that it is not fair that he enjoy the comfort of his home and his wife while his fellow soldiers are fighting at the front. As a last resort, David instructs his general to assign him to the front line so that he dies there, which is what happened. This event culminates with Uriah dead and Bathsheba in the palace and giving birth to a son by David. All this—says the text—did not please Yahweh. In this chapter, David is shown as a king drunk with power, who cannot and does not want to limit his desires when he sees his neighbor's wife from his window; he is presented as a cynic who invites his victim to drink and dine;[1] and as someone who despises the lives of his soldiers since, in order to hide a personal problem, he did not care that many others also died unnecessarily. From a theological point of view, the text does little to exalt David and much to show his errors, particularly those related to contempt for the lives of others.

The passage where David orders Solomon to be anointed (1 Kings 1:28-40) is ambiguous. It contrasts with the choices made by Saul and David by Samuel, who expressly mention that it is

---

[1]W. Brueggemann, First and Second Samuel (Louisville: John Knox Press, 1990), 279.

God who tells him to do so. In this case, it is David who orders the priest Zadok and the prophet Nathan to anoint him as king and present him to the people. It is through Benaiah's mouth that Yahweh is mentioned to bless Solomon, but David says nothing about the designation coming from God. At the end of the text, one has the feeling that the dynasty that was denied to Saul is now established by David, but without divine sympathy.

Solomon: Power and Glory

The narrative of Solomon begins before David's death. As with the texts about David that overlap with those about Saul, the presentation of Solomon as king is now superimposed on that of his father's last days, in both cases being a literary device to link the lives. The narrative presents two aspects of Solomon's life in an alternating manner: some offer a positive view, while others reveal his cruelties. For example, at the beginning of his reign, the murder of Adonijah, Joab and Semei is narrated, and the expulsion of Abiathar, the priest, all important figures of David's period. He does this because he needs to eliminate a potential competitor for the throne, like Adonijah, David's son who is older than Solomon and with aspirations to occupy that place; because he seeks to place a general and a priest of his confidence (Benaiah and Zadok); and because by eliminating Semei, he gets rid of a popular leader among the community. Within a few days, Solomon got rid of those who had accompanied his father and installed a new leadership similar to his own. After these actions, it is said that "the kingdom was established in the hand of Solomon" (1 Kings 2:46). So from the beginning there was bloodshed in his reign.[1]

It is no coincidence that in 9:6-9 Solomon is given a clear and strong warning in which we hear advances of the destruction of his descendants and the exile, events that will happen at the end of the Deuteronomistic history. The literary strategy consists of advancing the theme of destruction so that the reader keeps it in mind when evaluating the events that are now narrated. This allusion stands out even more when we contrast it with the first appearance of God to Solomon in Gibeon (1 Kings 3:4-15), a key text to understand his figure. In that dream, Solomon receives all the power and glory because his request to be able to discern between good and evil is granted to him. This request is an

---

[1]Compare these facts with 3:3-15 where he is described with these words: "He loved the Lord and walked in the ways of his father David;" see B. Birch *et al.*, *A Theological Introduction to the Old Testament* (Nashville: Abingdon, 1999), 248-49.

allusion to Gen 3:5 where the primitive couple is denied that gift, so that Solomon, upon receiving it, places himself in the position of being above all human beings of yesterday and today. He is the only one to whom God has granted what God denied to all humanity since the time of Adam and Eve. The garden closed to all is opened to Solomon, who stands as a new human being, of unlimited wisdom and whose relationship with God surpasses that of the patriarchs and matriarchs. This scene grants Solomon the legitimacy that he did not have to occupy the throne because he had been designated king by his father and not by God. Now he can develop his reign because he has received confirmation that Yahweh is with him. Hence, the contrast with chapter 9 — and then with his straying into idolatry in chapter 11 — is crucial to understanding the journey from glory to disgrace in Solomon's life.

Chapters 5-8 are devoted to Solomon's greatest work, the building of the temple. The text ironically places the story of the construction of his palace at the center of the story, already denoting certain doubts about his vocation and sincerity. It points out that his house took him thirteen years while the temple took only seven years, an indication that his love for God was less than his wealth and power. The construction of the temple is followed by the transfer of the ark from its place in the city of David to its new site, some four hundred meters to the north. It is a way of consolidating continuity and, at the same time, the replacement of David, of whom he says in his prayer, "you [David] will not build the house but your son..." (8:19). It is a solemn ceremony that cannot have errors and that culminates with the entry of God into the temple in the form of a cloud that evokes the entrance to the tent built by Moses in the desert (Ex 40:34-35). From a political point of view, it expresses the continuity of God's protection of Israel since the time of Abraham, something that Solomon needed to confirm his leadership. To the social, political and religious legitimation that he had received in Gibeon, he now adds the maximum religious support expressed in the acceptance of the temple. It is his triumph and Solomon himself proclaims it in the poem 8:12-13 ("... I have built this house for you as a dwelling place, a place for you to live forever") followed by an extensive speech and prayer. The depth of his words is the foundation for the later "theology of Zion" that will expand in the post-exile period until converting the mountain and the city into an eschatological reality in Ezekiel.[1]

Israel Finkelstein has questioned the historicity of Solomon's building work.[2] His argument is disputed by other archaeologists, but even if his opinion is correct that the narratives attribute to Solomon a splendor that he never had and that several of the buildings attributed to him were created a century later in the time of King Josiah, what interests theology is not historical accuracy but how that narrative presents a coherent and meaningful story for the reader even if it is so on the level of symbolic discourse. The question that should prevail is not historical rigor, but the meaning of the story. From this angle, the construction of the temple serves the narrative to consolidate the figure of the king, to give dignity to the God of Israel in front of the Canaanite gods, and to provide a house of worship that will serve as a place of pilgrimage for centuries. At the same time, the ideological side is revealed, since having a House for God allows the manipulation of the divine word. Anyone who wishes to know God's will — and everyone wanted to know it in order to plan their lives, crops and trade — will now have to come to Jerusalem to seek it. Until then, the ark had been temporarily resting in a tent built by David; now there is no longer any doubt about where Yahweh resides, that the solidity of the building indicates that it will not move from there, and who had been the builder of that temple.

The story shows Solomon as the wisest, but also the richest of all the kings. His ability to build provided a source of wealth to sustain him. The information is that, in addition to expanding Jerusalem and building the temple and his palace, he had the walls of Jerusalem, Hazor, Megiddo and Gezer built, all of them of enormous size. It is interesting to note that the text balances between exalting the king for his virtues and showing his weaknesses. But these are not limited to personal issues such as idolatry, but first of all the social ones are highlighted. According to 4:22-23, the daily provision of food for the palace was enormous

---

[1]Zion is a pre-Israelite name referring to the Jebusite city conquered by David (2 Sam 5:7), which later came to refer to both the mountain where Solomon's temple was located and the entire city of Jerusalem (1 Kings 8:1). The word does not appear again in pre-exilic historical texts or in Ezekiel, but it is abundant in prophetic texts (Isaiah, Jeremiah, Zechariah and others) and in Psalms (9:12; 74:2; 78:68; 132:13; 135:21; etc.); see R. Rendtorff offers a detailed study in *The Canonical Hebrew Bible* (Leiden: Deo Publishing, 2005), 575-85.

[2]I. Finkelstein, "King's Solomon Golden Age?" *The Quest for the Historical Israel* (Atlanta: Society of Biblical Literature, 2007), 107-16; In the same work see the position of A. Mazar, *The Search for David and Solomon*, 117-40.

and the maintenance of a fleet of chariots (4:46; 10:26) required a lot of money. That is why we are told in 4:7-19 that he had twelve provinces that each contributed taxes to the crown once a year. These provinces do not correspond precisely to the tribes, which denotes that the tribal system was not as clear as Joshua presents, but they are organized based on the political reality of Israel at that time. The general image given by the story evokes Samuel's warnings to the Israelites when they asked for a king: "...he will take the tithe of your crops and vineyards and give it to his servants..." (1 Sam 8:10-18). So all Israel had to contribute money and goods to support the crown. In addition, these projects and the life of the palace itself required a lot of personnel and soldiers, which implied that levies were made (9:15) among the non-Israelite populations resident in Canaan and although it says that he did not do so with his compatriots (9:22) it does not seem that this is consistent with the rest of the story.

The mention in 11:28 that Jeroboam was at the head of the levy of "the house of Joseph" suggests the existence of Hebrews who worked under this regime. The result of these levies was the availability of a significant number of people who worked for a very low salary in conditions of near slavery, an essential material base to be able to concentrate the wealth necessary to carry out the works attributed to him. It is therefore not surprising that chapter 10 describes the visit of the Queen of Sheba and then the immense riches accumulated by the crown and allows us to contrast this reality with what is related in the following chapter. To these sorrows, we must add that 11:14-25 indicates that he had as military adversaries Hadad the Edomite and Rezon in Damascus whom he could not defeat; this mention is presented as a consequence of his sins after idolatry, but the same text says that they were his enemies throughout his reign. The very existence of these situations suggests that his military power was more modest than described; Regarding Rezon of Damascus, it is likely that he even lost territories that had been conquered by David (2 Sam 8:6).[1]

Marriage with foreign women, expressly forbidden in Dt 7:3-5, is a characteristic of Solomon that follows the international custom of the time of exchanging wives as a gesture of political alliance with other nations. The text points to these women as

---

[1] P. Zamora in his commentary points out that the text disqualifies "the triumphalism of the *Cycle of Solomon*" [1 Kings 1-11] which "affirmed a seamless dominion over all the neighbors (5:14)," *El libro de Reyes I* (Estella: Verbo Divino, 2011), 232; also see M. Mulder, *1 Kings 1-11* (Leuven: Peeters, 1998), 565-78.

responsible for Solomon's idolatry (1 Kings 11:4) and for his subsequent misfortunes, although with little basis.[1] The worship of Canaanite gods, the construction of altars, and joining forbidden women destroy Solomon's former glory and deteriorate his relationship with God. The theology that emanates from the text highlights the king's fragility and his inability to remain faithful to the Law. But the story does not describe a total break between God and the house of David. So that although he announces to Solomon the break in their relationship (11:9-13), he establishes that he will sustain the kingdom as long as Solomon lives by virtue of three elements. These are the memory of "David, your father;" the chosen tribe of Judah, which will be under the rule of the successor; and the city of Jerusalem, "which I have chosen."[2] The Davidic line, the tribe of Judah, and the city of Jerusalem (Zion), mentioned together in this verse, will form the core of the theological and messianic expectations of later Israel.

The Kingdoms of Judah and Israel and the Cursed Kings

After Solomon, each kingdom had its own king. The schism of the crown highlighted, once again, the oppression and injustices exercised by Solomon's government, which his son, instead of repairing, sought to deepen and unleashed the rupture of political unity and, as a consequence, the breakdown of religious unity. The story begins to unravel the succession of kings, alternating those who reigned in Judah and those who reigned in Samaria, and offering the date of assumption in relation to the years of government of the neighboring king, a way of testifying that even in the separation there is a cultural and religious element that unites them. In fact, the traditions of the north — expressed in the Elohistic texts, to the extent that they can be identified[3] — reveal that the Yahwistic faith never ceased to be at the center of the religiosity of that sector and therefore remained within the scope of the faith common to both nations.

---

[1] Solomon is presented as the victim of his women. However, the formation of a harem in flagrant contradiction with the Torah (1 Kings 11:2) cannot be justified with the argument of the love he felt for them; a different reading that values these foreign women is given by Z. C. Insfrán, "Mujeres fieles. Mujeres idólatras," *Mujeres haciendo teologías* (2013): 167-89.

[2] P. Zamora, *Reyes I*, 230; he also points out that "it is the first time that it is said that Jerusalem is the city chosen" by God.

[3] We are not referring only to the texts of the Pentateuch but in particular to the collection of Elohistic Psalms (Ps 42-89 and others); the fact that Ps 14 and 53 are similar with the exception of the name of God reinforces that they came from different temples and places of worship.

Two elements make up the theological intention of this extensive section (1 Kings 12-2 Kings 25): the first is to keep alive the memory of David as the model of a king. David is the yardstick for measuring fidelity, which is seen in the repeated phrase "he did what was right in the eyes of Yahweh, *like David his father*" (15:11) or "he did what was right, although *not like his father David*" (2 Kings 14:3). The second is to show the responsibility of the kings in the moral and religious decline that will lead to the destruction of the temple and the end of the monarchy.[1] Deuteronomistic thought sustained this conviction throughout the work, particularly when it affirms the responsibility of each king in the permanence of idolatrous practices in Israel. Out of thirty-nine kings of the divided monarchy, only a few of Judah are rescued and none of the kings of Samaria will be rescued; Of Asa (1 Kings 15:11), Jehoshaphat (22:44), Joash (2 Kings 12:2), Amaziah (14:3), Uzziah (15:3) and Jotham (15:34) it is said that "they did what was right" but it is clarified that "they did not do away with the high places" where sacrifices were carried out.[2] The text reserves for Hezekiah (18:3-6) and Josiah (22:2) words of higher praise because they did suppress the altars to the Canaanite gods and promoted reforms, although they did not manage to straighten the paths of Israel permanently. All the rest are explicitly accused of straying from the path of God.

An event that foreshadows the end of Judah is the fall of Samaria (2 Kings 17). The plot is woven with the flagrant faults of the dynasty of Omri and then of Jehu. The first marked by idolatry and the rejection of the prophets Elijah and Elisha, and the second by murders and violence. The successive kings are presented as responsible for the breaking of the alliance by virtue of their actions, in particular by the inclination to idolatry and the departure from the Law. The long text of theological reflection of 2 Kings 17:7-23 attributes the fall to having failed in everything to keep the pact with Yahweh and having inclined to other gods. The story takes advantage of the opportunity to base the end of Samaria on the same reasons that later will base the destruction of Jerusalem in such a way that it acts as a sign for Judah. After a long reflection on the theological reasons for the fate of the Northern Kingdom, Judah is mentioned with words that in the context of the deportation of Samaria would cause horror to

---

[1] V. Fritz, *1 & 2 Kings* (Minneapolis: Fortress Press, 2003), 2-3.

[2] T. Vriezen & A. van der Woude, *Ancient Israelite and Early Jewish Literature* (Leiden: Brill, 2005), 302.

anyone who heard them: "...Judah did not follow the commandments of Yahweh and did the same as Israel" (17:19). With this phrase the fate of Judah is linked to that of Samaria and perhaps the description of the difficulties of the new inhabitants of that region brought by the Assyrians to recognize and worship Yahweh—facts that they do not manage to overcome even with the sending of an Israelite priest—should also be read as an allusion to the religious situation of Judah. It is difficult not to read with both references the final phrase "they revered Yahweh but served their idols" (41). Nevertheless, it is evident that the text of 17:24-41 will play an important role against the rights of the inhabitants of Canaan who populated the country when the returnees from Babylon claimed ownership of the land.

A characteristic of this period is that the voice of the prophets appears strongly. Not only are there more and more prophets who act in the story only once, but long cycles are dedicated to Elijah and Elisha. The prophets Ahijah (11:29), Jehu (16:7), Micah son of Jemlah (22), Jonah (2 Kings 14:25), the prophetess Huldah (22:14) act, and two anonymous prophets are mentioned in 1 Kings 13:11 and 20:13; to this, we must add that Isaiah has a long intervention (2 Kings 19-20). Elijah and Elisha will establish a tradition about their persons that will far exceed that of other "writing" prophets, and their influence can be seen even in the New Testament, in particular that of Elijah, who will be evoked on several occasions in the four gospels. This presence of the prophets reflects the esteem that the Deuteronomist has for them and considers them the true messengers of God to correct the path of Israel and the kings. Their conflict is evident in the case of Micah, son of Imlah, who is warned by the king's messenger before taking him before him that the prophets "announce good to the king" and that he must do the same; to this, Micah responds that he will announce what Yahweh communicates to him (1 Kings 22:13-14). This dialogue and the subsequent development of the scene show the distance between the ideology of the kings who seek to use the voice of the prophets to legitimize themselves and that of the Deuteronomist who reveals himself in the figure of the prophet who remains faithful to the word received.

The stories of the kings are profound and touch the reader's sensitivity. On the horizon of these stories is always the sad end of the history of the monarchy in Israel. They must be read bearing in mind that each infidelity contributes to bringing closer the tragic destiny of losing the temple and the land as if they were falling down a long slide of almost four hundred years that leads to the worst fate. But there is a turning point in the story, and it is when the recovery of the Torah among the ruins of the temple is narrated. This event will trigger Josiah's reform.

Josiah: The Insufficient Reform

From a theological point of view, Josiah's reform plays a central role. It is the confirmation that no matter how many efforts are made to repair it, Israel's distancing from the will of God is such that it is no longer possible to reverse the final and tragic destiny of its existence, and at the same time it is the culmination of a process that places the Law as the center and criterion for the life of Israel. Note that in this story the Law is placed above the temple and the monarchy. The temple was the ideological support of the monarchy but now it is minimized because, as the Law is found in it, it emerges as the foundation of the temple. While the temple will no longer be spoken of, the Law and its observance become the recurring theme of the entire period of Josiah. The Law is also placed above the monarchy from the moment that the king recognizes himself incapable of judging its content and therefore turns to Yahweh for confirmation, which will be done through the prophetess Huldah. He adds in this direction that Josiah's life will be remembered not for his military achievements or his economic successes, but for his attention to the Law and his effort to restore its observance. From this moment on, it will be the Law that will give meaning to the existence of the king and the temple.[1]

First, there is a mention of a reform carried out by Hezekiah (18:3-8). This acts as a precedent, but the act to which the story points is when the scroll of the Law is rescued from the ruins of the temple (2 Kings 22:1-10). Whatever the content of this scroll — it is believed to correspond to a version prior to the definitive one of Deuteronomy — what matters is that it produces a strong reaction in King Josiah, who is distressed and frightened by the prospects that arise from its content for the future of Israel; and he orders that, in order to certify the veracity of what is said there, he send a delegation to consult Yahweh. To do this, they turn to the prophetess Huldah.

The words of the prophetess Huldah provide two things: first, it confirms the truthfulness of the text; according to her words, what it says there comes from God. Second, her firmness in

---

[1]W. Brueggemann considers that this may have been the beginning of the process of canonization of the Scriptures that later made Israel the "people of the book," *1 & 2 Kings* (Macon: Smyth and Helwys, 2000), 548-50.

maintaining this provides the foundation for the reform that the king will carry out.[1] It is clear in the text that Josiah acts in accordance with Huldah's words and that the reform that Josiah undertakes seeks to rebuild ties with God, which would have the effect of avoiding disaster. In this enterprise, the idols that were in the temple and their objects of worship are eliminated, the rooms dedicated to fertility cults are demolished, human sacrifices in the Valley of Hinnon are suppressed, altars are destroyed throughout the territory of Judah, the horses that were at the entrance of the temple and that were associated with sun worship are removed,[2] and the destruction of Canaanite altars built by Solomon on the hill in front of Jerusalem is not left unmentioned (2 Kings 23:4-14). All these measures aim to establish the centrality of the Jerusalem temple as the only place of worship and sacrifices, since this place had been chosen by Yahweh, while the other sanctuaries were established by different people (Abraham, Jacob, etc.).

This centralization is so great that it helps to understand the development of the theology of Israel, which initially accepted a diversity of sanctuaries, but then, based on Deuteronomy (see 12:1-7), recognized only the Jerusalem temple as a place of worship. This change is due to the difficulty of maintaining a monotheistic (or monolatric) faith, while the multiplicity of places of worship made them easy prey to the surrounding polytheism. In turn, it has served as a criterion for dating many texts of the Old Testament, since a marked emphasis on the single temple in Jerusalem leads one to think that the text was written after the time of Josiah.[3] With the mention of Solomon's idolatry, David is

---

[1]M. Sweeney, *1 & 2 Kings* (Louisville: Westminster Press, 2007), 442; the author has a positive assessment of Hulda's intervention, which contrasts with the opinion held by Esther Fuchs who considers that the text gives a negative image of Hulda, see "Prophecy and the Construction of Women," *Prophets and Daniel: A Feminist Companion to the Bible* (ed. A. Brenner; Sheffield: Sheffield Academic Press, 2001), 62-64; in our opinion it is difficult to sustain Fuchs' position. W. Brueggemann, *1 & 2 Kings,* also highlights the importance of a woman being the prophetess linked to the palace and points out that the fact that the text does not highlight this is an indication of the acceptance that women had in that function, 550.

[2]It is not known for certain what cult these horses refer to; it is interesting to note that the Basilica of San Marco in Venice has four life-size bronze horses above its entrance, brought in the 13th century by the Crusaders from Constantinople; in this case, too, their presence is not understood, although we can infer that it is a sign of the political and military power of the Venetian church in those years.

[3]A. Rofé, "The Strata of the Law about the Centralization of Worship in Deuteronomy and the History of the Deuteronomic Movement," *Deuteronomy*

the only king who remains outside the period of social and religious decadence. It is then mentioned that Josiah seeks to extend the reform to the northern territories, which in his time were no longer under the dominion of Israel. This fact must be understood as the attempt to restore the ancient borders in the understanding that it was the territory promised long ago to the ancestors and granted by God to Israel during the conquest; the framework of a full reconciliation had to include the restitution of the lost land.

But Josiah's efforts proved insufficient. The announcement of his death in battle against Pharaoh Necho at Megiddo precipitates the end. Huldah had announced that she would die "in peace" so that she would not witness the humiliation of Israel; in effect, Josiah died young without seeing the collapse of Jerusalem, so that part of his words were fulfilled, but his violent death does not correspond to that prophecy. This fissure warns that the reform has not prospered, and that it has not been possible to restore the link between Israel and its God. The sentence of 2 Kings 23:26-27 ("... *I will also remove Judah from my presence, as I removed Israel, and I will reject this city that I had chosen, Jerusalem, and the house of which I had said, My name shall be there...*") seals the fate of Judah and opens the door to the unhappy death of Josiah.

The Tragedy: The Burning Temple and the Desolate City

The austerity of the story is striking. An event that has been on the horizon of the narrative since Deuteronomy and that has outlined a good part of the narratives is dealt with in a couple of pages. This is certainly not due to literary incompetence but rather reveals an intention of the author, who prefers a low profile to the bombast of a tearful description. The tragedy is too dense to allow for a scandalous or morbid story. Furthermore, the silence of God is perceived; not a silence motivated by disinterest, but one that accepts and allows what happens. Throughout the Deuteronomistic history, theological reflections have been punctuated, such as 1 Kings 17:7-23 after the fall of Samaria, where the reasons why God allows this to happen are given. But in this case the mention is brief and prior to the central events; they are given in 24:3-4 ("by order of Yahweh this happened in Judah"). The author does not want to add anything, he limits himself to

---

(London: T&T Clark, 2002); Rofé points out in Dt 12 the difference between the law against Canaanite cults (vs. 1-7) and against the idolatry of Israel (8-12).

narrating the facts because he considers that they speak for themselves.

The facts are as follows: A first invasion by Nebuchadnezzar sacked the temple, deported part of the population and appointed Zedekiah as king in place of Jehoiakim, who was taken prisoner to Babylon. This happened in the year 597. On this occasion, he took the riches of the temple but preserved its structure and that of the city. Then Zedekiah rebelled against Nebuchadnezzar and in retaliation Nebuchadnezzar invaded Israel again and took control of the city. He killed Zedekiah and his family and appointed an officer of his army, Nebuzaradan, to burn down the temple, the palace, destroy the houses and demolish the wall. This happened in the year 587. With the exception of the poor peasants, the king and all the inhabitants were taken into captivity. That is the end of the story. Nebuchadnezzar installed Gedaliah as governor, but he was later killed by the Israelites who had remained and fled to Egypt to avoid reprisals from the Chaldeans. The story ends with the information that thirty-seven years later, Jehoiakim, the last king, was released from prison and treated with dignity at the Babylonian court until his death.

The social and political impact of these events was incalculable and, like every significant event, it also generated its own word. The events of the fall of Jerusalem were recorded not only in Kings and Chronicles but also in the books of Jeremiah and Lamentations (attributed to Jeremiah but whose reading reveals a diversity of voices and authors) and in particular in the work of Ezekiel, who most profoundly expresses the situation of spiritual and social decline that led to the burial of the monarchy and the burning of the temple, events that changed the cultural and religious physiognomy of Israel forever. When Israel returns to Judah after several decades of exile, it will be a different people from the one that had been sent into exile.[1]

Like no other prophet, Ezekiel had to elaborate theologically on the most distressing experience of the people of Israel. In a long section spanning chapters 4-24, the prophet reflects on the lamentable situation of Israel. Idolatry abounds, the

---

[1] Jeremiah speaks of seventy years of captivity (25:11-12; 29:10), but this should be considered a symbolic number. Depending on the date taken for its beginning, the time in Babylon lasted fifty years (587) or sixty years (597). Another option is to consider that what he calls the captivity refers to the absence of the temple, since it was destroyed for seventy-two years, from 587 until its reconstruction in the year 515 (Ezra 6:15).

Law is forgotten and replaced by Canaanite cults, and religious practices inspired by those of neighboring peoples are carried out in every village. Social injustices arise as a consequence of valuing wealth and power more than caring for one's neighbor. All of this contributes to God reconsidering the divine relationship with Israel. It must have been very sad for Ezekiel to narrate how God's presence leaves the temple (Eze 10:18-22) and later also withdraws from the city of Jerusalem (11:22-23). Nothing like this had been heard since the time of Noah, when God announced divine regret for having created the Earth and flooded it to purify it. But this is a text from the origins, which has nothing to do with Israel as a chosen people but with the human condition as a whole. Now the break is not with humanity but with Israel. Enmity is not expressed with creation but with the chosen land. Moreover, God uses the other nations, those with which the Israelites should not unite, as a tool to show the divine will; and God sends them to a foreign land, toward an uncertain future, to those lands where God cannot be worshipped because God has established the divine dwelling in Jerusalem. Ezekiel knows how to get deep into the description of the situation. There are priests who worship idols (Ez 8), there are false prophets (13) and a corrupt ruling class (19); the prophet announces the destruction and suffers for it (24).

The five poems that make up Lamentations use the genre of funeral songs to express sadness and desolation with that strange cadence that characterizes them. In Hebrew it is called *eihah*, a title with hermeneutical value that means "How?" with the sense of being a cry of anguish and despair. In one of the most distressing texts it is narrated that those who remained in the city die of hunger to the point that mothers feel obliged to kill their children (Lam 4:10). The theology of Lamentations maintains that "they would never have believed that the enemy would enter the gates of Jerusalem" (4:12) but at the same time it does not doubt the reality that nothing has remained of the glories of the past and that a new world awaits the survivors. Like Ezekiel, Lamentations points out the rich (4:5), the false prophets and priests (4:13) and the monarchy (4:20) as responsible for the tragedy.

Every conquest of territories seeks money for today and slaves to continue the profits tomorrow. The Babylonians found money in the temple and the palace and slaves in the captives and the poor who were left to work the land for their new owners. From a theological point of view, everything has been subverted. The gold and bronze of the temple that were there to express the glory of Yahweh now finance the luxury of the imperial court; the

154

land that gave its fruits to support the people is now plundered for the benefit of a distant and foreign court. But the text does not offer a naïve reading of the fall, as if Israel were an innocent victim of the international political game; on the contrary, the interpretation it offers us is that it was the disobedience and attachment to other gods of the leadership of Israel that unleashed the tragedy. It was the greed of the kings and the hypocrisy of the priests who lost their way and turned the pact into a farce. They acted as if the continuity of Abraham's blood gave them the right to the continuance of the promises, or as if Yahweh were obliged to protect and sustain them by virtue of their ancient commitment. They believed that it was the seed of Abraham that gave them protection and did not perceive that every covenant is based on the fulfillment of the commitment assumed by both parties.

At the end of the story, the restoration of the royal dignity of Jehoiakim is mentioned, but nothing is said about the restoration of the temple. Conversely, the later story will show that the temple will be rebuilt but the monarchy will not be reestablished. The meaning of this ending is disputed, as it admits various interpretations. Some think that it expresses the recognition of the ancient hierarchy of the Israelite crown. In our opinion, the poverty of condition of this king whose only brilliance consists of eating as a subordinate thanks to the generosity of his master until his lonely death, without mentioning any possibility of returning to his land, is a way of pointing out the weak situation in which the crown that once rested on the head of kings like David and Solomon ended up.

For the Chronicler There is No End to History

If we delve into the theology of Deuteronomistic history, we must do no less with the work of the Chronicler. The work that encompasses the books of 1 and 2 Chronicles, Ezra and Nehemiah has been called the Chronicler. We have already mentioned that both the books of Chronicles and Ezra and Nehemiah in the Hebrew Bible are just two works called: Chronicles and Ezra. This and their contiguous location in the third section called Writings speak of their unity, although in the Hebrew Bible Ezra is presented before Chronicles.[1]

---

[1]Chronicles follows Ezra-Nehemiah, but although in that order the chronological line is inverted, the books are marked by the repetition of the Edict of Cyrus (2 Chr 36:22-23; Ezra 1:1-3) to indicate the correct order and continuity of the reading, P. R. Andiñach, *Introducción hermenéutica al Antiguo Testamento* (Estella: Verbo Divino, 2012), 220.

When we are faced with two texts that narrate the same events, in this case a second story, the practice of hermeneutics leads us to look for the differences between them. A story or a poem is not rewritten if there is no intention of saying something different; in turn, a second writing assumes that what was narrated in the first one no longer manages to say everything that those events are expected to say for the new times. Sometimes the difference consists of a total change of the narrative, as is the case of the two creation stories in Gen 1-2. In prophetic texts, it usually implies the application of a text whose origin responded to another context to a new situation; for example Isaiah 2:4 and Micah 4:3 with respect to Joel 4:10 which reproduces the same image but in the inverted sense: Isaiah and Micah speak of making plows from the metal of weapons and Joel announces that weapons will be melted from the metal of plows. In the case of the Chronicler's work in relation to the Deuteronomistic history, it consists of a change of perspective and also of evaluation of the history of Israel. Hence, he adds information and also omits other information.

The Chronicler conceives himself as a new history of the world, not as a work that seeks to complement the Deuteronomistic history. He does not begin with Joshua but with Adam, and although he quickly goes through the first periods he does not fail to mention them. From Saul to the fall of Jerusalem — the section where they coincide in time — he writes with an eye on the other history and seeks to contrast it with it. He deliberately omits to follow the events of the northern kingdom and not only does he not mention its kings but there is no reference to the prophets Elijah and Elisha who developed their ministry in the north but who exerted a profound influence on the religiosity of Israel and in the case of Elijah on the expectations of his return as an emissary of God.[1] What is striking is that he does not ignore the existence of the northern kingdom and proof of this is the account of 2 Chronicles 18, where the history of Jehoshaphat and Ahab is presented, the latter king of Samaria; what happens is that he rejects this tradition as illegitimate. This elimination of the tradition of Samaria is a theological choice and is due to the fact that its kings did not represent the line of succession of David and

---

[1]There is a single mention of Elijah in 2 Chr 21:12, but it has no parallel in Kings. It is also strange for a prophet to send a letter, suggesting that the writer considered him to be residing elsewhere (Samaria?). Chronicles appears to have relied for this event on a tradition other than that represented in Kings.

were therefore perceived as illegitimate and prone to corruption and idolatry.

Another element to highlight is that the Chronicler does not end his narrative with the fall of Jerusalem and the end of the monarchy but continues the story with the restoration and constitution of the new political and religious entity that is post-exilic Israel, Judaism proper, so called because its territory is limited to ancient Judah. And unlike Kings, the Chronicler has an open ending. In Kings we saw that its ending does not leave an open door to the future but ends with the poor king eating on borrowed time until his death, which is not even mentioned. The Chronicler closes in a different way; if we follow the order of the Hebrew Bible, it ends with Chronicles 36:22-23 where the liberation of the captives of Babylon is announced so that they can go to Jerusalem to rebuild the temple. If we prefer the order of the LXX—and our current Bibles—it ends with the words of Nehemiah 13:30-31, which narrate the restoration of the priesthood purified of idolatries and the establishment of norms for its exercise from then on. In both cases, time does not end there, there is no end of history, but it supposes the historical continuity of the relationship of God with God's people.

The Need for a Second Story

Until the production of Sara Japhet, most authors held that Chr-Ezra-Neh was the work of a single author. Japhet showed that the differences between Chronicles and Ezra-Nehemiah were sufficient to postulate the contrary and from his works there is a general consensus that we are dealing with two works.[1] However, this distinction should not hide the fact that both in the Hebrew Bible and in the LXX and later in the Christian Bibles, both works are linked.[2] It is not the question of authorship that is of interest—they are undoubtedly written in different ways—but rather that of recognizing a line of argument and history and the intention of constituting a work that expresses an alternative to the received

---

[1]S. Japhet, "The Supposed Common Authorship of Chronicles and Ezra-Nehemiah Investigated Anew," *VT* 18 (1968): 330-71; "The Relationship between Chronicles and Ezra-Nehemiah," *Studies in the Historical Books of the Old Testament* (ed. J. Emerton; VT Sup 30; Leiden: Brill, 1979), 52-64; and *I & II Chronicles* (Louisville: Westminster John Knox, 1993), 3-7.

[2]The repetition in Ezra 1:1-3 of the text of 2 Chr 36:22-23 is the author's marker to indicate the continuity of the reading between the two works. The existence of the marker is proof of the diversity of authors but also of the fact that this diversity was not a problem for those who organized the texts; see P. Ackroyd, *The Chronicler in His Age* (Sheffield: JSOT Press, 1991), especially chap. 14.

history. As they are in the Bible, it is evident that they are intended to be read as a single history and we will see that considering the unity of a work by the Chronicler allows us to explain the theological emphases present throughout all these books. On the contrary, reading Chronicles in isolation has led to interpreting its ending—without the reconstruction of the temple—as if it were a utopian work, a work that describes unfulfilled desires and therefore leaves open to the future the realization of the dream.[1] Unlike the Pentateuch, which ends without the conquest of the land but for that reason closes its story there and leaves it as an expectation of liberation, Chronicles gives no signs of closing its narrative but on the contrary, the superposition of its ending with the beginning of Ezra indicates the need to continue reading that book.

The differences with the Deuteronomistic history are perceived in numerous details, which are theologically significant. In addition to the gross omission of the kingdom of Samaria and the stories of Elijah and Elisha, there are other more subtle ones. We will give two examples. With all the affection that Chronicles has for King David, it does not like the fact that the city of Jerusalem is called "city of David." On several occasions, it changes the previous text based on this inclination. In 2 Sam 5:9 David gives his name to the city but in its parallel text it is others who call the city in this way (1 Chr 11:7). In 2 Kings 14:20 and 16:20 it is called the city of David but in its parallels 2 Chr 25:25 it is called the city of Judah[2] and in 28:27 it is called Jerusalem. In two cases, the Chronicler omits the mention that is in the first story (compare 2 Sam 6:12 and 1 Kings 2:10 with their parallels 1 Chr 15:25 and 29:26-28). In short, the expression "city of David" appears 19 times against 151 times when he calls it Jerusalem. What theological intention is there in this? There are those who see in this rejection the possible fact that the author identified with that name the ancient and small "city of David" and not the whole

---

[1] P. Beentjes, "Tradition and Transformation in the Book of Chronicles," (Leiden: Brill, 2008), 103-04; the author expresses surprise at this ending without a temple and at the irony of a foreign king ordering the construction of the future temple; however, continued reading avoids this question and the political situation of submission reflected in Ezra explains the mention of Cyrus the Persian in Chronicles.

[2] The Jerusalem Bible follows the LXX and translates it as "of David;" this is a variant that should be avoided because it is unnecessary and because it ignores the Chronicler's tendency.

post-exilic Jerusalem.[1] But that is relegating the problem to a question of geography and urban development. Our opinion is that the reason is deeper and has to do with the fact that the Chronicler was jealous of the sanctity of the city and that he must not have been pleased that neither David nor his subjects called Jerusalem in that way. However prestigious the figure of David may have been, the city of Jerusalem had been chosen by God and was "of God" and not "of David." Kalimi suggests that the Chronicler minimizes the relationship between David and the city to the point that in his account of the conquest of Jerusalem he expresses this by narrating that the first to enter it was not David but Joab (1 Chro 11:6).

The second example is the treatment of King Manasseh. While in 2 Kings 21:1-18 he is described as a godless king, in 2 Chr 33:1-20, following the first text, his conversion is added, which leads him to restore the city and remove the idols from the temple. For the Chronicler, Manasseh is a sinful king who becomes pious and who even composes a prayer that he bequeaths to posterity.[2] Regardless of the fact that the Chronicler may have had a source unknown to the Deuteronomistic author on the life of Manasseh, what emerges from this divergence is the intention to highlight everything that can contribute to mitigating the sins of the kings. It is not enough to affirm that this second source existed — which is improbable — because what is important is that the Chronicler did not hesitate to deviate from the received history to offer an alternative to it. This leads us to rethink the concept of sacred history that we apply to the work of the Deuteronomist and the Chronicler. It is sacred insofar as its primary interest is to offer an interpretation of the facts from the perspective of the relationship between God and God's people. But it was not sacred in the letter or as a narrative, therefore, it was liable to be criticized and even modified in a second version without affecting the status of the first. On the contrary, the coexistence of two stories does justice to the inclusiveness of ideas proper to biblical thought.[3]

---

[1] I. Kalimi, *An Ancient Israelite Historian* (Assen: Royal van Gorcum, 2005), 109-12.

[2] The custom of "adding" prayers missing from the received texts (see Jonah 2; the additions to Esther in the LXX; etc.) was reflected in a late text that was not incorporated into the canon, the so-called *Prayer of Manasseh* ; it is part of the Old Testament apocrypha and was composed in the wake of this mention in Chronicles, see L. Vegas Montaner, "Oración de Manasés," *Apócrifos del Antiguo Testamento II* (ed. A. Díez Macho; Madrid: Sígueme, 1982), 209-11.

[3] This cultural and hermeneutical attitude is characteristic of ancient Judaism. The reader should bear in mind that not only are there parallel narratives

The prolongation of history after the fall of Jerusalem in the books of Ezra-Nehemiah surprises us by the total omission of any reference to the time of the exile. It is foreseeable that during that time texts of a narrative nature were created, in particular if we remember that the literary genre "history" is for that part of the world almost an invention of ancient Israel; it is striking that if it was practiced throughout all the centuries of its existence, no record of this period was produced. If there were historical texts about the exile, none were preserved in the canon or outside of it. There are psalms composed in Babylon (137) and there are those who maintain that the same writing of Chronicles could have been done in Babylon, but about the period of captivity, almost nothing has survived. Of what happened there, we know little and it is difficult that this is so by chance or simple forgetfulness; nor because there was no one who devoted themselves to it. We must also avoid speculating about an absence and constructing a discourse on the lack of data. Rather, we are inclined to think that the experience of exile from a theological point of view was so traumatic that silence was chosen; a silence that reveals itself as a message in itself. Just as one could not worship in the land of Egypt (Ex 5:1, 3; 7:16; etc.), neither were the conditions for connecting with God given in Babylon and therefore there was no word to say. For the theology of Israel, if there is no connection with God, there is no possible word to be pronounced. And if there was, it did not deserve to be rescued.

The Theology of the Chronicler

Peter Ackroyd has described the Chronicler as an interpreter of history to distinguish him from a historian who seeks to record events with a certain degree of objectivity. Someone — we think of a school — who took the old traditions and incorporated new material into them, rewrote them, at times gave them a homiletic tone, at times assumed that the reader knew the previous history, at other times offered moralizing and didactic elements. In all cases, he acts as a theologian whose discourse is built on the scaffolding of history.[1] Although it is exaggerated to say — as has sometimes been said — that it is the first theology of the Old Testament, what is certain is that the Chronicler's work is

---

in the Old Testament, but that based on the same principle we have four versions of the life of Jesus and many repetitions of themes in the Pauline letters that, with their nuances, express inclusivity.

[1]P. Ackroyd, *The Chronicler in his Age*, 276; Ackroyd asserts that the same status of theologian applies to the author of Joshua-Kings.

a clear attempt to give a comprehensive theological interpretation of the history of Israel. This is built from documents that are already, themselves, theological works but which in his opinion require revision. This intention becomes dramatic when we see that he omits the entire history of the origins of the world and of Israel and begins with Saul; Thus, the Chronicler does not seek to conceal the fact that his interest is in a particular moment of history and not in the whole of it, nor does he pretend to disguise his desire to analyze history with theological eyes. Those who aspire to the utmost objectivity strive to pay attention to the details and to leave nothing out of the story; the Chronicler deliberately abandons centuries of history to concentrate on what, for him, is the central knot that will provide the foundation for a new stage in the history of Israel.

A first theological fact is the absence of the patriarchal and exodus stories. It is true that it assumes that the reader knows these stories, but their absence must be seen from another point of view: the Chronicler is interested in the future and not the past. He knows that God was with Israel in the past, but his reflection is that God is and will be with God's people. He does not look back in search of enlightenment, but rather he sets out to build a solid theological apparatus on which to base the new social, political and religious reality of post-exilic Israel. He does not ignore or eliminate the events of the distant past—that is why he includes them in the form of a genealogy—but he considers that it is the monarchy that must be revisited by the interpreter. As the restored Israel consists only of the tribe of Judah and its ancient territory, although even smaller, in his exposition he sticks to the kings of Judah, since those of Samaria, in his opinion, were illegitimate and disappeared from history forever. The greater distance in time and pious eyes soften the edges of the kings' lives and in some cases (David, Solomon, Manasseh) they are presented clean of the serious faults attributed to them in previous history. The kings continue to be responsible for the fall of Jerusalem and the destruction of the temple, but in the light of the restoration these events are now not seen as the end of history and the definitive abandonment of God's covenant with God's people; on the contrary, they are seen as a new opportunity that God places before them.

There is a clear monotheistic bias in the Chronicler's theology. The vestiges of bygone times where the polytheism of Canaanite culture made its influence felt in Israelite thought are left behind, and there are no traces of the monolatry enshrined in the first commandment, which recognized the existence of other gods but agreed to worship only one. The Chronicler's monotheism is probably the first in his history and was the product of contact with the Persian religion during the exile. Whatever the origin, what emerges from the reading is that in the new theology of Israel there is no space for the existence of other deities. This had immediate consequences in the social conformation because it consolidated the centrality of the temple of Jerusalem, which was an idea promoted in the time of Josiah but which would now be installed in the Israelite imagination so as not to be abandoned. It is striking that the unified monarchy of David and Solomon had not been able to centralize worship with all the political power that this implies for the king, and now the small and weakened Israel that returns from captivity achieves this as a consequence of a radical change in its theology.

The scarce geographical dispersion of the new Judah means that centrality does not add political power, but it does clarify the relationship with God and establishes a principle that will impact the incipient diaspora. This will be forced to make a pilgrimage to Jerusalem to worship in the indicated place and, in turn, will be the beginning of a process that will later lead to the creation of a fundamental institution in the subsequent development and continuity of Judaism: the synagogue. This "meeting house" (as it is called in Hebrew, *beit keneset*) will be a place of study, a place of meeting for the community, but not a temple. In this period, in the heat of monotheism, the expression "the God of heaven" will be coined, which is found only in the books of Ezra, Daniel and Jonah. This way of referring to God is a way of explaining that, unlike the Canaanite idols, the God of Israel is not a visible being and does not have a physical form. Far from understanding heaven as a material place where God dwells, what these words express is God's universal power, sometimes emphasized with the expression "the God of heaven, *who made the sea and the land*" (Jon 1:9). It implies that God is omnipresent, and that nothing escapes God's gaze and judgment. Israel does not worship a stone, a river or a star; it worships a God who dwells in Jerusalem, who is one, who governs the universe and that nothing escapes God's interest because God looks down on everything from above.

From what we have just said, it follows that Chronicles develops a theology of the city and the temple. This was described by Tamara Cohn Ezkenazi as a process of expanding the sanctity of the temple to the entire city. What was initially attributed to the temple as the "House of God" is now assigned to the city of Jerusalem and everything found in it. We see this in Neh 12:30 when the priests purify "the people, the gates and the wall" and in Ezra 3:8 where it is said that the Jews arrived at the house of God in reference to Jerusalem, a fact evident because the temple had not yet been rebuilt.[1] This transfer will also have its effect on the conception of the leadership of Israel. Personal figures gradually become blurred, and the community begins to have an increasing prominence. This is the price that the monarchy and the priests pay for their dark and dubious past of fidelity, since it was not possible to read the classical prophets and the Deuteronomistic history and continue to venerate the priesthood and the kings. The process has begun and in a few years we will no longer see figures that stand out and the narratives — wisdom literature and others — will become anonymous and little adept at praising human characters. Hence, in the political aspect, the theology of restored Israel will not seek to return to the monarchy.

The zeal to rebuild the temple has no equivalent in the restoration of the monarchy; the prophets Haggai and Zechariah raise their voices and cry out for the temple but say nothing about rebuilding the throne or the palace. We believe that this is so not only because the Persian empire would not have allowed it, but because there is a disenchantment with the monarchical institution. The kings are revalued as figures of the past, but there is no attempt to restore their power. It was Flavius Josephus who in the first century AD first used the word theocratic to describe the government of post-exilic Israel. He says in *Against Apion* (II.164-167):

> ...other nations concentrate power in monarchies, others in oligarchies, and others in majorities... our legislation was not attracted by any of these forms of government and assumed a form which may be called theocracy since it places all power and authority in the hands of God.

Jonathan Dick comments on this text by Josephus and says "to the extent that *governed by God* meant *governed by priests*, Judah was a theocracy during most of the Second Temple period."[2] Israel would be under the command of governors appointed by the

---

[1]T. Cohn Eskenazi, *In an Age of Prose* (Atlanta: Scholars Press, 1988), 2, 54-57; Cohn Eskenazi points out that the importance given to the construction of the walls is not because they ensure the defense of the city but because they are the new perimeter of the House of God.

[2]Jonathan Dick, *The Theocracy Ideology of the Chronicler* (Leiden: Brill, 1998), 2.

Persians, who could be Jewish or not, but would be accountable and pay tributes to the empire in a careful and regular manner.

Finally, it is important to highlight the Chronicler's theology that he seeks to provide a basis for the construction of a community separate from the surrounding peoples. Although this attitude has obvious political consequences, it was not understood in this way, but rather as a theological requirement that sought not to be contaminated by idolatry. The expulsion of foreign women narrated in Ezra 9-10 and Neh 9-10 is inscribed within the framework of this theology. In relation to this fact, it has been questioned whether they were really foreign women who were expelled and it has been postulated that they were Jewish women who practiced Canaanite cults within Israel.[1] If this were the case, there would be a justification for the expulsion because they would be practicing idolatry within their own people and would deserve the sanction. However, although it refers to idolatry practices within the Jewish community itself, the texts do not seem to refer to native women of Israel; In turn, if this were the case, it is not clear what the reason would be for hiding these practices if history testifies how throughout the centuries all social sectors of Israel fell into idolatry and were exposed and criticized. Everything leads to consider that those expelled were foreign women and their children and that it was a terrible and unjust act since the worship of other gods was undoubtedly shared by their husbands and relatives; therefore, it is one more example of the androcentrism of the culture of the ancient world that attributed social evils to women and held them responsible for the sins of all.

When investigating the meaning of the expulsion, we see that it is linked to the theology that sought to maintain the sacredness of the city and the people; the theology inherent to the Chronicler considers everything foreign as a vehicle of their gods that introduced into the bosom of the people contributed to distorting the inherited faith. Even language — and eventual bilingualism — is considered a threat to the religious integrity of Israel, as revealed by the concern for children who do not speak the language of the country (Neh 13:24). This theological current will find an adversary in the theology represented by books such as Ruth and Jonah, which are open to the presence of foreigners and value their ability and willingness to join the people of God.

---

[1]B. Becking argues that it was more a Jewish "witch-hunt" than the expulsion of foreign women, see "On the Identity of the Foreign Women in Ezra 9-10," *Exile and Restoration Revisited* (ed. G. N. Knoppers *et al.*; Someret: T&T Clark, 2009), 31-49.

We find the same in the universalist theology present in Isaiah 56:1-9, where foreigners who adopt faith in Yahweh are welcomed, and in texts such as 45:14-25, which announce the future conversion of foreign nations. But even stronger because of its concreteness is the instruction of the prophet Ezekiel (47:22-23), who during the exile had proposed giving land to the foreigner and integrating him into the tribe where he resides, and in this way he would be incorporated into the people of God. But some years have passed from Ezekiel to Ezra and Nehemiah, society has changed and with it theological thinking.

The Voice of the Prophets: Cry and Theology

The Voice and Writing

What characterizes prophets is their voice. The Hebrew words *dabar* (word, in this case in the sense of a spoken, proclaimed word), *kol* (voice) and the verb *shama* (to hear) have a stronger meaning in prophetic literature than they do in other texts. Here, they sound like that word that comes from the depths of communication with God and that is recited as a word that must be heard and acted upon. That is why it is unfortunate to call those whose words we have in a book (Isaiah, Jeremiah, etc.) "prophets writers" in order to differentiate them from those others whose stories are interspersed within historical books (Elijah, Elisha, Huldah, etc.). First, because the books only in a very small proportion include words written by the prophets themselves — if they have them — and second, and more importantly, because the prophetic vocation was never to write but to orally announce the divine word. The few cases in which a prophet is instructed to write are in particular circumstances and related to a specific situation (Is 30:8; Jer 36:2 where he instructs Baruch; Hab 2:2). And when the prophets call, they do so with the formula "hear the word of Yahweh" and do not invite the slow reading of any text. So the call to which they were summoned was to make their voice heard, a voice that, like all others, fades into the air, diluted in the very moment it is recited. This condition also explains why prophetic literature has a predilection for poetic discourse, although it does not use it exclusively. Unlike prose, which is linear, narrative and develops over time, poetry happens in the moment. It has no time and is consumed in itself. It is as volatile as the word that is proclaimed and whose powerful force in the ears of those who receive it dies the moment it leaves the speaker's lips.

This ethereal condition of the prophetic word is not a mere coincidence and calls for us to reflect on it theologically. It is necessary for Moses *to write* the laws because there is a halo of eternity in them, of regulations that present themselves as permanent, although later history shows us they also change and adjust to new contexts. The laws must be passed down from generation to generation and be an instrument for use by priests and judges; by definition, they must be objective and applicable to different situations and contexts and must be available to be read by many. Something similar happens with the stories of the founding fathers and mothers of Israel, which acquire legendary status and become permanent stories and therefore must crystallize into a stable work. At the same time, the narrative character is unavoidable in the historical exposition that supposes the existence of time as its first raw material. But everything changes when we face the prophetic texts, even those that are recorded in prose. The prophetic word comes to the forefront of emergency situations; it is an urgent word that cannot be postponed to be polished or to avoid exaggerations typical of the din of an unexpected or desperate act. The prophetic word explodes in its context and prophets do not have time to write and calibrate their words; and if they did, they would be failing in their vocation because they would spend hours taking care of this prose and that could endanger their mission. At the same time, in the discourse of the prophets, "the God who is" (*El Dios que está*) is proclaimed in its most concrete expression, since it always refers to a divine will or action that arises from the present and immediate situation that the prophet lives. The wise individual will meditate for days on end on their concerns; the prophet will shout their message at the very moment they is called to do so.

The above-mentioned characteristics of prophetic literature lead us to think about its access to canonicity. It is known that an essential condition for a text to be canonized is that the community attributes to it a value or message that exceeds the context in which it was produced. A statement that cannot be reread in the face of new episodes in history would have no meaning in a canon. The question therefore arises: How did prophetic texts become part of the canon if their discourse is linked like no other biblical discourse to the social and spiritual context in which they were produced? In exploring answers to these questions, we must remember that the process of canonization is one of the least known and most obscure chapters in the history of texts.[1] However, from the reading it can be inferred that the fact already mentioned that the prophetic books are works composed of the encounter of various texts allows us to glimpse that the canonized work is the product of a complex process of selection, elimination and rewriting of a variety of literary pieces, some of such different origins that in isolation they

---

[1]For a summary of the current state of canonical research see B. Childs, *Old Testament Theology in a Canonical Context* (Philadelphia: Fortress Press, 1985), 57-69; the work of A. Sundberg, *The Old Testament and the Early Church* (Cambridge: Harvard University Press, 1964).

could not be identified with the book in which they are found today. Thus, the canonized text no longer belongs to a context but presents in most cases the final product of successive readings and rereadings that were incorporated in written form into the primitive material. We estimate that the text that we have today in the prophetic books only in a very minor portion corresponds to the first context of the prophet.

Historical-critical research has revealed that behind every prophetic text, there is a succession of hands and authors. The discovery of this has led to the same discipline to seek to distinguish between the author's original texts and later texts, attributing superior value to the former and discarding the latter as additions, "second-hand." This idea contributed to conceiving a golden period of Israelite prophecy during the 8th century that would later have weakened both literarily and in its theological concepts.[1] The additions would be a product of this later period where the deterioration of theology was accompanied by a growing leadership of the priests whose interest was centered on liturgical questions and not on the relationship between God's message and social reality. Consequently, searching for the original text of the prophet is the main goal of historical-critical exegesis, in order to free their message from later interventions. The exclusive recourse to this exegesis has had a devastating effect on biblical interpretation. The fact of introducing an external element to the texts (the reconstruction of the original context of composition) that acts as a key that opens the meaning made them lose their hermeneutical perspective.

The meaning—in the genetic research of the texts—arises from their dissection into fragments and their classification according to the periods to which each one can be assigned. But this classification has been revealed to be so hypothetical and so debatable that it ends up tarnishing the message. In many cases, it destroys a literary fabric of delicate workmanship that in itself is a bearer of meaning and that by ignoring it prevents the message printed in it from being revealed. The Danish theologian Søren Kierkegaard complained already in 1850 about the way in which

---

[1]This conception, influenced by 19th-century evolutionist ideas, has lost its validity; see a detailed description of the relationship between history and biblical text from its origin to the present day in W. Bruggemann, *Teología del Antiguo Testamento* (Salamanca: Sígueme, 2007), 15-75; Leo G. Perdue's *The Collapse of History* (Minneapolis: Fortress Press, 1994), is the most significant work of recent decades on the character of Old Testament theology and its relationship to the various areas of the text.

the biblical criticism of his time considered the text; in his opinion it made it seem like a letter that a beloved sends to her beloved *but in a language that he cannot read* ... and that requires complex tools to be deciphered, so complex that the beloved may never know what their beloved is saying to them.[1] Even considering what has been said, it is necessary to consider that the patient work of historical reading had the inevitable consequence of revealing the fact that the text is not the product of a sudden illumination that produced it, nor of a single writer, however skillful he or she was with the pen. The text bears within itself the marks of its material growth and of those very human perceptions, ideologies, theologies and aesthetics that shaped it over time. Without understanding the history of prophetic texts, we might believe that God spoke only once to each prophet and then fell silent forever.

Prophets in Jewish Tradition, Christian Tradition, and Both

Prophetic literature has a different meaning if it is read from the perspective of Judaism than from the perspective of the Christian tradition. This difference can be seen in the different place and value that they occupy in the respective canons. In the Hebrew Bible, the prophets include Joshua, Judges, Samuel and Kings, who are called earlier prophets, while those called later prophets are four books: Isaiah, Jeremiah, Ezekiel and the Book of the Twelve Prophets.[2] This section called *Neviim* (Prophets) has a lower canonical value than the *Torah* (Pentateuch). This is because the prophets are understood as interpreters of the *Torah* or as its commentators and consequently cannot have the same authority as the Law that they comment on. In the Jewish tradition, the prophet is first of all the one who exhorts to "return to the Law," which in most cases means "return to Yahweh." Its function is to correct the people and warn them about the consequences of having deviated from the Law and the blessings of returning to it. This becomes clear when, during the time of exile, the prophet Ezekiel describes the temple that will be rebuilt as a replica of the Solomonic temple, so that the house destroyed by the Babylonians

---

[1]Søren Kierkegaard, *Para un examen de sí mismo recomendado a este tiempo* (Madrid: Trotta, 2011), 44-48.

[2]The fact that Joshua to Kings are prophetic books expresses the idea that the underlying meaning of the stories they narrate is primarily theological and not historiographical. As prophets, they do not tell a story but announce a message through it. This distinction already existed in biblical antiquity and can be seen in the literature of the Annals such as the Assyrian or Hittite, properly historical works, and in Israel in lost works such as "The Annals of the Kings of Judah and Israel" and other works cited as historical sources.

would once again be the same one where the people of Israel would gather in the future for their worship and sacrifices. Ezekiel does not think of a new era but of restoring the lost era. This message explains the fact that in rabbinical literature throughout the centuries there has been a certain inclination toward Ezekiel over the other books.

The Christian reading of the Scriptures did not see the prophetic texts as a group differentiated by their semantic level from the texts of the Pentateuch. Unlike the synagogue, the church does not give the Pentateuch a higher value than the other books, but values them according to their content. We already mentioned at the beginning of the section on the historical books that by separating the "earlier" prophets (Joshua to Kings) from the "later" ones (Isaiah to Malachi), on the one hand it gave historical value to the former and on the other hand it highlighted the properly prophetic function of the latter. Christianity reads the prophets not as those who call for the restoration of the betrayed Laws but as those who, as in the Jewish reading, call for conversion and reunion with God; but the Christian reading will ultimately be inclined to look forward in history by interpreting the prophetic text as preparing the ground for the arrival of the Messiah. Hence, the confusion about the supposed fact that the prophets predict the future as part of their ministry is much stronger in the Church than in the synagogue. The tendency to read them in terms of "what will come" led to exaggeration of this characteristic, which in prophetic literature itself is a secondary element. This conception led to including Daniel among the prophets for his apocalyptic content[1] and to considering the Twelve Prophets as separate works, each with its own particular message. It is significant that in this way the canon closes with Malachi, which toward its end announces the irruption of the "sun of justice" and the return of the prophet Elijah (4:1-5). Both images were read in Christianity as an announcement of the imminent arrival of the Messiah and as the door that opened to what was

---

[1]In our opinion, the apocalyptic theology present in Daniel and in brief texts in other books did not permeate the Old Testament. Its emergence occurred after the closing of the canon and, although the production of works was very extensive, it did not achieve the level of an integrative interpretation of biblical thought. However, it continued to grow and is part of the theological background of the New Testament and of numerous extra-biblical Jewish and Christian theological works, such as 2 Esdras or the Apocalypse of Ezra, 1 Enoch or the Ethiopic Enoch, the Testament of Abraham and other writings.

written in those early years and which we later call the writings of the New Testament.

What is common to both traditions is the recognition in the prophets of a special sensitivity to justice. The words *mishpat* (justice) and *tzedakah* (right, righteousness) are used in a sense that goes beyond their juridical and legal value. Justice or its denial has a cosmic dimension for the prophets; it is much more than the equitable distribution of goods, and it touches an area of life that goes beyond everyday coordinates. Abraham Joshua Heschel puts it this way:

> For our society, a single act of injustice — lying in business, oppressing the poor — is something accepted; for the prophets it is a disaster. For us, injustice is an offense to the well-being of the people; for the prophets, it leads to death; what for us is a fleeting episode, for them it is a catastrophe that threatens the existence of the world.[1]

The concepts of *mishpat* and *tzedakah* will be central to the formation of prophetic theology, which will find in them a criterion for judging the lives of people but also the human quality of Israelite society.

One aspect of God that the prophets of Israel present will be taken up and radicalized in Christian reading, and will permeate the texts of the gospels and the letters of Paul. We refer to the universal character of the sovereignty of Yahweh and Yahwistic dominion over every other possible deity. In the story of Isaiah's vocation (6:1-13) Yahweh is described in the temple and on a throne with the seraphim surrounding God, who represent minor deities. These act as intermediaries with Isaiah. They are the ones who act as spokespersons for God and perform the symbolic acts. The temple where the scene takes place is a space that mimics the universe. It is difficult not to see in this scene the description of Yahweh and the Yahwistic entourage of minor gods who make up God's heavenly "army" (6:3). When 6:8 speaks of God in the plural ("Who will go for *us*?" reminiscent of Gen 1:26) it confirms that God assumes God's self as the Lord of an army of gods who submit to God and carry out the divine orders. At a second moment in history, Israel will consolidate its monotheism, but

---

[1]A. J. Heschel, *The Prophets* (New York: The Jewish Publication Society of America, 1962), 4; this book leads the reader to engage with the prophetic text, not just to read it. His view of the prophets has not suffered the passage of time.

before reaching that understanding, monolatrism (also called henotheism) leads it to the idea of the universal power of its God.[1]

In the Old Testament, this conception of a God who exercises divine sovereignty over the entire universe is proper to the prophets and is undoubtedly different from the "theology of the covenant" which by its very theological conception emphasizes the exclusive link with Israel and relegates its international and cosmic interference. Only Jeremiah is sent to the international context (Jer 1:5 and 10) but this does not prevent the idea of the universality of the power of Yahweh from appearing in the other prophets, even if only in an embryonic form. The oracles to the nations present in all the long prophets (Is 13-23; Jer 46-51; Ez 25-32) and in several of the shorter ones (Amos 1-2; Joel 2:20; Ob 5-14; Zeph 2:5-15; the words of Nahum about Nineveh, 2:1-12) can be understood as a way of conceiving the sovereignty of the God of Israel over other nations, although sometimes they have been understood in a rhetorical sense, of creating a climate of judgment toward other nations so that the judgment of Judah and Israel is highlighted. David Petersen has pointed out that

> Israel lived in a political context, both national and international. They did not think that Israel could have a political position internationally without taking into account the plans of their God for that context.[2]

The gospels and Paul assume this universality of God and of Jesus' ministry, although not without some contradiction. In Matthew 10:6 and 15:24 Jesus seems to limit his ministry to "the lost tribes of Israel," which contrasts with texts such as John 1:9-10 ("The true light, which enlightens every person, has come into the world"), Mark 16:15 ("Go into all the world and preach the gospel to every creature") and its parallels, as well as other texts. For Paul's theology, the universality of God is not a matter of debate, and he merely limits himself to confirming this extension of God's power in passages such as Rom 3:6 ("otherwise how would God judge the world?"). The texts of the Apocalypse have an evident universal tone.

---

[1]L. Alonso Schökel calls this idea of Israel the "supracosmic greatness," *Prophets* I (Madrid: Cristiandad, 1980), 139.

[2]D. Petersen, *The Prophetic Literature* (Louisville: Westminster John Knox Press, 2002), 39.

Diversity within Prophetic Literature
The Prophetic Books

The sixteen works that we call prophetic are not all the same. From a theological point of view, there is a diversity of approaches to the relationship between God and the divine word and even to the conception of the prophet's mission. Although they all agree that the prophets are God's spokespersons, and that God calls them and instructs them on what word to announce, from there, a range of possibilities opens up. The issue is even more complex when we observe that this diversity of forms, styles and messages occurs within the same books, so that it is not possible to classify the books individually, but it is necessary to go to the texts present in them. Let us take Amos as an example. In it, we find oracles against the nations (chapters 1-2); oracles and words of judgment against Israel (3-9, 10); and oracles of salvation (9:11-15). Is it the same God who inspires the prophet with such diverse words? How can we reconcile an oracle of judgment, sometimes so critical and definitive regarding divine punishment, with those of salvation at the end of the book? Is God an amateur? Is a God credible who changes the divine discourse? Is the prophet credible? These and other questions arise from simply reading the prophetic texts, so full of comings and goings, of apparently contradictory statements, loaded with threats and blessings, proclamations of life and announcements of death.[1]

The history of the writing of the books helps us to understand the existence of diverse texts in the same work.[2] The oracles against the nations in Amos and in the other books reflect a time in which Israel suffered the threat or oppression of other nations. They contrast with those in which foreign nations are exalted as instruments of God — in some cases the same nations condemned in the oracles — as happens in Isaiah 45 with the

---

[1]This diversity has led to the belief that the office of prophet is late and that the books group together ancient texts by characters who were not prophets but poets; it is argued that Isaiah, Jeremiah, etc. did not consider themselves prophets. This position is supported by A. Graeme Auld, "Prophets and Prophecy in Jeremiah and Kings," *ZAW* 96 (1984): 66-82; also by R. Carroll, "Poets not Prophets," *JSOT* 27 (1983): 25-31; for an evaluation of both articles and their eventual refutation see T. Overholt, "Prophecy in History," *JSOT* 48 (1990): 3-29.

[2]A work that combines rigor with sensitivity in interpretation is that of J. L. Sicre, *Con los pobres de la tierra* (Madrid: Cristiandad, 1984); in it the author makes an exhaustive review of the details of the writing of the books and their internal thematic relationships.

Persians calling Cyrus "his anointed," or in Habakkuk 1:5-11 which celebrates the action of the Chaldeans against Israel itself; or in Jeremiah 25:9 which calls Nebuchadnezzar "my servant." The oracles of judgment on Israel are generally pre-exilic, a time in which Israel had a certain power and autonomy and injustices became evident within the community itself. The oracles of salvation, on the contrary, reflect the moment of exile and post-exile, a moment in which Israel strives to rebuild itself as a nation and the prophetic word drives them to do so with messages of hope and restoration. But this historical location — which is general and imprecise — accounts for the eventual origin of the texts and explains their difference, but it does not explain the combination of all of them in the same work.

A literary view that does not privilege the history of the texts as a key to reading will observe that, for the semiotic author, there is no contradiction between the texts. They are articulated effectively to offer a message. In the case of Amos, there is a warning to the nations and to Israel; a strong call to attention to Israel for its violence and hypocrisy in worship; and the announcement of restoration as a sign that God's love for God's people even goes so far as to cleanse them of the blunders into which they had fallen. It is the last literary stratum that adds the oracles of blessing and in this way establishes the theology of the entire work. It does not eliminate the previous ones — something that could have been done since the narratives were not yet canonical — but rather adds and completes a discourse in which God is shown in divine multi-facetedness but also in the God's vocation to save Israel. But even more, the same concept that shows that the text is not a mechanical accumulation of literary strata but a selection of them for the purpose of constructing a meaning supposes that, just as texts are added, others have also been eliminated.

The Cycles of Elijah and Elisha

The stories about Elijah and Elisha are found in Kings (from 1 Kings 17 to 2 Kings 13) and correspond to the time of the kings of Israel from Ahaz to Joash (869-786). In both cases, they act several decades before Amos (approx. 740-720), when after the division of the kingdom, the weight of idolatry was more noticeable in the Northern Kingdom because it was far from the center of worship in Jerusalem. Unlike the aforementioned prophetic books, in this case we are faced with stories that are, in turn, inserted in a larger history such as that of the kings of Israel.

This narrative nature of the deeds of Elijah and Elisha gives them certain distinctive characteristics: the narrative tells about them, instead of them speaking in the first person about others; their acts are described instead of being announced; they perform miracles that change people's lives, something unusual in other prophets. They say little about the future.

Only in the context of the Egyptian deeds is there another grouping of miracles, like those narrated by these two prophets. The function of the miracles in Elijah and Elisha is to show the power of God manifested in God's servant and act as a guarantee of the veracity of the prophet's ministry. Neither Isaiah nor any other prophet will normally resort to miracles as a basis for his credibility. The sacrifice on Mount Carmel (1 Kings 18) is an example of this. The bulls and the wood are prepared and after the priests of Baal unsuccessfully try to produce fire through their prayers to their God, Elijah sprinkles the wood with water from twelve jars and at the clamor of his prayer the fire of Yahweh appears and consumes the sacrifice. The only purpose of this action is to show that the fire that will engulf his sacrifice is the product of divine intervention and not of any natural phenomenon caused by the prolonged drought and heat. In this way, the story confirms that his action has the backing of the God of Israel. But that is not the only thing that the miracles and other stories of Elijah and Elisha express theologically. What is most important is that they show a God interested in the lives of people. A God who is sensitive to the pain of a mother who is about to die of hunger (1 Kings 17:7-16), to that of another woman whose son has died (2 Kings 4:18-37), who is enraged by the unjust murder of Naboth (21:17-24) and empowers Elisha to purify a poisoned meal or multiply the loaves of bread to feed the people (4:28-44). The contrast between this God and the Canaanite Baal is permanent. The message is that the God of Israel is the one who reveals the divine person in the action of these prophets and shows God's self as close to the needs and anxieties of God's people, both in collective matters and in anxieties in the personal sphere.[1]

The hardest battle of Elijah and Elisha is against idolatry, and this is present in the figure of the worship of Baal. King Ahab and his wife Jezebel are the greatest representatives of this attitude, which leads to the construction of a temple to Baal in

---

[1]This is akin to the name of God given in Ex 3:14 translated as "I am the one who is," see P. R. Andiñach, *El libro del Éxodo* (Salamanca: Sígueme, 2006), 82-85; S. Croatto, "Yavé, el Dios de la 'presencia' salvífica," *RevBíbl* 43 (1981): 153-63.

Samaria (1 Kings 16:32); the injustices and violence they commit are presented as consequences of their flagrant idolatry. In contrast, what is evident from the narratives of Elijah and Elisha is that Yahweh is the owner of life and death and that Baal is a powerless and non-existent God. The recourse to the death of the opponent can make us uncomfortable, both when it refers to the prophets of Baal after the sacrifice of Carmel and when it narrates the death of forty-two children by the attack of two bears (2 Kings 2:23-25) after they mocked the prophet. In both cases, what is at stake is the credibility of the prophet's mission and that is why the reaction is of that nature. The reader will remember that, as we indicated in the previous chapter, the stories in Kings have a theological purpose and are therefore prone to exaggeration in order to highlight the forcefulness of the facts. Hence, all these traditions — which may be built on a historical core — were later enlarged and magnified by the editor to transform them into emblematic cases in favor of the prophetic vocation and the respect due to his word.

The Prophetesses

The androcentric character of the biblical text has contributed to obscuring the presence of women in different historical periods and their role as social actors. Traces of the action of these women appear here and there, sometimes with greater prominence, although most of the time only mentioned in passing. The office of prophet does not escape this condition and if on the one hand we must affirm that there were prophetesses in ancient Israel as much as there were in the surrounding cultures of the ancient Near East,[1] we must also say that little information has reached us about their ministries and words. Brief mentions that confirm the existence of prophetesses are the wife of Isaiah (Is 8:3) and the prophetess Noadiah, of whom we have only the name and the information that she was associated with other prophets (Neh 6:14), which indicates that at least in this case she did not act separately from the community of male prophets. Of the prophetess Miriam, sister of Aaron and Moses, we know she was the leader of the women and that — in the story that has come

---

[1] J. Stökl, "Female Prophets in the Ancient Near East," *Prophecy and Prophets in Ancient Israel* (ed. J. Day; New York: T&T Clark, 2010), 47-64; in the same volume see the article by H. G. M. Williamson, *Prophetesses in the Hebrew Bible*, 65-80, where the author, after an excellent study, concludes that there were more female prophetesses than those mentioned and that, although little cited, "at least some biblical writers recognized this reality" and included them in their narratives.

down to us—she led them in song and dance (Ex 15:20-21).[1] The story then presents her confronting Moses because of his marriage to a foreign woman (Num 12), a fact clearly contrary to the Law. This reproach of Miriam is consistent with the prophetic office, however, she is reprimanded for it with leprosy and condemned to live a week outside the camp while the impurity in her body persists. Aaron, who had also confronted Moses together with Miriam, does not receive corporal punishment; and Moses, who had committed the fault so often denounced in dozens of texts, is supported by Yahweh. It is difficult not to notice that there is an underlying gender prejudice in the culture that gives body to this story to the detriment of Miriam. The story privileges the figure of Moses over that of his critics Miriam and Aaron, but places the weight of rejection on the prophetess, thereby taking away the authority of her word. And to take away the authority of the word of a prophet—in this case of a prophetess—is to leave it with nothing. Esther Fuchs presents an interesting analysis of this case. She argues that the statement that God speaks "mouth to mouth" with Moses (v. 8) but indirectly with the other prophets—in allusion to her and Aaron—is a way of affirming the insignificance of the word of Miriam, who is described as someone who exceeded her functions and deserves to be punished for it. In turn, she postulates that the voice of the prophetesses was not lost in the twists and turns of history but was suppressed to avoid competition with male prophets.[2]

Deborah, prophetess and judge, is the only one of all the judges who exercises the function of judging and at the same time the only one of them who possesses the office of prophesying (Judg 4-5). The account does not present her in the exercise of prophecy so that we cannot judge her action. If Fuchs is right, we would have another case in which her ministry, in the sense of her prophetic voice, has been omitted or suppressed. We know of her existence, but her words, that which constituted the very essence of her prophetic office, have not survived. Deborah has a strong character. She is a soldier, a leader and governs with intelligence, but nothing is said about her prophetic ministry.

---

[1]C. Meyers, "Miriam the Musician," *A Feminist Companion from Exodus to Deuteronomy* (ed. Athalya Brenner; Sheffield: Sheffield Academic Press, 1994), 207-30; the author postulates on the basis of other texts the existence in ancient Israel of a stable institution of choirs and dance groups made up of women.

[2]E. Fuchs, "Prophecy and the Construction of Women," *A Feminist Companion to the Bible* (ed. Athalya Brenner; Sheffield: Sheffield Academic Press, 2001), 54-69, esp. 59.

The case of Huldah is different. Her story is found in 2 Kings 22:11-20 and is repeated in 2 Chronicles 34:22-28. The fact that it is repeated already indicates the esteem that the textual tradition had for her figure. Given the patriarchal cultural context of the story, it may be surprising that a prophetess should have such recognition and authority; at the same time, we must observe that the text does not highlight her condition as a woman. It is not surprised or celebrated and thus suggests to us that the existence of women exercising this office was not something exceptional.[1] Huldah is a prophetess who intervenes in the time of Josiah and is consulted by the king regarding the authenticity of the scroll of the Law found among the ruins of the temple. She is the first person in the entire Bible to make a judgment on a sacred text, which is why she has been called the first biblical critic. The king instructs "to consult Yahweh" and his advisors direct them to go directly to Huldah, who lives in Jerusalem. The intervention of Huldah is crucial to define the future of the religious reform that the king will carry out and that will be remembered as the most important in the history of the kings of Judah. Renita Weems points out that "she knew what the king only suspected, she knew what the inhabitants of Jerusalem ignored."[2] In this case, Huldah's voice is heard clearly and her message goes beyond what is requested of her by addressing the king's life and death in the background. Her words are taken to Josiah, and he, based on them, undertakes the reform in Judah and in the territory of Israel. From the reading, it is clear that there was no intention on the part of the narrator to hide Huldah and that he assigns her a place of privilege, as in other cases they have been assigned to male prophets. It is inevitable to regret two things: that the words of other prophetesses have not been preserved for us; that only this brief episode was bequeathed to us from Huldah and not a complete book that compiled her wisdom and message.[3]

---

[1]This is the opinion of W. Brueggemann who in turn points out the interesting relationship that exists in this story between *Torah* and prophecy ("the law and the prophets"), where the first requires the second to be confirmed, *1 & 2 Kings* (Macon: Smyth and Helwys, 2000), 546, n. 2.

[2]R. J. Weems, "Hulda the Prophet: Reading a (Deuteronomistic) Woman's Identity," *A God So Near* (ed. Brent Strawn & Nancy Bowen; Winona Lake: Eisenbrauns, 2003), 330.

[3]We do not agree with E. Fuchs who in the work cited above (62-64) argues that in this case too the prophetess is relegated and her ability to prophesy is minimized; he says this in light of the violent death of Josiah that would have eventually left Huldah as a prophetess whose prophecy was not fulfilled; however, the fact that the fulfillment of her words was partial does not diminish their value

We should not forget that there were also records of false prophetesses. We are not referring to the case of the necromancer of En-Dor (1 Sam 28) who deceives Saul and is sometimes confused with a prophetess, but to the prophetesses mentioned in Eze 13:17-23 who are attributed the same actions as their male colleagues: they are denounced for their venality, their lies and for leading people away from Yahweh. According to the account, they are a community of prophetesses and seem more like a group within society than a sector separate from it. They are said to reject the righteous and support the wicked, a recurring theme that allows us to verify the falsity of their message and that equates them with false male prophets.

Other Prophets

We are surprised by the text where King Abimelech of Gerar receives in a dream the voice of God, who warns him that Abraham is a prophet (Gen 20:7). At the time when this observation was placed there, every prestigious leader of the past had to be considered a prophet as well, and 15:1 offers a certain basis for affirming this. Less surprising but equally strange is the consideration of Moses as a prophet, a title that is more forceful when we note that the prophet Hosea recognizes him in this way (Hos 12:14). In the case of Moses, it is clear that his story of vocation (Ex 3:1-4:17) has reminiscences of the prophetic stories of vocation, but it is stretching the text to consider him as a model that influenced the subsequent stories.[1] The nomination of Moses as a prophet (Deut 18:15-18, and especially 34:10) is also related to what was already said about Abraham, that the title of prophet was projected into the past on every figure who had acquired prestige in the present. In the case of Moses, it is added that he acts as a mediator and interlocutor with God, and in particular as a receiver of the Law. Considering the familiar and dialogical atmosphere on which he had with God, it will not be found again in any other biblical character. In this sense, we can understand

---

because it is known that there is a large number of prophecies of all kinds that were not fulfilled and that did not diminish the prestige of the prophets who announced them.

[1] D. Petersen says that he "probably" should not be considered a prophet. In his article he questions whether Moses was a model for other prophets and concludes that his attribution must have occurred when most of the prophetic literature had already been written and it was not appropriate for any new leader to surpass the figure of Moses, see D. Petersen, "The Ambiguous Role of Moses as Prophet," *Israel's Prophets and Israel's Past* (ed. Brad Kelle & Megan Bishop Moore; New York: T&T Clark, 2006), 311-24.

the expression of 31:10 that says before his death "there has not arisen in Israel a prophet like Moses." This transfer of the figure and attributes of the prophets to Moses contains, in any case, a certain artificiality. The role of the rest of the biblical prophets has little in common with Moses: they confronted the corrupt kings of Israel with the word of the Law; They were rarely community leaders but rather rejected and even condemned by the authorities and sometimes by the people themselves; the prophets brought to light the conflictual relationship between the Law and worship, between the memory of the liberation from Egypt and social injustices within Israel itself; between the sense and responsibility of being a chosen people and idolatrous practices that led to destroying the relationship with God.

Moses is associated with the seventy elders who gathered in the tent to receive part of his spirit and begin to prophesy (Num 11:16-30). The text makes it clear that it was only for that one time and that they never did it again, but it sets an important precedent. It is God who decides when, where and in whom the spirit of prophecy will be present. The prophetic character is not an attribute of the person but a faculty given and taken away by God based on the divine plan. When faced with two elders who prophesy outside the circle of the seventy, Moses is asked to prevent them from doing so. His response expresses a profound theological concept when he says "...I wish that all the people of God were prophets" (v. 29), words that in a certain way will be connected with Joel 2:28-29 [3:1-2] where it is said that "all flesh will prophesy... sons and daughters... old men and young men... male and female servants..."

The first prophet who delivers his message in a speech in keeping with the so-called prophets is an anonymous person mentioned in Judges 6:7-10. This prophet is sent to Israel in response to their cry to God in the face of the threat of a Midianite invasion. His message has all the elements of what will become a classic prophecy; it contains the formula "thus says Yahweh;" it evokes the deed of liberation from Egypt and how God freed them from that oppression; God reminds them that God fought the inhabitants of Canaan and gave them "their land;" and God closes the divine monologue by reminding them that God had instructed them not to worship the Amorite gods, but that they did not "listen to my voice."

The importance of this prophet from a literary point of view is that it shows the historical continuity between Moses and the prophets Samuel, Gad and Nathan, who will come later. It is like a link placed there to keep alive the bond between the first prophets and those who followed them, who will undoubtedly have a much greater role than those who were called prophets but whose performance does not articulate well with that function. The hermeneutical effort to locate prophets in the time of the patriarchs and matriarchs (Abraham, Sarah, Moses), however artificial and anachronistic it may seem, has proven effective in showing prophetic activity rooted in the times of the origin of the people of Israel. From the theological point of view, every word, rite or practice of faith that with the passage of time becomes significant for the practice of faith has to go back to the origin in order to be legitimized with divine support.[1]

Samuel, Gad and Nathan will be the prophets who accompany the rise and consolidation of the monarchy. As such, they will answer to God and not to the king and will lay the foundations for what will later be the sharpest preaching of the pre-exilic prophets. In no case are they under the orders of the king and, to the extent that they are the ones who anoint the kings, they are placed above them. The social dynamic is that the prophet is the one who receives from God the illumination to identify the future king. This was the case with Saul and David. Solomon's arrival to the throne omits this step and replaces it in the text with God's direct communication with him in the dream of Gibeon (1 Kings 3). This is how Solomon and his reign are legitimized. But they are not the only prophets of their time. Both in 1 Sam 10:5-6 and in 19:18-24, groups of prophets are mentioned who enter into a trance at the moment of receiving the message of God, including Samuel in the second episode. These ecstatic prophets are not described in detail, but they seem to precede those others who will build their discourses on visions or symbolic gestures.[2] After this period that we could call the formation of character, the prophetic institution will mature to acquire a dimension never seen before.

Martyrdom is not common among prophets, at least considering the information that has been recorded in the texts. But we wish to mention a case that reminds us of so many Jewish

---

[1]Note this same phenomenon in relation to the personification of wisdom in Prov 8:22-31; with Christ Rev 1:8; and with the figure of the devil Jn 8:44; 1 Jn 3:8.

[2]It is difficult to determine whether Jeremiah also participated in this way of prophesying. In Jer 23:9 the prophet recounts an experience in which he "became drunk because of Yahweh" and then denounced the false prophets of his time; see W. Holladay, *Jeremiah 1* (Philadelphia: Fortress Press, 1986); also in 1 Kings 22:10 there is mention of prophets in a trance before the king, but in this case they are prophets denounced as false by Micah ben Imlah.

and Christian martyrs throughout history and, closer to home, in our Latin America. We refer to the prophet Uriah, son of Shemariah, whose story is told in Jer 26:20-23. He preached alongside Jeremiah that God did not approve of the injustices and idolatry that were practiced in the royal palace. When the king, his courtiers and princes heard his words, they gave the order to arrest him and kill him; Uriah found out and fled to Egypt. But the king sent a retinue there that arrested him and brought him back to where he was killed in front of the king. As we have experienced on many occasions in our countries, the complicity of the oppressors among themselves has no borders and does not stop at nationalism when it comes to repression. Uriah's guilt was proclaiming what the powerful did not want to hear, and that is why his life was taken from him.

The False Prophets

There are numerous texts that mention or denounce false prophets.[1] The crux of the problem is that these denounced prophets are not those of Canaanite gods, but present themselves as speaking for the God of Israel. Thus, they pose a conflict of interpretations in its crudest form. How to decide when a prophet who claims to be Yahweh is true or false?[2] This dilemma is presented to us in the texts themselves and is also ours. The situations in which prophetic discourse is fractured and presents two opposing possibilities are numerous and generate a serious problem for kings and priests. Micah (2-3) mocks the prophets who gesticulate and drool; Jeremiah contrasts Ananias (28) and declares that he has lied to the people; the same happens with his denunciation of Shemaiah in 29:24-32. In these texts, the basis for the truthfulness or otherwise of the prophet remains somewhat nebulous, since it is based on the opinion of the prophet who has already been consecrated and deserves the reader's recognition. For example, in 28:2-7 Isaiah describes false prophets as drunkards who announce meaningless words, perhaps because they would be ecstatic prophets. In other cases, it is said of them that they

---

[1] A study and presentation in Spanish on false prophets is the section by L. Alonso Schökel & J. L. Sicre, *Profetas I* (Madrid: Cristiandad, 1980), 49-56; also J. Asurmendi, "Profetas buenos y malos, verdaderos y falsos," *Res Bib* 37 (2003): 41-50; J. L. Crenshaw, *Los falsos profetas* (Bilbao: Desclee de Brouwer, 1986); A. González, et al., *Profetas verdaderos, profetas falsos* (Salamanca: Sígueme, 1976) (consisting of three independent articles of great value).

[2] J. L. Sicre raises this question and presents the answers of the various prophets, see *Prophecy in Israel* (Estella: Verbo Divino, 2003), 145-47; includes bibliography in Spanish.

prophesy "in the name of Baal" (Jer 2:8). Others are more incisive and discuss the content of the prophecy and point out that false prophets like to announce "peace" when there is none and there will be none (Jer 6:13-14; 14:13-16; 23:9-32; Ez 13:1-6; Mic 3:5-11). Ezekiel points out that they say "thus says the Lord" when in reality God has not communicated with them and adds a political and social criterion by pointing out that false prophets do not denounce injustices (22:28-31).

Beyond the mockery of his alleged drunkenness and other personal behavior, we understand that the discussion must take place on the content of the prophecies. That is where the problem lies and where the credibility of the prophet is at stake. Two texts seem key to us to explore the distinction between false and true prophets. The first is Dt 13:2-6 and its context is that of the warnings about idolatry. But what makes this text a special witness is that it mentions that the fulfillment of a prophecy is not sufficient proof that it is inspired by God. If the prophecy is fulfilled but the prophet invites us to turn away from Yahweh, it is a sign that it is not from God and we must move away from God.[1] The criterion in this case, rather than having announced something that later happens, lies in the life proposal that the prophet has for his listeners. In that sense, it contradicts Dt 18:9-22 where, toward the end, the text indicates the fulfillment of what was prophesied as a sign of veracity; This discrepancy between texts from the same book highlights the difficulty of the subject. On the other hand, it is worth asking how someone who hears a prophecy can know at that moment whether or not what was announced will be fulfilled in the future, in order to decide whether the community is dealing with a true or false prophet. And if the criterion is only fulfillment, several of the prophetic texts of Isaiah and Jeremiah, whose fulfillments did not occur in the way they announced, should be considered false prophecies.[2] Micah demands strict ethics on the part of the prophets when transmitting the truth received from God, and yet Jeremiah lies when informing the leaders about the prophecy he had announced

---

[1]The same theological idea is found in Jesus' words when he says on the mountain: "Not everyone who says to me, 'Lord, Lord,' will enter the kingdom of heaven, but only he who does the will of my Father who is in heaven" (Mt 7:21). In both cases, the hermeneutical problem of distinguishing the discourse from its reference in reality arises.

[2]For example, the return announced in Is 40-55 does not coincide with what would later happen; many of the oracles against foreign nations did not come true in history; the prophecies about Zerubbabel in Haggai 2:20-23 do not seem to have been fulfilled.

to King Zedekiah (Jer 38:24-27). In truth, many of the prophecies of the true prophets were fulfilled when we read them in general terms, but not always if we take them in each particular case.

The second text is narrative and presents a scene that takes us straight to the relationship between the prophets of Yahweh and the false prophets. It is found in 1 Kings 22, where the intervention of the prophet Micah ben Imlah is narrated. Before an imminent battle, the king of Samaria consults the prophets around him and they predict victory. Then they look for Micah and he announces a flagrant defeat, which angers the king and orders him to be imprisoned and tortured there for his prophecies. Micah explains the conflict in terms of the sovereignty of God, who put a "spirit of lies" in the mouths of the king's prophets. The central thing in this scene is who is the lord of one and the other, to whom they respond, and what is the purpose of the prophecy? In the case of the king's prophets, they are described as pleasing him in everything they say. So the origin of their words is not a communication from God, but rather they are the product of observing the king's mood and acting accordingly. The purpose of this prophecy is to say what the king wants to hear and thus preserve their status as palace prophets. The sign of this prophecy is meanness. In our time, it has good representatives in the so-called prosperity theology that proclaims a plethora of material blessings for the believer simply for being one, particularly in reference to economic well-being and social advancement. Micah's words, on the contrary, do not arise from a calculation of what the king wants to hear but from what God has communicated to the kind. It is a word that is not constructed based on the king's plan but on God's plan. For this reason, the king may not like it — as in this case — and the prophet is willing to suffer the consequences; the backing of his words is his own life. The essence of this prophecy is to announce God's will in a crude manner, without personal calculations, and seek a sincere reunion between God and God's people.

In his study of Jeremiah 28, Jesus Asurmendi concludes that "it is the community that makes the selection, that chose the good and rejected the bad" prophets. And he would have done this based on two criteria, which do not necessarily have to do with the fulfillment of their words but rather with the recognition that there was a prophetic tradition, a way of communicating the word of God that responded to certain coordinates of conduct and theological signs that by presence or absence allowed the prophet to be qualified. He considers that the criterion was to perceive in the announced words a constant invitation to the "conversion of the whole life," and secondly that the prophet's discourse makes "a call to hope." It follows from this that the true prophet is the one who invites the people or his interlocutor to change their life, to approach God's project and abandon pettiness and sins. But in no case does true prophecy refer to a superficial hope or an illusory optimism, but rather it calls for the recognition of the reality of evil and sin so that these evils may be eradicated from life and society.[1] Asurmendi reminds us that the problem is not new, as Micah 3:5-8 attests, but it is aggravated by the political and religious crisis that came with the destruction of the temple and the captivity in Babylon. This demands that one take sides in the arena of history for one or another political option and therefore the consequent ambiguity arises as to whether the prophet — because he is one — can or cannot make a mistake in his decision.

Jeremiah chose to ally himself with Babylon and even calls Nebuchadnezzar "my servant" — a title that makes him similar to the Davidic kings- and lays the foundations of his throne in Jerusalem (Jer 42:9-11). At that time they reject his words (Jer 44:15-19) and without a doubt those who do so do not consider Jeremiah a true prophet, at least not at that time, but with the passage of time and history his words will be valued and finally recognized as truly coming from the God of Israel. Horst Preuss had already reflected on this and did so with a practical and direct sense, perhaps seeking to explain the phenomenon rather than delving into its theology. Preuss, in his theology of the Old Testament, concludes that the determination of false or true prophet was established after the events that generated them and by looking back at history. The criterion was not only the direct fulfillment but also the verification that what was announced was in accordance with the will of Yahweh for that situation.[2] This observation by Preuss explains the literary mechanism for judging the prophet but leaves us with uncertainty regarding the act itself at the time of its occurrence. From a theological point of view, it is the Spirit who illuminates the dilemma and will require an act of faith from the believer who must evaluate the relevance of the announced word in relation to God's liberating project. No precise formulas are offered but rather an invitation to experience God's action in history and make a decision.

---

[1]J. Asurmendi, "Profetas buenos y malos," 49.

[2]H. D. Preuss, *Old Testament Theology II* (Louisville: Westminster/John Knox Press, 1992), 86.

In the complex process of defining the canon, the prophetic books were evaluated long after the events and with sufficient conceptual distance to establish the soundness of the words or their weakness. Their discourse was compared with the *Torah*, of which they were considered its main interpreters, and to the extent that they fit with its message they were incorporated into the canon.

Isaiah: Where Words Explode

What happens with Isaiah is what happens with so many poets: what they want to say is beyond words and therefore they need to make them explode. Poetry plays with the limit between the rationality of the message (the objective meaning of the words) and the world that the text creates, which is more than the sum of its words. To overcome this barrier, language itself has strategies and one of them is to resort to metaphors and symbols. This is not exclusive to Isaiah, but he makes intensive use of this tool. The word explodes because in the symbol or metaphor it says "more" than its first meaning indicates. In the phrase "the people who walked in darkness saw a powerful light" (9:1), the words darkness and light do not mean what the dictionary tells us, but rather they are submerged in the condition of the oppressed and abandoned people to describe their state and give us a deeper and bolder message than the mere meaning of the words. The explosion makes them grow and allows the text to speak of a reality that would otherwise be ineffable.

In Isaiah, theology begins by contrasting the Law with the reality of the powerful and oppressors. In 30:9-10, he points out:

> They would not listen to the Law of Yahweh; they say to
> the seers, "Do not see;" and to the prophets, "Do not
> prophesy to us what is right, but tell us what is flattering,
> prophesy lies…"

This distance between the Law and daily life is a sin that "spreads like a crack in a high wall whose fall comes suddenly and suddenly" (30:13). He will then resort to the image of the vessel that breaks and whose remains are useless. The rejection of the Law leads to the denaturation of Israel's reason for being and to the destruction of its link with God.

The Formation of the Book of Isaiah

The process of formation of almost any book of the Old Testament can be shown in almost any other, but particularly in the prophetic books. In these works, the successive hands and strata are so evident that it is impossible to avoid them. At the same time, if confirming the condition of composite works is a major fact for the history of the text, it is even more so for its interpretation to the extent that it reveals the growth of the work in stages, its profound hermeneutical condition and its path toward meaning until arriving at the moment in which it was expressed in the current text. What biblical criticism described as the history of the formation of a text (of the Pentateuch or any other biblical book) and did so in search of identifying the original passages to find its supposed true message ended up in a dead end; but hermeneutics appropriate that description and considers it the best example to show the long process of creating meaning. A process that is eminently hermeneutical and that reveals how the message is the product of centuries of maceration.

In the description of Isaiah's growth, we can perceive that of the other works. It is now common to speak of First (1-39), Second (40-55) and Third Isaiah (56-66), and to attribute each section to the pre-exilic, exilic and post-exilic times.[1] This literary division is not in question, but the assignment to historical periods does not stand up to detailed analysis. Undoubtedly, for the first two sections, the thematic cores correspond to those times, but in both sections a volume of post-exilic text has been added that does not allow 1-39 to be identified with the pre-exile alone, nor 40-55 in its entirety with the exile. For example, chapters 13-14, which present oracles against Babylon and about the return from exile, were composed toward the end of that period or the first years of the restoration. Chapters 14-15, which present oracles against Babylon and about the return from exile, were composed toward the end of that period or the first years of the restoration. Chapters 15-16, which contain the oracles against Babylon and about the return from exile, were composed toward the end of that period or the first years of the restoration. Chapters 16-17, which contain the oracles against Babylon and about the return from exile, were composed toward the end of that period or the first years of the restoration. 24-27 and 34-35 are texts with an apocalyptic flavor that must have been composed in the late Persian period or even during the Hellenistic era.

It is disputed whether chapters 54-55 are the work of Second Isaiah or not, but in any case the theological relationship

---

[1]The first to observe this division was B. Duhm in his commentary on Isaiah published in 1892. L. Alonso Schöekel in the *New Spanish Bible* of 1975 printed Isaiah divided into these three sections, which is excessive; in the *Pilgrim's Bible* published in 1993 he continued with this practice.

between 40-55 and 56-66 is so strong that it leads one to think that the Third Isaiah school was responsible for a good part of the editing of Second Isaiah.[1] What has happened? What we observe is that the text of a mid-eighth-century prophet called Isaiah, of whom we know very little, was gradually added to in order to update it in light of successive events in history.[2] We call this the process of rereading, a hermeneutical dynamic present throughout the Bible that consists of visiting the text every time a new situation questions the current interpretation. This new reading modifies its understanding and new words are printed in the text to adapt it to the new meaning. Later, the same process was repeated when an anonymous prophet during the exile produced more oracles and compiled and then joined them with those from the first Isaiah, not without first materially modifying it by incorporating text to the received work.[3] Similarly, in the post-exile, a collection of oracles was added to the pre-existing work and the re-reading process again modified the texts of the first and second sections in order to adapt them to the new social and theological challenges. There is one more step to take, and it is revealed when we note that there are texts in the three sections that refer to the situation of the diaspora; they are brief texts that obviously correspond to the late post-exilic period, perhaps the middle of the third century. A list of the main mentions of the diaspora includes 11:9-16; 27:12-13; 35:9-10; 43:5-7; 55:12; 56:8; 60:4, 9b; 66:18-21. The texts on the nations (14:1-2; 14:26-27; 34:1-17; 43:3b-4; 51:21-23; 60:11-12, 14; 63:1-6) and the texts on the new Jerusalem (1:27; 16:5; 49:14-26; 54:1-17; 59:20a; 66:7-14) are also from the same pen. All of these belong to the stratum that Croatto calls Fourth Isaiah, who should not be confused with the editor of the three sections but should be considered an author since his

---

[1]C. Westermann, *Isaiah 40-66* (Philadelphia: The Westminster Press, 1975), 27-28.

[2]A key article for our topic is that of S. Croatto, "Composición y querigma del libro de Isaías," *RIBLA* 36/37 (2000): 36-67; in this article Croatto presents the relationship between the composition of the text and its message and highlights that the final form is part of its kerygma.

[3]R. E. Clements' article explores the development of themes from First Isaiah through Second Isaiah, but does not suspect that the process might have been different: the introduction into First of the theological concerns of Second Isaiah, see "Beyond Tradition-History," *The Prophets* (ed. Philip Davies; Sheffield: Sheffield Academic Press, 1996), 128-46.

task far exceeds that of a mere compiler of works and editor of sutures.[1]

It is striking that the complexity revealed by the formal growth of a work does not conspire against its coherence, but on the contrary, makes evident that part of its message resides in the laborious work of composition, its sum of contexts, of a combination of genres and perspectives, of metaphors and prose. It is the construction of what we call the final text that has been bequeathed to us as a word to enlighten the reader on the path of life. Theology — what the text tells us about the relationship between the people who are listeners or the reader who goes through the pages and the God whom it recognizes as the source of salvation — is the rich product of all that. But it is not a disordered or haphazard combination but a construction that has the harmony of art, of the work that even in its dissonance hides an intimate connection of meaning.

The Liberating Messiah of the Oppressed

Injustice and oppression hurt the prophet and in his denunciation he agrees with his contemporary Amos, although the latter preached a few years earlier and in Samaria. The harsh criticism of the powerful who sink the poor and who try to reconcile it with a religious piety built on ritual observance is the bold and vertiginous word of the first years of the prophet. The rebellions denounced in the first chapter — which are programmatic for 1-39 — become transparent when he describes them by demanding respect for the "right of the oppressed, to do justice (*mishpat*) to the orphan and protect the widow" (1:17), a denunciation that is repeated in v. 23.[2] But what distinguishes Isaiah from Amos and other prophets is having announced the arrival of a Messiah who would liberate the oppressed, texts concentrated in the so-called Book of Emmanuel (7-12) although they are also found in other passages. The whole is linked to the

---

[1]S. Croatto, "Isaiah 40-55," "Isaiah 56-66," and "Fourth Isaiah," *Global Bible Commentary* (ed. D. Patte *et al.*; Nashville: Abingdon, 2004), 195-221; P. R. Andiñach, *Introducción hermenéutica al Antiguo Testamento* (Estella: Verbo Divino, 2012), 255-57.

[2]Note that in the Hebrew Bible Isaiah follows 2 Kings. Thus the destruction of Jerusalem and the temple is followed by the denunciation of social injustice and religious hypocrisy in Judah; this relationship is obscured in the order of the books in the Septuagint and Christian canons, but it does not disappear and must be taken into account in the interpretation.

time of the Syro-Ephraimite war and the invasion of Sennacherib,[1] a time of great danger and fear for Israel, which makes the invocation of a Messiah who will liberate them from fear and oppression even more forceful. This Messiah will be a messenger of God who will bring justice and right to the people. When he reigns, violence against the weak will end and everyone will be able to live in peace from their work. It is no coincidence that this Messiah is described in relation to the figure of David and not to that of Solomon. While the latter could not rid himself of the image of an idolater with which he ended his life, David retained for himself the image of the generous, brilliant king, humane in his errors, but capable of repentance. In the "Davidic" Messiah, military force will be combined with religious devotion.

There is a profound theology in the presentation of the Messiah. A warrior is expected, and a child is announced; a new Israel is expected, and it is proclaimed that he will sit on the throne of David (a throne that was destroyed and defeated, non-existent at the time of the prophet). The name Emmanuel, which means "God with us" (7:14) defines his condition as one sent to bring the people closer to God after the prolonged estrangement. But this approach does not consist of an eschatological proposal — at least not in the first reading of the text — but in the direct action of one sent by God who will do justice and govern with equity. In successive texts, this condition of liberator becomes clear: in 9:1-6 it is announced that light is sent to those who are in darkness, a metaphor for the liberation from the economic and social yoke that weighed on the poor; In 11:1-9 the Messiah is described as the one who inaugurates a new time where the one who governs "will judge with righteousness" (*tzedek*) the poor of the Earth, in the sense that he will do so with honesty, with justice, which is at the same time a denunciation of those who governed without justice and led Israel to the humiliation of exile. It is a misguided reading to interpret these texts as the description of an ideal and celestial kingdom. Neither the child announced in 7:14 nor the actions that describe the Messiah are eschatological but consist of effective acts of doing justice to those who suffer his absence denounced on every page of the prophet.[2]

It is in a second reading that one perceives that the promise of the Messiah is not limited to the time of Isaiah and can

---

[1]The Syro-Ephraimite War consisted of an alliance between Samaria and Damascus against Judah; both nations invaded and besieged Jerusalem but Judah obtained help from Assyria and defeated Damascus; the story is in 2 Kings 16:5-9.

[2]S. Croatto, *Isaías 1-39* (Buenos Aires: La Aurora, 1989).

be reread in an eschatological key in a new level of reading that is far from obliterating the previous one adds to it. The dynamic and non-exclusive relationship between an eschatological and a historical reading preserves our theology from reducing to illusion that which the text has intended to be a living and concrete hope and in whose realization rests the hope of the oppressed. The prophetic word is always in tension between what would be realized in the near future and what remains as an expectation for future times. An example is 61:1-3 where the prophet proclaims that the Spirit calls him to announce freedom to the captives and liberation to the poor. This text in its first reading has an unavoidable historical referent, which is the oppressed of his time. As time passes and in the face of new social frustrations, its realization is postponed and it is read as a future expectation. However, this expectation was always understood in the perspective of its realization in history, a crucial attitude that allowed some much later to discover in the figure of Jesus of Nazareth the fulfillment of these prophecies and others to continue in the confidence that his arrival would occur later.

A Voice that Says: Shout!

The prophet's voice has an intimate relationship with the context in which it is proclaimed. If yesterday he had to denounce injustices, now he seeks to proclaim consolation for his people. Because those who were oppressed before are now oppressed and those who previously turned away from God now seek him to rescue them. Thus, the prophet exercises his role as God's spokesman by calling on people to remain confident because Yahweh has not forgotten them or the divine covenant. The debt has been forgiven because he has paid double the price for it. This is saying a lot to a people who have lived through the experience of the fall of Jerusalem and the burning of the temple with its most sacred objects and who now find themselves in a situation of captivity and solitude.

There is a new account of vocation in 40:1-6, but neither the prophet in question is mentioned nor does the work present itself as a new starting point. The hermeneutical intention is that the so-called Second Isaiah is a continuation of the first in order to announce the continuity of history and the possibility that God, who once harshly condemned God's people, may now have mercy on them and call them to hope. Thus, the form of the text is part of its message; instead of a new prophet, the text is ascribed to Isaiah himself, seeking to say that God is also the same. And this was necessary to reaffirm because, faced with what they perceived as God's abandonment of their city Jerusalem and their temple, many may have believed in the death of the God of Israel and began the search for a substitute to protect them. An anonymous voice, which personifies God, demands that the prophet cry out.[1] It is the call to the prophetic exercise of saying, of activating the voice. There is no demand for measured and thoughtful words, nor for reflection on the present and sharing of conclusions. On the contrary, there is recourse to a superlative of the voice, that word that comes from the depths and must be proclaimed in such a way that it can be heard by all.

The prophet must shout, but he does not yet know the content of the shout and asks: What should I shout? The answer surprises the listeners. If until a page ago condemnations and denunciation against Judah and Jerusalem dominated, now the prophet's message seeks to give the people the comfort of knowing that there is no anguish, no oppression, no pain that survives the passage of time because only the word of God is indelible. To the ears of the captives in Babylon, hearing that the strength of the muscle weakens just as the harmony of the flower corrodes (and they would think of the strength of the army that kept them in captivity, of the power of the political structures that supported the empire that subjugated them, of the sophisticated military technology on which it was based and which had no rival among other nations) must have sounded like a powerful message of hope that moved them to resist while awaiting the strong to weaken and for the time to come when, supported by their faith, they would return to their land to enjoy the lost freedom. These words, placed at the beginning of the second part of Isaiah, should not be read disconnected from 1-39, where judgment and salvation for Israel have been abundantly proclaimed. They act as a confirmation of those oracles because the announcement of the fragility of human oppression confirms the prophet's words of judgment, and the solidity of the word of God is support for his message of salvation.[2]

Exile is the time when the value of Scripture as a support for the identity and spirituality of the people begins to take shape.

---

[1]The Hebrew text uses an imperative from the verb *qarah* which means to proclaim, to announce. We translate "shout" based on the literary context which calls for a loud voice to be heard by all.

[2]B. Childs insists on the theological integrity of Isaiah and the interconnection between its different parts, an argument that we share, see *Isaiah* (OTL; Louisville: Westminster, 2001), 302-03.

Much time will still have to pass before Israel can be properly called "the people of the book," but in exile and early post-exile, the first shoots of what will later become a leafy tree can be seen. In the absence of a temple and a king, the community closes itself off on its ancient stories, many of which begin to be written in the heat of this new social and theological reality. During this time, the value of the written text that does not perish begins to be perceived. Other forms of human expression are volatile, like music, or deteriorate, like the plastic arts, but the written word is enduring because when recorded in the text it can be reread by successive and almost infinite generations. The ontology of the expression "the word of our God remains forever" is built on a material, palpable reality inherent to every text.

Toward the end of the section, there is another voice that shouts, and it does so with joy. It is the voice of the barren woman who is told that she will have many children and therefore — said with the extreme beauty of the poetic word- she is urged to stretch out the curtains of the tent, to strengthen the stakes, because the house will be too small for her to house all her children. In this case the Hebrew verb (danan, to shout for joy) is more specific than in 40:6 but this image of the woman who expands her house expresses the profound joy of the people who know that their liberation is near and that the blessing will be immense. That Israel that had to suffer the shame of captivity discovers that its God has not abandoned it and that he continues to nourish the hopes of God's people.

The Servant Who Frees the Oppressed

Servants are not expected to free anyone. Servant have no power to do so. They are subject to their master and owe obedience to their masters. But the servant presented in Second Isaiah finds the strength to be free from his own surrender and weakness. The text does not justify his strength. He is a servant of Yahweh and his strength resides in the one who sends him. That is its theology: that through a servant sent by God who will give his life for others, those who live in anguish and oppression will be freed. These are four poems[1] united by the common theme and language that were added to the preceding text in such a masterful

---

[1]There is a long discussion about the number and length of the Servant's poems. The most widely accepted view is that there are four poems (42:1-6; 49:1-7; 50:4-11; 52:13-53:12), but some see five and others seven. For an exposition of the possibilities and their foundations, see L. Alonso Schökel & J. L. Sicre, *Profetas I* (Madrid: Cristiandad, 1980), 272-75.

way that it is necessary to read them in their current literary context to understand their message. In principle, they act as a counterweight to the texts that mention Cyrus as Yahweh's anointed (41:2-3; 44:28; 45:1). This attribution is made in relation to the one who is seen as the victor of the Babylonians and liberator of all the peoples oppressed by them, including Israel. But if not even David is described in terms of a military redeemer whose only merit will be to defeat an enemy, even less can this title be attributed to Cyrus without further ado. The songs that concern us here come to the forefront of this attribution, perhaps a few years later. From this, it follows that the liberation and redemption[1] that the servant promotes through his suffering surpasses that of Cyrus because it is more than a political liberation and also transcends historical events to the extent that it is not exhausted in the possibility of returning to Judah. A second context is the successive texts on salvation, the restoration of Israel, the blessing and the establishment of a kingdom of justice, the new Jerusalem and others. All these texts create an atmosphere of optimism that the poems of the servant place in its proper place. Liberation will have a cost and it will be very high, but it is a price that the messenger of Yahweh must pay, the one who will put his life at the service of the people.

The ambiguity in the identity of the servant is part of the message and, as a work of fine literary quality, it does not answer all our questions. Depending on which aspects of the description of the servant are emphasized, he may be a symbol of Israel, of a particular person, of the Messiah — the most problematic because there are no messianic texts in Second Isaiah — or a mixture of all of them. Polysemy allows any of them to offer semantic value and be capable of opening up the text for us. However, what is interesting to highlight is that the servant is described as the one who is invoked to do justice (Heb. *tzedek*, 42:6); to be salvation (Heb. *yeshuati*, 49:6) for the nations; to encourage the weary (Heb. *yaeph*, 50:4). The last poem relates his death in favor of others (52:13-53:12). The story shows that the suffering that has value is that which is done with a meaning, with gain for someone. It is not the suffering itself that liberates, but that which is carried as a

---

[1]In Second Isaiah we find the Hebrew root *ga'al* (to redeem, to rescue) eleven times and only twice more in the rest of Isaiah but in the same poem (63:9, 16). The concept of rescue is essential to Isaiah's message to the point that it expresses the rejection of the ancestors but the faithfulness of God when in 63:16 he says: "Abraham ignores us and Jacob does not know us, but you Yahweh are our redeemer (*go'el*);" for the concept of *go'el* see the entry in *TDOT*.

burden for the benefit of others; in this case, the prophet declares: "He suffered the punishment that brought us peace" (53:5). The servant gives his life to free the lives of his community, and that is the justification of his pain and humiliation. Seen in this way, it matters little whether the prophet in his poems describes the people of Israel or has in mind a particular person. What matters is that suffering is blessed when it is done for the benefit of others. The servant, in his transcendent dimension, is the archetype of every person who in history has given his blood in the struggle for justice and equity for his community.

Rendtorff has observed that Second Isaiah ends as it begins.[1] In the first chapter, it speaks of the word of God "abiding forever," and in 55:10-11 the story is filled with metaphors whereby his word fertilizes the Earth and fulfills the purpose for which it was proclaimed. The images of rain and snow that give life and renew nature allude to the fact that "abiding forever" is not an ecstatic state, but rather implies a constant movement of renewal and restoration of life and history. Once again, the theology of the text surprises us with an ambiguous game that combines permanence with change and that leads us to perceive the action of the one who is and will be forever in contingent events, in the changing becoming of days and nights, in the fleeting nature of life.

Christian readers have seen in the servant of these poems the figure of Jesus of Nazareth, particularly in the last of them. This is reinforced by the episode of Philip and the Ethiopian, where Philip interprets 53:7-8 in reference to Jesus (Acts 8:26-35). The path is legitimate if we go from the New Testament to Isaiah to place Jesus of Nazareth in that prophetic line and not if we pretend that Isaiah spoke about Jesus, which would be an anachronism improper to the Scriptures. To a large extent, the entire New Testament is a rereading of the Old under a new key produced by the irruption in history of Jesus of Nazareth and this text does not escape this. But the process of rereading is always from front to back, where a new event redefines the past and is illuminated by it. On the other hand, the relationship between Jesus' life and these poems should not be overestimated, since texts such as 61:1-3 or Zechariah 9:9-10 had a major influence on the construction of the prophetic line of Jesus' message.

---

[1]*The Canonical Hebrew Bible* (Leiden: Deo Publishing, 2005), 194.

The Theology of the New Heaven and Earth as a Political Reality

Toward the end of the book, there are a series of oracles of judgement and blessing, and on two occasions it is announced that God will create a new heaven and Earth (65:17; 16:22). The lack of poetic sensitivity of the various commentaries has led to an understanding of this announcement as eminently eschatological. It is understood in such a way that heaven and Earth will be new in the last days or at the final judgement. This is the reading that Revelation 21:1-5 makes of this theme, and perhaps at the end of the first century it is a pertinent reading, but it is not the case in the early post-exile. Because poetic language, which is essentially symbolic and ambiguous, should not refer to a special reality far removed from everyday experience. The Jewish community that has returned to Jerusalem and settled there begins to feel the effects of having to rebuild its city and temple with very meager economic and human resources. They are few and have no money. What they produce from their work in the fields is taken by the Persian Empire, a situation described with complete clarity in Nehemiah 9:35-36:

> Behold, we are slaves today in the land you gave to our fathers to eat its fruit and its bounty; here we are slaves. But its abundant fruit is for the kings you have set over us because of our sins. They rule over our bodies and dispose of our livestock at their whim. Therefore, we are in great distress.

So the renewal of heaven and Earth is a way of referring to the construction of a political society with justice, equity and consequently in harmony with God. What they believe they cannot do, God will do for them, in the sense that God has demonstrated so many times in the past. Here it is necessary to remember Joshua 24:11-13 when the conquest is described as an act of God, not of the people of Israel, reminding them that they live in houses that they did not build and feed on vineyards that they did not plant; in fact, they did fight their battles and built their political destiny, but the theological interpretation is that nothing would have been possible if the will of God had not been on their side.

Third, Isaiah speaks in chapter 59 (see verses 4, 7, 9, 11, 14) of injustice and lack of righteousness. We did not expect to find these problems that we thought were typical of the pre-exile, the era of Israel's economic and military brilliance, in this new context of weakness and hardship. But human nature does not always resist the temptation to oppress one's neighbor, even when in this new situation it is a struggle between the poor. And in the face of this situation, the prophetic voice cannot remain silent. The gathering of the nations (that is, of the dispersed Jews, 66:18) will be a new act of God, but will have justice and equity as its sign. God will not gather them together so that they may once again attack each other and so that the strong may oppress the weak; God's act of liberation will not have as its goal the re-creation of a society where injustice is once again practiced. It is striking that the new heaven and Earth are described with very earthly words. Let us look at 65:19-24, which speaks of a society without infant mortality and where the elderly will enjoy a high life expectancy ("There will be no child who dies when only a few days old, nor an elder who does not live out his days; for every child will die when a hundred years old, and whoever does not live to be a hundred years old will be considered accursed," v. 20). Even today in the 21st century, according to United Nations statistics, a quarter of the world's population has a life expectancy of less than forty years and does not have access to health services or drinking water, and the next quarter, which exceeds these values, lives in conditions of so-called "non-extreme poverty." Furthermore, Isaiah continues his description by pointing out that they will inhabit the houses they build and eat from the vineyards they plant. The new heaven and Earth is described as a place where those who work can enjoy the product of their hands, a situation of justice so basic and human that it does not even need to be explained. The prophet had already said in 58:6-7 that what God wants is for those who are homeless to be welcomed into the home and for bread to be shared with those who are hungry.

After a few decades, this renewed and just society did not come to fruition; as the books of Ezra and Nehemiah show, social problems did not cease and differences between brothers and sisters did not cease to exist. Once again, injustice and inequality took hold in the concrete and human society that made up the people of God. It is from that moment on that the announcement of the renewal of heaven and Earth begins to be read as an eschatological reality that will later feed into apocalyptic theological reflection.

Jeremiah or the Seduction of the Word

Jeremiah differs from Isaiah in several respects and makes his own contribution to Israelite prophetic theology and to biblical theology. Not only is he later by more than half a century, since his ministry runs from 627 until the fall of Jerusalem in 587, when he is taken against his will to Egypt (43:4-7), but unlike Isaiah his prophecy is so intimately intertwined with the acts of his life that it is not possible to separate it from them. He also differs in that the narrative is all set in Jeremiah's time and although it is possible to perceive that there are texts that were incorporated in the exile or in the early post-exile, these remain at the textual level as an integral part of the prophet's work. There is no room to distinguish, as in the case of Isaiah, between dissimilar parts that were integrated; rather, the additions in Jeremiah were conceived as well-articulated literary extensions and not as a new chapter in history. This can be seen at the very beginning of the introduction (1:1-3) where the dates of the beginning and end of his ministry are established, thereby inviting the reader to read it as a unitary work and as a narrative that fits entirely within the life of the prophet. Like the Pentateuch, but with greater realism than the former, it presents itself as a literary work, dictated and written. It is Baruch the scribe who receives Jeremiah's dictation (36:2 and 27-32) or, in another case, it is written by the prophet himself (51:60). This condition of a written work creates a hermeneutical situation different from the rest of the biblical texts because in this case, instead of pretending that there is a full identity between reality and the story, its artificiality is assumed, its condition of a literary work, of being a mediation between the events and the message that the reader decodes. Although it refers to facts that may have been historical, the story is situated outside of them; This is common to all literary works, but what is unique about Jeremiah is that he makes it explicit. In doing so, we can also say that he creates the reader, since a work that presents itself as written transforms the reader into a necessary actor.[1]

The God Who Calls

The account of Jeremiah's vocation is striking because of its transparency. There are no supernatural acts or scenes foreign to everyday life, as in Isaiah. It begins with a simple "the word of Yahweh came to me" that establishes the intimate relationship

---

[1]An issue that remains unresolved is the relationship between the Masoretic text of Jeremiah and the Septuagint; the latter is an octavo shorter due to dozens of small absences of words or paragraphs throughout the text. Hebrew texts of both the long and short versions were found among the Qumran manuscripts, so that from that moment on we know that the Septuagint is not an abbreviated version of the Hebrew Masoretic text, nor is the latter an expansion of the former, but that the Septuagint is the translation of a Hebrew version different from the one later incorporated into the Hebrew canon.

between the action of God and the prophet: he speaks in the first person and narrates God's action toward himself. Then he continues with the words of God, where he tells him that his choice has been made since before his formation in his mother's womb.[1] He uses the expression "I consecrated you" (Heb. *qadash*), a verb that integrates the idea of the sacred, that which is chosen by God for a determined purpose. And that purpose is to be a "prophet to the nations." What is the theological novelty of this call to Jeremiah? We see that it establishes that the prophetic vocation is not a decision of the prophet himself but is an act of God. It is God who calls whoever wishes to do so. On the other hand, it is a decision from the very beginning of life so that it is presented as irresistible to the prophet. There are creational allusions in the fact that we speak of "before I formed you in the womb," a way of manifesting God's sovereignty over all creation, even those things hidden from human sensitivity. It implies that there is a plan of God for humanity and for each human being that is even prior to their own existence. Add to that the expression "I knew you," which in this context means that God is fully aware of whom God calls as a prophet and what their qualifications are. All of this creates the necessary climate to understand the significance of the election and that the mission entrusted to us will be like any other task that human beings do, but that it requires sanctification, an act of God that consecrates that life to carry out a project that belongs to God alone.

It is not clear what the expression "prophet to the nations" means. In Jeremiah's time, the international political context was confusing and changing. The tension between Assyria in Mesopotamia and Egypt in the south was as permanent as the outcome of an eventual fight between them was unpredictable. As had happened in the past, Israel was in the middle between both powers, and on this occasion this can be said both because of its geographical location and because of its hesitations regarding its political alliances; this led — once again — to it suffering the consequences of occupying that place. In this scenario, it is likely that the expression "prophet to the nations" means that his ministry will go beyond denouncing the sins and transgressions of Israel, that his mission will be imbued with the international

---

[1] We have developed the theme of election in our earlier discussion of the Pentateuch. In this case, the concept of election is strained because it is applied to the primordial time before being formed; in the Old Testament, only in the poem Prov 8:22-31 is it spoken of in this same way when referring to the origin of wisdom; in the New Testament it will be applied to Jesus in Col 1:16-17.

conflict in which Israel will be involved and which it will not be able to avoid. This speaks of a conception of God that expands beyond the borders of the divinely chosen people and that calls God's prophet to get involved with other nations as a way of showing divine sovereignty over the entire Earth. When describing the divine mission, God does so clearly, mentioning that it gives God authority over "peoples and kingdoms" to destroy and build. This authority must also be understood theologically from the moment that it is only recognized by Israel — who recognizes Yahweh as Lord of the world — but not by the authorities of the other nations for whom Jeremiah is nothing more than the prophet of the God of the Israelites who lives in Jerusalem and who in no way can extend divine sovereignty beyond the geographical borders of that nation and even less have any kind of power over the authorities of other nations.[1]

Jeremiah's response differs from that of Isaiah. The latter declares "here I am, send me" (Is 6:8) while our prophet interposes the excuse of his lack of eloquence and youth. In this he is similar to Moses' objection ("I do not know how to speak well" Ex 4:10) and we must note that in all three cases the mouth and the ability to express oneself with words are involved. In the case of Isaiah, God will send a seraph who will touch his mouth with a burning coal that will purify it from sins and enable him for the mission; with Moses, he will appoint his brother Aaron as his spokesman, who will speak for him; in the case of Jeremiah, it will be God who touches his mouth and by this means put "God's words" in it. In addition, God adds a central element: "I will be with you" (1:8 and 19); the guarantee for Jeremiah is that the God who calls and summons him is a God who is. There are, however, notable differences between the three: while in the case of Isaiah it is a question of purifying his mouth from sins and in Moses it is a question of responding to a physical difficulty in his speech, in the case of Jeremiah it is a question of training someone who feels that he is not up to the task. These are three different theological situations, but, in all three, the intervention of God leads to enabling the prophets for their mission. It should not surprise us that in the origin of the ministry of the prophets (and Moses) there

---

[1] The oracles against the nations in many prophets must be read as a message to Israel rather than to the nations mentioned. As the spoken word of the prophet they never heard it and if they had heard it they would not have recognized his authority to judge their peoples; on the contrary, for Israel they express the hope that their God judges and will judge the peoples who oppressed them.

is a symbolism related to the voice, the mouth and the word; this prominence is consistent with what we have already mentioned about the prophetic office in which the voice is not only its privileged tool but at times its exclusive one. The prophet cries out and speaks. The prophet does not write; the prophet calls to listen, not to read.

Then there are two visions where the implications of the call are materialized. In the first there is a play on words between almond tree (Heb. *shaqed*) and watchman (Heb. *shaqad*, a verb meaning to observe, watch, keep watch). God affirms that he will watch over the word given to Jeremiah. The second is a pot of food that is poured from the north, with the meaning that the invasion will come from there and that they must flee to the south, which in fact happened when the survivors of the fall of Jerusalem left for Egypt.

The account of Jeremiah's vocation opens a new scenario for prophetic action. Like no other prophet, he is clearly told to destroy in order to build, to uproot in order to plant. The accounts of vocation — like those of the hero's childhood — violate chronology. They are placed at the beginning of the ministry but were developed and written at the end of the journey and in light of events that have already occurred; so they are presented as a program to be developed, but in reality they describe what the prophet's action was. That is why it is notable that, since this account is a text written in light of events that have already occurred, it includes a mission that seems not to have been fulfilled. In Jeremiah's prophecy, the first part is fulfilled, but the second is elusive. His action appears to demolish all accommodating discourse that evaded responsibility in history, but the events did not give him the opportunity to build the society that he proclaimed in his vocation and program. Perhaps taking this into account leads us to interpret that his oracles of salvation were considered a promise that would remain pending in order to complete the work begun by the prophet when it was fulfilled in the future.

Seduce and Let Yourself be Seduced

It was not only Jeremiah who lived his mission viscerally. We must say the same of Jonah, Hosea, Habakkuk ("I heard and my bowels were troubled..." Hab 3:16). There are thematic links with other texts where the profound sneaks into the everyday: 12:1-6 with Hab 1:2-4; Jer 15:10 and 20:14-18 have echoes of Job 3:11 and 10:19; Jer 17:14 resembles Is 1:18; the same feeling is perceived in Psalms 3; 5; 7; 13 and others. But, in Jeremiah, this inner conflict is exposed in the story without mincing words. Although they have been called confessions, they have little of confession.[1] Rather, they express feelings and anguish for the rejection of their words and for the destiny to which Israel is headed due to its hardness of heart. They contribute to strengthening the idea that theology is a "second act," as Latin American liberation theology has affirmed, where the first thing is the experience of reality, the contact with social facts, the perception of what is happening, and then comes the theological elaboration that gives form to discourse and constitutes a tool for transformation. Jeremiah first suffers, curses, proclaims, and from there, in a second moment, arises the word that will be dictated to Baruch, theology, the reflection on praxis. In the case of these texts of Jeremiah, the anguish does not come from an existential or contemplative inner search — which also have their own value- but from his confrontation with history and the conflicts with his contemporaries.

It matters little whether or not the texts are autobiographical. It is the theological role that counts. We can describe four theological effects of these texts that, to a greater or lesser extent, feed all prophetic theology. The *first* is that they reveal the irresistible character of the prophetic vocation. By saying "you seduced me..." (20:7) he is affirming that the call has an erotic force, and therefore inexplicable, that makes it irresistible. He uses the Hebrew verb *patah*, which means to persuade, to seduce, and he uses it to describe the seduction of a woman or a man. The prophet does not want to be a prophet, and he shouts this out, but he cannot go against an impulse that leads him not to abandon his mission. God can do more than he can. The *second* corresponds to the continuation of his words "...and I let myself be seduced." In this he affirms his personality, his part in the decision, his intimate conviction that tells him that although he could not resist, his heart is where he has decided to be. Jeremiah is far from feeling that God has nullified his will by leading him down a path that he has rejected. Perhaps there are no words to express it, but Jeremiah is where he wants to be even though he has rejected his life and his destiny with such extreme

---

[1]There are six texts that make up the so-called "confessions:" 11:18-23; 12:1-6; 15:10-21; 17:14-18; 18:18-23 and 20:7-18.

words as "Alas! my mother, why did you give birth to me..."
(15:10; also 20:14-18).[1]

The *third* contribution is in tension with the previous one and consists of Jeremiah's profound conviction of his total dependence on God. It is expressed in 17:14 "Heal me, and I will be healed; save me, and I will be saved..." He needs health and needs to rescue his days, but he knows that he can do nothing to obtain what he seeks. The word that springs from the depths cannot deceive itself and understands that whatever the course of life—and for Jeremiah his life has been an experience full of challenges and pain- the decision regarding everything that happens to him resides in the will of God. Just as he was called for a mission, he could no longer resist his call; now he seeks health and can do nothing but ask for it and hope that God will grant it. The *fourth* theological aspect that we wish to point out is that the intimate discourse—all intimate discourse—involves the reader in a particular way. A relationship of complicity is established between the author and the reader because when reading these texts reader feels that they are being touched, that in one way or another the barrier between the external text and the person who, with more or less coldness or with a certain distance, analyzes a message is broken. When Jeremiah tells what happens to him and feels, he seeks to make the reader consider what their own situation is in the face of these experiences; the story leaves no room for indifference on the part of those who approach him. One can stop reading, but one cannot read without feeling involved in the drama of the prophet, which now becomes the drama of the reader.

The Crisis of Judah and the Crisis of the Prophet

A life so closely linked to the vicissitudes of his country could not fail to be influenced by historical events. Jeremiah's theology is revealed to be contextual to the very end, in this case modifying his thought and preaching to the extent that events so demand. The turning point in history that meant the death of King Josiah, and as a consequence the discontinuity of his reform, is also a turning point in the life of the prophet. This reform had

---

[1]This text is interesting because it shows the origin of his anguish. In the previous text (15:5-9) he laments the violence that has been brought upon Jerusalem and mentions the death of young people, husbands, and a mother of seven children whose "sun set in broad daylight;" he had to announce these words and his anguish comes from being the prophet who had to say them; R. Rendtorff, *The Canonical Hebrew Bible* (Leiden: Deo Publishing, 2005), 212-15.

brought hope that Judah would rectify its life and meet Yahweh again, but the crisis that his death produced changed the destiny of Judah and also changed the task of the prophet. The crisis of Judah implied the crisis of the prophet. His oracles prior to the death of the king in the year 609 are different from those that followed. We have only one oracle dated to the time of Josiah (3:6-13) whose content is an invitation to the region of Samaria — the Northern Kingdom had ceased to exist in the year 722 — to abandon their idols and return to Yahweh.[1] It is an optimistic oracle that reflects the time of the reform in which it expands toward the north and there is an expectation of recovering not only the territory but also the practice of the Yahwistic faith. In 4:1 he speaks to Israel as a lover would do who hopes that God's beloved who has rejected him decides to return to him ("If you would return, O Israel, return to me..."). It is a theology of reconciliation and forgiveness that accompanies a historical process that was cut short by the army of Pharaoh Neco, who defeated Josiah in the battle of Megiddo and ended his life (2 Kings 23:29-30).

Other words are spoken by Jeremiah from 609 onwards. The religious decline that will lead to exile begins, and the prophet sees it clearly and denounces it. Perhaps the clearest passage of this new stage is the speech proclaimed at the door of the temple. We have it in two texts that complement each other. The first in 7:1-15 and the second in 26:1-24 where the social context of his preaching is added and information on the reaction of the powerful to his words. This message happens during the reign of Jehoiakim (609-598), in the first year of his reign, when the death of Josiah was still a recent event but the impact of the frustration of his religious reform was already perceived.[2] Only one year has passed and the reform has already been betrayed by the new king.

---

[1]Jeremiah's attitude toward Josiah's reform is discussed. Some think that he opposed it because he considered it superficial and vain, and they support themselves on texts such as 8:8 ("as you say: we have the Law... but the scribes have changed it") and on the fact that Josiah consulted Huldah (2 Kings 22:11-20) and not Jeremiah when asking for advice about the scroll found in the temple. Others consider that Jeremiah supported the reform and this is seen in texts such as the cited 3:6-13; and 11:1-7; 17:19-27.

[2]There are authors who dispute the dating of this text. Beyond the date inscribed in 26:1, they think that the fact that it is in prose implies that the oracle was reworked during the exile by a Deuteronomistic editor who sought to justify the destruction of the temple with this narrative; see W. Brueggemann, *A Commentary on Jeremiah* (Grand Rapids: Eerdmans, 1998), 77-78 and T. Fretheim, *Jeremiah* (Macon: Smith & Helwys, 2002), 132-36.

In the scenario of a Judah that is vertiginously returning to idolatry, the prophet is called to announce the word of God at the doors of the temple. The temple is the most sacred place and is, at the same time, the symbol of political power. There, the king and the ruling class feel strong and protected by Yahweh.

Surely they could argue with the story of a century ago in the time of Sennacherib who could not conquer the city in the year 701 and they would repeat the words of 2 Kings 19:32-34: "Thus says Yahweh concerning the king of Assyria: he will not enter the city..." But now Jeremiah undermines the principle on which they built their theology of security through divine election, and he does so with three arguments that feed off each other. The *first* is the theological security that Yahweh will protect the temple just because it is God's temple. He announces to them that proclaiming "this is the temple of Yahweh" (7:4) is not enough reassurance for their existence or for those who worship there. God will decide to stay and protect the place if they change their behavior. If they stop oppressing the poor, the widow and the foreigner, and stop killing people; but that is an unacceptable demand for the powerful because their power is built precisely on injustice; without it, their power is diluted. The *second thing* that he denounces in front of the temple is that the idolatry that they practice is closely linked to the deviations of their personal and social lives: they steal, lie, murder while sacrificing to Baal and other gods. They have rejected the guidance of the Law and that separates them from God's plan. The situation is extremely serious because Jeremiah denounces that they have changed their sense: "How do you say: we are wise, and the law of Yahweh is with us? Surely the lying pen of the scribes has turned it into a lie" (8:8); and in 2:8 it is denounced that the prophets "prophesied in the name of Baal." The relationship with God is fundamental, but that relationship must be validated by the bond of love for one's neighbor, which they do not practice and which cannot be reduced to ritual orthodoxy. This violation of the Law and the first commandment is denounced as the origin of all other problems. *Third*, he compares the fate of the temple of Jerusalem with that of Shiloh (26:1-6). This was extremely irritating for those who trusted in God's unlimited protection. He reminds them that that sanctuary was the home of the Ark and yet the Philistines captured it without Yahweh defending it (1 Sam 4:1-11). For Jeremiah, there is no doubt that God will allow God's house to be destroyed. From a theological point of view, what he says is that the walls and objects of the temple are sacred to the extent that

Judah is faithful to the covenant; that there is no other sanctity in the temple than that which those who worship in that place grant it with their own lives; and that there will be no blessing if there is no justice. The stones of the temple make sense if they house a faithful community eager to live according to the Law.

In chapter 26, it is narrated that, in response to these words, the priests and prophets (v. 11) demand his death. Only the intervention of some elders and part of the people saved him from being executed, a fate that the prophet Uriah could not avoid (26:20-23), and he was able to continue his ministry. But his soul was hurt. His compatriots from Anathoth, his native land, also seek to kill him and say, "do not prophesy in the name of Yahweh, and you will not die at our hands" (11:21). Anguish, pain and sadness take hold of Jeremiah. He rebukes God and asks Him, "Why does the way of the wicked prosper, and why does the disloyal prosper?" (12:1). His bravest but also saddest pages will be produced during this period of his life.

Consolation and Hope for the Captives

There is no theology that only announces misfortunes and condemnation. Or if there is, it is a fragmented theology, with a short horizon. The very existence of a relationship between God and God's people supposes that ultimately there will be justice and reunion, although it will be a justice and a reunion promoted by God and not a mere human resource to smooth out violence and hide blunders. The composition of Jeremiah interspersed between the oracles of 1-25 (which are mostly condemnation and warning) others that spoke of hope and restoration. These show the literary character of the book, whose final composition reflects the time at the beginning of the restoration, when words of judgment could no longer be the only voice that the prophet announced. In 23:3-8, harsh words are heard against the shepherds of Judah, but they are opposed by the announcement of a messiah, of a king who will reign with justice. Just as important as the above is that the return of the dispersed to Jerusalem is announced from where they have been expelled. This indicates that at least the oracle is from the time of the exile, perhaps toward the end, when hopes of returning began to flourish among the captives. A second text in this direction is 29:1-23, which transcribes a letter from the prophet to the exiles. In it he urges them to continue their lives, build houses, form families, work each in his own field, because "after seventy years" God will rescue them from there and lead them to Judah. In both cases, he speaks to the exiles with affection, with words that seek to convey to them that God's love is still with them. These passages and others like them act as a preview of what is to come, so that the oracles of judgment do not end up discouraging those who are captive in a foreign land.

The heart of the message to the captives is found in chapters 30-33, sometimes called "the book of consolation."[1] Chapter 30 was originally addressed to those who lived in the region of Samaria in the heat of Josiah's reform; but in the final version they are reread from the perspective of the post-exilic restoration. Through a hermeneutical process, the texts were rescued from their original context and applied to the new situation of exile. But chapter 31 is a text specific to the post-exile. In this poem of extreme beauty, the hope of the return that God will promote for the captives is sung. The main actor is Yahweh, who will return "to build Israel." The message is not only for the captives in Babylon but extends to those who are "at the ends of the Earth," an allusion to the exiles of Samaria in 722 but also to Judah that had been scattered in various places throughout the empire. The beauty of the text is unparalleled; while Israel is mentioned as a virgin woman and God as her groom, it is said that the Lord has conceived something new in this relationship, since it is the woman who now stalks the man (31:22).

The consolation texts of Jeremiah weave a very delicate theological plot. At that moment, it was necessary to say the harshest words and there the prophet was, leaving even his health behind for it. But when the integrity of the spiritual life and the spirit of the people are at stake, he does not hesitate to seek to strengthen the community with his message. The prophet does not seek revenge; he knows that the people have sinned and that for that reason they have fallen into captivity, but he also knows that God's love for them surpasses all measure and that God will not hesitate to rescue them from where they are. There is undoubtedly a historical reference, but not in the sense that we must point out a particular event in which these promises are to be fulfilled, but in the sense that underlies the message that God continues to be active in history and that God promotes the reconstruction of God's people after the long experience of anguish and desolation. If after the demolition of the temple some thought that the God of

---

[1]Note that in the Masoretic text they occupy a place in the central core of the book, near the more conceptual chapters, which speaks of the author's intention to highlight his message. This is not the case in the Septuagint, where they are located almost at the end of the book, so they lose prominence; see J. Torreblanca, "Jeremías," *RIBLA* 35-36 (2000): 68-82.

Israel no longer existed, now they receive from the prophet the message that it was not the stone walls that gave life and meaning to Yahweh but that it was Yahweh who governed all the steps of history and continues to do so.

The highest point of Jeremiah's theology is when he prophesies that there will be a new covenant (31:31-34). It is not easy to conceive and communicate to Israel that the covenant "with the fathers" is expired and that God proposes a renewed covenant, not like the one he had made "when I took them by the hand and brought them out of Egypt." But the theological situation was so difficult that it was not enough to say that in this new time, God was restoring the old relationship with God's people. The prophet feels that the time that is about to begin supposes a new covenant, inscribed in the heart and not on stones like those that kept the Ark. This new covenant will replace the former and will be with the same people who have now matured in their faith and in their relationship with God. This passage has undergone numerous readings from Christianity that saw in it the announcement of the replacement of Israel by the future church; thus it is assumed that the Jews broke the covenant and that the new covenant will be with the new people that will emerge from the preaching of Jesus of Nazareth. This is the reading of the Letter to the Hebrews (8:6-13), which has marked Christian thought for centuries. Written in the heat of the conflict in the Jewish community between those who adopted the faith of Jesus and those who rejected it, it resulted in a limited and poor reading. The old and new covenant mentioned in Jeremiah is linked to the Israelite community and is resolved within it. It has to do with the message of restoration that, after the destruction of the temple and the city, demands a renewal of the Covenant. But the prophet announces something deeper than a renewal; what is new lies in the fact that this Covenant will be in the heart, not written in stones like the previous one, and that it will begin with the forgiveness of Israel's sins. On the other hand, at no time does the text suggest that there will be a change regarding the actors of the new covenant. Paul M. van Buren argues that both covenants have the same content, and that there is no true "new" covenant at play.[1] At the point of asking about the content of this new alliance, rather than speculating, we must place the answer in the literary context of Jeremiah. Everything indicates that the passage seeks to

---

[1] *A Theology of the Jewish-Christian Reality* (San Francisco: Harper and Row, 1983), 2: 155.

bring to its fullest expression the change that is expected of Israel and that the prophet preached throughout his life. We should not look for a different formulation of the terms of the covenant—in fact there is none in this or any other text of the Old Testament—but rather understand it as a rhetorical device to highlight the significance of the historical moment that is opening for Israel.

Ezekiel: The Mute Prophet

Ezekiel's theology aims to provide a basis for a message of hope for those anguished by exile. If in 1-24 the word of condemnation toward Israel predominates, perhaps with language so strong that it has no rival in the rest of the Scriptures, in 33-48 there is talk of peace, restitution and a new opportunity to meet God again. Without a doubt, this is not a naïve hope or one that does not arise from a previous traumatic experience, but what we find is a message that gives tools to build the social fabric and theological support of Israel in the context of the anguish and loneliness of exile in Babylon. Ezekiel is a book of exile, thought and written for those who felt that everything important and valuable for their life and their faith had been destroyed and there was no longer any point in hoping for a new encounter with the God of their ancestors. Unlike Jeremiah, who is sent "to the nations," Ezekiel is a prophet for Israel, who speaks to those who have been deported and have lost hope. Seeing that his message is not addressed to other peoples, we can see that his first objective is to shake Israel and make it aware of its responsibility in the tragedy they are experiencing, and secondly, to open the door to a new experience with God.

A fundamental contribution to nourishing hope is found in the vision of the throne of God with which the book opens. It is a complex vision, and it is not advisable to speculate too much on symbols that escape us because they are obscure, but we can say that the four wheels that turn between them (1:15-21) compose a fundamental symbolism: the throne of God is not chained to the temple of Jerusalem but is moved. If, until that moment, the link between the presence of God and the temple made the destruction of the sanctuary understood practically as the death of God, with the vision of Ezekiel, a new understanding of the presence of God is offered. God does not succumb with the stones of the temple and, in turn, can move wherever God's people are. God can accompany, console and watch over God's sons and daughters who are in Babylon because God's throne is independent of the fate of the temple. This affirmation is the cornerstone of the theology of hope that the captives need to recompose their relationship with God.

The Voiceless Prophet

To leave the prophet without a voice is to leave the people without a prophet. And it is to leave them without the company and guidance of God. The prophets spoke for God and when the prophets were silent the link with divinity was interrupted. For this reason, it was a serious fault to prevent the prophets from announcing their message or to order them not to prophesy, as denounced in Amos 2:12 and 7:12. But the novelty is that now it is not the rebellious people who silence the prophet but God, the voice behind the prophet. In Ez. 3:22-27, Ezekiel is locked up and left mute. If, until that moment, God had spoken through the voice of the prophets, then, in this case, he has decided to speak through the absence of the divine voice. It is the divine silence that "says" what the Lord seeks to transmit. However, God's intention is not absolute silence so that this resource was accompanied by another that consisted of the exercise of symbolic acts represented with his body. No other prophet cultivated them, like Ezekiel.[1]

In four successive symbolic acts, Ezekiel will express the imminent destiny of Judah and Jerusalem. In 4:1-3 he makes a model of the city in brick and then he will carry out all kinds of actions against it that represented the siege of the city. The custom of representing a city or a house in order to attack and destroy it is a gesture common to many ancient peoples. To facilitate hunting, the desired animal was painted on the wall and attacked with stones and arrows, thus anticipating its defeat. In the same way, by acting in this way, our prophet understood that a real attack was being carried out on the city and its defeat was foreshadowed. This first symbolic act provides the frame of reference for the three that follow. The next consists of lying on his left side for three hundred and ninety days and another forty days on his right side as a way of bearing the guilt of Israel on his body. The gesture is so excessive that it seems difficult to believe it was done as it is told; it can only be understood as a symbolic action, a literary construction. But, on the other hand, it has the persuasive force needed by a prophet who is prevented from speaking, the force of an incontestable act that denounces the rebellion of the people. To

---

[1] J. L. Sicre analyzes nine symbolic acts and suggests that their value is not in the eventual historicity of the acts but in their capacity to "transmit and visualize the message," see *Profetismo en Israel* (Estella: Verbo Divino, 2003), 180-83.

the muteness is added the paralysis of the body. Then Ezekiel is instructed to eat an impure and unworthy diet: bread baked with human excrement; after his complaint to God, it is replaced by ox excrement.

The first three symbolic acts describe the immediate fate of the city: the siege, the sins, the famine. The fourth will describe the fate of the people. In 5:1-4 (5-17) he is instructed to shave his head and separate his hair into three parts: one third he must burn in the city, another third he must cut into small pieces and throw around the city and the last third he must scatter to the wind; and from that portion he must take a little and throw it into the fire so that from that fire "the whole house of Israel" will be burned. The mute prophet speaks with his body and after four acts, he has announced the disaster that awaits Israel.

The acts described have generated many interpretations of diverse origins that seek to explain Ezekiel's personality.[1] However, the center of the stories is not the life of the prophet but his understanding of the events of history that, when put into words, reveal his theology. Ezekiel's theology follows the line initiated by Deuteronomistic thought, in the sense that the tragedy is not attributable to the actions of the imperial army but is considered a product of one's own faults and sins; even so, we must observe that it differs from Deuteronomistic theology in that it does not conceive of foreign nations as enemies of the faith of Israel and rescues them: it denounces that Israel has behaved worse than them because "they did not even act like them" (5:7). These words are the preamble to the most merciless description of Israel's future that has ever been made in the entire Old Testament (chapters 5-11), events that will culminate in Yahweh's abandonment of the temple.

Ezekiel's silence will last until the destruction of the city in 33:21-22, when Ezekiel will regain his speech and begin to announce a new message. In it, harsh words against the shepherds of Israel—that is, against the leadership that is assumed to have

---

[1]W. Zimmerli lists several authors who considered Ezekiel's behavior as pathological or as mystical raptures. Among others he cites Karl Jaspers who suggested that Ezekiel was schizophrenic; E.C. Browne who describes him as psychologically ill; and H.W. Hines who considers him an erratic mystic; see W. Zimmerli, *A Commentary on the Book of the Prophet Ezekiel 1-24* (Philadelphia: Fortress Press, 1979), 17-18. However, to seek the motive of the behavior in the psychology of the character is to reduce the density of the text to a medical register; we prefer to explore its symbolic and kerygmatic meaning.

abandoned the people they were supposed to lead — will alternate with words of encouragement and hope for the captives.

More Visions and Symbolic Acts

Chapter 8 combines visions with symbolic acts. Ezekiel does not speak, but he expresses himself. He does not shout like Isaiah, but he leaves his message. The literary construction of this text is delicate and profound. It begins with the prophet sitting in his house in the company of the elders when a strange being (made of fire and brilliance, a figure like that of chapters 1-3) transports him to Jerusalem and shows him the obscenities that are committed in the temple. Ezekiel is a priest and as such he has a zeal for the temple that we do not find in other prophets, even in Jeremiah, who was also a priest but not of Jerusalem but of a lateral lineage. The being who transports him — or God, it is not clear who speaks to him — tells him "they do this to drive me away from my sanctuary" (8:6); in this way, he leaves evidence of the reason for the imminent abandonment of the temple. In that place, the prophet will have three visions, each one more atrocious than the last.

The first vision takes place in the atrium. Ezekiel must pierce the wall and enter the temple. This scene has been interpreted in many ways, even psychoanalytically.[1] But what interests us is to observe how in the story of a prophet who is also a priest of Yahweh, what scandalizes him is the presence in the temple of old men together with reptiles and impure animals and decorative images. These animals transmitted impurity to whoever ate or touched them (Lev 11) at any time of life, but it was unthinkable to find them in the temple because they contradict the sanctity of the place. The same must be said of the images that adore the walls, which were prohibited in Lev 26:1. Basic laws of the faith of Israel are violated, and this abomination

---

[1] In a much-cited article by Edwin Broome he sets out his psychoanalytic analysis; in his interpretation, punching a hole in the wall would be a representation of the sexual act, see "Ezekiel Abnormal Personality," *JBL* 65 (1946): 277-92; the article was highly criticized at the time but later defended in D. Halperin's work, *Seeking Ezequiel* (University Park: Pennsylvania State University Press, 1993); Halperin analyses the rejections of various authors and seeks to defend Broome's interpretation. As we have already mentioned, this type of approach ignores the process of production of the text and assumes a close relationship between the message and the psychology of the author. In our opinion, even if it were possible to reconstruct the psychology of the author, nothing significant would be added to the message of the text.

is not provoked by those who worship other gods but by the leaders of the people themselves.[1]

The second vision takes place in the women's quarters at the entrance to the temple. We are told that they worship and sing to Tammuz, the Mesopotamian god who corresponds to Adonis in Egypt.[2] The worship of this god had begun with the Assyrian presence in Israel during the 8th and 7th centuries, particularly by foreigners who had been brought and forced to settle in the territory that was once Samaria; they practiced it as a domestic and marginal cult. What frightens Ezekiel is that the worship of Tammuz had reached the doors of the temple, and that those who practiced it in front of it did not consider it an alternative rite but rather did so as an act compatible with the worship of Yahweh.[3]

The third vision takes place inside the temple. There, twenty-five men turn their backs to the altar and prostrate themselves in the direction of the sun. Then they perform a rite that is unknown to us in which they smell a bunch of herbs. In this scene, there are several things that repel the prophet and priest Ezekiel. One is that they turn their backs on the place where Yahweh dwells, since in those times all Israelites had to pray in the direction of the temple. Another is that they worship the rising sun. The sun was a divinity common to all ancient peoples, but rejected by Israelite monotheism. It has been observed that in the story of creation, the sun and the moon are avoided for the sole purpose of not naming foreign divinities (they are called "greater and lesser stars" Gen 1:16). These idolatrous practices had entered Jerusalem during the period of kings such as Manasseh (2 Kings 21:5) and had been eradicated during the reform of Josiah. The gesture of the branch may allude to the rejection of the aroma of

---

[1]J. Kutsko has pointed out the paradox that the chapter 8 in which idolatry of images is most strongly denounced is also the one in which God is represented in the figure of a human being with heavenly features (vv. 1-3); Kutsko concludes that for the story a linguistic description is acceptable but not a physical representation; see *Between Heaven and Earth* (Winona Lake: Eisenbrauns, 2000), 89-90.

[2]Tammuz is the later name of Dummuzi, the Sumerian and later Babylonian god of vegetation. He was celebrated in the summer when plants died from the heat, and so it was celebrated with funeral songs. Later, his status as a foreign divinity was forgotten or relativized and he became the name of the fourth month of the Hebrew calendar.

[3]W. Zimmerli further points out that Tammuz's character as a god who died and came back to life made him even more odious to the prophet whose Yahwistic theology held that the God of Israel was a living God (Ps 42:3; 84:3) and therefore worshipping a God who dies was "an act of apostasy and one of the worst abominations." *A Commentary on the Book of the Prophet Ezekiel 1-24*, 243.

the temple or to repeating some Canaanite or Egyptian rite. In any case, it repels the prophet and, in conclusion, God declares that divine judgement will have no mercy on the divinely chosen people. That the Israelites now worship the sun disk was a sign of the religious and moral decline and backwardness into which the faith of Israel was sinking. The sum of the three abominations leaves the prophet in no doubt that the tragic destiny of Israel is inevitable and even desirable. These visions and symbolic acts open the door for God to abandon the temple. God can no longer consider it the divine home.

The Valley Where Dry Bones Come Back to Life

When archaeologist Yigael Yadin excavated the fortress of Masada in the Judean desert facing the Dead Sea, he discovered that beneath the floor of the small synagogue, in a cavity covered with a stone, two fragments of biblical texts had been hidden. Those who suffered the siege of the Roman army in that place, and died of hunger and thirst and fought to the end, chose them to bequeath to their successors. They were there for two thousand years. The texts chosen were Dt 32-34 (the song, the blessings of Moses and the account of the end of his life) and Ezekiel 35-38 (an oracle against Edom and then words of salvation). Among the words of restoration are 37:1-14, the vision and parable of the valley of the bones that come to life.

After the prophet's fierce declarations that end in chapter 25 — but whose theological culmination is found in 10-11 with the abandonment of the temple and the city of Jerusalem — words of hope follow. This has disturbed commentators, in particular because they consider it unlikely that these words could follow those words. But the problem is not in the texts but in the historicist reading that assumes the same author or a work written all at once. The unity of Ezekiel is not found in the process of formation of the text, but in the theological discourse and, in that aspect, there is no contradiction. The description of the disaster is followed by the words of restoration.

In chapter 37, there are two scenes that act together and that offer the theology of the story. The first is the vision of the bones, the second deals with the reunification of Judah and Israel. But already before in 34:25-31 there was talk of a new alliance built as a "peace pact" that King David would lead. And along the same lines there is talk in 36:1-12 and 25. These texts have prepared the ground to expose the new reality of the restoration, but the first obstacle is the people themselves. They are convinced that "our bones have dried up, our hope has vanished, everything is over for us" (37:11). Now the prophet has recovered his voice, he can already speak, and he is ready to do so in this case; at the same time, he has not lost the habit of expressing himself with physical symbols and special acts. On this occasion, the spirit takes him to a valley of human bones, places him in the center and makes him walk among them. For the Israelite tradition, human bones transmit impurity and this is even more serious if it is a priest: no priest could touch them (Lev 21:1). Ezekiel obeys and walks among the bones.

Then God orders Ezekiel to go to the bones and tell them that God will revive them. The bones listen to and obey the same prophetic words that the living did not hear.[1] The story contrasts the reality of the dry bones with that of the Spirit of God; the word bones is mentioned eight times and the word spirit as many times. The bones symbolize the dead, the past, that which is corrupted day by day to end up as dust; the bones are nothingness. On the other hand, the spirit of God is the vital force, the dynamism, that which has a future, that which enhances the recreation of reality and life. But the mastery of the story makes both realities not oppose each other but intersect when, at the prophet's command, the inert returns to life and the spirit is incarnated in those bodies. One should not look for an embryo of the resurrection of the body in this story. It is not the prophet's interest, nor does it affect his theology. The parable explains itself and the words of verses 11-14 confirm that it refers to the hopelessness of the Israelites who do not understand that time has changed and that now the same God who spoke harshly to them calls them to rebuild their lives and their relationship with God. They are immobilized by captivity and do not see the changes that God is promoting in their favor.

The second scene (37:15-28) shows Ezekiel taking two sticks representing Judah and Israel, which he must join in his hand to symbolize the reunion of both parts of the people of God. And he is instructed to announce that God will gather the dispersed members of Israel "from among the nations" and that they will have one king because "they will no longer be two nations." This mention tells us that the text is post-exilic and

---

[1]Note the irony that the prophet's voice was ignored for years and now the dead respond immediately. It has also been pointed out that at the beginning of the story there is a predominance of nouns and then, when God speaks, of verbs. This indicates the distance between the reality of death represented in the bones and that of life through the Spirit; see L. Alonso Schökel & J. L. Sicre, *Profetas II* (Madrid: Cristiandad, 1980), 820.

therefore acquires more value because it supposes a rereading in the heat of the possibility of the return of the diaspora to reunite in Jerusalem. But it is necessary to read the two scenes together to understand that the message is that the revival of the dry bones and the invitation to rebuild as a nation is not directed only to the captives of Babylon but to all the people of God who were dispersed after the fall of Samaria. This text is important because it bears witness to the fact that post-exilic theology — at least one theological line — is not exclusivist like that represented by Ezra and Nehemiah, but that there were those who sought to gather the ancient unified nation. We should not be surprised that the figure of David is invoked (v. 24) and that the possession of the land is mentioned as a sign of the new time; nor that it is given as a sign of the covenant that the sanctuary of Yahweh will dwell among the people.[1] It is not clear whether it refers to the temple or to the very presence of God, but the development of the story will show that a prophet/priest is interested in the physical temple as a place for sacrifices by virtue of the fact that the divinity dwells there. Any attempt to interpret the presence of God without a temple falls outside of Ezekiel's theology.

After the Ruin, A New City

Ezekiel's priestly character reaches its peak in the final section of the book. His concern about God's abandonment of the temple and Jerusalem in 10:18-19 and 11:22-23 leads him to proclaim the need to build a new temple and a new city for the Lord to dwell in and be worshipped; this is what 40-48 is about. As in 11-12, Ezekiel is taken from his home in exile to the place where a character will lead him in a vision. Here the account is uneven and at times the figure disappears or the literary genre changes from vision to description. But in any case, and although we recognize it as a composite text, the final form is homogeneous and leads from the beginning to a surprising ending: the city described will not be called Jerusalem.

The idea that the future city would have a different name had already been presented in Isaiah. This is seen in Is 60:14 and

---

[1]Ezekiel's idea of restoring the ancient unified monarchy and making the Temple the center of people's life coincides with the ideal of King Josiah which was cut short by his death in 609. This project was aborted but Ezekiel bears witness that it was never entirely abandoned; see M. Sweeney, "Ezekiel's Debate with Isaiah," *Congress Volume: Ljubljana 2007* (ed. A. Lemaire; VT Sup; Leiden: Brill, 2010), 555-74, spec. 571, expounds this point and points out that the same idea is already present in texts from the first part (11:14-21; 16-18; 20).

18, but explicitly in 62:2 where it says "...and you will be called by a new name, which will proceed from the mouth of Yahweh." The change of name is not a minor issue since it refers to both the name Jerusalem and the City of David. Neither of the two names will be used in Eze 40-48 (in fact it is never said that it describes Jerusalem) which must be interpreted as a criticism of the symbols and characters of the past. Everything indicates that the reasons that led to the destruction of the temple and the city (idolatry, breach of the covenant) remained, in the imagination of Isaiah and Ezekiel, closely linked to the city as such and to the names that identified it.[1] Although there is a sincere and profound lamentation for the loss of the temple and the city, there is also a feeling that the faults were not individual but collective and that with the deterioration of the relationship with God the link with its main physical symbols also deteriorated. In the imaginary journey, it is narrated that Ezekiel is taken to the land of Israel, to a "very high" mountain where there was *something like* a city (40:2); the literary game is that although the prophet thinks of Jerusalem he describes it as if it were another city with the intention of calling for reflection on its condition of a new city, different from the one that was rebellious and that no longer exists.[2] Anyone who read the text of Ezekiel in his days knew that Zion was not a high mountain but a low one, surrounded by hills higher than it. In addition, we must add that 40-48 devotes very little to the description of the city and all its interest is consumed in the description of the temple, the priestly office and a new distribution of the land among the twelve tribes.

It is striking to note that, in distributing the lands, he does so equitably, granting each tribe a similar portion of territory (48:1-49). Doing so confused many commentators who spoke of a hypothetical or utopian description; what happens to them is that

---

[1]Unlike Ezekiel, the prophet Isaiah does mention the new city as Jerusalem on repeated occasions (62:1, 6, 7; 66:10, 13, 20) but especially in 65:17-19 where it is associated with "the new heavens and Earth."

[2]*The Jerusalem Bible* places a note in 40:2 and indicates that it refers to Jerusalem. However, there is no textual basis for this statement, but rather a basis for suspecting the opposite; why does the prophet not call it by name here or in the rest of the section? The hypothesis that it refers to Jerusalem is also assumed by L. Alonso Schökel, *Profetas II*, 836; W. Zimmerli, *A Commentary on the Book of the Prophet Ezekiel 1-24*, 347-48; Zimmerli argues based on Is 2:2 that in an eschatological perspective Mount Zion will be understood as the highest among the mountains; however, it does not seem that the text presents the reality of the city and the temple in an eschatological key. We do not doubt that the city to which the exiles aspire to return is Jerusalem, but the prophet seeks to distance himself from it on a symbolic level.

they do not see the hermeneutical value of this distribution, which consists in doing justice, which was not present in the distribution before the exile, in which some tribes had been undermined or assimilated by the larger and more powerful ones. The text had already announced in 45:1-12 that one part should be reserved for the priests and another for the prince or king (Heb. *nasi*) with the severe warning that when he possesses his portion of land he must abstain from oppressing the people and live off the collection of taxes. The new land and the new city will be a place where human relations will be different from everything previously known. From the point of view of a theology that seeks to liberate and create fair conditions for the life and development of people, it does not matter whether the actual distribution that would later be made would follow these rules; what matters is that it is noted that the new relationship with Yahweh, in order to be lasting and not to be broken again, must be built on the basis of equality and justice. In the future Israel, the land will be for everyone and in equal parts.

This final section of Ezekiel has surprised us with a theological novelty. The prophet knows that the return and reconstruction will be in the place where the remains of the destruction of the old city still lie, but that it will not be the same even though the Israel and the city of the future are located in the geography that they occupied and on its ruins. The text leads us to another place. We notice that at the end there is the only text dedicated to the city (48:30-35) and that its gates are described in it. We must pay attention to it because it was chosen and placed there with the explicit intention of marking the end of the book. The city is a perfect square with twelve gates, three on each side and each one under the name of one of the twelve tribes. The symbolism of the gates is profound: through them the tribes will enter the presence of Yahweh. The text has a vortex, which is a vortex of the section but also of the entire book of Ezekiel, and in which the new name of the city is revealed. He keeps the secret until the last words and, as in a suspense story, creates a climate of tension that is not resolved until the final line. The last verse says: "...the name of the city from today will be *Yahweh is there.*"

Importance of Obadiah and Nahum's Theology for the Canon
The Experience of God and Human Cruelty

Biblical literature is the product of many hands that distribute meaning, construct theologies, and balance thoughts. For this reason, a reading that is only synchronic, which seeks to avoid historicist distortion, is also limiting and tends to lose depth rather than gain it. We have maintained throughout this book that we adhere to the final text and not to its previous stages, and therefore we privilege a synchronic reading; however, this reading must be done showing sensitivity toward the production process of the biblical texts that reveals their condition as a work that acquired its final form by the incorporation of the various contexts in which it was reread.[1] For this reason, in order to approach a biblical text, it is necessary to consider the history of its production in order to perceive in this evolution of authors, schools, and wisdoms, how the message is formed from a balance between meanings, particularly when there are texts that, taken in isolation, present contradictory perspectives. This is why we say that a fragmented reading of any book runs the risk of being partial to the point of incinerating the message or at least disfiguring it in such a way as if it were another text before us. This general principle that meaning is the product of a balance of texts that we consider crucial for any reading is difficult to apply to Obadiah and Nahum. It does not fit in with them. Their presence in the canon bears witness to something else.

The books of Obadiah and Nahum have in common that they both place the feeling of revenge at the center of their expectations.[2] The first one toward Edom, the second toward the city of Nineveh. In them there is no mercy for the enemy, cruelty is unleashed and no possibility of conversion of the sinner is glimpsed. In the formation of these texts, it seems that there was no search for a balance between contrasting meanings that we find in other books. The feeling of revenge and the joy at the misfortune of the other are present in numerous other biblical texts; we find them in the stories of the conquest in Joshua, in the Psalms, in other prophetic books. The thirst for revenge is present in the oracles against the nations that occupy long chapters in Isaiah, Jeremiah, and Ezekiel and in shorter texts in several of the other prophetic books. But, in all of them, the confrontation of

---

[1]The concept of historical *sensitivity* because it incorporates the history of the text into the analysis without it becoming the key to reading it; in the interpretation, the history of the text is taken into account but it is not granted the privilege of opening or closing its meaning; see L. Stulman & H. Chul Paul Kim, *You Are My People* (Nashville: Abingdon Press, 2010), 1-8.

[2]Psalm 109 also expresses the desire for revenge against the enemy, but it is the voice of one who is blasphemed and treated unjustly (vv. 1-5); from the place of impotence due to God's action against his enemies. In Obadiah and Nahum, a similar situation is not made explicit. See among others Ps 5:11; 10:15; 69:23-29; 137:7-9; 139:19-22.

thoughts and the perspective that the passage of time brings balanced their message to arrive at a theology that ultimately, and even though it may not satisfy our taste many times, expresses the love and mercy of God. There is none of that in these two books. If we were to incorporate them into a larger textual body, they would not attract our attention because their words would not stand out as novel or more aggressive than others; but being complete and closed works, the vengeance and cruelties expressed in them have no counterpart to qualify them. That is why we must ask ourselves the question: Why were both books preserved in the canon as autonomous works?

We can answer this question in two ways. The first, which does not excite us, is that they are not autonomous works but parts of the larger book of the Twelve Prophets. This would avoid the problem of isolating the message of vengeance by subsuming it in the set of oracles of salvation and hope present in the other books; but it creates another problem of a different kind, which is that there is no literary basis for organizing the prophets from Hosea to Malachi in a single work. Attempts have been made, but all are unconvincing.[1] The second answer is theological: they were preserved as they are because they express a deep and true human experience, and as such, it deserved to leave its mark as a word in the universe of theological thought. It is the experience of the mother who saw her children murdered; of the husband who was forced to witness the rape of his wife; of the sons and daughters who were torn from their parents' arms and sold to foreign peoples; of the weak old woman who was cruelly slaughtered; of the babies that a young warrior throws into the abyss because he was ordered to do so by his superior. From these terrible places emerge the words of Obadiah and Nahum, words that we must oppose and even criticize, theology that will not be ours nor will it contribute to our preaching, but that we cannot deny that they take root in the inner self of those who suffered humiliation and ridicule.

---

[1] This is a much debated and still unresolved issue. In favor of unity, see P. House, *The Unity of the Twelve* (Sheffield: Almond Press, 1990) and M. Shepperd, "Composition Analysis of the Twelve," *ZAW* 120 (2008): 184-93; against, see the article by Tchavdar Hadjiev who shows that the book of Zephaniah was not written as part of a larger work, see "Zephaniah and the Book of the Twelve Hypothesis," *Prophecy and Prophets in Ancient Israel* (ed. J. Day; New York: T&T Clark, 2010), 325-38; a work that is not defined but provides valuable insights into this issue is B. A. Jones, *The Formation of the Book of the Twelve* (Atlanta: Scholars Press, 1995).

Obadiah builds his theology on hatred of Edom, while Nahum celebrates that "fire will consume" Nineveh "and the sword will destroy it." Edom did not help Judah at the time of the destruction of the temple and the city (587 BC), but rather collaborated with the enemy. In some way, it took advantage of Israel's tragedy, gained territory and profited from the produce of the foreign land it occupied for many years. Before, around the year 612 BC — the order of the books is not chronological — Nahum had witnessed Assyrian cruelty, its torments and desire to destroy the subjugated peoples. We are convinced that the experience of a God who loves his sons and daughters, who promotes justice and respect for all human beings, does not allow us to build a theology based on the search for revenge for aggressions suffered; But their presence in the canon gives us a perspective to consider and reject the cruelty and humiliation to which some human beings subject others. They are there to show to what extent someone who has been cornered and exposed to humiliation has the right to utter the words that come from their experience. It is their biography and we cannot deny them the right to say what they feel.

Obadiah and Nahum in Theological Perspective

Old Testament theology is born from the search to interpret how God loves God's people, how God is always there and protects and corrects them, preserves and challenges them; also from reflecting on the role that this people has to play in God's plan for all nations. It is evident that, in these two books, the experience of God helped us to see that even the most aberrant behavior must be integrated into a greater understanding of history and contribute to clarifying what we call the human condition. Obadiah calls for vengeance on Edom and sings of the tragedies that will fall upon this people while Nahum celebrates the fall and destruction of the city of Nineveh, the capital of the empire (other texts are Ps 79:11-13; 137:8-9). These books should not be read as texts that show what God expects of God's people, but as testimony that the abominable is part of human nature and that it is necessary to always be alert to oppose it. The 20th century was the scene of the genocide of one and a half million Armenians in its first years (1915), the Jewish genocide of 6 million people toward the middle of the century during the war that ended in 1945, and ended with the genocide in Rwanda (1994) where 800,000 people were massacred in three months. Unfortunately for humanity, there were others as well. Latin America and Spain had their own deaths due to violence in the 20th century and we hope they never have any more. The list of horrors would be endless.

The books of Obadiah and Nahum are in the canon—and it is important that they are there—to bear witness to the fact that humanity is capable of such atrocities. However *inhumane* these behaviors may seem, in truth only human beings commit them and only humans use their intelligence to perfect the means of aggression and extermination, today of infernal sophistication. A beast, a wild animal, a spider, kills to feed itself or to ensure the space necessary for its survival. We humans do this to accumulate power and dominance over others, or to prove that we are stronger than our neighbors. Life is cut short in the name of absurd things, of despicable values.

The destruction of Edom in Obadiah is celebrated as a condition for Israel to return from exile and for the land to be restored to it. It will be revenge for what they suffered. The end of the book (Ab 19-21) says it clearly but adds something disturbing: that at the culmination of this action it will be Yahweh who will reign. Throughout Nahum, but in particular in 2:14 and 3:5, it is also suggested that Yahweh's dominion is manifested from the divine actions of extreme destruction. In turn, the idea of restoration associated with the destruction of the brother people is found in Nahum 1:15-2:2:

> Behold, upon the mountains
> the feet of the one who brings good news,
> of the one who announces peace.
> Celebrate, O Judah, your feasts, fulfill your vows;
> For the wicked will never again pass through you; he has utterly perished.
> A destroyer has come up against you;
> guard the fortress, watch the way,
> Gird up your loins, strengthen your power greatly.
> For Yahweh will restore the glory of Jacob like the glory of Israel;
> because plunderers have plundered them and destroyed their branches.

Contrary to many other biblical pages—but in harmony with others—peace in this text is the fruit of violence. In Obadiah and Nahum, the death of the enemy is announced so that the dominion and power of Yahweh may be exercised and manifested. As readers of this text, we cannot help but consider it and seek to understand its meaning as such and as part of the Scriptures.

There is a theological lesson that these books leave behind. They show how violence and hatred lead to the deterioration of humanity in both the aggressor and the victim. The relationship is not symmetrical and in no way comparable, because someone had to kill the child so that the mother now wishes the death of the aggressor's child or celebrates it; and in both cases the link between the person and God's plan for that person has been broken. The aggressor places the victim in the place of a non-being, who does not recognize the right to live or the meaning of his existence; the existence that for the aggressor has no meaning makes him consider the other a hindrance and a being who does not deserve to live. The neighbor is transformed into an object of use whose only purpose is to be functional to the oppressor and then be discarded. That is why he kills without remorse. On the other hand, the one who has been humiliated, if he is dominated by revenge, becomes dehumanized and his thinking becomes blurred that the other, the aggressor, is also a human being. And for that reason he cannot consider that the person who has attacked him is liable to be confronted with his crime and still has the possibility of repenting and confessing his faults. The expectation of revenge prevents him from reconstructing his own life and considering the human aspect of another's life — that of his aggressor — even though he will always carry in his memory those who have been taken from him or on his body the marks of horror. He needs peace to reconstruct his damaged fibers and this will not be the fruit of revenge but of the justice to which he is blinded.

Biblical theology considers murder to be an act against God, a distortion of life as the Creator conceives it; every death caused by hatred and violence is fratricide and deicide. Every time someone murders, it is done to a sister or a brother and by destroying the image of God imprinted in them, God is being murdered. The response that emerges from biblical theology in the face of crime is the search for justice. Nahum and Obadiah express human anguish and its drive for revenge, but they do not show the relationship that God establishes with the victims; they express the realism of biblical thought regarding the human condition but they are not exponents of God's proposal in the face of injustice. Only justice heals the wound and restores the tissues to heal life. The victim is not required to forgive the aggressor, but it is hoped that truth and justice, acts that are only human and unknown to animals, will create the conditions for someone who has suffered so much at the hands of others to rebuild their lives and live their days in peace.

The Day of Yahweh in the Twelve: Judgment to Redemption

The Book of the Twelve Prophets is both a collection of works and a book in itself. Jewish tradition recognized it as a work from the beginning and indicated this in its manuscripts by separating each of the twelve books with three lines, while the rest of the works of the Old Testament are separated by four lines; also because the combined length of the twelve books is equivalent to that of Isaiah and consequently they were all included in a single scroll; however, this did not prevent them from being read as individual works. In the Christian sphere, it was the Latin authors of the 4th century who first called them "minor prophets" (they are called this in *The City of God* by Saint Augustine) on the basis that they are shorter than the other three prophetic books, a name that suggests that each book should be read in isolation, an attitude that was followed from then on in the Church. However, it is not difficult to find examples in current literature of works that meet both conditions of diversity and coherence[1]. Individual stories or poems are grouped together, read and studied in isolation, but they are not thrown together at random within the book, but rather respond to an order established by the author. The same can be said of the Book of the Twelve Prophets. We know that all the prophetic books — as well as almost all the other books of the Old Testament — were composed by the concatenation of previous texts, but in most cases sutures were made to conceal the union; we have seen that the final editor wanted Isaiah to be read as a whole and not as three separate parts. But in the case of the Twelve, each work has a well-identified beginning, where biographical data of the prophet are given, in some cases the date and place where he carried out his ministry, and there are no textual signs that such identification was attempted to be concealed. Given this, it is surprising that within the books sutures were made to give literary unity to works that are clearly composed; as examples, we see the passage from Amos 9:10 to the final oracles of vs. 11-15; the psalm of Jonah 2; or the passage from chapter 8 to 9 of Zechariah; in all these cases and others the editor sought to give unity to the work and to minimize the literary seams. In turn, the fact that there are three books that quote or allude to the same text of Isaiah 2:2-4 (Joel 4:10; Micah 4:1-5; Zechariah 8:20-23) is a sign that we are dealing with works that

---

[1] We think of Julio Cortázar's book *Final del juego* (3rd ed.; México: Nueva imagen, 1987) which brings together eighteen individual stories grouped into three sections where we can glimpse internal relationships, somewhat obscure, but which connect the stories. Literature offers countless examples of this type.

were composed separately. It is therefore recognized that each book enjoys autonomy, a message, and structure that are its own but that have not been placed there in a haphazard manner.

From Judgment to the Redemption of Israel

As we look for what links the twelve books, we find several very significant signs.[1] We initially rule out that they respond to a chronological order because Joel is one of the last books written and occupies the second place; Jonah is late and is written before Micah, which is much earlier; there are also other inconsistencies that weaken the chronological argument. More semantic benefit is obtained by forgetting the chronology and observing that Hosea begins with the image of a broken marriage as a symbol of the rupture between Israel and God (chapters 1-3) and that at the other end of the collection Malachi presents his frontal rejection of divorce (2:16) and a proposal for present and future restoration. This relationship is not accidental but establishes that the path to follow goes from the judgment of Israel's infidelities to the redemption that Yahweh promotes through the observance of the Law and the eschatological perspective present in Malachi. The mention of the Day of Yahweh is linked to this plan.

Only in the prophets is this special day mentioned, and within them the Twelve are the ones that concentrate most of the references to the Day of Yahweh. Outside of this, it is found in Isaiah 2:12 and 13:6-9, where the first text is an exaltation of Yahweh and the second is within an oracle against Babylon in the section that groups together other oracles against foreign nations. The mentions in Ezekiel 13:5 and 30:3 also do not have the forcefulness that they will have in the Twelve; the first reference corresponds to a speech against false prophets and the second an oracle against Egypt in the context — as in Isaiah — of other oracles

---

[1]Here we assume the order of the books of the Hebrew Bible followed by the Vulgate and reproduced in Western Bibles. The Greek tradition of the Septuagint — followed by the Orthodox Churches — has a different order for the first six books, which it presents in the following sequence: Hosea, Amos, Micah, Joel, Obadiah, Jonah, while the rest is common to both canons. The order of the Septuagint privileges the concern for the Northern Kingdom (Samaria) while the BH does so for the fate of Judah and Jerusalem; for further information see the various works of M. Sweeney, *The Prophetic Literature* (Nashville: Abingdon Press, 2005), 168-69; *The Twelve Prophets* (Collegeville: Liturgical Press, 2000), vi-xlii; and "The Sequence and Interpretation in the Book of the Twelve," *Reading and Hearing the Book of the Twelve* (ed. J. D. Nogalski; Atlanta: Society of Biblical Literature, 2000), 49-64.

of the same tenor. In both prophets, the Day of Yahweh is instrumental to the subject they deal with and does not acquire the cosmic dimension that we perceive in the Twelve. What is observed in the Twelve is a tension between the Day understood as a battle in the military field in history and an eschatological battle. It is likely that the concept was born in reference to the desire to defeat in battle whoever had attacked Israel and that it later acquired a transcendent and universal value, but the truth is that even when it is addressed only to Israel and Judah, it does so by hinting at an action with consequences that go beyond historical events. As with other concepts in the Old Testament, it is difficult not to see that it is playing positively with ambiguity and that the reader is left in doubt as to whether to interpret in one sense or another or in both at the same time. Rendtorff points out that what really causes panic is that this day of misfortune is recognized and called as "the Day of Yahweh" while God calls again and again to repentance.[1]

The first mention of the Day of Yahweh in the Twelve is in Joel, where it is found four times. In fact, it is the book that mentions it the most and where it runs through the entire work. Its placement as the second book of the set is crucial because it places the theme of the destiny of Judah and Jerusalem at the center of interest and at the same time establishes that on that day Yahweh will judge the nations that humiliated Israel but Judah and Jerusalem will be rescued. He says this at the end (4:1-17) after the Day has been presented on three previous occasions as a judgment toward Judah itself. The identification of that day with two ecological tragedies, such as drought and then a plague of locusts that devastates the city and the surrounding fields is significant. Both are events that occur in history and we can even consider them regular in the natural course of climatic phenomena. But the text takes advantage of the dramatic nature of a drought and a plague to allude to a military invasion from the north that, far from being locusts, are enemy squadrons with their bows and arrows.[2] The tension grows throughout the book and when it is expected to culminate with the judgment and destruction of Jerusalem in foreign hands, the last scene changes dimension and develops in a transcendent climate where the words are of

---

[1] R. Rendtorff, *The Canonical Hebrew Bible* (Leiden: Deo Publishing, 2005), 276; the author emphasizes that the successive texts on the Day of Yahweh will concentrate the act of salvation in Jerusalem.

[2] For a development of locusts as a symbol of a military army see P. R. Andiñach, "The Locust in the Message of Joel," *VT* 92 (1992): 433-41.

judgment on the aggressors and of salvation and rescue for Judah and Jerusalem.[1] In accordance with the literary dynamics of the book, on the day that the judgment of Jerusalem was expected, it turns out that the other nations will be summoned and judged by the God of Israel at the gates of the city. So if the Twelve begin with the prophet Hosea, whose recurring theme is the rupture of God's relationship with Israel, and ends with a verse of wisdom where he urges to be wise to understand God's message (14:10), in Joel he found a first response to that sermon when he says that on the Day of Yahweh the people of God will be defended and rescued.

Amos, who follows Joel in the canon, will offer a different vision of the Day of Yahweh for Israel. In his sermon, he denounces that those who commit injustices and mistreat the poor have confused their thinking by believing that on that day they will be rewarded for their liturgical and dogmatic rectitude. The prophet proclaims that being orderly and meticulous in bringing their offerings and celebrating religious festivals will not exempt them from the wrath of God on that day. It is not the formulation of a correct doctrine that God evaluates in order to grant salvation but the coherence between doctrine and life. For Amos, the Day of Yahweh will not be a day of judgment for the nations that oppressed Israel but a time of tragedy for those who practice the hypocrisy of being faithful in the temple but unfaithful in life. He likes the contrast between the call to return to faith ("...seek the good and not the evil, that you may live..." 5:14) and the immediate change to "in every street there will be lamentation... for I am passing through your midst..." (5:16-17). He reveals that there were those who understood that day as one of light and blessing, but the prophet announces to them that it will be "dark and without clarity" (5:18-20). The recourse to the Day of Yahweh in Amos supposes a balance with the words of Joel. The latter is placed before Amos to mark the direction toward which the theology of the Day of Yahweh will go, but Amos is there to remind us that this protection on the final Day does not imply that in the present the responsibility toward the poor and marginalized disappears.

It is remarkable to note that Obadiah, which follows Amos, acts in relation to Joel and frames it. Obadiah returns to the conception of Joel, who announces that on that day it will be the

---

[1]P. R. Andiñach, "Lenguaje de la resistencia ante el poder imperial," *RIBLA* 48 (2005): 62-75.

foreign nations that oppressed Israel that will be judged (15a). The entire book is dedicated to condemning Edom for having mocked the fate of Judah and having taken advantage of its misfortune to enrich itself. Edom is considered a traitor because it is the people descended from Esau and therefore a blood brother of Israel, from whom help and protection were expected. The succession of Joel, Amos and Obadiah in relation to the Day of Yahweh shows that concern for the fate of Judah and Jerusalem leads to rereading the message in search of understanding where history is heading and what means God will use to rescue God's people.

Turning the page and finding Jonah, it becomes clearer that its location once again seeks to offset the message against the nations to present a story where the foreign people repent and are forgiven by God. Jonah must be read as an autonomous work, but the place it occupies in the order of the Twelve is not naïve. If Obadiah proclaimed the destruction of all nations for their sins against Israel, Jonah points out that every people and every human being (including Jonah himself) have the possibility of changing course and finding the grace and blessing of the God of Israel. He does not mention the Day of Yahweh, but his theology seeks to show that God in divine love awaits the repentance of the sinner in order to save him, and therefore it is not appropriate to celebrate the tragedy of the adversary as Obadiah does. In the sequence of the first five books in relation to the Day of Yahweh, we observe a search to balance the concepts of judgment and blessing as well as those of judgment of Israel versus judgment of foreign nations; This search aims to direct the reader toward a specific theological statement that will be made explicit at the end of the set of books.

The next mention is in Zephaniah, which gives the time of King Josiah as the date of his ministry. His purpose is to urge the people to accept the religious reform that the king promotes and, therefore, his first concern concerns the fate of Judah. Even though there are very strong oracles against the other nations, the mention of the Day of Yahweh is reserved for Judah and Jerusalem (1:2-18) which is an indication that although the judgment will be on every nation, there is a particular judgment for the people who have been chosen. The election as the people of God supposes a responsibility on the part of Israel that has not been sustained and therefore, with the recourse to a highly sensitive poetic figure, he says that on that day "...Yahweh has prepared a sacrifice..." in which the victim is his own guest in allusion to Judah and Jerusalem (1:7). Zephaniah's contribution is to point out that the reason for the judgment is idolatry, the presence of Baal in the midst of Judah. Although this criticism is understandable in Josiah's time, it might be surprising to find it in the late and post-exilic writing of this book; but what has been done is a hermeneutical transfer of a theme from the 7th century to the new situation of the 5th or 4th century. The context is not the same, but Israel's infidelity was never definitively eradicated and this passage responds to that reality.

The balance will come in the words of Zechariah. This book dedicates the final chapter to describing the Day of Yahweh and does so in great detail. On that day, the nations will gather to fight against Jerusalem; it will be a special day in which the succession of light and night will be altered; the Mount of Olives will split in two and spring waters will spring forth from the city; the mountains of the Earth will disappear and a plague will degrade the bodies of Jerusalem's enemies. In short, it will be a day where reality will be altered and a new order will emerge from creation. But beyond the description of the last day, what is new about the Day of Yahweh in Zechariah is that the judgment will consist of an eschatological battle and that both foreign nations, Judah and Jerusalem, will be judged; and that from that judgment there will be a remnant of both who will be the rescued ones who from then on will make a pilgrimage to Jerusalem every year to celebrate a feast before Yahweh. Until now, the judgment was for one or the other, but now every creature must face the judgment of God.

This model does justice to the general theology of the Old Testament, according to which salvation comes as a consequence of repentance and not by belonging to the seed of Abraham. Such is the preaching of the prophets and the conclusion of Deuteronomistic theology. However, in the development of the theology of the Day of Yahweh, which goes from the judgment of Israel to its redemption, it is the first time that it is formulated explicitly. In doing so, it opens the door to the last mention in Malachi. In this book, the Day of Yahweh occupies half of its content (2:17-3:24) and is a message built on the fact that on that day Israel will be purified and the broken relationship between God and God's people will be restored. In this case, the enemies are not foreign peoples, but those who oppressed the poor, widows and foreigners, those who did not observe fidelity to God and those who did not show fear for Yahweh. The criterion for condemning or saving is the fear of God.

When Malachi complains about the withholding of tithes and offerings, he is not doing so to demand money for the temple, but rather to confront the people with the observance of the Law. When he says, "Return to me and I will return to you," he is urging them to rebuild the bond broken by disobedience and lack of love for their neighbor. It is not by chance that Malachi ends with the creation of a memorial document in which the will to return to him is recorded and of which God says that those who are there will be God's "personal property." It is a concrete restoration in history, a way of reaffirming the old covenant and leaving in writing that the promises and responsibilities assumed by the ancestors are still valid. Given this reconstruction of the relationship between God and the people, it remains to define the theme of judgment and justice. This is announced in the final paragraph. Malachi's theology needed to go one step further, otherwise the historical reality of impunity would testify against it. This step consists of announcing that at some point before the Day of Yahweh is realized, the prophet Elijah will return — note that with this observation the arrival of the Day is delayed — and that on that day the wicked will be consumed by fire while for those who fear Yahweh there will be redemption and "the sun of justice will shine." In this final text, the figure of Elijah is linked to that of Moses (3:22) to create a climate of union between the founding Law of Israel and the prophet of the end times. In turn, Elijah's task will be to reconcile parents with children, which reinforces the symbol of uniting the old with the new, all with the explicit aim of avoiding a general destruction of the Earth.[1]

The Day of Yahweh served to convey a message of hope to the post-exilic community. From a theological point of view, it brings the conviction that all injustice and cruelty will not be forgotten and that at some point they will be judged by God. To the questioning of Mal 3:14:

> ...what is the value of serving God? What does it profit if we keep God's law, and walk afflicted before the Lord...?

---

[1] We have pointed out that the theology of the Day of Yahweh is the germ of later apocalyptic literature. But we must remember that despite the significant number of apocalyptic works produced between the 2nd century BC and AD, their near absence in the Old Testament implies that there was explicit resistance to incorporating them or that they simply arrived late, when the canon had already been consolidated. Thus it is understandable that they survived because they were held in high esteem even though they did not participate in the canon. It is interesting to note that the New Testament did not fully embrace this theology either, but rather integrated it into its discourse where it made it coexist with other perspectives.

We say: Blessed are the proud and those who do
wickedly...

The answer is that there will be a just judgment and that God's
judgment is not merely physical death, but that there will be a day
when the violent and oppressive will have to give an account of
their actions. Gustavo Gutiérrez, in his book on Job, says it this
way:

> What has Job understood? That justice does not rule in
> God's world? No. What he has perceived, and has led him
> to contemplation, is that justice alone does not have the last
> word in speaking about God.[1]

The Redemption of the Oppressed

Israel was, for most of its history, an oppressed people.
Even more so in the post-exilic era when most of the biblical books
were written and completed. It is a poor people who work for
others, whose meager earnings go to paying taxes, leaving them
very little for their own material development. In this era, there
are no new buildings or developments in the city. It is the Israel
that no longer has a Davidic dynasty or strong leaders like
Solomon's. The powerful voice of the great prophets no longer
vibrates and the new generations have opted for calm thought and
wisdom that will leave great works and profound thoughts but
that does not seek to consolidate a historical project but rather to
rescue the words that founded the faith and the nationality to
preserve them for the future. Even so, there are objects from the
past that retain their force. The symbolic objects they possess are
the restored temple, and the memory inscribed in the Scriptures,
many of which are still in the process of being consolidated. It
should not surprise us that this is the time of the foundation of
Judaism as a theological and religious entity, and that its
foundations are precisely the monotheism expressed in the
worship of the one God in God's only temple in Jerusalem, and —
as a value in tension with the above — the consolidation of the
Judaism of the diaspora. This will be characterized by upholding
the principle of the centrality of the temple of Jerusalem but will
create a theology that will distance itself from the culture of its
ancestors and will accept that the faith of Abraham can be poured
into cultural molds different from those that gave it life. The most
impressive fruit of this new theological conformation of Judaism is
the translation of the Scriptures into Greek in the middle of the

---

[1] G. Gutiérrez, *Hablar de Dios desde el sufrimiento del inocente* (Salamanca:
Sígueme, 1986), 160.

third century BC called the Septuagint, an enterprise of a magnitude never seen before and that will influence Judaism and then Christianity as no other element will.

This oppressed and poor Israel is the one that generates its written word. The stories of the patriarchs and matriarchs loaded with camels and riches or of the first kings who lived in palaces and enjoyed power no longer have the same impact as they did in the past. They are fundamental texts of incalculable religious and social value, but they must be reread so that they are significant for the new times. The psalms where God listens to and attends to the needs of the poor are consolidated, such as the alphabetical psalm 9-10 (which together form a single poem) or Psalms 12; 18; 74; 76; etc. Psalm 37 is dedicated to the people who do not own land and who are announced as their legitimate heirs.[1] There are texts such as Zechariah 9:9-10 where, in contrast to the memory of David and Solomon, the future king and messiah is described as humble and poor. Others such as Isaiah 25:1-6 ("...you were strength for the weak, strength for the poor...") and 66:1-2 ("...I will look upon him who is poor and of a contrite spirit, and who trembles at my word...") resonate with a different value when they are understood as the word that arises from the same experience of weakness and the conviction that the God of Israel is on the side of the oppressed.

It was in this theological context that the theology of the Day of Yahweh was born. It was undoubtedly a pre-exilic concept, but it was in the heat of a society that suffers oppression, that is only allowed to work and worship its God, and that bears the marks of having suffered the humiliation of losing its sons and daughters and of having lost dominion over the land that God had given them as an inheritance, that this theology was born and developed. The tension that we have already mentioned between historical and eschatological realization is nothing other than the theological expression of the feelings of those who cry out for deserved justice here and now but who see that social conditions do not allow it to be realized. But the transfer of justice to a transcendent sphere does not mean that history is forgotten as the scene of God's action and for that reason the theology of the Day of Yahweh is also a critique of any model of human justice that is

---

[1]There is a wide range of work on the Psalms and the poor in Latin America; see J. de Freitas Faria, "Esperanza de los pobres en los Salmos," *RIBLA* 39.2 (2001): 57-68; A. Ricciardi, "Los pobres y la tierra según el Salmo 37," *RevBíbl* 41.2 (1979) 227-37; and S. Gallazzi, "Señor reinará eternamente," *RIBLA* 45.2 (2003): 59-67.

distorted and ultimately is not true justice. It served as a yardstick for measuring the truthfulness of any project that claims to represent divine justice but in reality hides its own lust for power. Justice for the oppressed on that day will be a perfect and definitive version of the justice that men and women are capable of applying in this life.

Prophetic Theology as a Response to Imperial Power

We have pointed out that the prophetic discourse was an oral act. But that discourse was soon transformed into a written text and, in that transfer, it acquired the characteristics of any text. We refer the reader to the Introduction, where we analyzed the condition of the Scriptures as text. On this occasion, we want to highlight three aspects that relate to this topic. First, what has already been said, that the text survives the passage of time while the word fades away almost at the same moment of having been pronounced. Second, observe that the text has a material support (papyrus, parchment, stone, ceramic, etc.) that allows it to reach where the prophet cannot reach: to be read by kings and peasants, to be read by exiles and by future generations; if it is destroyed, it can be copied again; if it is censored, it can circulate clandestinely. For all these reasons, we affirm that the text is immensely more powerful and versatile than the prophet in person. Stulmann and Kim point out that "despite its passivity, the scroll—as a symbol, literary object and powerful presence—compensates for the absence of the prophet,"[1] A third element characteristic of texts in general and of prophetic texts in particular is that the oral prophetic word seeks to radically change a specific situation, while the word, once written, changes its audience to now address the survivors of that first moment; those who write it down and read it no longer participate in the events that generated it but seek guidance and encouragement in it for what happened after the time to which the prophet referred. The same authors cited above say "the change from oral to written implies a reformulation of intentionality, context and audience." The text refers to a new context with respect to that of the prophet: he has before him other people and another political and social situation.

The Theology of Empire

The context for reading most of the prophetic texts is the world of the great empires to which Israel was subjected from the

---

[1]L. Stulmann & H. Kim, *You are My People*, 10.

6th century BC. Of these, the almost fifty years of Babylonian captivity (586-539) and the two hundred years of the Persian Empire (539-333) are those that give their imprint to most of the texts. The theology of the empire gave religious support to the regime of exploitation and attempted to sustain under its columns the heavy social burden that rested on the shoulders of the subjected. Each imperial power brandished a theology that was shown to be totalizing, exclusive and — even more serious — very attractive to the vassal peoples, who at times felt the temptation to adopt it as their own in replacement of the faith of their ancestors. This was induced by the popular belief that when a people defeated and subjugated another, its gods were also defeated and subjugated by those of the victor.

The prophets were those who saw this most clearly and their texts are largely a search to counterbalance imperial publicity. It should not surprise us that the insistence on the power of Yahweh, on the divine creative capacity and on the divine condition of being the God who is (*El Dios que está*) above all gods is a counter-theology to that which the empire proclaimed regarding its own gods. Isaiah mocks Bel, the Babylonian goddess of the sky and the god Nebo considered to possess all wisdom, but he does so to ridicule the Israelites who were attracted to them: he tells them "Bel collapses, Nebo collapses..." (46:1), "they call upon him and he does not respond" (46:7). When Jeremiah denounces that Bel has been put to shame (50:2) after the fall of Babylon, he shows the weakness and inability of the goddess to defend her people and her city. Even stronger is the countercultural discourse in 51:44 which says that Yahweh will judge her "in Babylon," a way of affirming that the God of Israel has jurisdiction over the entire Earth and even power over the Babylonian gods in their own territory, something that had already been manifested in the narrative of the Tower of Babel (Genesis 11:1-11) and in the story of the exodus in relation to the Egyptian gods.

The theology of the Babylonian empire proclaimed that its gods were the owners of the world and therefore no people could oppose them. In their Akkadian language, the name of the city Babel (Akkadian *bab-il*) means "the door of God;" this name implied that the Babylonian king had the exclusive key to access the gods. One can argue that something similar is said by the prophets of the God of Israel, who reserved the right to interpret the will of God, and that seen in this way one and the other theology are the same structure with only a change of perspective or culture. But what differentiates one discourse from another is that while the empire uses theology as a tool to consolidate and give foundation to the exploitation of the vassal people, in the discourse of the biblical prophets the protagonism of Yahweh contradicts all projects of oppression and even preaches against the interests of the Israelite ruling classes or against a quietist "political realism" sometimes installed even in the poor sectors of the people. The message of the prophets is not the ideological support of the most favored sectors within Israel, but quite the opposite; they announce divine support for the claims of the poor, the victims, the marginalized, and they urge the political and religious leadership to act in accordance with the Law of God received from their ancestors.

The Problem of the Theology of Captivity: Pain without a Plan

The prophets must fight against the theology of captivity embedded in Israel itself. It is the theology that expresses the pain and anguish of having lost what is most precious without being able to glimpse a new project to overcome the present situation. It is born from a genuine pain and even from the emptiness of feeling that they have been disappointed by God because they have perceived him as weak and vulnerable. If God does not hear their cry, who will? If God is not powerful enough to change their destiny, what space is left for the hope of a restoration that will redeem the lost lives and rebuild the broken covenant? The present is perceived as static and definitive and no alternatives for change are seen on the horizon. It is a deceptive attitude because it leads to the manipulation of this feeling by those in power and the consecration of "the end of history" and "the end of ideologies," as it has been proclaimed in our midst since the end of the 20th century through a clear ideological formulation that pretends not to be such and that has caused so much harm to the vast majority of our people.

Disillusionment with the difficulties in building a more just society led many to resignation and habituation, a situation that the hegemonic power takes advantage of to reinforce the idea that no change is possible and that one should not entertain expectations of a society built on different values. The same thing happened back then and Ezekiel expressed it with the image of dry bones ("...they say: Our bones are dried up, and our hope is lost, and we are utterly destroyed..." 37:11); Isaiah calls them deaf and blind ("Hear, you deaf! Look, you blind! Who is blind but my servant?" 42:18-19) because they do not recognize that God is inviting them to rebuild their lives. Jeremiah uses the image of

235

buying a field, something that is done if one trusts in the future and hope, and he says "houses and fields and vineyards will once again be bought in this land" (32:15). In 33:24, God asks the prophet, referring to Judah and Samaria: "Have you not seen what this people say? Two families that Yahweh had chosen, Yahweh has now rejected."

This is the theology that arises from assuming the victim's situation as immovable and as a way of being. One is a victim and a loser and one recognizes the oppressor as the victimizer and the winner. It is the theology that, by not perceiving the dynamism of history and its constant invitation to novelty, ends up reproducing the social and political *status quo* not because it considers it just and desirable but because it considers it inexorable. The problem that the prophetic texts face when they were rewritten and consolidated in the post-exilic period does not reside in the idolatry of corrupt kings and the priests linked to them, nor in false prophets, since the former no longer exist and the latter have lost validity in a subjugated community; the problem resides within the very people of God who, due to their condition as captives, have lost the vision of a liberating God and creator of the future. It is not that they do not want to listen to the prophet, as has been denounced so many times, but that they have lost faith that God wants or can free them from the oppression and humiliation in which they live.

There are numerous texts that reveal this theology of captivity, as well as numerous prophetic texts that denounce it and offer a word that may sometimes seem naïve or unrealizable but which in reality is rooted in the ancient traditions of the desert and God's constant will for justice. Ezekiel 37 denounces this quietist theology, but so does the entire section 40-48 (the description of the rebuilt temple), which must be read as an antidote to a theology of captivity that does not believe that there is a temple ahead in history. However, where it is expressed most clearly is in psalms such as 79 and 137, where the lack of a liberating project in history leads to the feeling of revenge prevailing as a last resort — fallacious, of course — to obtain justice. Psalm 22:1-12 expresses the anguish of feeling that God "is far away" and 44 expresses that God's accompaniment to the patriarchs and matriarchs has ceased and it is perceived that God is asleep and cries out, "Wake up! Why do you sleep?... why do you forget our oppression and our misery?" (vs. 24-25). The feeling is genuine, but the only way not to be trapped in self-victimization is through the construction of a theology that liberates, that opens the horizon to perceive that God's project is beyond our limited gaze.

A Theology of Liberation, A Theology that Liberates

The prophets' distancing from oppressive power, their attentive eye on events and their sensitivity to being interpreters of history led them to formulate a theology of liberation. If in the context of the Pentateuch the theology of liberation is constituted in the relationship between the memory of the exodus from Egypt and the covenant as a legal body that provides social support for its sustainability as a political structure, in the discourse of the prophets liberation is expressed in the link between the Law and present events. For the prophets, the Law is no longer a set of amalgamated elements but a single, solid reality. What was a relationship between parts became a unified reality where liberation from slavery and the giving of the laws are ingredients that constitute the dough with which a single bread is baked. Now the theology of liberation is that which is born from confronting the Law with the event that the prophets have before them.

What stands out in prophetic theology is the intimate conviction that transcendent values are at stake in historical events. What happens today is a sign not only of the future but of the eschatological destiny of each person and of Israel as the people of God. They see the transcendent in the fleeting, what remains in those events that pass but are pregnant with eternity. Their theology affirms that there is a future in history and therefore the prophets look to the future and are convinced that God's project did not end with the destruction of the temple in Jerusalem in the year 587, but neither is God deceived when it was rebuilt and re-inaugurated in the year 515. Neither in the tragedy that immobilizes nor in superficial optimism does prophetic theology find its culmination. The action of God and the divine project of liberation are not reduced to an event or to a privileged time. On the contrary, it is embodied in history and participates in the vicissitudes of human societies, but always preserving a remainder, an ontological plus, that will allow it to be part of the historical process while at the same time being critical of any deification of any social order. It is a theology of liberation, but even more so, it is a theology that liberates.

By questioning the foundations of every system that becomes stagnant and betrays its origins, what the prophet Jeremiah calls "the fidelity of your youth" (2:2) creates the conditions for new historical challenges to have adequate tools to build a renewed theology. For this reason, a theology of liberation can never be dogmatic, because it would die after the first generation when history generates new scenarios. But a theology that liberates is a wealth of theological and social criteria that will be put into action as soon as the people of God perceive that their theology no longer responds to the demands of their time and that they need, for their mission, a renewed reading and a hermeneutics that respond to new challenges.

Hence, the process of the formation of the prophetic books with their fascinating layers of superimposed texts is also a symbol of their own message. It shows a word that never stops being written, a message that is written over and over again in the face of each new event and that seems to have no end. It rescues the past—and for this reason the attribution of new texts to prophets of the past abounds—but does not hesitate to reform its message to give a word that is truly inspiring in the face of the challenges of the present. They are also a symbol of the creative activity of God who does not let the course of history stop and who always surprises with something new and unexpected.

Prophetic discourse feeds two great concerns that come together in the same place. The first is justice, basic and human, which every person, by the mere fact of being a person, has the right to enjoy. In principle, it is not a heavenly justice, but the imperfect and regular justice that people administer. But it happens that the prophet sees in that justice—or in its absence—a sign of the relationship with God and an x-ray of the soul. To violate rights is to deny the identity of the other. It is to not see the image of God in his body. The prophet cries out because what is at stake when facing injustice is the very identity of God, which in the mistreatment of one's neighbor appears as nonexistent or weak. He discovers that only if one does not fear God can one commit a conscious act of injustice. In turn, the prophet is the one who most clearly goes beyond personal acts and denounces what is today called structural injustice, those economic and political structures that give rise to oppression and make injustices persist. Denouncing this dimension led the prophets to prison, exile, and death.[1]

The second is worship. Amos does not accept that people attend the temple with offerings and sacrifices while subjecting the poor to injustice. Micah is scandalized because he sees how the

---

[1]Jeremiah was imprisoned (32-33; 38); Amos was deported (7:12); Uriah was killed by order of the king (Jer 26:20-23).

powerful jealously attend religious services while putting poor farmers in debt to take their lands. Hosea burns with rage when he sees the priests consecrated to officiate the most sacred rites involved in crimes, lies and theft. No one like them denounced that there is no legitimate worship without justice, nor are there valid prayers if one does not love one's neighbor in a real and concrete way. As an extension and logical consequence of this, the prophets are bearers of the most consistent denunciation against idolatry and give their full support to the sovereignty of Yahweh. This proclamation of monotheism is radical and born of experience; Croatto asserts that the prophets do not fight against the cult of Baals because they are monotheists, but that their preaching leads to monotheism to the extent that Israel recognizes that only Yahweh freed them from slavery in Egypt.[1] Therefore, monotheism, far from being a dogma that is imposed on the believer, becomes central to the faith of Israel as a consequence of the historical experience of liberation brought about by a single God. It is the experience of acts of oppression and God's proposal of liberation that is the raw material for defining the content of faith.

The theology of the prophets liberates because it does not allow itself to be caught by the seduction of power—neither the power of the kings of Judah nor later the power that shone seductively in the successive empires. In the development of their ministry, the prophets were not themselves political leaders and they do not seem to have aroused the popular will around their person. In no case did their life project consist of leading a social revolt, but rather they worked to create the conditions that would make evident the causes of economic inequalities and the decline of faith. Their discourse is theological—which seems obvious to say but it is necessary to emphasize it—and has strong political consequences, but, at its root, it is not a political discourse. It is a proclamation of the Word and its goal is the conversion of the sinner; and if this does not happen it calls out or confidently awaits the intervention of God.[2] Prophetic theology will encourage social dynamics and will not deny them because it feels that the first fruits of what is to come are present there.

---

[1] S. Croatto, *Liberación y Libertad* (Buenos Aires: Mundo Nuevo, 1973), 80; this is a foundational work whose value and depth have not been diminished by the passage of time.

[2] S. Croatto, *Liberación y Libertad*, 90.

The Word that Comes from the Depths
The Theology of the Psalms

The Bible Hymnal: Song and Prayer

In the three-part division of the Hebrew Bible (*Torah, Neviim* and *Ketubim*), Psalms presides over the third, and from that position it sets the tone for the rest of the books grouped there. There is a significant element in this: while in the Pentateuch and in the prophets the text is presented as if it were God who speaks and addresses the people, in the psalms it is the human voice that dominates the texts. In the Pentateuch, we saw how a theology that is expressed through stories reveals the will of God and proposes a path that human beings can follow or resign themselves to, or can choose to meditate on and postpone a decision; in the prophets we find that their voice is understood as the almost distanceless mediation of the same voice of God who manifests the divine will through the men and women God calls together. Later we will see that, in the wisdom texts, it is the voice of a one who addresses brothers and sisters in a horizontal manner. But in the psalms there is a shift in perspective: it is the human voice that calls out to God, cries out for help, expresses its gratitude, tells of its anguish and trusts in God's response.

If the image is appropriate, we can say that if through Moses and the prophets the word of God "comes down" to the people so that they may receive it and act on it, in the psalms the human word "rises" to them as a prayer of whoever or those who know that there is someone there who will receive it. In no other text, like in the psalms, is the word of God presented as that word that comes from the depths of human beings.[1] And in no other genre is that word that comes from the depths of the soul better expressed than in poetry. In 45:1 the author presents himself with this credential: "My tongue is the pen of a skilled writer." By saying tongue (Heb. *lashon*) he reveals the character of a work to be recited, declaimed aloud in prayer or song; But then he warns us that the poem has become a written text and that the author is a quality poet who knows his craft. What is said here about this psalm undoubtedly applies to the entire collection.

---

[1] N. Sarna, *Song of the Heart* (New York: Schocken Books, 1993), 1-2.

The book is divided into five parts that emulate the division of the Pentateuch. If in the Talmudic conception the Pentateuch was written in its entirety by Moses, this new collection of psalms that emulates that *Torah* has King David as its author.[1] We know that both Moses and David are not the material authors of the works, but the attribution has theological consequences in both cases that should not escape our reading.[2] On the one hand, the attribution to David explains the human-like language of the poems; on the other hand, the same attribution grants them a value as Scripture that only the most beloved king could grant them. It is a hermeneutical resource, and it does not cause any conflict that many of the titles of the psalms attribute the authorship to Solomon (72; 127), to the sons of Asaph (50), to the sons of Korah (42-49), even a psalm points out Moses himself as the author (90); The Psalms are "David's" because it is a theological affirmation that grants the work the seal of authenticity that eliminates all suspicion in the face of a text whose human condition is undeniable. Attributing the psalms to the beloved king blesses them and avoids all discussion about their condition as texts that must be treasured as part of the Word of God, even when their verses are human to the core. In this way, it also allows us to glimpse that all Scripture is the word of God created through the human word, which reveals the richness and mystery of the incarnation of an eternal God who agrees to be known and represented by weak and contingent words. This, which is true for all Scripture, is made evident in the Psalms, although it is usually partially veiled in many texts. When the poorest, those who suffer injustice, those who suffer an absurd illness cry out in the Psalms, their words are not only an expression of their personal anguish but also privileged spokesmen for God. God speaks through his pain as God speaks through a prophet and wants that word to be understood as another instrument through which the divine will is communicated with human beings.

We note that each of the five parts concludes with a doxology (41:14; 72:18-19; 89:53; 106:48; 150) that reveals the ultimate character of the collection as a work of praise and

---

[1] Thus says a medieval Talmudic source: "…just as Moses gave the five books of the Law to Israel, so David gave the five books of the Psalms to Israel…," see W. Braude, *Midrash on Psalms* (New Haven: Yale University Press, 1959), I, 5.

[2] We expound the importance of the theological conception that points to Moses as the semiotic author of the Pentateuch in P. R. Andiñach, *Introducción hermenéutica al Antiguo Testamento* (Estella: Verbo Divino, 2012), 63-64; the same can be said of David in relation to the Psalms.

exaltation of the glory of God. At the same time, it also highlights its condition as an organized work that follows a scheme orchestrated by the editor. Psalms 1 and 2 are introductory and show a sapiential bias: "Blessed is the one who does not walk in the counsel of the wicked or the way of sinners..." (1:1); Psalm 2 concludes in this way: "Now, you kings, be wise; take warning, you judges of the Earth. Serve Yahweh with fear... Blessed are all who trust in him" (2:11-12). With this language that urges meditation and trust, the reader is introduced to the entire book. At the other extreme, Psalm 150 is a doxology that closes the fifth book but also concludes the entire collection of psalms. This final exaltation and praise of Yahweh, which begins with Psalm 145, is a theological conclusion that affirms the unconditional acceptance of the greatness and wisdom of God. In the psalms we find much passion and anguish, but the final word will always be praise. Does this structure not suggest that ultimately the sorrows of life that the psalms abundantly recount should lead the believer to the recognition of the greatness of God? We understand that this is so, but in the same way that a New Testament theology that celebrates the news of the resurrection must not ignore the tragedy of the cross, the conviction that in the psalms the community of faith is called to praise and gratitude to God cannot be done by hiding the deep anguish of life expressed in its poems. On the contrary, this praise has a much deeper meaning because it is born from the experience of injustice, from the absurdity of pain, and from what is sometimes perceived as God's silence toward them.

It is necessary to pause to consider the theology present in the title of the book. In our language, Psalms comes from the Greek *psalmoi* or *psalterion*, which refers to the stringed musical instrument that is assumed to have accompanied the psalms. In Hebrew, they are called *tehilim*, which means "songs of praise," a word whose linguistic field shows it related to words such as prayer, worship, and the Hebrew *hallelujah*, which means "we praise Yahweh." Psalms is the hymnal of the Old Testament, the book where the songs and prayers that were recited in the temple or repeated at home were grouped together, and as with our current hymnals, when organizing the book, very old and other recent songs were grouped together, words of gratitude and supplication, songs for particular occasions and others more general, local songs and others that came from far away lands. In turn, various musical instruments are mentioned in them, such as the harp (33:2; 57:8), the lyre (33:2; 43:4), the horn (47:5; 98:6) which was used more to give notice or to call the assembly than as a musical instrument; the flute (150:4), the cymbal (150:4), and a kind of small drum (149:3; 150:4). This diversity of both concepts and musical instruments should not be understood as casual but rather as a sign of the capacity to absorb different languages and traditions and fuse them into a new and same theology. Diversity is celebrated in the psalms in a textual way, in their very literary constitution, and this, far from disaggregating the faith, helps to outline a thought that values the experience of what is different but at the same time integrates it within the same perspective. The diversity of voices is a theological value and therefore contributes to the unity of thought.

The Poetic Word: The Aesthetic as a Message

The fact that the author of Psalm 45 considers himself a good poet lets us know that the psalms were conceived as works of art, as literary pieces. They are not the simple transcription of spontaneous prayers but the product of the delicate work of an artist who, as such, knows that words skillfully interwoven create beauty, and this contributes to accessing dimensions of human experience that are not reached by plain language. But it is necessary to point out from the beginning that it would be unfair to consider that only Psalms resorts to beauty to strengthen its message. There is no doubt that this is the case in the psalms, but extensive parts of the prophetic books are also written in good poetry and at the same time there are psalms and songs of fine workmanship present in the narrative books (Ex 15; Dt 32; Judg 5; Jo 2; 1 Sam 2 and many others). In reality, the Book of Psalms stands out because it is full of poetry and because the psalms face the world in its entirety and therefore combine a great diversity of themes. This distinguishes it from other poetic books that focus on one theme or perspective: the Song of Songs expounds the erotic experience; Job the meaning of human suffering; Ecclesiastes explores the ephemeral nature of life; Proverbs offers wise perspectives on everyday life. Psalms, on the other hand, cannot be classified into a single genre or theme because they encompass a range of personal and collective life experiences.

What characterizes the psalms as literature is their commitment to poetic language.[1] Although there is much written

---

[1] On the poetic language of the Psalms we would like to mention the work of B. Green, *Like a Tree Planted* (Collegeville: Liturgical Press, 1997), 9-23, where the author makes an analysis of the poetic language and explores in particular the use of metaphors; J. D. Pleins makes a reading that takes into account

about what defines poetic language, here we describe it with three elements: first, as that form of language that seeks the beauty of saying, the aesthetic. Second, that this aesthetic condition is an integral part of the message, not a mere ornament. The third is that, unlike prose, which develops over time, poetry is timeless and is consumed in the moment. The first two characteristics also apply to prose texts, where the beauty of the narrative or the plot plays an important role in shaping the message. However, in relation to these two, poetry also has its own codes. The repetition of a concept that would be boring in prose is an opportunity to create a climate that deepens the message in poetry. The multiplication of images and symbols that would delay and even make the narrative in prose, particularly the tight Semitic prose, burdensome, are essential raw material in the poetic text because they refer to those experiences that cannot be expressed with the rationality of a narrative. There is in the psalms what has been called an eroticism of the text, an approach to the exposition of an experience in such a way that it places beauty — which has no rational explanation, it is only perceived and enjoyed — as a privileged actor in the reading.[1] This non-rational element that poetic language provides creates a space for the meaning of the text to manifest itself.

The third element is specific to poetic language. While prose narration assumes the passage of time because it "tells" something that happens or happened at a given moment and that something narrated had a beginning and an end, or at least a development in the timeline, the language of poetry happens in the instant, it cannot be "told," it is by definition timeless. The depth of its message is achieved not by the growing progress of a situation that is narrated nor by the information it offers to the reader who finds out about this or that event and its development

---

the poetic in *The Psalms* (New York: Maryknoll, 1993); also see L. Alonso Schökel, *Treinta Salmos* (Madrid: Cristiandad, 1980), 24-34.

[1] The concept of the eroticism of the text belongs to Susan Sontag, and she presents it in *Against Interpretation and Other Essays* (New York: Farrar, Straus & Giroux, 1966); in Spanish (*Contra la interpretación*) there are several editions of this complete work or of the essay in question. In this essay she argues for reading with greater sensitivity toward the text (which she considers in a broad sense: literary work, painting, theatre, cinema, etc.) as an object of art and expresses her complaint about the excessive rationalization that requires identifying "a meaning," which Sontag characterizes as typical of interpretation when it ignores the pleasure inherent in the mere contemplation of the object. In our opinion — and contrary to Sontag — the "erotics of the text" contributes to the creation of meaning and the text is capable of being interpreted without falling into unnecessary rationalizations.

(think of the stories of the patriarchs and matriarchs, of Jonah or of Esther) but by the investigation into the life experience that the author wants to share and exposes in a timeless space, where metaphor, wordplay and repetition create the climate that leads to the message. This timelessness gives poetry a particular universal bias because, in the same way that it exhibits this condition, it records a real, concrete human experience that was felt in the flesh and blood of the person who suffered it. In the poetry of the psalms, their timelessness does not dehumanize them, but on the contrary, transforms them into incorruptible witnesses of all pain and suffering, of all gratitude and praise. Whoever reads them today joins their voice to that of a brother or sister more than two millennia away and perceives the solidarity that the same feeling generates.

The lament of a persecuted person becomes that of all those who live in fear:

...Yahweh my God, in you I have put my trust; save me from all who persecute me... (7:2)
... The Lord is my light and my salvation; whom shall I fear?
Yahweh is the strength of my life; of whom shall I be afraid?
When the wicked gathered against me, my enemies and my tormentors
To eat my flesh, they stumbled and fell... (27:1-2)

The cry of a sick person is a word that resonates in every sick person who feels their life threatened:

I said, "Have mercy on me, O Lord;
Heal my soul, for I have sinned against you.
My enemies speak evil of me, and ask:
When will he die and his name perish? (41:4-5)

Those who suffer from loneliness and anguish can identify with these words:

I cried to the Lord in my distress, and he answered me.
Deliver my soul, O Yahweh, from lying lips,
And of the deceitful tongue. (120:1-2)

Gratitude for blessings echoes the gratitude of other times and latitudes:

...I will praise you, O Yahweh, with my whole heart;
I will tell all your wonders.
I will be glad and rejoice in you;
I will sing to your name, O Most High. (9:1-2)

The prayer of the oppressed is the cry of all the oppressed:

How long will the wicked, how long, O Yahweh, will the wicked rejoice?

How long will you speak arrogant words,
And all the workers of iniquity will boast?
They have crushed your people, O Lord, and afflicted your
inheritance.
They kill the widow and the foreigner, and they slay the
orphans. (94:3-6)

The effect of understanding in successive future contexts the message that was conceived in a particular one is the same hermeneutical process that is present in all biblical texts; we have already pointed out that the validity of the biblical message is the product of this process of rereading that always renews the meaning for the reader. But in poetic texts in general and in the psalms in particular, this identification between the text of the past and the situation of the reader of all times is present in the very skin of the text.

The God Who Is *(El Dios que está)* Far Away: The Silence of God

The experience of marginality, of inexplicable poverty, of the proximity of death due to absurd causes has been present in times past as it is today in our society. Those who are sensitive to pain have always experienced this situation as an act of injustice, as something that should not be that way, because there is no justification for hunger or violence against the innocent. People do not come into the world to suffer anguish or to destroy their bodies in heavy and meaningless work. Numerous psalms tell of people who suffered in this way and who, from that situation, raised their prayer to the one they considered was the only one who could understand their anguish and listen to them; but various psalms testify that the expected response was not heard and that those who prayed did not always receive strength in their anguish. It is at that moment that what is perceived is the silence of God.

This distressing experience of a God who remains silent has disturbed many throughout history and has been a cause for reflection. It is the question of understanding a God who allows the genocides of the 20th century to happen or of questioning his silence in the face of what seems to be the meaninglessness of the life that led and leads many people to disillusionment and resignation. From philosophers and poets to anonymous people have felt this emptiness of God in the moments of greatest need for him. This is how the poet César Vallejo expresses it in the poem *The Black Heralds*.[1]

> There are blows in life, so harsh... I don't know!
> Blows like God's wrath; like before them,
> the backwash of all that has been suffered
> was embedded in the soul... I don't know!

Or as in the *Oración de un desocupado* from the poet Juan Gelman:[2]

> Father
> From the heavens come down, if you are, come down then,
> I'm starving on this street corner
> that I don't know what good it is to have been born,
> That looked at my rejected hands,
> that there is no work, there is not,
> Get down a little, contemplate
> This that I am, this broken shoe,
> This anguish, this empty stomach,
> This city without bread for my teeth, the fever
> digging my flesh (...)

What surprises us is that there are psalms that bear witness to a similar experience.[3] In them, the experience of suffering is presented at a personal or collective level and they are a verbalization of that which is eating away at the psalmist's insides. Psalm 10 is an impressive example of a plea from someone who perceives God as distant at the moment he needs him most. It is the moment of anguish and, even though he seeks him out, he feels that he is hiding from him. As happens with all the biblical texts where dismay is expressed at God's inaction, the author does not lean toward atheism but toward something that may be even more terrible, which is the intimate conviction that God intentionally distances the divine self from him and seems indifferent to his suffering. He asks:

> Why are you far away, Yahweh,
> and you hide yourself in the time of trouble? (10:1)

Can this question arise from any other source than the deepest uneasiness before the God from whom we expect protection and justice? This leads us to think that the psalms were not written to justify God but to testify with complete crudeness the human experience before the creator. This anguish expressed in the question becomes more radical when the sufferer perceives

---

[1]The work of the Peruvian poet César Vallejo (1892-1938) expresses this anguish in a radical and beautiful way in numerous poems.

[2]Juan Gelman (1930-2014) was an Argentine poet who was awarded the Cervantes Prize in 2007.

[3]See Psalm 10; 13; 22:1-22; 27:8-14; 28:1-5; 42; 60; 69; 70-71; 77; 88; 89; 102; 142.

that the oppressor (Heb. *rasha'* evil, impious, enemy, criminal) has no interest in the things of God; the one who oppresses him mocks God:

> With arrogance the evil one pursues the poor...
> For the oppressor boasts of the desire of his soul,
> blesses the greedy and despises Yahweh.
> The oppressor, in his pride, does not seek God;
> God is not in their thoughts. (10:2-4)

The persecuted person (v. 2) cannot understand how God forgets them and allows those who exercise violence against them to prosper in their acts. However, they find an answer in their inner self when they meditates on the distance of God who lives high in heaven, far from evil. God seems to say to them with Juan Gelman "come down" and expresses it with all irony when God says:

> Your judgments on high are far from him (10:5).
> Later he will say what the oppressor thinks of his own crimes:
> God has forgotten; he has covered his face; he will never see him. (10:11)

It is impossible not to see in this Psalm, and in particular in these last two quotations, a judgment on God that is reversed into a judgment on all theology that ignores human anguish. God is questioned because, by remaining high in heaven, God's words and judgments, so celebrated in worship and in a multitude of psalms, do not make a dent in the oppressor's practice. God is "high" when what really matters happens here on Earth. And the worshipper questions God by saying that God's judgments should serve to stop the violence the worshipper suffers in his own body or else they seem useless and incomprehensible. Those who suffer injustice have no time for meditation or to consider strategies; they cry out and demand a response to their situation because they have the right to do so.

In v. 11, which we quoted above, the worshipper puts into the mouth of the oppressor what may be the worshipper's own suspicion: God is absent, God does not see injustice. This is the contemporary position of those who consider that there is a creator God but that God has ignored human fate or was never interested in it. It is the image of a God who, after six days of laborious creation, lay down to rest on the seventh day and continues to rest, asleep, without being interested in the fate of the universe God created.

We could say that the psalm, insofar as it questions God for the divine silence, also questions those who do theology without taking into account the place of the one who suffers. And if the pain and injustice of the persecuted transcend all times, its criticism also applies to theologies of all times. Jorge Pixley has expressed this with great clarity in his book on Job.[1] Pixley points out that the theology of Job's friends is academic, formal, undoubtedly orthodox, but it has no answer for those who suffer a radical injustice in their lives because in this way of theological thinking, human suffering is not considered an offense to God. What's more, Job's friends distrust his integrity. It is a theology purified of the human, which believes itself to be heavenly and devoted to the "things of God" although in reality it has distanced itself from God because any theology that in the face of pain and injustice does not incline in favor of the victim will express the voice of a God who is not the one who frees the oppressed and opens the door for the repentance of the oppressor. It will be a theology that will say nothing significant and will not respond to the needs of the liberation of the oppressed or the oppressor; and that with its indifference to pain and injustice will only contribute to perpetuating them.

In Psalm 10, those who suffer do not receive an answer, but their faith sustains them because, even without understanding God's ways, they trust that God is on their side. The last verse expresses the wish that what they have suffered should not be suffered by anyone else, and they do so from the place of pain that has not ceased. It is wonderful to see how, from anguish, one can also clearly see the origin of oppression:

> You strengthen the heart of the humble, and your ear is attentive,
> so that no more will man commit violence on Earth. (12:18)

The God Who is (*El Dios que está*) Near: The Encounter with God

When God reveals the divine identity to Moses in Ex 3:14, God says to him "I am the one who is," and God confirms it in verse 15 where God reinforces the divine will to be with God's people. At the same time, God calls them for a mission, a way of telling them that the divine presence will not be incidental but that it has a specific purpose for their lives and that of the slaves. In this statement, God makes evident God's own condition as the one who accompanies the people and is attentive to their destiny. The meaning of the name given in 3:14 should not be reduced to a play on words or an enigmatic phrase because what the story tries to

---

[1] J. Pixley, *The Book of Job* (San José, Costa Rica: SEBILA, 1982).

give us is the true identity of God and not an expression that leaves us confused. This presence of God where God is needed has also been an experience of the believing people throughout the centuries that has been captured in numerous texts of different kinds within the Old Testament. When we refer to the psalms, we see that many of them bear witness to this profound experience of "the God who is" (*El Dios que está*). A superficial reading might lead one to think that these psalms contradict those presented in the previous section. However, if we delve deeper into them, we see that the former express the same search for God that we find in these psalms, with the difference that while the former show the moment of anguish and the silence of God, the ones presented here refer to the encounter and perception of the response of the divinity. In both cases, there is a cry for help and in both cases, a particular way of relating to God is perceived.

There is anguish in the words of Psalm 3 as the psalmist says:

> Oh Yahweh, how greatly have my enemies multiplied!
> Many are those who rise up against me
> and they say about my life:
> "There is no salvation from God for him." (3:1)

To then say:

> With my voice I cried to Yahweh,
> And he answered me from his holy mountain. (3:4)

The speaker points out that his enemies are thousands and that they announce that God will not be there to save him (v. 3). With extreme beauty, the poem expresses the tranquility of the persecuted with the images of "I lay down and slept, and I awoke, for Yahweh sustained me." The moment of sleep is when persons cannot protect themselves and lose control of what happens around them; it is the moment of greatest vulnerability. The fear of dying during sleep or of not waking up because of being killed while sleeping is put aside due to the security of God's sustenance. The basis of such security is based on the testimony of having been heard by God and having received a concrete answer expressed in the words "and he answered me." Psalm 4 continues with the testimony of the God who answers the cry but not without first establishing that the relationship with God is complex and does not arise naturally as a simple response to a request. The psalm begins with words of supplication:

> Answer me when I call, O God of my righteousness.
> When I was in distress, you gave me a place;
> Have mercy on me, and hear my prayer.

Then he points out the superficiality of the lie and affirms that "Yahweh has chosen the godly; Yahweh hears when I call upon him." This game of demanding an answer and then affirming that God hears the voice of the one who cries out must be understood as the dynamics of meaning proper to poetic discourse that does not follow the laws of regular logic. It is what John Day calls "certainty of being heard" when analyzing the theology of the psalms and their condition of prayer that accepts the presence of God, even in desperation.[1] It is not a saying and unsaying but a literary way of creating a climate and then resolving it by announcing its opposite and thus highlighting the protective action of God.

Psalm 23 follows the one that begins with "My God, my God, why have you forsaken me? Why are you so far from my salvation and from the words of my cry?" (22:1). The succession is not accidental and thus the words of 23:1 sound even more powerful: "Yahweh is my shepherd, I shall not want." In verse 4, it uses an uncommon Hebrew expression: *tzalmavet*. We translate it as "shadow of death" because it is a compound word that brings together the two ideas of gloom and death. It deserves our attention because in Hebrew there are few compound words that are not proper names and we find *tzalmavet* seven times in Job and a couple more in the prophets. In Job, it has the meaning of a place where death reigns, a territory from which there is no return (Job 10:22; 12:22; 16:16; 24:17; 34:22; 38:17). It is striking that in five instances it appears in Job's mouth to describe his own situation of suffering and anguish comparable only to life in *Sheol*, the place of the dead; and Yahweh also uses it (38:17) to describe death and the world of shadows. In Is 9:1 there is talk of a "land of the shadow of death" to describe the desperate state of the people of Israel before announcing the imminent arrival of a liberating child. In light of this use of the word *tzalmavet*, what is interesting to note about the theology of Psalm 23 is that it is the only text that uses this word to describe the condition of the place one passes through (a "valley") where shadow and death prevail, but at the same time to say that one passes through it with tranquility and without fear. Only in this psalm do *tzalmavet* and the protective presence of God come together:

> Even though I walk through the valley of the shadow of
> death (*tzalmavet*)
> I will fear no evil, for you are with me.

---

[1]J. Day, *Psalms* (Sheffield: Sheffield Academic Press, 1993), 30-32.

Your rod and your staff, they comfort me (23:4).

Fearlessness does not come from the walker's strength or courage, but from the certainty of God's company. The experience of God who is near is expressed with great depth in this psalm, in which not even passing close to death puts at risk the trust in God's saving presence. We find the same game of denying and then revealing in 6:7-9:

Every night I flood my bed with tears. I water my bed with tears.

My eyes are worn out from suffering;

They have grown old because of all my troubles.

Depart from me, all you workers of iniquity;

for Yahweh has heard my cry.

The LORD has heard my supplication; the LORD has accepted my prayer.

First, the psalmist's weeping and anguish are described; then, it is stated that God has heard his cry and his prayer. Those who harass him will have to turn away from him because God has rebelled as the one who is at his side. It is the God "who is" who allows those who suffer persecution or are humiliated to continue their lives and have hope that God will finally do justice to their cause.

The God who reveals the divine self in the psalms is also the God of concrete and effective presence in the personal life of the believer. There are many examples: Ps 3; 4; 6; 23; 46; 80; 89; 91; 130. Ps 139 is a poem that uses enumeration and mentions the aspects where God is near: on the road, in sleep, in the heavens and in *Sheol*, in the sea, in thought, in the mother's womb. To such an extent that it makes him exclaim with joy: "Where shall I go to flee from your presence?" (v. 7). The intimate conviction that God accompanies does not lead to conceiving it as a presence that leads to delegating human responsibilities to divine action or that assumes that God will solve problems. Nor is it a theology that proclaims an easy life for the believer. On the contrary, the experience of God's company arises after a sometimes anguishing search to find God and to hear God's word.

The Righteous and the Wicked as Social Categories

It is no coincidence that the Book of Psalms opens with a psalm that establishes the opposition between the righteous and the wicked. It ends with the sentence, "For Yahweh knows the way of the righteous; but the path of the wicked he will destroy" (1:6) and from that moment on the successive psalms will resort to this distinction again and again, although they do so using other words. Along with the righteous (*tzadik* and its plural *tzadikim*) we also find the pious, the saints, which translate the word *chasid* and its plural *chasidim* used in numerous psalms to refer to those who remain loyal to the faith and have mercy on their neighbor (12:1; 16:10; 18:25). This term is not common outside the psalms and the few times it appears (Is 57:1; Mic 7:2) it coincides with the sense of a faithful, just, upright person or group. Along with these are also the *ani* (oppressed), the *anawim* (poor) and *'ebiyon* (poor, needy). These concepts refer, in the first instance, to poverty and material oppression, to those who do not have what is necessary for a dignified life or are exploited in their work, and therefore must be considered to express social categories. And although it may have derived at a later moment in an idea of spiritual poverty and not necessarily economic, a plethora of texts leaves no doubt about their condition of being marginalized from the social system. Thus we see them in 35:10; 41:1; 49:2; 82:3-4; 112:9; 113:7; 132:15. From their situation of anguish due to poverty they cry out to God for justice and protection and trust that their word will be heard and their situation understood. It says in 40:18 (repeated in 70:5):

Even though I am oppressed (*ani*) and poor (*'ebiyon*),
Yahweh will think of me.

You are my help and my deliverer; O God, do not delay.

The certainty that he is addressing his liberator (from the root *palat*, to free, to escape) does not inhibit the psalmist from calling for God's swift action, since his situation can no longer be tolerated. He asks God not to delay divine liberation, just as in other cases he urges God with imperative verbs to carry out the divine will in his defense without delay (109:21-22).

The psalms contrast the wicked with these poor and pious people. The word *rashah* (wicked) and its plural *reshaim* (which we translate as "wicked" or "evil") do not refer in the first instance to a certain group of people as if it were a religious sect, but to those who oppose the liberating will of God and trample on the rights of others for their own benefit. However, in the particular context of Israelite society, it refers to the ruling class that oppresses those who work for them. They are the doers of injustice, those who do not listen to Yahweh, and those who, driven by this social rapacity, bow before other gods who seem more benevolent to their practices. When *rashah* is applied to those outside of Israel, it refers to foreign enemies insofar as they are nations that oppress or oppressed Israel, as is evident from Psalm 9:5:

You rebuked the nations, you destroyed the wicked (*rashah*).

There are other possible interpretations that have been attempted, such as that the wicked refer to sorcerers (14:4) or to those who were outside the covenant and worshipped other gods, but this possibility does not fit with the evident relationship of opposition that exists between the righteous and the wicked in the context of the same social and religious space. If they were only foreigners, they could not cry out to the God of Israel for protection because in those times it was not thought that the God of a people could exercise authority over a neighboring nation; if they were sorcerers and witches, there would not be so much to say or cry out because the same Israelite law condemns them with complete clarity. The righteous and the wicked are two actors who need each other so that the written discourse is coherent with the social reality that it seeks to testify to. Both terms are presented as theological categories, but they reflect two social categories that act as the faces of the same coin: the oppressor and the oppressed.

In this opposition, we see a profound theological affirmation that is, to a large extent, exclusive to the psalms. As a human word that rises to God it cannot fail to leave its mark on the text and consequently bequeaths us the intimate conviction that every material need, every empty stomach and every hurt life is an affront to God whose perpetrators, by virtue of being so, become God's enemies. The wicked and the impious (*reshaim*) are so because they have acted in opposition to the will of God by exercising their power against their brothers, condemning them to poverty and marginality. The political and social oppression that in other texts of the Old Testament is presented as an aggression against the law of God is here presented in a poetic language that, far from resorting to the legal, prefers the realm of experience and gives way to the voice of the victim. From that place, the oppressed does not see in his victimizer a social adversary or a person who has had better fortune in the distribution of goods and power; he sees his aggressor as someone who has no mercy and as an enemy of God. For the psalmist's theology, the wicked are persons who let themselves be carried away by their desires of excess and rapacity and who, in order to satisfy those desires, do not consider the harm they inflict on others. Poverty seen from the perspective of the theology of the psalms, whatever its social or historical explanation, is always unjust and unacceptable.

Our time is not given to this kind of characterization. Poverty is a statistical fact — often distorted to hide its dimension — unfortunate for some and inevitable for others. For some, it is an undesirable consequence of the economic system. For others, an opportunity to exercise piety toward the poor. However, today we know that oppression and injustice are political acts and respond to social dynamics that are consolidated or combated in the evolution of those same social dynamics. We would do a disservice to biblical interpretation if we wanted to oppose it to the social analysis of injustice, as is done today with sociological and economic tools; the only thing that would be achieved is to marginalize faith and theological reflection from social events and their dynamics. The biblical testimony itself interprets that God's action is carried out in history and through human instruments, and in most cases it analyzes historical facts and considers that the divine presence acts invisibly behind or within visible events. Now, having said this and affirmed it with determination, it is necessary to take into consideration that the theology of ancient Israel did not subsume people into the social conglomerate as if they had no identity or conscience. Poverty and wealth were social realities, but the poor and the rich were people who were aware of their place and were responsible for their decisions.

The rich are spoken to in order to warn them of the painful situation they find themselves in before the eyes of God. The psalmist at one point confesses having envied the wicked and their wealth ("when he saw the prosperity of the wicked," Ps 73:3) but then he saw the emptiness of that project and he declares about them almost with pity for their fragile destiny:

> They say: How does God know? Is there knowledge in the
> Most High?
> Here are these wicked people, without caring about others,
> they accumulated wealth.
> (Ps 73:19)

In another text he will construct an antithetical parallelism between the value of the righteous and the association of wealth and sin:

> Better is a little from the righteous,
> Than the riches of many sinners. (Ps 37:16)

The righteous and the wicked, the poor and the rich, are recognized as people who can (and should) be confronted with their social responsibilities. For Old Testament theology, the two do not occupy the same place in the social dynamic and, as in other themes, biblical thought does not remain silent about this reality. The abundance of a few in contrast to the scarcity of the majority is, for Old Testament theology in general and for the psalms in particular, an unjust social act and a product of sin. It says:

> The wicked arrogantly persecutes the poor (10:2).

The Liberating Will of God

The psalms have their own way of expressing God's liberating will. Poetry has different resources from prose discourse. In the latter, the narrative that unfolds over a period of time prevails and usually involves a variety of actors; in contrast, poetry is always urgent and stripped of characters, where there is usually only one voice, at most two. It is also by its nature more intimate; if a battle is narrated in prose, it will be done without mentioning the people involved or without speaking about their lives, but in poetry it is very likely that the same event will be given space to the words of a warrior, his anguish at the risk of dying and his hope of coming out alive. We see this in Psalm 18:33-36 where the psalmist expresses his gratitude for receiving strength in combat, a skillful hand for the bow and the assurance that God is his shield. Or in 144:1-2 where he says:

> The Lord guides my hands in battle, and my fingers in war;
> My mercy and my fortress, my fortress and my deliverer,
> my shield, in whom I trust.

For the warrior in battle, liberation consists of being protected by God, in God not allowing him to lose his life in the fight. The shield and the fortress (two images typical of the war world) are in this poem the presence of God, who protects the fighter and gives him the confidence he needs to know he is free from this essential fear.

In the psalms, the vocation of the God of Israel to free human beings from their bonds is presented in the various dimensions of experience. They bear witness to the God who frees us from the fear of death and its corollaries: loneliness, anguish, feeling disoriented ("… you who raise me from the gates of death" 9:13; 18:4-5; 33:16; 48:14). There are psalms that express this will in the social and political sphere where God shows the divine self on the side of the oppressed, giving them hope ("The oppressed will see and rejoice" 69:32; 145:14); in many of these cases, it is also a discourse that seeks to be concrete and for this reason the expectation of justice does not remain in mere words and is based on the liberating antecedents in the time of Egypt (78:12). On other occasions, and encompassing the above in a broader discourse, the overcoming of sin and God's vocation to free the human being from his bonds is announced (32:5; "Wash me thoroughly from my iniquity, and cleanse me from my sin" 51:2).

Liberation from death is presented in many psalms, also in a perspective that is unique to them. It refers neither to the violent death of war nor to the inexorable fact of leaving the world of the living, but to the anguish of living in Sheol, the place of the dead where God is not and where no one there praises God. *Sheol* is *not* a place of reward or punishment, but it is the abode of those who have died and lead a ghostly life far from God; in 6:5 it says it with total clarity: "In *Sheol,* who will praise you?" Psalm 16:9-11 tells of the joy of knowing that one's life will not end in *Sheol* but that "you will show me the path of life." This opposition between *Sheol* as the place of residence of the dead and the abundance of life that God offers is an important theological step. There are those who have wanted to see in these passages an allusion to the theological concept of eternal life and try to unite the promise of not inhabiting that place of misfortune with the still rudimentary affirmation of the existence of a place of eternal reward. But it does not seem that this affirmation can be sustained since *Sheol,* although an unpleasant place, supposes a kind of eternity in the state of the soul, given that, there, existence is not consumed or degraded. In truth, the opposition is not between *sheol* and eternal life but between a grey and empty existence in the place of the dead and another where the soul praises Yahweh and celebrates divine protection. In these texts that allude to what happens after physical death, what is at stake is the believer's impossibility of recognizing and praising God if he is to inhabit *Sheol forever*. The psalmist does not conceive of himself without the possibility of giving thanks and celebrating God in praise, something that in his conception only the living can do. Unlike Greek rationality, which in order to persevere in praise should postulate the need for eternal physical life, Semitic thought does not get stuck with that question and only affirms that in death there will be no place for praise and leaves it in the hands of God to resolve how this will be made possible.

Death is also the triumph of the righteous over political "enemies." These can be divided in the psalms into three types: local oppressors, conquerors who dominated Israel, and the rulers of Babylon during the exile.[1] It is not always possible to identify which of the types a psalm refers to, but regardless of the original reference, the enemy is always both the psalmist's and God's enemy. In 30:2, the psalmist says:

...you did not allow my enemies to rejoice over me.
Yahweh, my God, I cried to you, and you healed me.

---

[1]To expand on this aspect see J. D. Pleins, *The Social Visions of the Hebrew Bible* (Louisville: Westminster Press, 2001), 428.

O Yahweh, you have brought my soul up from *Sheol*;
You gave me life, so that I would not go down to the grave.

In Psalm 49:14, death is personified and mentioned as the guide of the lives of people who boast of their riches toward *Sheol*. They are described as those who trust in their material power and it is said that although they believe that this power can redeem them (v. 7), they do not know that it is death itself that leads them to the end:

They are led like flocks to *Sheol*; death will shepherd them...

The rich and powerful—like the oppressed—will not be able to escape this human destiny, but it is said that they will reach their final days convinced that nothing will happen to them; the poem compares the rich and proud to animals who know nothing of the destiny that awaits them: "They behave like beasts" (49:20). There is vanity in their lives, but this will be forgotten from the moment they settle down with the other dead. Having said this, the psalm then establishes that the descent into the shadows is not the only possibility, since it is in God's hands to prevent the righteous from being sent there and for their life and days to be rescued. As in the previous case, it is hoped that God will offer an alternative that mere rational thought cannot glimpse. Faced with the proximity of death, Psalm 116:6 does not hesitate to affirm that "Yahweh cares for the weak. I was prostrate and he saved me." Salvation in this case means liberation from death and oppression.

It is striking to see that in the psalms based on the history of Israel, the acts of God in freeing God's people from oppression are given priority, but their hardships are not described. The sufferings of slavery, which was the central point of the narratives in Exodus, do not seem to have aroused interest in the psalms. Psalms 78 and 106 describe the history from the time of Egypt, but speak of Israel's rebellions and their disagreements with God as those acts that motivated their liberating action and their leadership through the desert to the promised land. But nothing is said about the anguish and oppression to which they were subjected during slavery. There is nothing similar in these psalms to Ex 3:7, where God's action is presented as a response to the cry of the slaves; On the contrary, in the psalms built on the history of Israel (77; 78; 105; 106; 114; 136) God is moved to act to rescue a people who have sinned, who have built altars to foreign gods, who have forgotten the divine covenant. Psalm 105:25 gives the origin of the oppression of the Egyptians as an act of God and not as the greed of Pharaoh and his desire for profit (Ex 5:6-14). It says that after multiplying them in Egypt, God "...changed their [the

Egyptians'] heart to hate God's people, to think evil against God's servants..." In Psalm 136, which is a thanksgiving for God's accompaniment in the history of Israel, the exodus from Egypt is included but without mentioning the slavery or the suffering of the Israelites.

We believe that there are at least three reasons for this silence. The first is formal and has to do with the fact that poetry does not feel comfortable with narratives. Although there are some and of high literary quality, it is not the strong point of the genre.[1] Poetry seems to be injured when approaching an expository narrative discourse, and therefore can suffer from certain deficiencies that begin as formal and lead to conceptual ones. The next two reasons are theological: the second is that it seeks to avoid giving the image that God acted in response to a request from the people. For the psalmist, if that had been the case, God's sovereignty would be weakened by making God dependent on a human request. It is of little use that we can cite several psalms that show the opposite (Ps 3:4; 22:24; 120:1) those where God responds to the cry of the one who suffers and acts accordingly; but the examples are not pertinent because at this point it is about the understanding (theology) of the history of Israel in the psalms and not about a believer who at that very moment raises prayer. The theology conveyed by the psalms regarding the role of actors in the history of Israel is different from that of Exodus and the prophets. This can be seen from the fact that in all the historical psalms mentioned above God acts on God's own initiative and in no case in response to a request from the people. The third reason is related to the previous one. We already mentioned at the beginning of this chapter that the psalms are presented as human words directed toward God. The psalms recognize themselves in this way and therefore their word goes toward God, but they do not feel authorized to place themselves on God's lips and express the divine will, whether it responds to a need raised by Israel or in any other way. The psalmist knows that he is not a prophet and leaves it to them to be God's spokesperson.

We have already mentioned that there is also in the theology of the psalms an awareness of the social and political liberation that God promotes in history. Obviously, this is not the

---

[1]We think of works such as the Cantar del Mio Cid, the Divine Comedy or Martín Fierro, which develop a linear novelistic plot. But the question arises as to whether in this type of work the poetic aspect has not been subordinated to the formal needs of a story, such as temporal succession and the inclusion of characters and dialogues.

language that the Bible uses, but its conception of reality as "social" cannot be evaded. In 69:32 and in 145:14 and other texts, this is attested. We find it explicitly in Psalm 146, when the psalmist says of God:

> Who does justice to the aggrieved,
> Who gives bread to the hungry.
> Yahweh frees the captives;
> Yahweh opens the eyes of the blind;
> Yahweh raises up those who are fallen;
> Yahweh loves the righteous.
> Yahweh protects the foreigners;
> He supports the orphan and the widow,
> And the way of the wicked is turned aside. (Ps 146:7-9)

This psalm has prophetic reminiscences that bring it close to the language about the servant of Yahweh (Is 42:7) and the expectation of a liberating king as announced in Isaiah 61:1-3, a text that will be taken up in the gospels by Jesus of Nazareth, applying it to his own ministry and rereading it within a new dynamic of salvation and liberation inaugurated by his presence (Lk 4:16-22). The richness of the text allows it to be read from different places and with different hermeneutical interests. However, as a first reading, it would not be correct to read these verses in an intimate sense, as if they referred to an inner experience of the believer, or in an eschatological way, as if they referred to a final and definitive time. Without a doubt, in the exercise of an inclusive and generous hermeneutic such as the one we promote in this work, this text can be read in this way and thus respond to realities as concrete as these and others. But in terms of biblical language and the psalms, the announced justice and the captives who will be freed refer to real acts of liberation of those who are oppressed and imprisoned. All language is built on a reality that acts as a referent, which makes the volatility of words consistent. In this case, they refer to a concrete reality of oppression in which it is said that Yahweh acts in favor of the liberation of the hungry and obstructs the plans of those who oppress them. When 145:7 says that "Yahweh frees the captives" and "opens the eyes of the blind" it uses the same words that Isaiah 49:9-10 uses to speak of the captives who are freed from prison and receive light in their eyes after many days of confinement. In Isaiah, it is a reference to prisoners in exile who were freed or had the expectation of being freed. The psalm evokes that experience and now announces it as a testimony to God's will to bring justice to where it has been violated.

The Theology of the Psalms: Passion and Justice

The ancient poet who reveals himself in 45:1 is representative of a multitude of artists who lived their experience of faith with passion and depth and expressed it beautifully when they put it with pen and ink on the surface of the parchment. An example of literary beauty is the way in which he presents one of the deepest questions of humanity, a statement that is often disconcerting: "The fool says in his heart: there is no God" (14:1 and 53:1). It is not a declaration of intellectual atheism but of a practical character. It could be translated in a dynamic and dull way as "the fool says: I care not for the opinion of God." Also in 36:2 there is a variant: "the wicked has no fear of God" and in 10:4 another: "the wicked, in his pride, does not seek him; there is no God in his thoughts." The problem that this attitude poses to the biblical thought of that time is that the lack of interest or fear of God implies surrender to injustice and the oppression of one's neighbor. Taking God into account had concrete practical consequences for ethical conduct, and not taking God into account meant ignoring the obligations of the covenant made with the ancestors by which the Law and all its social implications were to be respected. The real problem is not the declaration of indifference toward God but the passivity and lack of interest in the fate of one's neighbor, in particular the poorest and most marginalized. This is also reflected in other aspects of the theology of the psalms.

The Creator God

The theology of the psalms exalts God's status as creator but has its own way of understanding it and only alludes in a very subtle way to the Genesis account. Psalm 104, which follows the order of creation in Genesis, is marked by sapiential theology to the point of saying: "How innumerable are your works, O Yahweh! You made them all in wisdom (*hokmah*);" Psalm 136:4-9 lists the acts of creation but then leans toward the epic to emphasize the gift of the promised and delivered land. Psalm 8 comes close to the creation account by saying, "You made him to rule over the works of your hands; you put everything under his feet" (v. 7), but even here the verb used (*mashal*, to rule, to govern) is not the one used in Gen 1:28 to describe the function of dominating nature, which suggests a conceptual distance. These examples and others lead us to observe that in the psalms God's creative condition is presented differently, in particular as a conflict with nature expressed in the dominion over chaotic waters and sea monsters. This is a reflection of the Canaanite myths but in the psalms it is framed within the language of Yahweh without contradicting the rest of the theology of the Old Testament. In 74:12-15 the creative act is described thus:

> You divided the sea by your power; you broke the heads of
> the sea monsters.
> You crushed the heads of Leviathan and gave him as food
> to those who dwell in the wilderness.
> You opened the fountain and the river; you dried up the
> mighty rivers.

Or in 89:9-10:

> You rule the sea; when its waves rise, you hold them back.
> You broke the storm like a mortal wound…

In this creation, the conflict is present between chaos and order and reflects the social condition of Israel, which lives in a situation of almost permanent conflict and struggle. A harmonious and ordered creation responds to a stable and consolidated spirit, but the psalms reflect the anguish and search for meaning of a psalmist who perceives the social context as hostile, whatever the time in which the psalm was written. It is not a question of the context of the writing and its theology but of an approach to reality. For a people who have had to fight for their survival throughout almost all of their history, conflict is something inherent to life. Hence, while other authors place themselves in a perspective of continuity with the main social actors, the psalmist perceives social dynamics in a conflictual manner and aspires to a rupture. And this particular way of reading reality is also reflected in his conception of how God created the universe: it is not the product of an act of moderation but the result of a conflict from which the God of Israel emerges as the victor and dominator of the world.

The Mighty God

The psalms recognize the power of God and represent it sometimes by using the figure of the king and other times by using what is perceived as the most sublime. In 24:7-10, God is humanized to the point of asking that the doors be opened so that "the king of glory may enter." In a text of extreme beauty, it is stated that the king "is Yahweh, the mighty, the mighty in battle." The psalms where God is linked to the king are numerous (29:10; 48:2; 74:12; 93:1; 95:3; 96:10; 97:1; 98:6; 99:1), and they seek to avoid his deification by establishing the essential opposition between

God and the human condition of the king, who in the psalms is always a representation of David. We see this in 132:10-12:

> For the sake of David your servant, do not turn your face away from your anointed. The LORD has promised David and will not go back on his promise: his descendants will be on your throne... and his sons will sit on your throne forever.

These words walk the ledge because they suggest a mechanical relationship between God's protection and God's commitment to preserve the Davidic dynasty. At the same time, we must bear in mind that although many psalms may have arisen as an exaltation of King David or another monarch, later interpretation saw in them a messianic suggestion. Thus, the initial theology printed in the psalm was later modified when it was reread in terms of liberation; from that moment on, it no longer represented the powerful figure of the king of Israel but that of the humble messiah, who would inaugurate the time of definitive justice.[1]

The greatness of God is expressed by the name *elyon*, which means "the high one" or "the most high" and which was the name of a Canaanite deity that was appropriated by Israel and reinterpreted according to its own theology. In 46:4 it says "the dwelling place of *elyon is sacred*" which is usually translated as "the Most High." And in 47:2 the greatness of God is combined with God's reign in a magnificent verse.[2]

For Yahweh the Most High (elyon) Is Awesome: A Great King over all the Earth.

In 82:6-7, the powerful figure of God is again contrasted with the weakness of human beings; in this case, addressing powerful men: "I said: You are mere human beings, and all of you are sons of the Most High; but as human beings you will die, and as princes you will fall." This is said of the rich in a psalm that calls for justice for the oppressed and marginalized and holds the

---

[1]The one who has emphasized that the context of reading the royal psalms is not that of the Judahite monarchy but that of the messianic theology that preserved them and gave them a new meaning is B. Childs in his *Introduction to the Old Testament as Scripture* (Philadelphia: Westminster, 1979), 515-17.

[2]J. Day, *Psalms*, 126; Hans-Joachim Kraus points out that this denomination is often accompanied by the term "king" and that it contributes to forming a "monarchical theology," a concept that according to Paul Tillich –whom he quotes, is "a border between polytheism and monotheism," since the monarch would reign over a pantheon of lesser gods. See *Teología de los Salmos* (Salamanca: Sígueme, 1985), 29-31.

powerful responsible for their impiety toward the needy. The theology reflected here consists of recognizing that God's power is based on justice and sensitivity toward the helpless and not an anonymous force that is applied without distinguishing one from another. Along the same lines, the image of God as holy, chosen for a mission, is subscribed to. God's holiness highlights the divine uniqueness and exclusivity and is constructed in opposition to the pretensions of those who sought to worship the Canaanite gods. Thus, when after recognizing the divine acts of justice and mercy he is called "the holy one of Israel" (71:22) or in the psalm that reviews the history of Israel it is said "...they turned and tested God, and defied the Holy One of Israel..." (78:41), in both cases this is done to establish the distance between the God of Israel and the Canaanite divinities that in the eyes of the Israelite faith have no power and could not save. The holiness of the God of Israel consists in the divine condition of being at the side of the weak and marginalized to liberate them; it is not a holiness that separates God from reality but rather one that proclaims God as a God immersed in human problems.

The God of Justice

What surprises us about the theology of the psalms is that it understands God as the only one who can ultimately do justice to the oppressed. The psalms say this in two different ways. In one, the ethics that every believer should practice are affirmed. Psalms 15 and 24 are good examples. They establish the conditions for entering the temple and, in both cases, they are linked to a righteous life in relation to one's neighbor. Psalm 15 says:

> Yahweh, who will dwell in your house? Who will reside on your holy mountain?
> He who walks uprightly and works justice, and speaks the truth in his heart.
> He who does not slander with his tongue, nor does evil to his neighbor,
> nor does he admit any reproach against his neighbor.
> He who despises the vile, and who honors those who fear the LORD.
> He who, even when testifying against himself, does not change his word.
> He who does not give his money at usury, nor accept a bribe against the innocent.
> He who does these things will never slip.

Note that none of these behaviors are related to ritual or religious acts, but rather they are an enumeration of ethical behaviors that emanate from the Law, all related to the figure of the neighbor and are required as a precondition for access to the temple and worship. It is striking that the strict restrictions of the purity laws of Leviticus 11-16 or the holiness laws of 17-26 are not mentioned, and that it is telling the truth and doing justice to one's neighbor that enables one to enter the temple; this says much about the central role of justice and righteousness in the relationship with God.

The second form is the recognition of the existence of a divine justice distinct from human justice. We see it in 50:6 "...the heavens will declare their justice, for God is the judge..." Pleins has pointed out that Psalm 37 shows God promoting justice toward the poor while providing land to the peasants who lost it through the action of "the wicked," the "enemies of Yahweh" (v. 20).[1] The mention of the poor to whom justice must be done abounds in the psalms. The expression "poor and needy" is found in texts, such as 40:18; 70:6; 86:1 and others. The mention of "poor" as such is found in many more (9:19; 10:2, 9; 14:6; 18:28; 68:11 and others). If we look for its derivatives such as weak, needy, etc. the citations multiply. Although there was a debate at the beginning of the 20th century about who these poor people referred to, today there is majority support that they refer to the economically poor people of Israel.[2] They are the victims of the system of exploitation who were denounced by the prophets and of whom the texts of wisdom speak. Psalm 72:13-14 says it this way:

He will have mercy on the poor and the needy,
and will save the lives of the poor.
From deceit and violence he will redeem their souls,
and their blood will be precious in his sight.

It is the lives of the poor that are at risk and God saves them; it is violence that is exercised against them and their blood is shed. With the beauty that we have already highlighted from other texts, it is said here that the innocent blood shed on Earth and despised by the powerful who oppress them is valuable in the eyes of God. The disposable life for some is precious to God and

---

[1] J. D. Pleins, *The Social Visions*, 436.

[2] At first it was postulated that the poor in the psalms were those belonging to a Yahwistic party or a spiritual community that shared a common vision of worship and cult. Later the opposition between poor and enemies was taken into account and they were described as those who, having no power, were oppressed by their enemies, generally the dominant sectors of the Israelite community. For an analysis of the different schools of thought on this subject see H.-J. Kraus, *Teología de los Salmos*, 201-07.

consequently an effective justice is announced that will be exercised here on Earth.

This concept is even more important when we consider it in the context of a theology that ignored any kind of retribution in a life after physical death. Although there are two psalms that could express a transition toward an understanding of a life beyond death—and therefore the possibility of a final judgment where the justice postponed on Earth would be made effective (49:14-15; 73:23). It is difficult for that to be the correct reading, and if it were, we can see that it did not permeate the rest of the theology of the psalms. Thus, in the psalms, the search for an effective justice in the present reality is more than giving each person what they deserve and need, but rather it is recognizing the dignity inherent in the human condition and making their life have the meaning that God gave it when God decided to bring it into the world. In them, God expresses the divine self through this human justice, weak and imperfect, but it is the one that the Lord has given to human beings to administer. It will take a long time for Israel's theology to grasp a different dimension for justice and to transfer it, as a final and finished work, to eschatological expectation. This will have as a consequence that the human sphere will become a space of preliminary testimony, of showing the first fruits of God's justice here on Earth while awaiting that full and definitive justice in which all creation will be judged.

The Texts of the Sages
Theology and Counter-Theology

Meditation and Justice

When approaching the biblical texts of wisdom, we must leave aside the widespread image that points to them as written by wise sages who lived in the comfortable rooms of palaces. It is often heard that they enjoyed the tranquility that comes from belonging to a wealthy class and therefore oblivious to the troubles and conflicts of their society. However, indolent humans do not describe reality with words such as:

> To do righteousness and justice is more pleasing to Yahweh.
> that the sacrifices (Prov 21:3)

This proverb uses the words *tzedaka* (righteousness, right) and *mishpat* (justice), both of which are the facets of prophetic theology and of those who seek to denounce the worst abuses. In 31:9, *tzedaka* is mentioned again, now in clear allusion to defending the rights of the poor and marginalized:

> Open your mouth, judge righteously,
> And defends the cause of the poor and the needy.

Those who wove the theology of Ecclesiastes and Job suffer from deep anguish because of the experiences of injustice and distress that they have to live through and because they cannot understand how a God of love and justice allows such calamities to happen and affect the poorest in particular. Neither the character Job nor Solomon (the king that Ecclesiastes suggests as the semiotic author of book's reflections) represent the poor of their time, but their theology is not constructed to sustain a system of injustice or to give ideological support to the dominant classes. On the contrary, both unmask the link between a theology that boasts dogmatic purity but is not sensitive to the pain of others and ends up harming the rights of those who have no one to defend them.

Wisdom texts have their own coordinates and constitute a distinctive theological discourse. They depart from the dynamic established between the *Torah* and the prophetic texts — here, as in the oldest tradition of reading, when speaking of prophetic books we include the books from Joshua to 2 Kings, which were later called "historical" — in which the latter apply and comment on the

267

former (the Law) in the context of the course of history. It is necessary to remember that the prophetic texts conceive of themselves as a historical continuity with the narratives of the patriarchs and matriarchs and the exodus and in this way they are presented in biblical literature where we find a coherent line from creation to the end of the monarchy, which has been called the Enneateuch. This is reinforced in the prophetic books (Isaiah to Malachi) by the fact that most of them include in the first lines the information necessary to place them in a precise moment in history, although later this precision becomes blurred. From the semiotic point of view, even post-exilic books such as Jonah or Joel—which do not indicate their time—admit to being read as if they referred to specific moments in the history of Israel established on Earth.[1]

However, when we turn to the books of wisdom, we see that they are linked in a different way with the biblical traditions. The books allude to the Law (Prov 3:1: "My son, do not forget my law, and let your heart keep my commandments;" 4:2; 28:7 and others; Job 22:22) but this relationship is not mediated by ancestoral stories nor by the preaching of the prophets. The wise one understands the Law to be the highest expression of the Law in the double instruction to "fear God" and to "keep the divine commandments" (Eccl 12:13; Prov 1:7). We can say that the wisdom tradition is not attracted by the "narrative" theology that demands reflection on past events, but rather it concentrates on responding to life's challenges by applying these two basic principles. This disregard for the past as a source of inspiration also reveals that the wise sages were not urged by the events of the immediate present and that they found in time a theme and a concern, as well as an inexhaustible element. We can see this in the fact that no wisdom text conveys to us the feeling of urgency or of the definitive, and that this condition defines their theology to a large extent. It is a thoughtful theology, matured over time, which focuses on the careful observation of both the workings of the immense sky that dazzles with its mystery and the inaccessible "trail of the eagle in the sky" (Prov 30:19).

---

[1]Of the sixteen prophetic books, only six do not mention a specific date for the prophet's ministry, namely, Joel, Obadiah, Jonah, Nahum, Habakkuk and Malachi; but even they include information that allows them to be placed in real or semiotic history. Daniel, whose first part is fictional (Dan 1-6), is also concerned with establishing the moment in history in which the events narrated take place, even though they do not correspond to its own time.

At first glance, we might assume that meditating and worrying about justice in human relations are incompatible activities. The latter is a concrete act that is exercised on society and one's neighbor, while the former is an inner discipline, an act of personal reflection. However, the wise sages who wrote these books did not feel alien to the historical and social events they were thinking about, but rather they conceived of them as the space in which divine action and human action were played out. Meditating on injustices and expressing the contradiction between them and the world as God had created it and expected it to function was, for them, a way of beginning to repair the imbalance in reality. In this delving into society and its troubles, wise thought makes evident the crisis in which that society and the thought that interprets it find themselves. On the one hand, the foundations of society are undermined by social inequalities and by the meanness of the rich who oppress the weak. This is not the way the Lord expects God's creatures to relate, but it is the real situation that the wise one observes and denounces. Armando Levoratti has pointed out that "the revelation of this crisis is undoubtedly one of the essential purposes of the teacher,"[1] to which it should be added that this vocation to bring to light what is hidden is also an essential part of his reason for being and the sage's mission as a spokesperson for God. On the other hand, the wisdom writers discover that this crisis is prolonged and seems permanent because it reflects the vanity of the human heart, the intimate inclination to take advantage of one's neighbor for one's own benefit.

Because of this condition of revealing hidden social and spiritual relationships, we can affirm that the meditation of the wise one and the denunciation that it provokes are not escapist forms of passively accepting reality but a way of conceiving intervention in social reality that prepares the way for rebellion and action. It is understood as the previous and necessary step to understand what is happening and then plan an action that can modify that situation. In the so-called "discourse of wisdom" (Prov 8:12-36) the thinker describes the goods of wisdom in such a way that riches pale:

---

[1] A. Levoratti analyses the discourse of Ecclesiastes in this way and points out that "Qohelet claims to have discovered a reality that usually remains hidden from the eyes of the majority. This reality is as current today as it was in his own time, because disorder, nonsense, contradiction and incoherence are not mere contingencies or secondary and casual accidents, but unavoidable components of the human condition and of social life," *CBL II* (Estella: Verbo Divino, 2007), 841.

My fruit is better than gold, even than refined gold;
And my profit is better than the chosen silver.
I will walk along the path of justice,
Through the paths of justice. (Prov 8:19-20)

Justice (*tzedaka*) and right (*mishpat*) are dense and meaningful words in biblical theology. The wise one uses them with the intention of avoiding any ambiguity so that the choice they make is clear. Gold and silver are precious goods for which people killed and continue to kill. The accumulation of wealth and power seems to be the driving force of societies of yesterday and today, without stopping to think about the damage and destruction they cause in their quest for profit. To achieve their petty goals, human lives are destroyed, the environment is polluted and species that have been evolving on Earth for millions of years are eliminated, jewels of divine creation; this is common currency in our time. But the wise one puts this practice into crisis by pointing out that living according to the will of God makes all wealth and power pale.

Wisdom as Access to Reality

Gerard von Rad has pointed out that the preferred discourse of wisdom texts is poetry.[1] Although there are several literary genres that the wise sages used (proverbs, riddles, narratives, tales, psalms, speeches and others) the poetic form is the one that is at the base of all of them. This is not only an aesthetic option—although it is that—but even more so it is the recognition that what one wishes to convey demands a language inclined to metaphor and ambiguity. Poetry is by its very nature an open and suggestive discourse, which, like no other, calls for interpretation and for choosing a meaning in conflict with others. Just as prose aspires to be precise and clear, although sometimes it does not achieve this or deliberately seeks to break out of that mold, poetic discourse calls us to taste the words and to bet on a meaning. But even though it is inclined to poetry, it happens that wisdom literature is little affected by myths, those narratives that are symbols put into a story and, therefore, where prose comes closest to poetic discourse. One would have expected a certain sympathy for mythical language and for its narrative forms as an extension of what is presented as a search to find answers both to current questions and to the great mysteries of life. What happens is that the wise avoid mythical language because, although they

---

[1] G. von Rad, *Sabiduría en Israel* (Madrid: Fax, 1973).

discuss an ambiguous and changing reality that leads them to the poetic word, they consider that it is reason that guides them in their disquisitions. Wisdom (*hojmah*) and reason (*heshbon*) go together in the thought of Ecclesiastes (7:25):

> ...I turned and set my heart to know and to examine and to seek wisdom (*hochmah*) and reason (*heshbon*).

Also in Prov 2:6 we find this idea expressed with words like knowledge and intelligence:

> For Yahweh gives wisdom, and from God's mouth comes knowledge (*da`at*) and understanding (*tebunah*).

It may seem like a contradiction, but the wisdom discourse that uses poetic images to express its ideas and vision of the world considers itself to be a rational discourse. McEvenue has postulated that wisdom theology should be understood as "an invitation to science to expand in the direction of faith."[1] We share this to the extent that rational thought in this theology coexists with faith without generating contradiction. But in our opinion, the invitation is also an invitation in the opposite sense, for faith to recognize the autonomous sphere of human thought that addresses the issues of life without the need for an explicit mention of the sacred. In their self-understanding, wise persons let reason guide them to understand and describe the world created by God and its laws and to elaborate practical and theoretical consequences for life without the divine appearing as a recognizable actor, which sometimes makes it appear as a "secular" thought. However, biblical wisdom literature is not an isolated fact, nor should it be read as a theology separate from the rest of the Scriptures. They are not secular pages simply incorporated into the texts of the faith of Israel, but rather they express a different way of linking human experience in its relationship with God. Wisdom walks between the rational discourse of "common sense" and the poetic word that investigates reality beyond that common sense. This tension between reason and poetic discourse is also found in other sections of the Old Testament, often expressed as a tension between the marvelous and the everyday or between the surprising of God and its necessary articulation in a human language that allows it to be transmitted. In this sense, wisdom literature represents an outstanding aspect of elements that underlie and are already present in the rest of the Scriptures.

---

[1] S. McEvenue, "Wisdom," *CBI* (ed. W. Farmer *et al.*; Estella: Verbo Divino, 1999), 687; the author writes Wisdom with a capital letter because he recognizes a transcendent value almost equivalent to divinity.

Another issue to consider is the following. If in the Hebrew Bible the works of wisdom (Proverbs, Job and Ecclesiastes) were located in the third section of the *Ketubim* or Writings, this does not prevent us from finding the influence of wisdom theology in other texts. Moreover, in light of the examples that are found scattered in numerous works, the question arises as to whether there was not a "wisdom" writing of all the biblical works. This does not seem to be the case, since if it were, a greater influence would be noted in the set of texts, but a cursory review makes it evident that passages that were foreign to it were imbued with wisdom. Hence, we find that wisdom theology is present in places whose general content does not belong to this school. We see them in the creation narrative (Gen 2-3); in historical texts such as the story of Joseph (Gen 37-50)[1] and that of Solomon (1 Kings 3); in Psalms (1-2; 32; 34; 48; 73; 104; 112; 128);[2] in prophetic literature (Is 5:21; 40:13-14, 21; 41:20; 44:18-19, 25; Jer 18:18);[3] in the Song of Songs (1:1 and 8:6-7). In the case of Psalms, it is worth noting that the book opens with two wisdom psalms in order to establish from the beginning the salvific nature of what makes up the body of the work. It says of the blessed person:

...his delight is in the law of the Lord,
and in his law he meditates day and night (1:2).

and

...Yahweh said to me: You are my son; today I have begotten you.
Ask of me, and I will make the nations your inheritance...
(Ps 2:7-8)

The rest of the book only sporadically uses wisdom language, but these two psalms, located at the opening of the book, point to the Law as a source of wisdom and to dependence on the Creator as the starting point of everything the wise person thinks and does.

We are even more surprised to find that biblical wisdom literature shows no interest in the stories of the patriarchs and matriarchs or prophetic discourses, nor is there any mention of the founding institutions of Israel, such as the temple or the

---

[1] See the already classic article by G. von Rad, "La historia de José y la antigua *hokma*," *Estudios sobre el Antiguo Testamento* (Salamanca: Sígueme, 1975), 255-62.

[2] The status of "wisdom psalm" is problematic because they generally only include wisdom parts within the psalm. A classic article on this subject is R. Murphy, "A Consideration on the Classification of Wisdom Psalms," *VT Sup* 9 (1963): 156-67.

[3] J. Fichtner, "Isaiah Among the Wise," *Studies in Ancient Israelite Wisdom* (ed. James Crenshaw; New York: Ktav Publishing House, 1976), 429-38.

monarchy. Even though most of these narratives and spheres were known and popular in post-exilic times, the sages do not rely on them to develop their thinking. Those elements of Yahwism that make up the faith of Israel and distinguish it from other Canaanite peoples are absent among the sages. One could cite, on the contrary, the so-called "prayer of the fathers" in Ecclesiasticus 44:1-50:24 and the extensive text of Wisdom 10:1-19:22 where central moments of Israel's history are reviewed in a wisdom key, but in the set of its books these passages seem foreign and strange to the literary spirit of the work, as if they were in the wrong place. The same thing happens with these texts as with the passages of wisdom in works that are not wisdom: they are there to remind us of a different way of thinking, but they are not fully integrated.

This absence of the great foundational stories of Israel is a theological fact that should not be overlooked. It can be understood as ignorance or disdain for the received traditions, which is not probable; rather, we are inclined to think that, in the universe of wisdom, the coordinates for interpreting reality are different. The wise live in a radical present and, when they see the stories of the past, they do not believe that the stories serve to resolve the problems before them; and they are equally uncomfortable with the prophetic expectations of a future that seems uncertain and nebulous. Neither the memory of the promises nor the anxiety for their fulfillment are things that sensitize the wise. They live the present as the only place where the relationship with God is played out. Far from the examples of the past, the wise are interested in affirming that this or that person is "blessed" today because that one remains faithful to the law of Yahweh; that in the decisions we must make, "it is better to do this thing than that other thing...;" and they are interested in highlighting the distance between the righteous and the wicked, between the kind and the wicked. The wise are concerned about the issue of retribution and injustice when they see that the wicked are usually rewarded and the righteous suffer the blows of life. They devote much effort to meditating on the destiny of the righteous and the wicked and although they do not agree to understand the reason for existential injustices, at least they recognize and integrate them as an undesirable part of reality. In the teaching process they feel like a "master" when they are next to a young apprentice, or when they speaks like parents in front of their child whom they instruct in the ways of life, because the wise understand age hierarchies as levels of wisdom that the elder must transmit to the younger.

Another aspect is related to the absence of Yahwistic traditions in wisdom literature. That literature is built on the confession that Yahweh is the God who brought Israel out of the land of slavery and gave it a good land to live in. That confession is not, in principle, an affirmation of the people of God but an affirmation of the divinity itself that reveals itself and says in the first person:

> I have seen the affliction of my people in Egypt, and have heard their cry because of their oppressors. I know their affliction, and I have come down to rescue them from the hand of the Egyptians and to bring them up out of that land to a good and spacious land, to a land flowing with milk and honey, to the place of the Canaanite, the Hittite, the Amorite, the Perizzite, the Hivite, and the Jebusite. The cry of the Israelites has come before me, and I have seen the oppression with which the Egyptians oppress them. (Ex 3:7-9)

God then has to confirm this liberating vocation by declaring that the divine identity is "I am the one who *is*" (Ex 3:14), the one who accompanies God's people. But wisdom theology does not resort to these affirmations to modulate its discourse, but rather it does so from the observation of reality and from meditating on what it perceives. In its reflection, it considers that there is a distance between the reality of God and that of human beings, a distance that cannot be shortened by human action. The text affirms in one of its most transparent verses about its conception of the relationship with God that "God is in heaven and you are on Earth" (Eccl 5:2). Therefore, human experience is not enough to describe or encompass the knowledge of the divine. The wise person perceives that what separates the divine sphere from the human does not appear so clearly in the stories where there is a God who converses with Abraham and Moses, who becomes a column of fire or a cloud to direct the people or who writes the laws with the divine finger on the stone.

The difficulty of the wise assuming this way of understanding reality and doing theology leads us to wonder if for them the knowledge of God through the observation of life and nature is an alternative source of revelation to that of the great stories of the patriarchs and matriarchs.[1] This is supported by observing that their exploration of reality omits the texts that have served as the foundation of the faith of Israel and the vehicle of its

---

[1] W. Zimmerli, *Manual de teología del Antiguo Testamento* (Madrid: Cristiandad, 1980), 180-83.

theology and yet it does not fall into discredit or apathy but comes out vigorously affirming that "the fear (*yr'ah*) of Yahweh is the foundation of all knowledge (*da'at*)" (Prov 1:7). It is from this declaration that a double reference is established to found their theology: one grows in faith from the knowledge (*da'at*) of the world, but knowledge is not born from the sagacity of humanity but from the fear of God. Far from the wise is the arrogance of those who believe themselves to be the possessors of the keys to the universe, of a privileged path to its knowledge and of the mechanism that governs it. In their understanding, it is not human reason that opens the secrets of the cosmos, nor is it deceived by the deceitful devices of those who claim to possess wisdom as a personal property. On the contrary, the wise perceive the fragility of their knowledge and recognizes the limitations of their task, but finds that God supports them in their search by saying "do not feel wise, but fear (*yr'ah*) Yahweh" (Prov 3:7); or when they ironically state, "Have you seen one who is wise in his own eyes?" (26:12, also Is 5:21; this expression means "wise by their own wisdom"). And the writer forcefully declares:

> The fear of the Lord is the beginning of wisdom,
> The knowledge of sacred things is intelligence. (9:10)

It is through recognizing the immensity of the Creator and human finitude that we gain access to knowledge of the world and can perceive in it the signs of the divine presence and its will to instruct human beings in order to correct them and direct them toward a better life. The simplest beings and things cease to be insignificant and reveal the profound reality of life and of God's will. Thus, ants and lizards are signs of what God wishes to teach human beings (Prov 6:6-11; 30:24-28); a storm (10:25) or oxen are an opportunity to understand God's will (14:4); vegetables open the way to a good relationship with one's neighbor (15:17).

Creation according to the Sages: Seeing for the First Time

The wise one observes creation and wonders about its origin, which is a way of wondering about its meaning. In Genesis 1 the foundation of the cosmos is carried out through the word, which is expressed in the phrase "And God said..." repeated every day of creation. The second account (Gen 2:4 onwards) is not very concerned with the details of creation but emphasizes the care that God puts into protecting human beings: God plants a garden, provides it with water, creates a woman who harmonizes with the man, provides them with food. When we go to the wisdom texts that deal with creation, we find none of that. These texts are not interested in the process of creation or in the first avatars of humanity, but we are simply told that God creates "with wisdom." However, it is not strange to hear it said that the theology of Israelite wisdom is creational theology. When one reads it, one feels that one is in contact with things as if it were the first time that they are being named; The wise see the simplest side of things in such a way that it seems that they see things as they have never been seen them before or as if they were naming them for the first time. As if God had put them there on the day of creation and we had come now to discuss them and to draw lessons for life from the primitive wonder that contemplating the scene of human adventure produces in us.

There is a faith in creation among the wise which can be seen in how they marvel at it and how they are able to see the action of the creator behind every aspect of nature. For them, snow and hail (Job 38:22) or birds such as the turkey or the ostrich (39:13-18) are proof of God's wisdom and of the divinely masterful way of organizing the world. We find in the wisdom texts the same conviction that runs throughout the Old Testament that there is an unbridgeable distance between the creator and the creature, between God and nature, a distance that prevents the deification of any created thing. But while outside the wisdom texts this attitude tends to desacralize creation and present it in its full materiality in opposition to the idolatry that tempted Israel and that was built on giving divine rank to the stars or other objects, in the thought of the wise, creation is elevated to the rank of a magnificent jewel where the hand of the creator can be appreciated, acting as a goldsmith carving a masterpiece. Hence, instead of desacralizing nature, it is sacralized because it is the work of God's creative will, and this sacralization of its condition as the work of God prevents its divinization, a fact unacceptable for biblical theology. Understood in this way and from the theological point of view, it is not far from the expression of Gen 1 that before each finished work says that "God saw that it was good," an expression that we saw also has an aesthetic value ("God saw that it was *beautiful*"). Only the wise take the opposite path: they observe the goodness and beauty of creation and from there infers the greatness of its creator.

In Prov 3:19, it is said that "by wisdom the Lord laid the foundation of the Earth; by understanding he established the heavens." Wisdom and understanding (*hojmah* and *tebunah*) are the attributes of God who worked in the creation of the Earth and the heavens. Far from the anthropomorphisms of Genesis, here, divinity remains hidden and linked only to abstract nouns that do not allow God to be confused with the divine attributes. This is significant because, on several occasions, wisdom is personified and can give the impression that it is conceived as a being associated with the action of God. This is how Prov 8:14-15 reads:

> With me is counsel and good judgment;
> I am the intelligence; mine is the power.
> Through me kings reign,
> And the princes decree justice.

And

> When he formed the heavens, I was there;
> When he drew a circle on the face of the deep… (8:27)

However, the set of texts makes it clear that wisdom was also created by God and leaves no room to think otherwise. In 8:22, it is stated, "Yahweh acquired me in the beginning, before the divine works of old." The fact that wisdom speaks in the first person may suggest that wisdom is an autonomous personality, but this must be taken as a literary device to express the importance of wisdom, which is also made to say that "whoever finds me finds life" (8:35). The same happens when it is mentioned that wisdom was created "from the beginning," "before the deeps were." This suggests that there was a privileged treatment for wisdom at the time of creation, but it is difficult to accept this if we see that in the poem that is crucial to this theme (8:22-31) wisdom is described as a spectator of creation and not as helping in the creative act.[1] At no time does wisdom appear as a being in parallel with the creator, but as an entity created before other things and a witness to creation. The presence of wisdom in the moments of creation does not disturb the creative action of Yahweh, but rather enhances it in the sense that it seems to act as a guiding element of divine action. Wisdom participates in the creative act as a primordial witness and as the first creature that had the fortune of being present at the initial moments of the cosmos.[2] For sapiential theology, wisdom is an attribute and, as such, it has no ontological

---

[1] M. López Torres suggests that this poem gives rise to a feminine understanding of the deity, see, "Danzando en el universo - Proverbios 8,22-31," *RIBLA* 50 (2005): 65-68; it is an interesting idea, but v. 22 speaks of Yahweh "acquiring" her (*qanah*), as if she were a tool for his creative action and not as part of his very being; for *qanah* see G. Yee, "The Theology of Creation in Proverbs 8:22-31," *Creation in the Biblical Traditions* (ed. R. Clifford and J. Collins; Washington: Catholic Biblical Association, 1992), 89, note 7.

[2] W. Zimmerli considers that wisdom was never deified and that it has always been considered a privileged witness of creation but without divine attributes, see *Manual de teología del Antiguo Testamento*, 184.

condition; for that reason, it is not described as an independent being but as a *criterion* that applies both to the action of God and to that of human beings, although with a different meaning in each case.[1] For the former, it is an ingredient of God's infinite knowledge and of the divine action that never ceases; for the latter, it is a good to be achieved and protected because finding it gives blessing but losing it causes harm to the soul (8:35-36). Because by seeking it and trying to incorporate it into one's personal life, one will discover that it is not a product that can be bought but that it is Yahweh who gives and administers it, as is reflected in the poem 2:1-6 and in the story of 1 Kings 3 where Yahweh says to Solomon "ask for whatever you want and *I will give it to you*" and then when the king asks for wisdom and God grants it to him, God culminates with a subtle statement full of meaning: "*I have given you* a wise and intelligent heart" (3:5 and 12).

It is in Job that creation is exalted by the spirit of the wise as nowhere else because there it is made evident that God has created everything "with wisdom." Job has been arrogant before God and reviews creation in the divine response "from the storm" and shows Job the smallness of Job's thoughts and power to act. God mocks Job's knowledge and tells him:

> Who is this that *darkens* counsel by words without wisdom?
> Now strengthen your back like a man;
> I will ask you, and you *will instruct me.* (Job 38:2-3)

Through the divine irony, God points out that the absence of wisdom in Job's words leads to the obscuring of instruction; then, and for the first time in Job, God will challenge him and ask him questions while waiting to be instructed by Job through his answers. But the speech is overwhelming and forceful so that it leads Job to recognize that he has been careless in his judgments and to cover his mouth with his hand (40:3).

There is another aspect of creation that we are interested in exploring. Wisdom theology that observes creation also observes people and their social relationships and is not unaware of the marginalization and devaluation of the poor by the fortunate. There are two sentences where the poor are related to God as creator and two others where "rich and poor" are mentioned as the work of the divine hands. In Prov 17:5 it says:

---

[1] L. Schiavo and L. Lago analyze wisdom as one of the personified attributes of God (hypostasis) and how later in Christianity it derived into the feminine form of divinity, see "Sofía – los mitos del amor reflexivo y del amor en la alteridad," *RIBLA* 57 (2007): 86-96.

He who mocks the poor insults his maker...

And at 14:31 Proverbs says:

He who oppresses the poor dishonors his Maker;
But he who has mercy on the poor honors him.

The first proverb is completed in the second case with its antithesis. In these proverbs, not only is the poor linked to the creative action of God (who is called maker, 'osehu) but a direct relationship is established between the dignity of the poor and that of the Creator. To offend one is to offend the other. Hermisson wonders whether, following the logic of wisdom, it could not be thought that the poor are responsible for their poverty by not cultivating wisdom and the fear of God, but then God will make us observe that the intention of the wise one is to show that although poor, the person does not cease to be a creature of God, and therefore their life and human condition deserve the respect of all.[1]

Recovering the proverbs that express the defense of the poor helps to overcome the opinion that has been quite widespread for some years now — and which we already mentioned at the beginning of this chapter — that the texts of wisdom and wise persons in general belonged to the dominant classes associated with the palace. It is not unusual even in our days to hear this opinion, as if the texts that were produced without the social pressures of the prophets should be pigeonholed into the category of palace texts and are in themselves insensitive to poverty or injustice.[2] A supposed "material basis" of wisdom has been postulated that places it as a product of palaces and centers of power, whose ideological purpose would be to sustain the unjust social order.[3] In our opinion, this reading has no textual support, nor does it take into account the numerous texts of wisdom that express the anguish over injustice and the longing for a more balanced society. We will return to this later, but for now let us note that in a large number of proverbs where creation is not abundant, the few that we find are referred to proclaiming due respect for the weak and poor. To the above, we add two more proverbs:

The rich and the poor meet;

---

[1] H.-J. Hermisson, "Observations on the Creation Theology in Wisdom," *Israelite Wisdom* (ed. J. Gammie *et al.*; New York: Scholars Press, 1978), 45.

[2] See the article by R. López, "La liberación de los oprimidos, ideal y práctica sapiencial," *RIBLA* 9 (1991): 7-20, where he analyzes the commitment of the wise to justice and social inequality.

[3] See M. Clevenot, *Materialist Reading of the Bible* (Salamanca: Sígueme, 1978), 99-100; the Presentation and Judgment by X. Pikaza, 9-38, is enlightening.

The Lord made them both. (22:2)

and

The poor and the oppressor meet;
Yahweh enlightens the eyes of both of them. (29:13)

The expression "enlightens the eyes" refers to the act of birth when God opens the eyes of the newborn. In both cases, the existence of the poor and the rich is at stake, and the wise affirm that both the rich and the poor owe their lives to the Creator. The text also establishes that the rich cannot boast of the weak and the poor because their lives are worth as much as anyone else's. Although these proverbs can be read in such a way as to justify the oppression of the poor and encourage their patience and tolerance — and not their rebellion — based on the common destiny that ultimately awaits them both, what we see in them is that they establish that their economic weakness does not make the poor less worthy and places them on an equal footing with their oppressor. Both have been brought into the world by the same God and both deserve the respect that is denied to the poor. In these cases, the wise do not ask about the origin of poverty, nor do they seek to explain or condemn it. They are interested in the dignity of those who are marginalized because they are poor and sees in this a contradiction with God's creative intention.

Wisdom and Everyday Life in Proverbs

The thinking of the wise is clear. People are considered either wise or foolish, and there is nothing in between. The former walk the earthly path in harmony with God and God's creation and thus enjoy life and its pleasures, while the foolish direct their steps toward perdition and will see their days ruined. The wise person is therefore the person capable of distinguishing between good and evil. It is a simple theology, perhaps too simple, but it has the virtue of being easy to apply to everyday life. It is not a theology that tries to explain or understand life, but rather seeks to give instructions for living life in agreement with God and to warn about the dangers of straying from the right path.[1] This is how Psalm 1 puts it, in order to establish a starting point for the entire collection of psalms: the one who meditates on the law and seeks

---

[1]G. Gorgulho argues that the antithesis righteous-wicked expresses the social order of the economic system at the end of the Judean monarchy; in this sense, faced with the threat of the Babylonian invasion, "the righteous" see themselves "liberated from violence" and live in the justice promoted by God, see "Proverbs," *CBL II* (ed. A. Levoratti; Estella: Verbo Divino, 2007), 810.

the way of God will be "like a tree planted by streams of water" for whom everything will prosper; Another fate will befall the wicked, who will be swept away by the wind and will have no place in the "congregation of the righteous" nor will he "rise on the day of judgment," a way of saying that the unwise will not participate in that final day of just judgment for those who remained faithful. The psalm closes with an image much loved by the wise, that of the two paths:

> For Yahweh knows the way of the righteous;
> but the way of the wicked leads to death.

In this case, the verb to know (*yada*) has the meaning of "blesses," "recognizes," "illuminates." This condition of conceiving reality as belonging to one path or another is reflected in the preferred literary form of proverbs, which is antithetical parallelism. One sentence exposes a situation and the next its opposite. Although the text also uses other literary forms, it is not by chance that this is the one the text uses most. Examples abound:

> The hope of the righteous is joy;
> but the hope of the wicked will perish. (10:28)
> The righteous will never be removed;
> but the wicked will not inhabit the land. (10:30)

There are various behaviors that preserve life and all of them are linked to being responsible in the family and daily relationships. To be on the right side, one must respect one's parents (4:1; 6:20; 13:1); one must be prudent in the decisions of daily life (10:19; 16:23); one must control one's passions and excessive impulses (14:29; 15:1; 15:18; 16:32). We have already mentioned that respect for the poor is an attitude appreciated by the wise (14:31; 17:5); also honesty in business (10:2; 12:17; "it is better to have a little with justice than a lot without it" 16:8); accepting being corrected ("He who loves correction loves knowledge..." 12:1). Loyalty to friends and relatives has a privileged place when it says, "Do not forsake your friend or your father's friend..." (27:10). And although there are many and varied proverbs that point out the right path and warn about the dangers of abandoning them, they all have, as a common basis, the recognition of the Creator so that life may be abundant and blessed. In 10:27 it says it this way:

> The fear of the Lord prolongs life;
> But the years of the wicked will be shortened.

It is not very far-fetched to think that the wise saw an automatic relationship between living many or few days and the reverence given to divinity. Increase and shorten, although clear words, acquire in this case a particular dimension that makes them

281

allude to plenitude or decadence. Thus the days of those who fear God will be lived in plenitude while the others will be a burden for the soul. This symbolic use of the terms has not always been well understood, which has led to simplifying wisdom theology as if it were a mere retributive game by which good behavior adds days to the calendar and bad behavior subtracts them. Sometimes it is thought that proverbs and wisdom theology offer us a path of good behavior that ensures wealth and material prosperity. But experience testified that this was not always the case and the use of poetic language allowed us to account for this contradictory reality. A clear example of this symbolic use of certain key words can be seen in this sentence where the reference to food transcends the possible proteins it may provide:

The righteous eats to satisfy his soul,
But the stomach of the wicked will be empty. (13:25)

"Soul" (*nefesh*) is placed in parallel with "stomach" or "belly" (*beten*) so that both realities are considered symbolic because food is not sent to the soul nor will the stomach of the wicked be empty just because that one is wicked.

As expected, wisdom theology also strives to clarify which behaviors lead to perdition and the abandonment of the blessed life. They are in principle the opposite of those already mentioned, but there are also particular aspects that it is interested in highlighting in order to warn people about the risks to which they are exposed. There are many texts dedicated to this, but the common denominator is the distancing of the will to please the Lord. Fools are carried away by their impulses and do not consider the consequences of this. In wisdom theology, there are several behaviors that lead to losing one's life and days.

Wisdom theology places a high value on the corruption that adultery produces. The key texts are Prov 2:16-19; 5:1-23; 6:24-7:27. In all cases, they refer to the man who unites with a married woman. The weight of the betrayal is placed on the conduct of the woman, who is described as seductive and eager to deceive her husband. In turn, the woman who commits adultery is considered indolent:

The behavior of an adulterous woman is this: She eats,
wipes her mouth,
and says: I have done no wrong. (30:20)[1]

---

[1]Eating is also associated with sexuality in the story of Joseph, when his master says that he kept for himself "the bread that he ate" in reference to his wife (Gen 39:6); also Prov 6:26, see G. von Rad, "La historia de José y la antigua *hokma*," 255-62.

Her conduct causes the loss of the man who is trapped by the sexual offer and this leads him to death, "her steps are leading to the *grave*" (5:5). As in other texts of the Old Testament, the weight of patriarchal culture is reflected in these thoughts where the woman is found responsible for the deviations of the man. But having recognized this condition as abnormal, it is necessary to point out the significance of wisdom considering sexuality as that aspect of life that can most complicate existence. The man is warned that he must be content with his wife (5:19) and it is said of the woman who deceives her husband that she is worse than the one who prostitutes herself because the latter only seeks bread or money while the adulteress lies and traps the man's soul (6:26). Wisdom thought recognizes the need for an economy of sexuality that establishes rules of coexistence and at the same time understands that these rules are violated and warns about the tragedy that the violation of these rules brings to life. In the context of wisdom theology, this does not mean that the woman's adultery puts creation in crisis, but that it impacts someone closer and more visible: the husband. It is a theology of the everyday and consequently the problem is posed by the deceived man, since "jealousy infuriates the husband, and he will not show mercy on the day of vengeance" (6:35).

If adultery destroys life, so does excess alcohol. In 23:29-35, the man is described as drunk, losing his sense of reality and becoming involved in fights and lamentations. This is not a criticism of wine itself, which is celebrated on several occasions and recommended as a way of forgetting sorrows or lulling the one who will soon die (31:6-7), but what is condemned is the excess that disturbs the mind and makes the mind cloudy. As with adultery, what happens here is the loss of the sense of what benefits life and falls into the error that leads to destruction. A proverb points out that drunkenness leads to poverty and poverty is considered a misfortune:

A poor man is he who loves pleasures,
And he who loves wine and ointments will not become
rich. (20:17)

But the most serious thing is that it makes people lose the path of wisdom:

Arrogant is wine, alcohol disturbs,
And he who errs in them is not wise. (20:1)

And makes kings forget the law and the rights of the poor:

It is not for kings, O Lemuel, it is not for kings to drink
wine,
Nor alcohol from princes;
Lest they drink and forget the law,
And pervert the justice of all the poor. (31:4-5)

Other behaviors are also denounced as responsible for
losing the right path and leading to death. Laziness (6:10-11) and
excessive talk pervert people's lives (10:19). What emerges from
this quick review of condemned attitudes is that wisdom considers
that life and death are at stake in everyday situations. It would be
a mistake to understand that this way of thinking has a limited
concept of the value of life. If a drunken binge or being lazy were
enough of a fault to lose one's judgment and God's blessing, one
would be faced with a superficial theology that is not very
understanding of human behavior. Another way of understanding
this way of thinking is to consider that its theology seeks to
identify in everyday acts the signs of a positive or negative
relationship with God. It does not ask about what one thinks or
declares but about what one does; it does not seek to confirm a
doctrine but to perceive how life itself is a reflection of God's will.

James Crenshaw has clearly pointed out that in order to
avoid falling and losing one's life and days, one's own strength is
insufficient.[1] Relying on oneself has no future and will lead to
frustration, and that is why it is said in 3:5:

Trust in Yahweh with all your heart,
and do not rely on your own intelligence.

On the other hand, the search to follow the right path and not get
lost supposes the guidance of God, not an individual discernment
product of one's own sagacity. This is where the notion that
wisdom is an attribute of divinity that is offered as a gift (grace)
from God to illuminate the path gains strength. In the poem of
Prov 8:22-31 wisdom almost takes on an entity of its own and is
placed next to Yahweh helping in the design of the cosmos (8:30)
but we already mentioned above that its personification is a
literary resource and in the story it has no entity of its own. Proof
of this is the little or no influence that this poem has had on the
rest of the Scriptures. Walter Brueggemann has characterized it as
a poem that "stands out alone" in the concert of the theology of

---

[1] J. Crenshaw, *Old Testament Wisdom* (Atlanta: John Knox Press, 1981), 91.
It is noteworthy that in late wisdom texts such as Ecclesiasticus the idea of one's
own inner strength as a way of conducting oneself in life is found: "Hold fast the
counsel of your heart / For no one is more faithful to you than it" (37:13) and "In
all your acts trust in yourself / For this is also keeping the commandments" (32:23);
this thought is dissonant with the general theology of the Old Testament.

the Old Testament and that, although it deserves our attention, it did not impact the elaboration of other texts.[1] But if the idea of a personified wisdom does not thrive in biblical theology, the concept of a God who "is wise" and concentrates all knowledge in the divine person does thrive. The attributes of wisdom are those of God and therefore these words put into the mouth of wisdom are read as if they were from the very mouth of God:

> To the simple he says: Come here.
> To those lacking in sanity he says:
> Come, eat my bread,
> and drink the wine that I have mixed.
> Leave the silliness and live,
> and walk in the path of understanding. (9:4-6)

Counter-Theology of Ecclesiastes: All is a Vapor that Vanishes

Ecclesiastes is a work of wisdom, but it differs greatly from Proverbs. Together with Job, they can be considered the two works of wisdom that present a kind of counter-theology to the thinking of the wise. If Proverbs expresses the intimate conviction that wisdom and the observance of God's will grant protection and prosperity to the pious, these other books question this theology from different places and raise the anguish and desolation that comes from seeing that the opposite also abounds in the experience of life: faithful who suffer, believers who perceive life as meaningless, fearful of God who find no comfort for their sorrows. Ecclesiastes[2] shares in common with Job that both give theological answers to situations that are their own and that they face with passion and firmness. But it differs from Job in that Ecclesiastes is attributed to Solomon, while Job is considered a foreigner. It is not foreign to this game of canon that Job challenges God like no other character in the Old Testament—and therefore it is an attitude that could be tolerated in the mouth of a foreigner[3]—

---

[1]W. Brueggemann, *Teología del Antiguo Testamento* (Salamanca: Sígueme, 2007), 370.

[2]The Hebrew name of the book is *qohelet* (from the root *qahal*, "assembly," "community," see Dt 9:10; 10:4; Ezra 10:12) which can mean either the representative of the community or the one who addresses it (hence Martin Luther translated it as "the preacher"); it is not a proper name but rather an office or function of the person. We use it to refer both to the book and to its semiotic author.

[3]L. Alonso Schökel takes up this argument and calls Job "a pagan;" he also points out that his name would have sounded similar to the word for "enemy" (see the Hebrew text in 13:24); in our opinion, the first observation of this author is excessive, since Job is not treated in the story as a pagan, but his condition as a

while Ecclesiastes expresses a profound reflection on the meaning of life and existence, something that could be understood as a natural product of the ingenuity of Solomon, considered the wisest of kings. But their greatest difference is that Job questions God and divine conduct while Ecclesiastes confirms the work of God but looks at it with skepticism and disdain. Rabbinic tradition has attributed Proverbs, Ecclesiastes and Song of Solomon to Solomon and has explained their strong differences by assigning them a different place in the life of the king. In a passage of the Midrash it is said:

> Rabbi Jonathan said: First he wrote the Song of Songs, then Proverbs and then Ecclesiastes (...) When a man is young you compose songs; When he grows and matures he writes proverbs and sayings; when he is old he speaks of the vanity of things. Rabbi Jannai, father-in-law of Rabbi Ammi said: We all agree that he composed Qohelet at the end of his days."[1]

Aside from the material authorship, what interests us here is that for the author of Ecclesiastes life does not have enough entity to be worth living and although the author recognizes God as creator the author can only see emptiness and monotony in the days. If Job suffers because of what happens to him, Ecclesiastes does so because of what is expected from life but does not happen.

Vapor of Vapors, Everything is Vapor

The word *hebel* means vapor, and is present in the short book of Ecclesiastes about thirty times. In the form *habel habelim* it indicates a superlative that could be translated as "the greatest of illusions" or "the most fragile of the fragile" or in a more interpretive way as "the height of absurdity," and it is used twice at the ends of the work (1:2 and 12:8) in order to frame the entire book with these words. By beginning and ending with "Vapor of vapors," or as it is usually translated in a classical way "vanity of vanities," it establishes a conceptual framework on which its theology will be built. This linguistic structure (a noun in the singular plus its plural) is used to highlight things that in themselves have a relative value but that in the superlative stand as models of excellence, such is the case of "king of kings" and "song of songs;" In this way, it indicates that one seeks to bring an act, a virtue, or a calamity to its maximum expression. There is

---

foreigner is part of the idea that there was of ancient wisdom see L. Alonso Schökel & J. L. Sicre Díaz, *Job* (Madrid: Cristiandad, 1982), 98.

[1]*Midrás* (Estella: Verbo Divino, 1991).

perhaps no stronger image to speak of the futility and fleetingness of life than to compare it to the vapor that dissolves in the air, that has nobody and does not survive the breath of a breeze. This volatility of life does not lead in Ecclesiastes to the denial of God, but the existential emptiness affirms it in a faith that dares to doubt and question reality. The author does not name God, but still knows God behind everything that happens and shows curiosity to know the ways of divinity, even though the author acknowledge a lack of capacity to understand it. The author understands that the divine dimension exceeds the capacity of human understanding and that any pretension in that sense is vain and mistaken. In a clear criticism of the author's wise colleagues who proclaim themselves to be the possessors of all the secrets of creation, the author of Ecclesiastes says:

> ...and I have seen all the works of God, which no man can find out, the work that is done under the sun; though a man labor and seek it, he will not find it; though a wise man say that he knows it, he will not be able to find it. (8:17)

For the wise of Ecclesiastes, the secrets of the cosmos and of life are hidden from the human mind, and this is a reality that, on the one hand, establishes the limits of the human being, but on the other, produces anguish and uneasiness. The almost inconceivable statement in 4:2 and 6:3 that it is better to be dead than alive is understood in the context of considering that to live is to be immersed in a world where the main questions have no answer and reality is hostile both because of the injustices that are observed and because of the inability to reverse them. In life, which is recognized as a gift from God, painful injustices are observed and no political or religious way out is perceived to overcome them. It is not believed that a more skillful or honest ruler can generate the justice that reality denies to people, particularly if we remember that the semiotic author of these pages is Solomon, the wise king par excellence, whom no one can expect to surpass.[1] Nor is the exercise of sacred rites and the repetition of prayers — unlike the experience of the prophets who sometimes rescue and value them — perceived as a path to achieving social justice and peace of mind. This situation leads to

---

[1]Why not think that in Ecclesiastes his attribution to Solomon could have had the sense of saying that if the wisest king of all and whose wisdom was expressed in his capacity to be a fair arbitrator could not organize a society with justice and without violence, it is a sign that inequalities are so difficult to eradicate that they lead honest and sensitive person to uneasiness and skepticism.

living life as a space where pain and lack of plans dominate the days.

In the complexity of the book's thought, it seems that 9:4 reverses this idea ("There is still hope for everyone who is among the living; for a living dog is better than a dead lion"). But this phrase is said in the context of lamenting that the righteous and the wicked go to the same fate when they die and that their loves and hatreds will be lost together and forgotten in the same way; thus, it seems that the righteous gain nothing with their commitment and the wicked will lose nothing with their lack of concern for the things of God. When evaluating this situation, one will think that there is nothing better than enjoying the moment and concentrating life on personal gestures that give us momentary satisfaction. There is hope because we are alive and can enjoy some of the delights of life, but nothing will change. Life is nothing more than a vapor that mysteriously dissolves into the air.

Injustices Are The Wound That Does Not Close

On the basis of this conception of life as an ephemeral and inconsistent entity, the theology of Ecclesiastes builds three pillars to support faith. The first is the perception that life is a constant attempt by human beings to "fight against the wind." There is a thirst to understand the world and to find meaning in the days that is frustrated in everyday experience. The following text is a clear expression of this thought:

> I turned and saw all the violence that is done under the sun; and behold, the tears of the oppressed, with no one to comfort them; and power was in the hand of their oppressors, and for them there was no comfort. And I praised the dead, who are dead, more than the living, who are still alive. And I considered him more fortunate who has not yet been, who has not seen the evil deeds that are done under the sun. I saw that every labor and every skill arouses envy in a man against his neighbor; this too is vanity and striving against the wind (4:1-4; also 6:4-5).

In this text it is clearly presented that the essential anguish is caused by the injustices that the oppressors exercise on the poor and oppressed. It is the combination of violence against the weak and seeing that power is in the hands of the oppressors that leads Ecclesiastes to dismay. Fighting against the wind means facing an impossible and absurd task because the forces are so unequal that whoever seeks justice will have no chance of achieving it. At this point we can observe the difference with the theology of the

288

exodus, there in the face of genocide and oppression a God is revealed who liberates and generates the conditions for the people of God to walk toward freedom. That of Deuteronomy when it says "See, I have set before you today life and good, death and evil..." (30:15) and urges to choose life. This is not the case in Ecclesiastes, where injustice is seen as established and where God does not appear to promote a change of situation but as those who can serve as a consolation to carry on with life despite the anguish that this produces.

We may not agree that nothing is possible to do against injustice, but what emerges from the thought of these wise people is that they see their strength overwhelmed by the magnitude of the violence that is exercised on the weak and they do not find in God an ally in the fight against injustice. That is why we call Ecclesiastes counter-theology. Ecclesiastes questions the image of God presented in Proverbs where God is a benevolent being and is described as the promoter of justice and peace. However, Ecclesiastes perceives God as indolent in the face of the ever present oppression. If we have to describe Ecclesiastes' relationship with God, we see it rather as the last resort before rejecting life. By saying "I hated life" (2:17) or by testifying that formal excuses are given for oppression (5:7), Ecclesiastes closes off any possibility of finding a way out that would give dignity to the crushed human being and meaning to those who are sensitive to the pain and anguish suffered by their fellow humans. It is then that the proposal arises to distract the mind with feasts and good food in order not to become even more frustrated. The author says this in verses that respond to 5:7:

> Behold, the good thing which I have seen: that it is good to eat and drink and to enjoy the goodness of all his labor and toil under the sun, all the days of his life which God has given him; for this is his portion. Likewise to every man to whom God gives riches and possessions, and gives him the power to eat from them, and to take his portion, and to enjoy his labor, this is the gift of God. For he will not long remember the days of his life, for God will fill his heart with joy. (5:18-20)

Ecclesiastes does so from a resigned and quietist theology. Ecclesiastes does not question society but the image of God that is offered and that does not correspond to the situation of injustice and violence that the poor suffer. One can be convinced that God wants to free God's people from these humiliations but in the thought of Ecclesiastes the theology that is criticized has prided itself on being a theology of everyday and practical facts and that

289

has done nothing more than justify God by avoiding contrasting God with the shameful reality of daily violence. This pillar shows that there is something in the conception of God that does not close the circle and opens to the intuition that another God is possible.

The Opportune Time and the Time of Justice

The second pillar of the theology of Ecclesiastes is what we call an opportune time. Things do not happen by chance or at any time. According to the theology of Ecclesiastes, each event occurs at the precise moment at which it has been destined by God. However, there is no simple determinism, since a lack of wisdom can cause the original plan to fail and make things happen in an incorrect and untimely manner. In 7:17, there is a warning about the risk of falling into impiety and that this can lead a person to "die *before their time;*" in 8:5-6, it is pointed out that the wise one knows how to discern the times and knows when things must be done. These texts show us that there is not always a fatalistic sense in Ecclesiastes and that the human being's capacity to do things at the right time or to make mistakes is recognized. For this reason, it does not fall into simplistic thinking and affirms that the strong also lose and that "there are wise men who have no bread" because "a bad time comes to everyone." Ecclesiastes reflects that life and its vicissitudes do not discriminate between the righteous and the sinners and that one should not expect a reward for having been a faithful follower of the rules. Ecclesiastes adds that people, however wise they may be, do not know "their time" (9:11-12), an expression used to indicate that the day of death is known only by God and will come "like fish caught in a net or like birds in a trap."

Unlike the Greek word, the Hebrew word for time (*'et*) contains both the sense of the density of a moment and that of simply "moment," any moment. If we are to compare it with the Greek, in the quotations to which we refer here, it should be noted that it is close to *kairos*, the special time when something is to happen or when several things come together and produce a particular moment, and not to *chronos*, time in the plain sense that passes. This is how the Septuagint translates it (*kairos*) in its version of Ecclesiastes, and it privileges the density of time rather than its mere passing. In the Old Testament texts, the word *'et* refers both to a particular moment, to a suitable climate for something to happen, and to the current use of the term (Gen 38:1; Ex 13:10; Dt 1:18, etc.). But, in our book, it is not the simple becoming of moments but the instant in which something special happens with the person or with the people. The times that Ecclesiastes says time (*'et*) corresponds to the moment in which something happens because everything has been arranged for it by God.

The major poem on the opportune time is found in 3:1-8. It lists fourteen pairs of contrasting actions (destroy, build; save, throw away; tear, sew, etc.). The number fourteen, being the doubling of seven, evokes a superlative degree of positivity.[1] Only the first pair is outside the human being's will (birth, death), while the rest are concrete acts that are in the divine hands. He reserves the last two for the most visceral actions:

> a time to love, and a time to hate;
> time of war, and time of peace.

Let us note the game of reversing the pairs so that in the first the positive value opens the verse and in the second it closes it. In this way the end is left for the "time of peace" (*'et shalom*) which consists of much more than the absence of war and includes the establishment of harmony, coexistence, balance between people, nations and therefore being in friendship with God. And after the poem, Ecclesiastes is carried away by favored themes, the futility of life, eating and drinking as an alternative to uneasiness, the repetition of events and the well-known monotony of the succession of days and hours expressed in 3:15 which says:

> That which was, is already; and that which is to be, was
> already; and God restores what has passed away.

But the fact that each thing happens again and again and at the opportune moment does not take away from the shame that where equity and justice should reside, evil dominates and the wicked sets up their seat. That wound remains open and is not healed with the tranquility of suspecting that the hand of the creator is behind everything. The theology of the wise one does not forget that the central core of existence is justice and that this is violated in life; that is why Ecclesiastes glimpses one of the most solemn and profound affirmations of the book when it says:

> And I said in my heart, God will judge the righteous and
> the wicked;
> because there is a time for everything and for every work.

---

[1]See Gen 4:15, where it is established that whoever kills Cain will pay for it fourteen times over; also Ps 12:6; 79:12; Prov 6:31; Isa 30:26; in all cases the number seven is used in its dual form to express a superlative, although most Spanish translations render it as "seven."

In God's time, there is a time for judgment. Injustices will not go unpunished because every work will be judged at some point. The *shalom* of the last verse of the poem is not built on impunity even when in life, and even in history, the wise one feels that he will not find the justice desired and deserved by the poor. When it says in v. 20, "everything goes to one place; everything comes from dust, and everything will return to dust" it seems like a repetition of his already known pessimism but in this case it is not because Ecclesiastes announces that God's justice is effective and that on the final day the equality that did not exist on Earth will become reality in the dust from which we were all formed by the creator.

An Ordered and Disordered Cosmos

An ordered universe is the third pillar of the theology of Ecclesiastes. It is ordered because, in accordance with the purest doctrine of wisdom, everything happens under the supervision of God and the divine will is behind every event. The times, the cycles, the life that is born and dies, everything is guided by the wise hand of the creator. Even the rewards and punishments are dominated by the divine will and thus the righteous receive their reward and the wicked their punishment. That is the order as the wise one conceives it. However, if everything could be summed up in that equation, the world should be harmonious and just without equal. In a world where nothing happens without God's will, there would be no pain or injustice. And the author of Ecclesiastes—as will the author of Job—knows that this order hides a deep disorder within it. Because he feels that not everything is going well, nor does everything happen as God's will wants it to happen. He perceives a gap between theological discourse and reality, but he does not question this perception, nor does he try to bring the parts together to unite them in a coherent discourse. He assumes that this is how things are and limits himself to describing them. His thought contains an inner contradiction, and he makes no effort to resolve it.

The vision of an ordered universe is based on the conviction that within the historical process, each thing has its assigned place. In the words of Brueggemann, "Yahweh is the hidden guarantor of an order that makes life in the world possible."[1] Things happen, benevolent or tragic, guided by the hand of God and therefore everything will ultimately be for the

---

[1] *Teología del Antiguo Testamento*, 362.

best. This differentiates him from the concept of God's action present in Genesis and in the Deuteronomistic history. There, God is in favor of what is good, what is just, and is committed to acting in that way. Evil is the product of human disobedience or of the action of "the enemies" represented by idolatry, social injustice, and the humiliation of one's neighbor. God supports those who work and fight for liberation from all servitude while other human forces, sometimes within the same community and sometimes from outside it, oppose this project. The dynamic of the story that begins with the account of creation and continues with the testimony of the prophets consists in presenting the scenario of the struggle between impiety and justice, between the vocation of the oppressed human beings to become free against the will of those who oppress them. But, in Ecclesiastes, the idea of an order that is responsible for both the good and the bad prevails. In a certain way, the bad (what he calls "the evil days:" the time of injustice, violence) is also the will of God and hides a beneficial end for the human being. This end, which we are not given to know but which we must accept, is a spring of God alone and not even the wise have access to its key. Thus it is understood that on several occasions he recommends that we should enjoy the good weather with banquets and joy because the bad days are also marked by God on the path of the human being and whatever the divine conduct, in any case they will also come in due time.

And yet, even accepting this reality, Ecclesiastes does not fail to perceive the disorder at the very core of human experience. This conception where even the bad will be for the good because everything comes from God, is crossed by the intimate conviction that undeserved suffering, violence toward the innocent and injustices suffered by the weak can never be a blessing, however mysterious it may be presented. This is the origin and crux of the anguish that the wise one suffers. Not only because he perceives that cruelty cannot come from God even if it is attempted to be presented in this way, but also because he questions the meaning of a life in which one must work so that the next generation can enjoy the product of his work without realizing that perhaps he will pass his effort on to a fool who does not deserve it. The statement that life is "hateful" (2:17), something unthinkable in the rest of biblical literature, is understandable when it is the expression of someone who feels that their days are the space to toil in tedious work whose product will then have to be bequeathed to a possible impious person who will enjoy it. This conviction that injustices are irreparable contradicts the theological orthodoxy that speaks of the benevolent God but at the same time disqualifies Ecclesiastes from finding the necessary strength to question that theology. It is at this crossroads — where the author finds himself with a desire to die, with a disdain for life — that Ecclesiastes must be understood. Deep down, Ecclesiastes carries the burden of feeling that even God has failed humanity, but that the search for the true God has not ceased because of the knowledge that God does not fail.

At the end of the book, the editor has introduced a conclusion. In a historicist reading, this text would be marginalized as secondary and foreign to the main body. However, the reflection on the canon must be made on the entire text and not on what a supposed reconstruction indicates as older and therefore more legitimate. In this conclusion, the content of the book is evaluated, and Ecclesiastes concludes that "there is no point in writing many books; much study is wearisome for the body" (12:12). These words are not, as might be expected, an invitation from a wise one to ignorance or intellectual frivolity, but rather they seek to place human thought in its proper place. They can be read as self-criticism, as a warning to the reader about everything said in this book. Ecclesiastes then states what is the cornerstone of wise thought: "The end of all the discourse that you have heard is: fear God and keep the divine commandments."

The Counter-Theology of Job: Unthinkable Suffering

If the theology of Ecclesiastes is counter-theology because it challenges the supposed perfect order of creation, Job is so because it poses the inconceivable for sapiential theology: that the just and faithful should be subjected to suffering. But his theology is not limited to this theme but addresses several other aspects, always walking on the edge of what for many in his time could be considered an affront to God: why do we suffer? Can I sin without knowing it? Is God guilty of our ills? And the most powerful: can a human being challenge God and question God's conduct? All these questions and others of the same tune are present in the book and shape more than a theology. They shape a theological *attitude*. This condition of Job's theology is also reflected in his literary style, since the prose and poetry sections present different theological themes. In the prologue, what is at stake is whether Job practices devotion and fear of God selflessly or whether he does so because he expects to be blessed with a peaceful life as a reward. Is his upright life based on a heart that only seeks to be just with the Creator God, or is it aimed at acquiring the benefits that will be bestowed upon him for his uprightness?[1] In this approach, the suffering of the innocent occurs as a test to verify the integrity of his faith and therefore is presented in function of that, not as a central theme. We will return to this later. In the poetic section, the crux of the discussion will be the origin of the suffering of the righteous.

Two Ways of Doing Theology

Jorge Pixley is the one who most clearly stated that in Job there is a radical critique of the way of doing theology.[2] He points out that Job's so-called friends question his claims based on an artificial and disembodied theological foundation that is constituted from the simple affirmation that all suffering corresponds to a committed sin. Then they do not stop questioning Job, insisting that, if he suffers, it is because he has committed some fault, even if he does not want to recognize it. Faced with this formal way of doing theology, Job replies with the reflection of someone who knows he is innocent and intuits that although the reasoning of his friends has the logic of the classical theology of the wise, their experience is different and this leads him to confront the theology of his friends with that which arises from his experience. Job's theology is made with flesh and blood, while that of his friends is built from coherent reasoning but alien to the suffering they have before them.

The question at the bottom of this is the conception of who the biblical God is and how humans relate to God. In the theology of Job's friends, God is far away and we can speak of God only through previously agreed premises. The reflection is as follows: If nothing happens without God's permission and if God's will is to bless the just and pious, then whoever suffers does so because they have not been as just and pious as they should have been. The same reflection applies to the sick and the poor, because the Lord would not allow just persona to suffer any of these calamities in their body or in their family. In their view, divine oversight protects from suffering and ensures that the innocent will never suffer ridicule. In his first speech, Eliphaz responds to Job and says:

Remember... what innocent person has been destroyed?

---

[1]J. Crenshaw points out that the suffering of the innocent is a secondary theme in the prologue, as it is presented as the way of resolving the dispute between God and Satan. *Old Testament Wisdom* (Atlanta: John Knox Press, 1981), 101.

[2]J. Pixley, *Job* (San José de Costa Rica: DEI, 1982), 14-15.

And where have the upright been cut off? (4:7)

These words of Eliphaz express a theology and a way of understanding the relationship with God that is consistent with the logic of retributive wisdom. But such a theological task loses its relationship with the human and, in particular, with human pain. It thinks about God, but is insensitive to the lives of people and their problems. Hence, it has been said that the theology of Job's friends describes an anti-God and is an anti-theology; a way of speaking about God without taking into account life and creation.[1] A God who is perceived outside of life, as a syllogism and not as a responsible creator attentive to the divine creation, is not the God that the Scriptures show us but one who will adjust to our intellectual or social needs, distorting the true divine identity. Rather than liberating, such a God will reinforce the mechanisms of oppression because that God will insist on personal sin as the origin of poverty, illness and misfortune. This God will not be a God who grieves over suffering, but on the contrary one who inflicts it on those who are supposed not follow the divine ways or are unaware of the divine Law. The theology of Job's friends is not only the expression of their coldness in the face of Job's pain but mainly that of God's coldness and indifference to Job's tragedy and the proclamation that God actually becomes the author of the misfortunes that happen to the wicked.

Job has a different vision of the God in whom he entrusts his days. The theology that is presented in Job's speeches is not a closed scheme nor is it organized as such. It is a claim and a denunciation against what is presented to him as an absolute and therefore indisputable truth. He speaks from what happens to him and reflects from his inner self where he feels that a tremendous injustice has been done to him and his family. He says that he is a victim of God's action:

Have I sinned? What can I do to you, guardian of men?
Why do you make me your target?
to the point of becoming a burden to myself? (7:20)

His theological attitude is that of someone who understands that his anguish is meaningless and is not the result of his actions. He suffers and does not know why. And as the pages go by, in his

---

[1]See L.A. Solano Rossi, "Los caminos de la teología y de la anti-teología en el libro de Job," *RIBLA* 50 (2005): 53-55, the author critiques the current "theology of prosperity" based on the case of Job; he considers it the postmodern version of the theology of retribution, according to which riches and well-being are gifts given by God only to the faithful and all misfortune has as its origin the sin committed by the one who suffers it.

speeches, he will denounce that his suffering is not linked to the sins he may have committed. That the calamities he suffers are not consistent with his pious life and that the righteous can suffer just as much as the wicked. Circumstances lead the reader to understand that misfortunes can happen to the righteous as well as the sinner. Slowly but surely, in Job's words, the understanding of human suffering is revealed as a part of life that we do not understand and for which we can demand an explanation from God.

Job Curses and Accuses Himself

Job's dialogue with his three friends is framed by two solemn speeches by Job. In the first, he curses the day he was born (chap. 3). In the last, he declares his innocence with a formula by which he accuses himself and demands that they prove his fault (chap. 29-31). In both cases, he expresses a judgment against God with radical firmness and confirms the criticism of sapiential theology by opposing it with its counter-theology. Already in 2:9 — in the narrative section — Job's wife, seeing how calamities fell one after another in her husband's life, had recommended that he curse God and die. Both actions went together in the mind of a pious believer, since to reject God's blessing and to curse God was to put oneself outside the reach of divine protection and to reject any gesture in divine favor. On that occasion, Job responds to his wife by calling her a fool for what she says and urging her to accept that everything comes from God, whether good or bad. This response is still in tune with wisdom theology, but in the poetic section there is a shift in the theology of the book. Now Job raises his claim to God, although he does so indirectly to avoid his speech being discredited by being considered as disrespectful to divinity.

Job's theology does not shy away from presenting his anguish:

> May the day I was born perish,
> And in the night when it was said, A man is conceived.
> That day will be one of darkness,
> And may God not take care of him from above,
> Nor may light shine upon it.
> Darkness and the shadow of death darken it;
> Let the clouds cover it
> And make it horrible as a dark day. (3:3-5)

Both birth and the night of conception are cursed. Both were days of glory for any couple, but they are devalued by Job's anguish. In his cry, he calls for darkness to come upon him, which is a way of sending him back to the time before creation when there was nothing but darkness and the voice of God had not yet organized and blessed the world. This condition places his own life outside of creation, and it is this very thing that he reinforces later when he declares:

Why did I not die in the womb, or expire when I came out
of the belly?
Why did my knees welcome me?
and the breasts for him to suckle?
For now I would be dead, and at rest;
I would sleep and be at rest. (3:11-13)

In verse 16 Job says that he wishes he had preferred to have been aborted and to never have seen the light.

Ecclesiastes had raised the same issue from the anguish of the lack of flavor in life and the meaninglessness of the days; routine and insipidity undermined his faith and overwhelmed him. At the other extreme, Job lives full of experiences and is overwhelmed by the things that happen to him, but his problem is that he cannot understand them. In Job, his uneasiness about life comes from feeling that everything that happens to him escapes his understanding and that his experience of pain questions his most precious treasure, which is the trust that God does everything for the good of those who fear God. That faith has been eroded by events and leads him to proclaim his rejection of life and to long for darkness and oblivion. Job, "a man of integrity and justice, fearing God and eschewing evil," arrives at the conviction that his God is unjust and that nothing justifies the suffering to which he has been condemned. Dying, or not being born, is better than waking up every morning to face that terrible reality. How far and how dissonant is this theology from those affirmations of the wisdom thought of Proverbs that say:

My son, do not forget my law, but let your heart keep my
commandments; for your days and years of life will be
many, and peace will increase in you (3:1-2);

or in 9:11:

For through me your days will be multiplied and your
years of life will be added to you.

The life announced here is that of someone who enjoys it and hopes to prolong it and has little to do with the experience of Job. The prophets also affirm life with the recurring idea of returning to God as a means to acquire life (Am 5:4).[1]

---

[1] J. Crenshaw, "The Shadow of Death in Koheleth," *Israelite Wisdom* (ed. J. Gammie *et al.*; New York: Scholars Press, 1978), 206.

The central part of the book is a dialogue in which the three friends try to convince Job of God's righteousness and that he must seek within himself the origin of the evil he endures. A central text is the intervention of Eliphaz, where he goes into detail about Job's sins that justify his misfortune (22:1-30). There, he accuses him with words such as "your wickedness is great and your iniquities have no end" (v. 5); Eliphaz accuses Job of taking advantage of widows, of the poor, and of "denying bread to the hungry" (v. 7). Then he urges Job to turn to God "and prosperity will return to you" (v. 21). Eliphaz does not present proof, but infers from Job's misfortune that he has sinned greatly and that is why he suffers. But Job's theology is not nourished by axioms but by life and he persists in maintaining his innocence. The literary structure gives us an indication of its choice for Job by placing his second solemn speech as the closing of the dialogues. In it Job accuses himself. It is a recourse to irony, to question the reasons that God may have for treating him in this way, and it is a way of demanding that the evidence of his crime be exhibited. He responds to Eliphaz and the other friends and says:

> If I have walked falsely, and if my foot has made haste to deceit,
> May God weigh me on the scales of justice,
> And you will know my integrity. (31:5-6) (…)
> If I have hindered the joy of the poor, and made the widow's eyes fail;
> If I ate my morsel alone, and the fatherless did not eat of it. (31:16-17) (…)
> If I have seen someone die without clothes, and the needy without shelter;
> If I lifted up my hand against the fatherless, when I saw that they were helping me at the gate;
> My back falls off my shoulder,
> And the bone of my arm will be broken. (31:21-22)

Only those who know they are innocent will seek to demand that God measure them on the divine scales or break their bones if they are guilty. They want to disassociate themselves even from a possible love of their riches ("If I rejoice that my riches were multiplied, and that my hand finds much… it is an evil deserving of judgment, because I have denied God" 31:25, 28). This second discourse is as bold as the first, but for different reasons. God is challenged both by rejecting the life that God has given them and by demanding that God reveal the evidence of the failure that causes their sorrows. Job seeks to be shown what his crime was. Job's bet in this case is that God will not be able to prove his faults and, thus, his innocence will become evident. The three friends would be made ridiculous, but it would also reveal *God's inconsistency and cruelty*. In this we see again Job's counter-theology. If God mistreats a person, this is denounced and questioned because there is no prior agreement that grants God impunity.

Is God Innocent?

Ecclesiastes and Job suggest that reality and human experience must be taken into account as the raw materials of theology. A theological exercise that is built only on statements of thought or on theoretical concepts will always be limited in its perception of the world and of life. Hence the scandal that these counter-theologies produce in the ears of Job's friends or of the reader accustomed to a thought purified of discordant elements. Elihu, a fourth interlocutor of Job, censures his attitude of complaining before God and addresses Job with these words:

...in this you have not spoken justly;
I will answer you that God is greater than man.
Why do you fight him?
For he will not give explanations for his actions. (33:12-13)

According to Elihu's theology, the obvious affirmation that God is superior to human beings means that there is no room to ask or question what we do not understand about what happens to us, as if everything should be accepted without the possibility of demanding explanations. This way of thinking is opposed by what we call counter-theology, which consists of theology that is formed in the midst of the ups and downs of personal and social life and which makes these areas a constitutive part of its reflection. Therefore, for counter-theology to become theology *per se*, it is necessary to assume that the theoretical formulations necessary for reflection cannot omit the human factor or the analysis of external reality.[1] Doing theology is not only "talking about God" but is also talking about people and their sorrows, their expectations and frustrations, and, centrally, their dreams and utopias.

---

[1] This openness is called in Latin American liberation theology "socio-analytical mediation;" it means that knowledge of reality is achieved through the tools provided by the social sciences. It is an attempt to avoid an idealistic approach that does not consider the social dynamics inherent to every society. However, there remains a pending discussion about the ideologies behind the different social schools and their impact on the analysis.

Job takes a theological journey in his speeches. He begins by defending himself from the accusations of his friends, but soon understands that they are only repeating a mechanical pattern of thought and that his main problem does not lie within them. He understands, with regret, that the origin of his problems is in the actions of God. Chapter 9 is where Job sets out this new scenario with great clarity. First, he establishes the immense power of God (9:1-12), to such an extent that no one can hold God accountable for God's actions. "He commands the sun, but it does not rise; and he even seals the stars" (v. 7) and Job insists on highlighting the mystery of God's actions by saying "He does terrible and incomprehensible things, wonders without number; he passes before me, but I cannot see him" (v. 10-11). Then he recognizes that no one is capable of dealing with God and if he did, he would have no chance of imposing his criteria: "even if I declared myself perfect, I would be corrupt" (v. 20). His speech is a profound reflection on the power of God and the smallness of the human being, and he comes to wonder what would be the point of forgetting his complaint if he were consumed by the sorrow of knowing that his Lord considers him guilty; and if he were truly guilty, what would be the point of trying to clean up his life if he felt that he would sink into the mire of his sins? With profound pain, he understands that there is no act of justice between him and God (it is usually translated "arbitrator" or "mediator"[1]) that can establish objectively whether he has truly sinned or not (v. 33). But he demonstrates his intimate conviction of innocence by closing this speech and saying that he will not stop speaking without fear of God "because I do not believe that I have committed a fault." This last statement shows Job in all his theological splendor. He knows that he is weak and incapable of comparing himself with divinity, but he maintains his truth and dignity as an honest and faithful man, even at the cost of facing God.

The complexity of Job's thought is also seen in that even when he recognizes the inconsistency of God's actions, he does not hesitate to cry out for his protection. Despite everything that has happened, Job trusts that God is just, although in a way that he cannot explain. This is proven when Job asks to be preserved in the world of the dead, waiting for God to call him on the day of judgment and for him to answer (14:7-17). Job trusts in God's

---

[1]The Hebrew uses a verb and says "there is no *mohiach* among us" which should be translated as "balanced judgment" or an act of impartial justice.

ultimate justice but cannot accept God's present injustice and laments that "man cannot argue with God as with his neighbors" (16:21). He points out that even though his friends condemn him and even though God does not give him respite in his pain, he knows that he is innocent; and when it seems that no one on Earth will trust in his honesty, he proclaims that the truth resides beyond the Earth:

...behold, my witness is in heaven
and my testimony in the heights. (16:19)

In this line, Job's strongest bet is to announce that he has a *go'el* (19:25). The Hebrew word *go'el* refers to the world of laws and describes the person who, when faced with a murder, has the obligation to avenge that fault.[1] It is a noun with the meaning of "avenger" and a verb (*ga'al*) that can be translated as avenge, redeem and sometimes defend. In current versions, it is usually translated as "avenger" or, forcing the meaning but sometimes correctly, "redeemer."[2] God is called *go'el* at various times in the theology of Israel. In Isaiah, this identification of Yahweh with the one who rescues God's people abounds and uses this expression (Isa 44:24; 48:17; 54:8; in 47:4 they call him "our redeemer"). Psalms 74:2; 77:15; 78:35 identifies Yahweh as the *go'el* of the people of Israel. An important text is Prov 23:11 which says "Do not move the ancient border, nor invade the heritage of the orphans; for their defender (*go'el*) is strong, and he will judge against you." This is not only because it belongs to wisdom literature but because it establishes that God is the defender of the poor in the face of territorial abuse. In this case, it does not apply to murder but to an act of trampling on the rights of the poor and orphans. But where we most appreciate its meaning is in the cases in which this root appears in the narrative of the exodus of liberation. In Ex 6:6 it says: "...I will take you out of the heavy tasks of Egypt, I will free you from its servitude and I will redeem you (*ga'al*) with a strong arm;" and in the triumphal song after crossing the sea, "You led in your mercy this people whom you redeemed..." (Ex 15:13).

---

[1] This tradition was so strong that to avoid a spiral of blood, cities of asylum were established where those who had killed unintentionally could take refuge (Ex 21:13; Num 35:9-34; Dt 19:1-13).

[2] The Reina-Valera version translates it as "redeemer;" the Jerusalem Bible "defender" and notes in a footnote that it is an imperfect translation. Although the meaning of redeemer has a theological value that is not in the origin of *go'el*, we consider that it responds to the meaning that Job seeks to convey: that of someone who rescues his life.

Redemption in these texts is intimately linked to the action of freeing the people from slavery and leading them to possess a land. In a certain sense, it expresses that God has such a close relationship with God's people that God goes out to defend them and avenge them.[1] The *go'el* of Israel is the one who frees them from all forms of oppression and rescues them to give them a new life. The proclamation of Job must be read within the framework of these textual traditions. In 19:23-24, Job declares:

> Oh that my words were written!
> Let them be written in a book!
> That with iron chisel and lead
> were engraved in stone forever!

At first, we see that Job fears the oblivion of injustice and that is why he longs for his experience to be captured in writing. He knows that memory is the only refuge from the impunity of the present, so that justice can be done at some point. And Job also knows of the durability of the written word and seeks to have his claims printed in stone with chisel and lead so that posterity can work the justice that eludes him. Then he adds:

> I know that my redeemer lives,
> and that in the end (*'ajarón*) it will rise above the dust;
> And after my skin is destroyed, yet in my flesh I will see God.
> Whom I shall see, and my eyes shall see him, and not another, though my heart fails within me. (19:25-27)

The question we must ask ourselves is who is the redeemer that Job claims to have and who will rise from the dust. There are those who identify Job's *go'el* with God. But this has two problems: the first is that Job's adversary is God, not a human being, and therefore God cannot be a defender against God's own person; the second is that the expression "will rise from the dust" implies death and subsequent resurrection, which does not seem appropriate to apply to divinity. To this we must add that the text considers that "in the end" (*'ajaron* is an expression that alludes to the end of time, to the day of God's judgment) not only will Job's *go'el* rise but that Job himself will be raised and see God face to face. It will be the long-awaited moment in which Job will have the now denied opportunity to proclaim his innocence in the judgment and ask God to account for his aggressions. Job's *go'el* is not God but is a figure of justice who will defend him before God.

---

[1]G. Gutierrez links it to a family relationship by which God has the responsibility to care for and avenge Israel every time it is subjected to injustice, see *Hablar de Dios desde el sufrimiento del inocente* (Salamanca: Sígueme, 1986), 123.

We have already mentioned that Job has spoken of a mediator (9:33) and of a heavenly witness (16:19); now these figures are concentrated on the defender who will redeem him, the *go'el*.[1] At a time when his friends condemn him without considering his hardships and even God exposes him to ridicule and does not protect him, Job maintains his innocence against God and proclaims that in the universe created and dominated by that God to whom he recognizes all power, there lives someone who will be a witness and defender of his cause. Job does not know who God is, but Job affirms with certainty that God exists. Job is innocent and he will maintain this until the day when his skin is rebuilt into his flesh to face his Lord on that last day and ask God for explanations.

But the theology of Job has one last and unexpected declaration from God. God has one last word after God's long speech "from the storm" (38-41) where God does not declare Job innocent but neither guilty and exposes him to the reality that all creation is under the divine dominion and that Job can do little or nothing to modify the divine designs. It is a strong rejection of anthropocentrism by which everything must be understood by the human being and nothing that humanity does not master has meaning for human life. Faced with this speech, Job recognizes his ignorance of the mechanisms of the universe and of God's plans and assumes that he has spoken about things that are beyond his understanding. It is when God addresses Eliphaz of Teman and tells him that it is he and his friends who have not spoken the right thing about God "as my servant Job has done" (42:7). It is in vain to pretend that this opinion of God refers only to the prose section—which would take up the story abandoned in 2:13—because it is evident that it refers to the speeches of the friends and of Job in the poetic section.[2] At the end of the work, God takes the side of those who have questioned God and rejects those who did not take into account the pain of their neighbor; the friends believed that they were defending God and what they were doing was overshadowing God's action. In an unthinkable scenario throughout the work, it will be Job's prayer—and not that of the friends—that rescues their lives from disgrace because God says to

---

[1] J. Pixley rightly points out that Job's *go'el* must be understood in line with the texts where desperation leads Job to cry out for a mediator or a witness to act against God to defend him, see *El libro de Job* (San José de Costa Rica: DEI, 1982), 105.

[2] L. Alonso Schökel & J. L. Sicre Díaz, *Job* (Madrid: Cristiandad, 1982), 602-03.

Eliphaz, "I will hear his prayer" in favor of you. The roles have been reversed. Now it is the friends who must be rescued from the wrath of God because they were not as faithful as the Lord expected of them by not showing sensitivity and love in the face of the pain of others. And it is Job — the rebel, the shameless, the irreverent — who is recognized for the integrity of his faith and who, through his prayer, will save those who had no mercy on him and mistreated him.

The Unfinished Book

The Book That Continues

A work—any work—is unfinished when what it pursues does not come to fruition and remains a promise. Biblical theology tells of the path of salvation for humanity, of its anguish over injustice and inequality, of the thirst for justice that follows the above; of the hope in the redemption that only God can effect (to redeem means to rescue from slavery, to free from oppression, to restore lost freedom, to put an end to an affront or a humiliation). The Old Testament testifies to this hunger and gives a glimpse of the direction in which bread is to be found. It does not satisfy but announces the time when pain will be healed, the final space in which every stain, however dark, will be purified. For this reason, its story remains unfinished. Humanity has not completed its journey and lives in the constant challenge of knowing that the truth and justice of God await it ahead. This is true for the two great hermeneutical families that these texts treasure. Judaism patiently awaits the arrival of the Messiah, who will redeem Israel and humanity from its hardships. Christianity sees in the New Testament the continuity and fulfillment of the expectations of the Old Testament, but it is the recipient of another new expectation that also remains a promise: the second coming of Christ to bring about the just and definitive judgment that will wipe away every tear. In this perspective, Christians reread certain passages of the Old Testament and discover their validity and continuity in the course of history until the definitive consummation of time and space.

Walter Eichrodt, in his *Theology of the Old Testament*, says that in its texts "one can perceive the presence of an internal force that pushes it powerfully and incessantly forward."[1] We share this interpretation even though Eichrodt conceives this force as an almost explicit proof of the "textual" necessity of Christ; for us, this reading limits the literary integrity of the Old Testament by explicitly defining the object of its anxiety while the text itself leaves it ambiguous. We agree that there is such a force, and a

---

[1] W. Eichrodt, *Teología del Antiguo Testamento I-II* (Madrid: Cristiandad, 1975), 1: 22.

306

destiny hinted at, but the place and the name remain pending revelation. They remain unfinished. It is not by default that the Messiah is not defined in detail nor that all speculation about the date of the irruption of this new David is imprecise; on the contrary, the reluctance to give precisions is an integral part of its message and is what makes it a book with an open ending; moreover, we can even speak of an unfinished theology. This is not the first time that the biblical narratives use the resource of what remains to be completed to hint that God's action still has surprises in store and new challenges to faith. We have already seen how the Pentateuch ends before the people cross the Jordan and therefore without the possession of the land, and leaves the fulfillment of that promise made to Abraham unfinished. Several prophetic books end in an open manner and leave their own prophecies unfinished. Note the end of Amos (9:11-15) where the restoration of the house of David is announced but remains pending. Zephaniah ends with the promise of the return of the dispersed ("At that time I will restore to the peoples pure lips, at that time I will gather you..." 3:20) but the expression "at that time" denotes that it is an action to be developed in an indefinite future. The entire book of Ecclesiastes must be considered an unfinished reflection from the moment it describes the flow of time and rivers as a metaphor for life, for God's plan and for the human experience that is incessant and incapable of being captured and consummated.

This condition of Scripture as an unfinished work deserves our reflection. It is not enough to say that the force that we recognize active within the texts ends with the arrival of Jesus Christ, because that is to reduce its power to a specific and concrete response. If this were the case, with the arrival of Christ the message of the Old Testament would have come to an end and it would no longer have any value other than that of being the antecedent of the Christian faith, a historical and referential value, but already devoid of enigma, challenge and any capacity to give rise to new interpretations. If this were the case, the message would have been closed in terms of an exclusive and totalizing response that leaves no room for reconsidering the texts and their messages. We believe that the condition of unfinished work has an intrinsic value and carries a theological message to which we must do justice and not ignore. This message consists of saying that when the texts of the Old Testament are concluded, God's work has not ceased and that the texts reflect the unstoppable activity of God. In this way, we are invited to be attentive and discover where God works and to allow ourselves to be surprised by the divine will. At the same time, this condition of being open to what is new in history is something that keeps us awake and committed to the search to discern God's action in our days.

The arrival of Jesus as Messiah as testified by the New Testament—a faith that this author shares—should not be understood as the correct answer to a riddle, which when discovered annuls and disables it as an enigma. On the contrary, the texts of the New Testament challenge the Christian reader to reread those of the Old to search in them for the foundation of Christ's preaching and his faith. Without the Old Testament, there is no New Testament. For the Jewish faith, which does not consider the testimony of the Christian Scriptures of the New Testament to have theological continuity with its Scriptures, there remains the expectation of God's intervention at the time and place of divine choosing. This acts as an incentive to project forward the confidence that God's definitive justice will be exercised on the day when every wound that throughout history has gone unpunished will be vindicated. The salvation promised to Israel and longed for in its devotion is still pending fulfillment and is expressed in the fact that the end of the testimony of its Scriptures is left open.

A second element resulting from the biblical text's condition of being an unfinished work is that it carries within itself the germ of its continuation. The expectation that something will happen later has various exponents in the texts (the arrival of a messiah, the reunion in Jerusalem of the dispersed, the restitution of the "house of David," the establishment of a new heaven and a new Earth, and others) but in all cases it is an open door to what Yahweh has in store for God's people and for humanity. There is no passage that suggests that this novelty in history will be the product of human activity. On the contrary, the sign is that of preparing for what God is going to do, not for what humanity is inclined to do. The image of the woman who spreads out her tent and strengthens its stakes (Is 54); that of those who in the psalms are invited to "wait on Yahweh" (Ps 27:14; 32:10; 33:20; 42:5; 43:5; and others), texts that originally referred to specific situations but are reread in terms of future expectations; the very end of Malachi—chosen by Christian tradition to close the canon—that announces the future arrival of the "sun of justice" and Elijah as his precursor in order to reconcile the enemies; these and others are examples that speak of the space that the same texts open for the future. In turn, these examples that we mention serve to establish that the expectation generated in the texts of the Old Testament defines itself as a consequence of its own internal coordinates but in combination with the surprise that every action of God provokes among those who receive it. The Old Testament prepares us for something, but that something is not clearly defined, but is drawn between the extension of certain theological lines such as the prophetic, the legal and priestly, the monarchical, the one that connects with the wise, the piety of the psalms; and the radical novelty that God imprints on the divine acts.

It was John McKenzie who took to its highest expression the idea that the Old Testament is so specifically Christian that it does not require any justification on the part of the Old Testament theologian. Observing that the Old was written when the New did not yet exist leads him to consider that it is not necessary to show the use of the Old Testament in the texts of the New Testament, and that in any case that would be the task of someone who explores the New Testament, but not of someone who analyzes and presents the thought of the Old Testament. He also notes that the New Testament deals with a person sent by God (Jesus of Nazareth) who proclaims that his words and life fulfill the prophecies announced in the Old Testament at the same time as initiating the period "of the end of time." McKenzie points out that there is nothing comparable to this in the Old Testament. We quote his words and he says "I do not find the Old Testament so foreign to the Christian faith, as I profess it, that the relationship between the two Testaments should be a serious problem."[1]

Extreme as it is, this position is interesting because it raises headlong the problem of the relationship between the testaments. For Christianity, whose canonical Scriptures are the Bible from Genesis to Revelation, there is a temptation to go for the simple and consider the Old Testament as old letters and beautiful exemplary stories. At various times in the history of the Church, it was treated in this way, considering the Old Testament as a witness to the development or evolution of the faith of Israel or a source of historical and sociological data. However, read in this way, its religious dimension is lost because its pages are not a record of facts but a testimony of faith in Yahweh, the God whose son was acknowledged as Jesus the Messiah. The message of the Old Testament is weakened by relegating it to being a preparatory text for what is considered the "true" message of God revealed in

---

[1] J. McKenzie, *A Theology of the Old Testament* (Eugene, OR: Wipf and Stock, 2009), 27-28.

Christ. The words in favor of the need for the reader or researcher of the New Testament not to omit its links with the Old Testament are numerous and it is not justified to expose them here. We do not feel that the Marcionite risk is a threat in our days.[1]

We have only mentioned that a reading of the New Testament in isolation from the Old Testament would cause Christianity to lose all cosmogony, all theology of creation, and all possibility of considering time as a raw material that, over the centuries, polishes and perfects the journey of faith. If Christian theology has a tendency to be more interested in eschatology (in the sense of *telos*, the ultimate end) than in creation, more interested in where we are going than where we come from, the reading of the Old Testament is a powerful force that reminds us of all the human experience, personal and social, historical and existential, that the journey of faith has accumulated and that supports the conviction that we will reach that final place that every believer yearns for. At the same time, what should also challenge us is to recognize that the Old Testament has its own light, and that this does not in any way diminish the value and authority of the New Testament for the Christian faith. Christological readings of the Old Testament miss the mark by ignoring the fact that in the course of God's self-revelation in Scripture, it was God who arranged for there to be first and second scriptures, and that in this journey and advance, nothing from before should be eliminated. The layers of biblical texts should not be interpreted as meaning that the new ones surpass the previous ones and annul them, but rather that the process of growth of the texts is the product of an act of creativity and therefore they complement and nourish each other with the text that they retouch and continue; the same must be said of the relationship between the Old and New Testaments: the attentive and careful reading of the Old Testament fertilizes the reading of the testimonies of the New.

The Christian reader must not forget that three-quarters of the New Testament was written by pious Jews who at that time felt themselves within the faith of their ancestors and who understood that they honored it by adhering to the movement that

---

[1] In the second century, Marcion of Sinope rejected the entire Old Testament as Christian Scripture, as well as any text of the New Testament that he considered to be Judaizing. In his theology, he insisted that the God of the Old Testament was not the Father of Jesus the Son, but that the latter revealed the true God. The nascent Christian church did not follow in his footsteps and confirmed the integrity and continuity of the Jewish texts with those of the New Testament.

in their understanding confirmed the veracity of their prophecies. They were what we would call today experts in what was later called the Old Testament, but which at that time were the only Scriptures that Christian communities recognized as inspired.[1] And the other quarter was written by Gentiles who adopted the faith of the Jews as their own by joining in the following and worship of the Jewish Jesus. If relegating the Old Testament to the past and closing it ignores that condition of a work that asks to be opened to what is missing, considering the New as its definitive fulfillment, without remainder and without challenges because it closes the expectations of the Old, is to minimize the semantic potential of both Testaments.

The Apocalyptic Horizon: Theology and the End of History

This condition of unfinished work also found a theological expression that interpreted it. We refer to apocalyptic literature. Toward the end of Old Testament times, the combination of a certain disillusionment regarding human justice, the growing feeling that humanity was sinking into its own contradictions and moving further and further away from the law of God, and the intimate conviction that even in the midst of this situation the God of Israel had not abandoned God's people but was still with them, gave rise to a new form of theology. Apocalyptic literature answers the questions: Where is God in the midst of this situation of persecution, anguish and death that we live in? What is the meaning of life and history in this context? And in our words: Is it true that "God is"? These questions are answered by pointing out that there were hidden things that explained God's apparent silence or the enigmatic nature of his actions. Hence, its emphasis—and its name: apocalypse means revelation—was placed on God, revealing new aspects of God's way of being with God's people and of the divine plan for history. New things that the ancients had not known were now announced so that those who remained in the faith would know the final destiny of history and of creation. If the political and religious powers hostile to the faithful could govern over their bodies and organizations, they did

---

[1]The New Testament, from the point of view of the texts, belongs to the Jewish tradition and largely expresses the thought of a section of that community in the first century. M. Zvi Brettler concludes his essay "The New Testament Between the Hebrew Bible and the Rabbinic Literature" with the statement that "the New Testament is to a large extent part of Jewish history," see A. Berlin and M. Zvi Brettler, *The Jewish Study Bible* (eds.) (Oxford: Oxford University Press, 2004), 504-06.

so convinced that by dominating them they would win in the struggle for power; but the apocalyptic announced that this triumph was superficial and mendacious. The true victory was on the side of the poor and humiliated, those to whom God had revealed the true plan that advanced behind visible history. They could persecute them and destroy their bodies, but they *knew* that salvation was on their side and that after the terror there would be no more pain or crying but the justice of the God who never sleeps and who sees and repairs everything.

This theology is both a continuity and a break with prophetic literature. It is a continuity in that it occupies the social place that the former occupied in the formation of theological thought and in the search for answers to new contexts and challenges for the faith of Israel. At some point between the 3rd and 2nd centuries BCE, apocalyptic thought bursts forth and becomes the literary expression of the search to theologically understand the new social and religious situation. It shares with the prophetic movement the condition of being the expression of its moment and the product of an intricate process of collective elaboration where the prophets of yesterday were the apocalypticists of the new historical stage. As far as the texts allow us to see, they seem to show that there has been no conflict between the two "schools" but rather a slow replacement of one way of doing theology by another. The presence of fragmentary texts or apocalyptic features in various prophetic books (Isaiah 24-27; Daniel 7-12; Joel; Zechariah 9-14) shows a non-traumatic transition, as if the texts accompanied a gradual process of social and religious transformation. But it is also a rupture in the measure that the object of theological reflection changes from being the factual history in the prophets to being, in apocalyptic, the history that God promotes *beneath* factual history. Apocalyptic does not consider the facts as they are but rather what it understands to be a hidden message between the folds of history. Having said this, it is necessary to point out that at the culmination of the transition process, profound changes have occurred in theological language that show a different way of understanding reality and of creating its own theological expression. We see these in particular in two aspects.

First of all, if the prophets are characterized by their voice, by declaiming their message and only at a later moment this message becomes a written text, apocalyptic theology defines itself as literature, as a written work from its origin. It is full of scrolls, books that are opened, texts read aloud. Now there is no prophet who denounces directly with the typical phrase "thus says the Lord" but in apocalyptic there is a seer who is an interpreter of the revelation that exposes what is hidden.[1] Interpreters are taken away or the heavens are opened to them and in their vision they are shown the reverse of reality; and this experience between mystical and concrete is what the seer relates. In its discourse, apocalyptic theology shows the contradiction between what humans believe to be true and real and what is so for God. It is not interested in "things past" because it considers them to be part of the old world, of what must be left behind. That is why apocalyptic literature, in its most refined sense, does not narrate past events, but rather likes to express itself in the first person and in the present tense. In doing so, it does not hide its literary nature, but rather constructs its discourse with images and symbols that are presented as such; apocalyptic literature, although it does not expressly formulate it, is the biblical literary genre that most clearly assumes itself as a literary work.

The second aspect that characterizes it is a different understanding of history and its end. History runs toward a goal and reflects little on its past. On that day, justice and truth will be exposed and the wicked and oppressors will be condemned while the faithful will attain salvation. The change of perspective is evident: while the prophets cry out for justice and righteousness in the present and conceive this human justice as a sign of divine justice, the apocalyptic yearns for and announces that the long-delayed justice will be consummated in the final judgment when the Lord judges humanity directly and in person. Apocalyptic thought does not believe in the effectiveness of human justice and although it does not resign itself to suffering or preach giving up in the face of pain, it proclaims that justice and redemption go together and will be realized on the day when all things are renewed by the action of God. On that day, time will cease and history will stop flowing.

The end of history has been widely proclaimed in our midst over the last two or three decades. As it is presented, it is a strange end, since it is supposed to occur in history itself and that it does not consist of the cessation of the coordinates of reality but,

---

[1]See the interesting analysis by W. Zimmerli, who points out that the unveiling of the secret can be transformed into a song of praise or of disturbance, but that ultimately what is revealed is the crisis of the relationship between humanity and God and the resolution of that crisis in the proximity of the goal to which divinity leads the world, *Manual de teología del Antiguo Testamento* (Madrid: Cristiandad, 1980), 269.

on the contrary, of its continuity and — we cannot help but view with suspicion — in the stubborn assertion that nothing will change. It is proclaimed that a definitive stage of history has been reached where changes in the economic, social and political structure of our society should no longer be expected. According to this conception, the capitalist model has consolidated itself to such an extent that it is no longer possible to expect substantial changes in its conformation. Because of this, it is understood that the course of history has ceased and the only task left to us is to improve what we already have. The ideology underlying this conception is petty because it does not seek to overcome challenges but to create resignation in the face of poverty and injustice. It replaces the utopias of a more just society with that of unlimited consumption for the few and the desperation of many to find the means (and anything goes to that end) to become part of those privileged few. It is, on the other hand, a fallacious ideology; because there is no such end of history and women and men today are creating new social movements that react to the inhumanity of the economic and social system. What is proclaimed is a false end of history.

We should not be confused by the sometimes similar language because the end of history as announced by apocalyptic theology is something else. Although apocalyptic theology does not become the central theology of the biblical message, we must point out that as such, it challenges and questions any pretension of ending history through human actions. It is the prerogative of the creator to decide the day and the hour and anyone who arrogates such power to themselves will be exposed in their intention to manipulate theological discourse to justify their own personal or group interest. In apocalyptic, the end of history and the end of days are understood in two dimensions: first, it refers to its direction and meaning; history is not a random succession of events, but has a direction indicated by God and a meaning that justifies creation and the life of people. The meaning is that creation must give glory to the creator God and, in this recognition of divine glory, people discover the value of their own life and that of their fellow humans. The second dimension of apocalyptic is that this direction of history leads to a final and just judgment, in its understanding, the only just judgment to which humanity can aspire. The unpunished oppressions and anguish of the present will be rewarded on that day of justice and truth.

We must ask ourselves whether apocalyptic is the final stage of Old Testament theological thought. In doing so, we wish to inquire whether, over the centuries and the constitution of the literature that became canonical, the apocalyptic interpretation of reality and of the Scriptures permeated biblical thought, particularly when taking into account its presence in the New Testament. The temptation to answer in the affirmative comes from observing that the 2nd century BCE to the 2nd century AD were the time of the expansion of this mode of expression and theology and therefore it could be said that the entire tradition was reread in this key. However, several indications point in another direction. First of all, the abundance of apocalyptic literature that emerged in Jewish culture and then in Christian culture far exceeds the few pages that were incorporated into the canon of the Old Testament (as well as the New). This should warn us against a possible overestimation of the influence of apocalyptic on formal theological thought. Of the multitude of texts, only fragments were incorporated into other works and in no case a complete book. Perhaps the most significant thing in relation to this is the opposite: in a context of apocalyptic ferment, there is a perceived resistance to incorporating works of this nature into the Scriptures.

If we wish to investigate Jewish apocalyptic thought, we must go to works that did not find a place in the canon: 4 Esdras, 2 and 3 Baruch, Jubilees, the Apocalypse of Abraham and various texts from the Enoch cycle. It has been said that this is so because at the time of their writing, the canon was already closed and they were not considered—as in reality they were not—prior to the time of Ezra. We think that there are deeper reasons and of a theological nature, since Daniel is a late work and yet it was incorporated into the *Ketubim* and we have no news that it has ever been questioned. It is noteworthy that Jewish thought that survived the destruction of the temple in the year 70 was not rebuilt on the hope of a transformation of time and space or of an immediate final judgment. It perceived that God's way of being with God's people was no longer expressed in the divine residence in Jerusalem or enjoyed in the sacrifices received in God's honor in the temple that no longer exists. The Pharisaic Judaism that structured the faith of Israel from that moment on understood that the new revelation was not that of a hidden message to be deciphered but that of God being with them even when there was no temple where God received prayers and sacrifices. God's new way of relating to God's people consisted in accompanying them in the different challenges that the new condition of a people in diaspora presented to the faith and to the preservation of their status as the chosen people.

One element that confirms this is the observation that several works of apocalyptic literature have a strong interpretative bias with respect to the ancient scriptures. Works such as 1 Enoch, Jubilees or 2 Esdras are to a large extent re-readings of texts from Genesis that they seek to update. On the contrary, the few apocalyptic texts that were incorporated into the canon are characterized by not having references to the ancient stories but rather being new texts, which incorporate new narratives and with little or no reference to the ancient biblical characters.[1] Thus, we see that the apocalyptic texts present in the Old Testament were, in all cases, incorporated into non-apocalyptic works, to which they contribute a nuance of their own but which in no case come to dominate the consensus of their theology. This even applies to Daniel, the only canonical book where the apocalyptic extends over six chapters.

That said, we can consider what contribution apocalyptic theology made to the concert of Old Testament theology. Without a doubt, apocalyptic theology was also incorporated into biblical thought just as it was resisted. We can infer that resistance arose from a fear that an understanding that emphasized the end of time would leave aside the semantic richness and the message inherent in narratives and prophetic texts. It also called into question the *Torah* as the guiding work of faith, insofar as it speaks for "this life" and not of things to come. But, at the same time, it was perceived that there was something in the apocalyptic message that bore witness to a genuine experience of faith and interpretation of reality. Its presence in various places is not a slip but a recognition of its place in the economy of faith. In our opinion, the apocalyptic literature that was incorporated into the Old Testament contributes to opening the door to other possibilities of understanding salvation. Without them, everything must be resolved in factual history, and the experience is that there is more impunity than justice in the balance of history. Thus, the touches of apocalypticism that we find in prophetic literature suggest that not all of God's plan is exhausted in our understanding of history, but that there is also another dimension that we still have to understand. That the expectation is of a final

---

[1]We prefer to speak of pre-apocalyptic texts since in general the link is more formal (images, vocabulary, discourse, etc.) than theological. See the cases of Is 24-27; Ez 9; 38-39; Joel 2:28-32 [chap. 3]; Zech 9-14.

and just judgment in which God's justice will repair all unpunished actions is a conviction that we receive from apocalyptic theology and for which we must not fail to be grateful.

Christian Interpretation of the OT and the Jewish Community

Christianity has acted throughout the centuries as if the Old Testament belonged only to it; in doing so, it ignores the fact that the texts have no owner and that they are offered, like landscapes, to anyone who wishes to admire them. However, by recognizing the diversity of possible readings, what we call the polysemy of the text, it is implicitly accepting that there are other readers who also have the right to interpret it and express their interpretation. Of these multiple readers, the Jewish community must be recognized as an interpreter of the utmost value and must be taken into account. In our understanding, this only partly has to do with the fact that they are, by physical or religious continuity, the descendants of those who wrote the texts and that the language in which they are written and the culture they express is their own language and culture of origin. This is so, first of all, because through the rabbinical and Talmudic reading of the Bible, Judaism has persevered in the faith of its ancestors throughout its long history. Unlike other ancient peoples who succumbed to the passage of time, the Jewish community has remained vital and active, even if one considers the natural changes that come with the cultural transformation that every society is subjected to. It has lived anchored to these texts and with them it has survived anti-Semitism—of which the Holocaust, or the *Shoah*, as we prefer to call it—has been its maximum expression but not the only one. That the persecution and contempt of Judaism has been and still is an enterprise that originates in societies with a Christian veneer and that it has even had ancient and recent expressions in theological thinking cannot fail to shame and make those who profess that faith reflect. Furthermore, it is necessary to recognize and say that God also shows divine wonders today in the Jewish community of faith, in examples of humility and commitment, in its martyrs, in its zeal to observe "the things of God," in its devotions. A Christian author who addresses Old Testament theology—like the person writing these lines—must always remember that for treasuring these texts, Jewish men, women and children were despised, mutilated, treated like animals and killed.

It is understandable that the Christian community read the Old Testament as a document that founded its own faith. It did so in several aspects. Walter Brueggemann points out five: the identification of the Messiah with "the Messiah;" understanding the Church as the continuation of the people of God; the assumption by the first Jewish-Christians that the way to be true Jews was to accept the "new covenant;" the challenge to the supremacy of the Law in order to balance it with "grace;" and finally, the "incarnation of the Word" in the person of Jesus. [1]

It is legitimate for the Church to make this reading because the Old Testament has a semantic wealth that allows its meaning to be explored in the light of a novelty in history, such as the emergence of Jesus of Nazareth. But this legitimacy corresponds to the reading that is made from the New Testament and in the face of the historical fact that has already taken place. Faced with the experience of Jesus' preaching, there were those who perceived that the ancient scriptures contained in germ elements that were now illuminated and that pointed in that direction. This perception was made explicit in many texts of the New Testament. What is not correct is to assume that the events of the New Testament were already announced in the narratives of the Old Testament. The Christian faith would do well to affirm that the prophecies of the Old Testament are only partially fulfilled in the New Testament, and this is firstly because the Old Testament is far from being precise regarding how this condition of unfinished text was to be completed; there is no passage that clearly states how revelation was to continue in history. But also because the life and preaching of Jesus of Nazareth breaks with the expectations that were held about the Messiah, about the irruption of the kingdom, about the role of priests and Levites in the economy of faith, about the place of the temple in the devotion of Israel, among other aspects. The expression repeated several times that it was necessary for such-and-such an event to be carried out "so that what was said might be fulfilled..." is undoubtedly acceptable but it must be understood as a testimony of the first Christians who interpreted *their* Scriptures in search of connections with their religious tradition. This does not mean that the message of the New Testament can be deduced from the texts of the Old Testament or that each phrase understood as a promise in the Old Testament must have its corresponding fulfillment in the New Testament. If this were the case, the text that would be superfluous would be that of the New Testament, since it would

---

[1] W. Brueggemann, *Teología del Antiguo Testamento* (Salamanca: Sígueme, 2007), 770.

be reduced to a mere confirmation of what the ancients had already said.

What is observed is that the Old Testament allows itself to be interpreted in this way — in the Christological sense, as it can be in other ways — but it does not demand that it be so. Those who claim that the Old Testament has been surpassed by the New Testament in view of the fact that the latter would fully fulfill the prophecies announced, what they really do is to disregard the novelty of the New Testament and present it as a simple witness to the truth already announced in the Old Testament. However, what is at stake is not the veracity of the Old Testament or the New Testament but the condition of the New Testament as the written expression of one more step in the incessant revelation of God already begun in the Scriptures prior to it.

The richness of the Old Testament and its capacity to accept and multiply its interpretation is what motivated the nascent Christian community to read in its pages. Those things that it understood confirmed the veracity of the new revelation in Christ. This is a natural and legitimate process to the extent that it is recognized that the inconclusive nature of the text leaves the door open to new readings and, in a certain sense, to its "prolongation" in successive texts. What the creation of the New Testament meant in the Christian community was expressed in the formation of the Mishnah in the Jewish community and then in the Talmud. Both theological enterprises see themselves as continuators of the message of the Old Testament. In the case of Christianity, the enterprise is presented as a small break, as a certain rectification of the course of thought of the ancient scriptures, something that is clearly expressed in the expression of Jesus in the Gospel of Matthew "you have heard that it was said, but I say to you" (5:21-48) called "antitheses" although several are not; The Scriptures are not rejected, but they are made more precise in view of a new theological context. In contrast, the production of Judaism in the Mishnah and the Talmud is presented as a reflection on the things of daily life in continuation and adaptation to the changing situations of the dispersed Jewish communities that must face the challenge of living their faith in adverse conditions, sometimes hostile and at other times with the threat of assimilation and loss of identity.

It is not uncommon to say that Christian reflection on the texts must be "biblical," in the sense that it must be constructed as a joint reflection of the entire Bible, the Old and New Testaments. In practice, and with regard to a work that includes a significant amount of critical tools in approaching the text, we only know the work of Brevard Childs.[1] It is undoubtedly an excellent work that deserves to be studied. From reading it, it emerges that what unites both testaments is more than an obvious chronological succession in the preparation of the writings or the fact that both bodies were written by people of the same Jewish faith; what is evident is that the unity is theological and transcends the formal. An identity of the New Testament with respect to the Old Testament is revealed that cannot be ignored. Jesus' Jewish condition could be considered an eventuality, but reading the texts of the New Testament does not allow us to think in that way, since everything contributes to showing that it could not have been otherwise.

As valuable as it is, Childs' work nevertheless leaves a taste of reductionism when one considers the image of both testaments placed one in conjunction with the other. In hermeneutical language, one would say that the meaning of the Old Testament is closed by limiting itself to reading it only in the perspective of its impact and influence on the New Testament; and in the opposite sense, the dimension of the New Testament is closed and limited by reading it "in reference to" the Old Testament and placing it in the box that the latter imposes on it. Childs' book is creative and valuable, but it gives the impression that it walks within narrow limits that inhibit the potential of both testaments. This is not the case with him, but in this type of reading there is a certain tendency to consider a text from the Old Testament that "it says such a thing but meant such another thing" in reference to a fact from the New Testament. We should rightly ask ourselves if it is true that he meant such another thing, why he didn't say it. However, a Christian theology of the Old Testament must highlight what is constituted in those Scriptures and that must remain as a theological support even when in the New Testament other winds blow and other themes are emphasized.

We refer to three elements that are key in the formation of theological thought of the Old Testament. First, *the* reality is that God manifests the divine self to a people and although God chooses them as such, God does not discard other peoples. The world of the New Testament is more global and international and the expansion of the message to the Gentiles can make us lose sight of that fundamental reality. If now people outside the people

---

[1] *Biblical Theology of the Old and New Testaments* (Minneapolis: Fortress Press, 1992).

who gave rise to the Christian faith are incorporated into the new concept of the people of God, in this incorporation one can think that the "transnational" vocation of God is fulfilled. Then one could infer that those who remain outside the Church would not have the possibility of accessing salvation. On the other hand, when the gospel is centered on the person of Jesus, there is always the latent risk of remaining in the person and falling into individualism and the weakening of the community's understanding of faith. The *second* is the radical materiality of creation (of every creature) which in the faith of Israel makes everything that does not belong to the sphere of God remain under the divine dominion and power and any deviation is seen as an affront to the first commandment that prohibits the worship of other gods or their images. The testimony of the New Testament is as radical as its predecessor but does not point it out so explicitly, which may be due to the fact that it assumes it as a *de facto* condition of the Jewish faith of the apostles. But the later history of Christianity left aside the prohibition of the veneration of objects and people to fall into practices that would have scandalized the prophets or the apostle Paul. This material condition of "everything but God" is a contribution of the Old Testament that gives health to the practice of the Christian faith. Finally, in *third* place, we wish to mention the intrinsic acceptance in the theology of the Old Testament of the diversity of opinions and theological expressions. It is true that everything contributes to the same testimony that Yahweh is the God who is (*El Dios que está*), but this affirmation is made from different places, sometimes very differently. This openness to theological diversity can be seen in the acceptance in the canon of the New Testament of four different gospels that express a diversity of perspectives; while distinguishing tendencies, they reveal unity in the central themes, but this inclusiveness is less clear in the testimony of faith of the Pauline letters. That Christianity in the first centuries was not very willing to accept dissent within the Church may have to do with having lost this heritage of the ancient Scriptures from its theological horizon.

The Jewish or Christian believer who immerse themselves in the world of the Old Testament enters a fascinating space, filled with questions and challenges, with ancient words that resonate as if they were new, and where a flame burns that many waters cannot extinguish.

Bibliography

Ackroyd, Peter. *The Chronicler in His Age*. Sheffield: JSOT Press, 1991.

Aharoni, Yohanan. *The Archeology of the Land of Israel*. Philadelphia: Westminster Press, 1987.

Alonso Schökel, Luis. *Profetas I-II*. Madrid: Cristiandad, 1980.

_____. *Treinta Salmos: Poesía y oración*. Madrid: Cristiandad, 1980.

_____. Luis y J. L. Sicre Díaz, *Job. Comentario teológico y literario*. Madrid: Cristiandad, 1982.

Alter, Robert. *The Art of Biblical Narrative*. New York: Basic Books, 1981.

Álvarez Valdés, Ariel. "Levítico 26: Una síntesis de alianzas como clave de lectura." *EB* 61 (2003): 155-81.

Anderson, Bernhard. *Contours of Old Testament Theology*. Minneapolis: Fortress Press, 1999.

Andiñach, Pablo. *El libro del Éxodo*. Salamanca: Sígueme, 2006.

_____. "Estudio de la leyenda acádica de Sargón." *OrArg* 11 (1994): 67-84.

_____. *Introducción hermenéutica al Antiguo Testamento*. Estella: Verbo Divino, 2012.

_____. *El fuego y la ternura*. Buenos Aries: Lumen, 1997.

_____. "Un amor clandestino. Aproximación al Cantar de los Cantares." *Acta Poética* 31 (2010): 89-112.

_____. "The Locust in the Message of Joel." *VT* 42 (1992): 433-41.

_____. "Lenguaje de la resistencia ante el poder imperial: El Día de Yavé." *RIBLA* 48 (2005): 62-75.

_____. "Génesis." *Comentario Bíblico Latinoamericano I*, 363-420. Ed. A. Levoratti. Estella: Verbo Divino, 2005.

Auld, A. Graeme. "Prophets and Prophecy in Jeremiah and Kings." *ZAW* 96 (1984): 66-82.

Avioz, Michael. *Nathan's Oracle (2 Samuel 7) and Its Interpreters*. Bern: Peter Lang, 2005.

Barr, James. *The Concept of Biblical Theology*. Minneapolis: Fortress Press, 1999.

_____. "The Theological Case Against Biblical Theology." *Canon, Theology and Old Testament Interpretation*, 3-19. Ed. Gene M. Tucker *et al*. Philadelphia: Fortress Press, 1988.

Barret, Rob. *Disloyalty and Destruction: Religion and Politics in Deuteronomy and the Modern World*. New York: T&T Clark, 2009.

Becking, Bob. "On the Identity of the Foreign Women in Ezra 9-10." *Exile and Restoration Revisited: Essays on the Babylonian and Persian Periods in Memory of Peter R. Ackroyd*, 31-49. Ed. by Gary N. Knoppers *et al*. New York: T&T Clark, 2009.

Beentjes, Pancratius. *Tradition and Transformation in the Book of Chronicles*. Leiden: Brill, 2008.

Bellis, Alice Ogden & Joel S. Kamisky (eds.). *Jews, Christians, and the Theology of the Hebrew Scriptures*. Atlanta: Society of Biblical Literature, 2000.

Berlin, Adele & Marc Zvi Brettler (eds.). *The Jewish Study Bible*. Oxford: Oxford University Press, 2004.

Berlin, Adele & James Kugel. "On the Bible as Literature." *Prooftexts* 2 (1982): 323-32.

Birch, Bruce, *et al.* (eds.). *A Theological Introduction to the Old Testament*. Nashville: Abingdon, 1999.

Blenkinsopp, Joseph. "Abraham as Paradigm in the Priestly History in Genesis." *BL* 128 (2009): 225-41.

Boff, Leonardo. *Teología desde el cautiverio*. Bogotá: Indo América, 1975.

_____. *Teología del cautiverio y de la liberación*. Madrid: Paulinas, 1978.

Botta, Alejandro & Pablo R. Andiñach (eds.). *The Bible and the Hermeneutics of Liberation*. Atlanta: Society of Biblical Literature, 2009.

Braude, William. *Midrash on Psalms*. New Haven: Yale University Press, 1959.

Broome, Edwin. "Ezekiel Abnormal Personality." *JBL* 65 (1946): 277-92.

Brueggemann, Walter. *Teología del Antiguo Testamento: Un juicio a Yahvé*. Salamanca: Sígueme, 2007.

_____. *Old Testament Theology: An Introduction*. Nashville: Abingdon Press, 2008.

_____. *1 & 2 Kings*. Macon: Smyth and Helwys, 2000.

_____. *Genesis. Interpretation*. Atlanta: John Knox Press, 1982.

_____. *A Commentary on Jeremiah: Exile & Homecoming*. Grand Rapids: Eerdmans, 1998.

_____. *First and Second Samuel*. Louisville: John Knox Press, 1990.

Carroll, Robert. *From Chaos to Covenant: Prophecy in the Book of Jeremiah*. New York: Crossroads, 1981.

_____. "Poets not Prophets." *JSOT* 27 (1983): 25-31.

Childs, Brevard. *Biblical Theology of the Old and New Testaments: Theological Reflection on the Christian Bible*. Minneapolis: Fortress Press, 1992.

_____. *Old Testament Theology in a Canonical Context*. Philadelphia: Fortress Press, 1985.

_____. *Introduction to the Old Testament as Scripture*. Philadelphia: Fortress Press, 1979.

_____. *Isaiah*. OTL. Louisville: Westminster, 2001.

Clements, Ronald. *Old Testament Theology: A Fresh Approach*. Atlanta: John Knox Press, 1978.

_____. "Beyond Tradition-History: Deutero-Isaianic Development of the First Isaiah´s Themes." *The Prophets: A Sheffield Reader*, 128-46. Ed. Philip Davies. Sheffield: Sheffield Academic Press, 1996.

Clevenot, Michael. *Lectura materialista de la Biblia*. Salamanca: Sígueme, 1978.

Cohn Eskenazi, Tamara. *In an Age of Prose: A Literary Approach to Ezra-Nehemiah*. Atlanta: Scholars Press, 1988.

Collins, John. *Introduction to the Hebrew Bible*. Minneapolis: Fortress Press, 2004.

Creach, Jerome. *Joshua*. Interpretation. Louisville: John Knox Press, 2003.

Crenshaw, James. *Old Testament Wisdom: An Introduction*. Atlanta: John Knox Press, 1981.

_____. "The Shadow of Death in Koheleth." *Israelite Wisdom: Theological and Literary Essays in Honor of Samuel Terrien*, 205-16. Ed. John Gammie *et al.* New York: Scholars Press, 1978.

Croatto, Severino. *Historia de salvación: La experiencia religiosa del pueblo de Dios*. Estella: Verbo Divino, 1995.

_____. "Yavé, el Dios de la 'presencia' salvífica: Éx 3:14." *RevBíbl* 43 (1981): 153-63.

_____. "Composición y querigma del libro de Isaías." *RIBLA* 36/37 (2000): 36-67.

_____. "Isaiah 40-55." "Isaiah 56-66." & "Fourth Isaiah." *Global Bible Commentary*, 195-211. Ed. Daniel Patte *et al.* Nashville: Abingdon, 2004.

_____. *Isaías 1-39*. Buenos Aries: La Aurora, 1989.

_____. *Crear y amar en libertad. Estudio de Génesis 2:4-3:24*. Buenos Aries: La Aurora, 1986.

_____. *Exilio y sobrevivencia. Tradiciones contraculturales en el Pentateuco*. Buenos Aries: Lumen, 1997.

_____. *Hermenéutica bíblica*. Buenos Aries: Lumen, 2000.

_____. *Experiencia de lo sagrado: Estudio de fenomenología de la religión*. Estella: Verbo Divino, 2002.

Davis, Ellen. "Losing a Friend: The Loss of the Old Testament to the Church." *Jews, Christians, and the Theology of the Hebrew Scriptures*, 83-108. Ed. Alice O. Bellis & Joel S. Kaminsky. Atlanta: Society of Biblical Literature, 2000.

Day, John. *Psalms*. Sheffield: Sheffield Academic Press, 1993.

de Sepúlveda, Juan Ginés. *Tratado sobre las justas causas de la guerra contra los indios*. México City: Fondo de Cultura Económica, 1986.

de Vaux, Roland. *Instituciones del Antiguo Testamento*. Madrid: Herder, 1976.

Del Olmo Lete, Gregorio. *Mitos y leyendas de Canaán según la tradición de Ugarit*. Madrid: Cristiandad, 1981.

Delcor, Maties. *Mito y tradición en la literatura apocalíptica*. Madrid: Cristiandad, 1977.

Dick, Jonathan. *The Theocracy Ideology of the Chronicler*. Leiden: Brill, 1998.

Doorly, William. *The Laws of Yahweh: A Handbook of Biblical Law*. New York: Paulist Press, 2002.

Edenburg, Cynthia. "Ideology and Social Context of the Deuteronomic Women's Sex Laws." *JBL* 128 (2009): 43-60.

Eichrodt, Walter. *Teología del Antiguo Testamento I-II*. Madrid: Cristiandad, 1975.

Faria, Jacir de Freitas. "Esperanza de los pobres en los Salmos." *RIBLA* 39 (2001): 57-68.

Finkelstein, Israel. "Archeology and the Text in the Third Millenium: A View from the Center." *Congress Volume Basel 2001*, 323-42. Ed. A. Lemaire. VT Sup. Leiden: Brill, 2002.

Finkelstein, Israel & Amihai Mazar. *The Quest for the Historical Israel: Debating Archeology and the History of Early Israel.* Atlanta: Society of Biblical Literature, 2007.

Fichtner, Johannes. "Isaiah among the Wise." *Studies in Ancient Israelite Wisdom,* 429-38. Ed. James Crenshaw. New York: Ktav Publishing House, 1976.

Flavio Josefo. *Obras completas de Flavio Josefo.* Buenos Aries: Acervo Cultural, 1961.

Fretheim, Terence. *The Pentateuch.* Nashville: Abingdon Press, 1996.

_____. *Jeremiah.* Macon: Smith & Helwys, 2002.

Freedman, David Noel. *Pottery, Poetry and Prophecy: Studies in Early Hebrew Poetry.* Winona Lake: Eisenbrauns, 1980.

Fritz, Volkmar. *1 & 2 Kings.* Minneapolis: Fortress Press, 2003.

Fuchs, Esther. "Prophecy and the Construction of Women: Inscription and Erasure." *Prophets and Daniel: A Feminist Companion to the Bible,* 86-122. Ed. Athalya Brenner. Sheffield: Sheffield Academic Press, 2001.

Frolov, Serge. "Rethinking Judges." *CBQ* 71 (2009): 24-41.

Fuchs, Esther. "Prophecy and the Construction of Women: Inscription and Erasure." *Prophets and Daniel: A Feminist Companion to the Bible,* 54-69. Ed. Athalya Brenner. Sheffield: Sheffield Academic Press, 2001.

Gallazzi, Sandro. "El Señor reinará eternamente: una contestación a la teocracia sadoquita: Templo, sacerdote y poder en los salmos." *RIBLA* 45.2 (2003): 59-67.

García Bachmann, Mercedes. "El libro de Proverbios." *RIBLA* 52 (2005): 53-69.

García López, Félix. "La formación del Pentateuco en el debate actual." *EB* 67 (2009): 235-256.

Gerstenberger, Erhard S. *Theologies in the Old Testament.* Minneapolis: Fortress Press, 2002.

Goldingay, John. *Theological Diversity and the Authority of the Old Testament.* Grand Rapids: Eerdmans, 1987.

Gordon, Robert. *I-II Samuel: A Commentary.* London: Paternoster, 1986.

Gorgulho, Gilberto. "Proverbios." *Comentario Bíblico Latinoamericano II,* 805-24. Ed. A. Levoratti. Estella: Verbo Divino, 2007.

Grabbe, Lester. *Ancient Israel. What Do We Know and How Do We Know It?* London: T&T Clark, 2007.

Gray, John. *1 & 2 Kings. A Commentary.* Philadelphia: Westminster Press, 1970.

Green, Barbara. *Like a Tree Planted. An Exploration of Psalms and Parables Through Metaphors.* Collegeville: The Liturgical Press, 1997.

Gutiérrez, Gustavo. *Teología de la liberación. Perspectivas.* Salamanca: Sígueme, 1972.

_____. *Hablar de Dios desde el sufrimiento del inocente: Una reflexión sobre el libro de Job.* Salamanca: Sígueme, 1986.

Gyllmayr-Bucher, Susanne. "Framework and Discourse in the Book of Judges." *JBL* 128 (2009): 687-702.

Hallo, William & K. L. Younger (eds.). *The Context of Scripture*. New York: Brill, 1997-2003.

Halperin, David. *Seeking Ezekiel: Text and Psychology*. University Park: Pennsylvania State University Press, 1993.

Hadjiev, Tchavdar. "Zephaniah and the Book of the Twelve Hypothesis." *Prophecy and Prophets in Ancient Israel*, 325-38. Ed. John Day. New York: T&T Clark, 2010.

Hasel, Gerhard. *Old Testament Theology: Basic Issues in the Current Debate*. Grand Rapids: Eerdmans, 1991.

Hermisson, Hans-Jürgen. "Observations on the Creation Theology in Wisdom." *Israelite Wisdom, Theological and Literary Essays in Honor of Samuel Terrien*, 43-75. Ed. John Gammie *et al*. Atlanta: Scholars Press, 1978.

Hayes, John & Frederick Prussner. *Old Testament Theology and its History and Development*. Atlanta: John Knox Press, 1985.

Heller, Roy. *Power, Politics and Prophecy. The Character of Samuel and the Deuteronomistic Evaluation of Prophecy*. London: T&T Clark, 2006.

Heschel, Abraham J. *The Prophets*. New York: The Jewish Publication Society of America, 1962. Trad. castellana: *Los profetas I-III*. Buenos Aries: Paidós, 1973.

Hess, Richard *et al. Critical Issues in Early Israelite History*. Winona Lake: Eisenbrauns, 2008.

Hofmann, Yair. "The Deuteronomistic Concept of the *Herem*." *ZAW* 111 (1999): 196-210.

Holladay, William. *The Psalms Through Three Thousand Years: Prayerbook of a Cloud of Witnesses*. Minneapolis: Fortress Press, 1993.

_____. *Long Ago God Spoke*. Minneapolis: Fortress Press, 1995.

_____. *Jeremiah 1- 2*. Hermeneia. Philadelphia: Fortress Press, 1986-1989.

House, Paul. *The Unity of the Twelve*. Sheffield: Almond Press, 1990.

Houtman, Cornelis. *Exodus I-IV*. Kampen: Kok Publishing House, 1993-2002.

Japhet, Sara. *I & II Chronicles. A Commentary*. Louisville: Westminster John Knox, 1993.

_____. "The Relationship between Chronicles and Ezra-Nehemiah." *Studies in the Historical Books of the Old Testament*, 52-64. Ed. J. Emerton. VT Sup 30. Leiden: Brill, 1979.

_____. "The Supposed Common Authorship of Chronicles and Ezra-Nehemiah Investigated Anew." *VT* 18 (1968): 330-71.

Jacob, Edmond. *Theology of the Old Testament*. New York: Harper & Row, 1958.

Jobling, David. *1 Samuel*. Berit Olam. Collegeville: Liturgical Press, 1998.

Jones, Barry A. *The Formation of the Book of the Twelve: A Study in Text and Canon*. Atlanta: Scholars Press, 1995.

Kalimi, Isaac. *An Ancient Israelite Historian: Studies in the Chronicles, His Time, Place and Writing*. Assen: Royal van Gorcum, 2005.

Kenik, Helen. *Design for Kingship: The Deuteronomistic Narrative Technique in 1 Kings 3:4-15*. SBLDS. Chico: Scholars Press, 1978.

Kessler, Martin. *Battle of the Gods: The God of Israel Versus Marduk of Babylon*. Assen: Royal van Gorcum, 2003.

Kierkegaard, Søren. *Para un examen de sí mismo recomendado a este tiempo*. Madrid: Trotta, 2011.

Knierim, Rolf P. *The Task of Old Testament Theology*. Grand Rapids: Eerdmans, 1995.

Knoppers, Gary & Lecter Grabbe (eds.). *Exile and Restoration Revisited: Essays on the Babylonian and Persian Periods in Memory of Peter R. Ackroyd*. New York: T&T Clark, 2009.

Kraus, Hans-Joachim. *Teología de los Salmos*. Salamanca: Sígueme, 1985.

Kutsko, John. *Between Heaven and Earth: Divine Presence and Absence in the Book of Ezekiel*. Winona Lake: Eisenbrauns, 2000.

Lemche, Niels Peter. *The Old Testament Between Theology and History*. Louisville: Westminster John Knox Press, 2008.

Levoratti, Armando. "Eclesiastés." *Comentario Bíblico Latinoamericano II*, 835-64. Ed. A. Levoratti. Estella: Verbo Divino, 2007.

Lópes Torres, Mercedes. "Danzando en el universo - Proverbios 8,22-31." *RIBLA* 50 (2005): 65-68.

López, Rolando. "La liberación de los oprimidos, ideal y práctica sapiencial." *RIBLA* 9 (1991): 7-20.

Lowery, R. H. *The Reforming Kings: Cults and Society in First Temple Judah*. JSOTS. Sheffield: JSOT Press, 1991.

Mazar, Amihai. *The Archeology of the Land of the Bible*. New York: Doubleday, 1990.

McEvenue, Sean. "La Sabiduría, una forma de pensar sobre Dios." *Comentario Bíblico Internacional*, 687-92. Ed. William Farmer *et al*. Estella: Verbo Divino, 1999.

McKenzie, John. *A Theology of the Old Testament*. Eugene, OR: Wipf and Stock, 2009.

Meier, Samuel. *The Messenger in the Ancient Semitic World*. Atlanta: Scholars Press, 1988.

Meyers, Carol. "Miriam the Musician." *A Feminist Companion from Exodus to Deuteronomy*, 207-30. Ed. Athalya Brenner. Sheffield: Sheffield Academic Press, 1994.

Milgrom, Jacob. "The Biblical Diet Laws as an Ethical System." *Interpretation* 17 (1963): 288-301.

Miller, Patrick. "The Absence of the Goddess in Israelite Religion." *HAR* 10 (1986): 239-48.

_____. *Deuteronomy*. Interpretation. Louisville: John Knox Press, 1990.

Miscal, Peter. *1 Samuel: A Literary Reading*. Bloomington: Indiana University Press, 1986.

Muilenburg, James. "Form Criticism and Beyond." *JBL* 88 (1969): 1-18.

Mulder, Martin. *1 Kings 1-11*. HCOT. Leuven: Peeters, 1998.

Murphy, Roland. "A Consideration on the Classification Wisdom Psalms." *VT Sup* 9 (1963): 156-67.

Myers, Jacob. *Invitation to the Old Testament: A Layman's Guide to Its Major Religious Messages*. Garden City, NY: Doubleday, 1966.

Na´aman, Nadam. "The Discovered Book and the Legitimation of Josiah´s Reform." *JBL* 130 (2011): 47-62.

Nelson, Richard. "The Altar of Ahaz: A Revisionist View." *HAR* 10 (1986): 267-76.

_____. *Joshua*, OTL. Louisville: Westminster Press, 1997.

_____. *The Historical Books*. Nashville: Abingdon Press, 1998.

_____. "Judges: A Public Canon for a Public Theology." *WW* 29 (2009): 397-406.

Niditch, Susan. *Judges: A Commentary*. Louisville: John Knox, 2008.

Noth, Martin. *The Deuteronomistic History*. JSOT Sup. Sheffield: Sheffield Academic Press, 1981.

O'Connors, M. "The Women in the Book of Judges." *HAR* 10 (1986): 277-94.

Overholt, Thomas. "Prophecy in History: The Social Reality of Intermediation." *JSOT* 48 (1990): 3-29.

Perdue, Leo. *The Collapse of History: Reconstructing Old Testament Theology*. Minneapolis: Fortress Press, 1994.

Petersen, David. "The Genesis of Genesis." *Congress Volume: Ljubljana 2007*, 27-40. Ed. A. Lemaire. VT Sup. Leiden: Brill, 2010.

_____. "The Ambiguous Role of Moses as Prophet." *Israel´s Prophets and Israel´s Past*, 311-24. Ed. Brad Kelle & Megan Bishop Moore. New York: T&T Clark, 2006.

_____. "Israel and Monotheism: The Unfinished Agenda." *Canon, Theology and Old Testament Interpretation*, 92-117. Ed. Gene M. Tucker *et al*. Philadelphia: Fortress Press, 1988.

Pikaza, Xabier. "Presentación y juicio." *Lectura materialista de la Biblia*, 9-38. Ed. M. Clevenot. Salamanca: Sígueme, 1978.

Pitkaen, Pekka. *Central Sanctuary and Centralization of Worship in Ancient Israel: From the Settlement to the Building of Solomon's Temple*. Piscataway, NJ: Gorgias Press, 2003.

Pixley, Jorge. *El libro de Job*. San José de Costa Rica: SEBILA, 1982.

_____. *Historia de Israel desde la perspectiva de los pobres*. Madrid: Palabra Ediciones, 1993.

Pleins, J. David. *The Social Visions of the Hebrew Bible: A Theological Introduction*. Louisville: Westminster Press, 2001.

_____. *The Psalms. Songs of Tragedy, Hope and Justice*. New York: Maryknoll, 1993.

Preuss, Horst Dietrich. *Old Testament Theology I-II*. Louisville: Westminster John Knox Press, 1992.

Provan, Iain. *Hezekiah and the Books of Kings*. Berlin: Walter de Gruyter, 1988.

Rendtorff, Rolf. *The Canonical Hebrew Bible: A Theology of the Old Testament*. Leiden: Deo Publishing, 2005.

Reventlow, Henning Graf. *Problems of Old Testament Theology in the Twentieth Century*. Philadelphia: Fortress Press, 1985.

Ricciardi, Alberto. "Los pobres y la tierra según el Salmo 37." *RevBíbl* 41 (1979): 227-37.

Rofé, Alexander. "The Strata of the Law about the Centralization of Worship in Deuteronomy and the History of the Deuteronomic Movement." *Deuteronomy: Issues and Interpretation* 97-101. London: T&T Clark, 2002.

Sarna, Nahum. *Song of the Heart: An Introduction of the Book of the Psalms*. New York: Schocken Books, 1993.

Schiavo, Luigi & Lorenzo Lago. "Sofía – los mitos del amor reflexivo y del amor en la alteridad." *RIBLA* 57 (2007): 86-96.

Shepperd, Michael. "Composition Analysis of the Twelve." *ZAW* 120 (2008): 184-93.

Sicre, José Luis. *Profetismo en Israel*. Estella: Verbo Divino, 2003.

_____. *Con los pobres de la tierra: La justicia social en los profetas de Israel*. Madrid: Cristiandad, 1984.

_____. *Los Dioses olvidados: Poder y riqueza en los profetas preexílicos*. Madrid: Cristiandad, 1979.

Silberman, Neil & David Small. *The Archeology of Israel: Constructing the Past, Interpreting the Present*. JSOTSup. Sheffield: JSOT Press, 1997.

Ska, Jean Louis. *Introducción a la lectura del Pentateuco*. Estella: Verbo Divino, 2001.

Steussy, Marti. *David: Biblical Portraits of Power*. Columbia, SC: University of South Carolina Press, 1999.

Soggin, Alberto. *Introduction to the Old Testament*. Louisville: John Knox Press, 1989.

_____. *Josuah*. OTL. Philadelphia: Westminster Press, 1972.

Solano Rossi, Luiz Alexandre. "Los caminos de la teología y de la anti-teología en el libro de Job." *RIBLA* 50 (2005): 53-55.

Stern, Philip. *The Biblical Herem: A Window on Israel´s Religious Experience*. Atlanta: Scholars Press, 1991.

Sternberg, Meir. *The Poetics of Biblical Narrative: Ideological Literature and the Drama of Reading*. Bloomington: Indiana University Press, 1985.

Stökl, Jonathan. "Female Prophets in the Ancient Near East." *Prophecy and Prophets in Ancient Israel*, 47-64. Ed. John Day. New York: T&T Clark, 2010.

Strawn Brent & Nancy R. Bowen (eds.). *A God so Near: Essays on Old Testament Theology in Honor of Patrick D. Miller*. Winona Lake: Eisenbrauns, 2003.

Stulmann, Louis & Hyun Chul Paul Kim. *You Are My People: An Introduction to the Prophetic Literature*. Nashville: Abingdon Press, 2010.

Sundberg, A. C. *The Old Testament and the Early Church*. Cambridge: Harvard University Press, 1964.

Sweeney, Marvin. *1 & 2 Kings: A Commentary*. Louisville: Westminster Press, 2007.

_____. "Ezekiel´s Debate with Isaiah." *Congress Volume: Ljubljana 2007*, 555-74. Ed. A. Lemaire. VT Sup. Leiden: Brill, 2010.

_____. *The Prophetic Literature*. Nashville: Abingdon Press, 2005.

_____. *The Twelve Prophets I*. Berit Olam. Collegeville: The Liturgical Press, 2000.

_____. "The Sequence and Interpretation in the Book of the Twelve." *Reading and Hearing the Book of the Twelve*, 49-64. Ed. James D. Nogalski & Marvin Sweeney. Atlanta: Society of Biblical Literature, 2000.

Talstra, E. *Solomon's Prayer: Synchrony and Diachrony in the Composition of 1 Kings 8:14-61*. Kampen: Kok Pharos Publishing House, 1993.

Torreblanca, Jorge. "Jeremías: Una lectura estructural." *RIBLA* 35-36 (2000): 68-82.

Trible, Phyllis. *Rhetorical Criticism: Context, Method and the Book of Jonah*. Minneapolis: Fortress Press, 1994.

van Buren, Paul M. *A Theology of the Jewish-Christian Reality: Part 2: A Christian Theology of the People of Israel*. San Francisco: Harper and Row, 1983.

Vegas Montaner, Luis. "Oración de Manasés." *Apócrifos del Antiguo Testamento II*, 209-211. Ed. Alejandro Díez Macho. Madrid: Sígueme, 1982.

Vogt, Peter. *Deuteronomic Theology and the Significance of Torah: A Reappraisal*. Winona Lake: Eisenbrauns, 2006.

von Rad, Gerhard. *Estudios sobre el Antiguo Testamento*. Salamanca: Sígueme, 1975.

_____. *Teología del Antiguo Testamento I-II*. Salamanca: Sígueme, 1976.

_____. *La Sabiduría en Israel*. Madrid: Fax, 1973.

_____. "La historia de José y la antigua hokma." *Estudios sobre el Antiguo Testamento*, 255-62. Madrid: Sígueme, 1975.

Vriezen, T. & A. van der Woude. *Ancient Israelite and Early Jewish Literature*. Leiden: Brill, 2005.

Weems, Renita J. "Hulda the Prophet: Reading a (Deuteronomistic) Woman's Identity." *A God So Near*, 321-39. Ed. Brent Strawn & Nancy Bowen. Winona Lake: Eisenbrauns, 2003.

Wells, Bruce. "What is Biblical Law? A Look at Pentateuchal Rules and Near Eastern Practice." CBQ 70 (2008): 223-43.

Westermann, Claus. *Genesis: A Commentary* (3 vols.). Minneapolis: Augsburg, 1985-1986.

_____. *Isaiah 40-66*. Philadelphia: Westminster Press, 1975.

White, Marsha. *The Elijah Legends and Jehu's Coup*. Atlanta: Scholars Press, 1997.

Widengreen, Leo. *Fenomenología de la Religión*. Madrid: Cristiandad, 1976.

Williamson, H. G. M. "Prophetesses in the Hebrew Bible." *Prophecy and Prophets in Ancient Israel*, 65-80. Ed. John Day. New York: T&T Clark, 2010.

Wright, G. Ernest. *El Dios que actúa: Teología bíblica como narración*. Madrid: Fax, 1974.

Yee, Gail. "The Theology of Creation in Proverbs 8:22-31." *Creation in the Biblical Traditions*, 85-96. Ed. R. Clifford & J. Collins. Washington: Catholic Biblical Association, 1992.

Yunis, Amer. "The Sacrifice of Abraham in Islam." *The Sacrifice of Isaac in the Three Monotheistic Religions*, 147-57. Ed. Frederic Manns. Jerusalem: Franciscan Printing Press, 1995.

Zamora García, Pedro. *El libro de Reyes I*. Estella: Verbo Divino, 2011.

Zimmerli, Walther. *Manual de teología del Antiguo Testamento*. Madrid: Cristiandad, 1980.

_____. *A Commentary on the Book of the Prophet Ezekiel 1-24*. Philadelphia: Fortress Press, 1979.

Author Index

Made in the USA
Monee, IL
14 March 2025

13861182R00193